Well-Known Trade Marks

This book considers the effectiveness of well-known trade mark protection at an international level. It particularly considers EU trade mark law from Japanese perspectives, and provides a practical and critical overview of trade mark law in Japan, including the historical development of the law and the recent development on cases and policy.

The book includes detailed coverage of the Japanese Unfair Competition Prevention Act, and contains the first systematic analysis of Japanese jurisprudence and legislative amendments of law in relation to well-known trade marks and unfair competition. The book goes on to comparatively analyse Japanese trade mark law alongside that of the European Community Trade Mark system. The book critically considers the difficulties in comprehensively defining a 'well-known trade mark' in the relevant international trade mark instruments. In breaking down the traditional definition of the 'well-known trade mark', the book works to address existing theoretical ambiguities in the application of trade mark law.

The book will be of great interest to academics and students of legal theory and intellectual property law.

Hiroko Onishi is a lecturer at Kingston University London, UK.

Routledge Research in Intellectual Property

Available:

Re-thinking Intellectual Property
The Political Economy of Copyright Protection in the Digital Era
Yijun Tian

The Development of Intellectual Property Regimes in the Arabian Gulf States
Infidels at the Gates
David Price

Intellectual Property, Community Rights and Human Rights
The Biological and Genetic Resources of Developing Countries
Marcelin Tonye Mahop

Intellectual Property in Global Governance
A Development Question
Chidi Oguamanam

Intellectual Property Overlaps
Theory, Strategies, and Solutions
Robert Tomkowicz

Private Copying
Stavroula Karapapa

The Law and Economics of Intellectual Property in the Digital Age
The Limits of Analysis
Niva Elkin-Koren and Eli Salzberger

A Politics of Patent Law
Crafting the Participatory Patent Bargain
Kali Murray

Copyright Industries and the Impact of Creative Destruction
Copyright Expansion and the Publishing Industry
Jiabo Liu

Health Technologies and International Intellectual Property
A Precautionary Approach
Phoebe Li

Intellectual Property, Traditional Knowledge and Cultural Property Protection
Cultural Signifiers in the Caribbean and the Americas
Sharon B. Le Gall

Intellectual Property and Traditional Knowledge in the Global Economy
Translating Geographical Indications for Development
Teshager W. Dagne

Well-Known Trade Marks
A Comparative Study of Japan and the EU
Hiroko Onishi

Forthcoming:

Intellectual Property and Conflict of Laws
Moral Rights and Alternatives to the Copyright Qualifications
Hanan Almawla

The Object of Copyright
A Conceptual History of Originals and Copies in Literature, Art and Design
Stina Teilmann-Lock

Intellectual Property Policy, Law and Administration in Africa
Exploring Continental and Regional Co-operation
Caroline B. Ncube

Well-Known Trade Marks

A Comparative Study of Japan and the EU

Hiroko Onishi

Routledge
Taylor & Francis Group

LONDON AND NEW YORK

First published 2015 by Routledge

2 Park Square, Milton Park, Abingdon, Oxon OX14 4RN
711 Third Avenue, New York, NY 10017, USA

Routledge is an imprint of the Taylor & Francis Group, an informa business

First issued in paperback 2017

British Library Cataloguing in Publication Data
A catalogue record for this book is available from the British Library

Library of Congress Cataloging-in-Publication Data
Onishi, Hiroko.
Well-known trade marks : a comparative study of Japan and the
EU / Hiroko Onishi.
    pages cm. — (Routledge research in intellectual property)
    Includes bibliographical references and index.
    ISBN 978-0-415-52131-4 (hardback) — ISBN 978-0-203-79814-0 (ebk)
    1. Trademarks—Law and legislation—Japan.   2. Trademarks—Law and
    legislation—European Union countries.   I. Title.   II. Title: Well-known
    trademarks.
    K1555.O55 2014
    346.2404'88—dc23   2013024951

ISBN: 978-0-415-52131-4 (hbk)
ISBN: 978-1-138-71333-8 (pbk)

Typeset in Baskerville by
Keystroke, Station Road, Codsall, Wolverhampton

Contents

Acknowledgements

This book has grown out of the PhD thesis that I completed in 2010 at the University of Southampton. I am extremely grateful for all the support I received while I was doing my studies at the University of Southampton, and the support and encouragement I have received since I started working at Kingston University. My special and deepest thanks and gratitude go to the following people:

To Caroline Wilson:

My greatest appreciation goes to Caroline as my main supervisor and later my mentor. What I have received from her is beyond compare. The lessons she has taught me have not been easy, and sometimes we disagreed. However, we shared both good and bad times, and she witnessed me becoming an independent researcher. I do not think I will ever meet a supervisor and a mentor like her. I treasure the relationship I have with her. Thank you very much, Caroline.

To Prof. Steve and Susan Saxby:

I would also thank Prof. Steve as my second supervisor and Susan as my rock. Steve was here for me when I was devastated and he gave me strong and warm support. I have also received the warmest welcome from Steve's wife, Susan, and the Saxby family. Thanks to them all, I have never felt lonely.

To Southampton Law School and members of staff:

Special thanks go to the Southampton Law School and members of staff. Throughout my studies and while writing my thesis, I received constant encouragement, support and warm hugs – in particular, from Jill, Aloma, Liz, Leo, Caroline, Ed and Filipo. I am so grateful for their great support and encouragement.

To Kingston Law School and members of staff:

I would like to thank Kingston Law School and members of staff for the moral support and encouragement that I have received while transforming my thesis into this book. It has been a challenge for me to complete the book, as it has been very easy to get carried away. Thank you so much to those who were there to listen to me and gave me a shoulder to cry on.

To Routledge:

I would like to thank my publisher, Routledge, my editor, Mark, and Katherine. They have been so supportive and understanding. I don't think I receive this level of support from anywhere else. Thank you very much.

To my dearest friends:

Since I was doing my studies at Southampton, and since I have moved to Kingston, I have made a number of very good friends, who have shared my emotional and intellectual journey and unbearable frustration. When I felt as if I was in the middle of the forest not knowing which way to go, they gave me a torch to find my way. We have shared a lot of bad and good moments, and the important thing is that they are always there for me. Without you all, I would have lost my way. Thank you very much for being there for me.

To my parents, Tsuyoshi and Yaeko Onishi, and my dearest brother, Shintaro:

This book is dedicated to my parents, in particular, dad – Tsuyoshi Onishi – whom I respect the most in this world. He has devoted himself to making my dream come true, and he is always there for me. When I completed a PhD degree, he did not congratulate me; instead, he said, 'There is a higher mountain to climb next', which was a great encouragement. When I have experienced hardship (even now), he always said, 'Come home; you have done a lot, you don't have to do too much.' This made me stronger and has got me through my PhD studies and professional life until now. I am so thankful that my parents let me pursue my dream. I just want them to know that my love for them is unconditional. Thank you very much, and I am the most fortunate person to have been born as their child.

List of abbreviations

AC	Appeal Cases (House of Lords)
All ER	All England Report
BoA	Board of Appeal (of the European Communities)
BUJ Sci & Tech L	Boston University Journal of Science and Technology Law
Bus Law	Business Lawyer
Bus L R D	Business
CA	Court of Appeal, England and Wales
Cal L Rev	California Law Review
Cal W Int'l L J	California Western International Law Journal
Cardozo Art & Ent L J	Cardozo Arts and Entertainment Law Journal
CEC	European Community Cases
CFI	Court of First Instance (of the European Communities)
Ch	Law Report Chancery Division
Ch D	Law Report Chancery Division
Chi-Kent L Rev	Chicago-Kent Law Review
Chi-Kent J Intell Prop	Chicago-Kent Journal of Intellectual Property
CIPA	Chartered Institute of Patent Agent
CIPAJ	Chartered Institute of Patent Agent Journal
CLJ	Cambridge Law Journal
CLR	Commonwealth Law Reports
CMLR	Common Market Law Revive
Colum Bus L Rev	Columbia Business Law Review
Colum L Rev	Columbia Law Review
Comms L	Communication Law
Conn L Rev	Connecticut Law Review
Corp Brief	Corporate Brief
CMLR	Common Market Law Reports
CTLR	Comminute and Telecommunications Law Review
CTM	Community Trade Mark
CTMR	Community Trade Mark Regulation
CW	Copyright World
EBL Rev	European Business Law Review

ECC	European Commercial Case
ECJ	European Court of Justice
ECLR	Electronic Commerce and Law Report
ECR I	European Court Reports (European Court of Justice)
ECR II	European Court Reports (Court of First Instance)
ECTA	European Communities Trade Mark Association
EEA	European Economic Area
EFTA	European Free Trade Association
EIPR	European Intellectual Property Review
Ent LR	Entertainment Law Review
ETMR	European Trade Mark Report
EU Focus	European Union Focus
EWCA	England and Wales Court of Appeal
EWCA Civ	England and Wales Court of Appeal Civil Division
EWHC	England and Wales High Court
Fla L Rev	Florida Law Review
Fordham L Rev	Fordham Law Review
Fordham Int Pro	Fordham Intellectual Property Media, and Entertainment Law Journal
FSR	Fleet Street Report
GATT TRIPS	Agreement of Trade-Related Aspects of Intellectual Property Law
Geo Wash J Int'l L & Econ	George Washington Journal of International Law and Economics
GI	Geographical Indication
Harv L Rev	Harvard Law Review
HC	High Court
HL	House of Lords
Hous L Rev	Houston Law Review
ICCLR	International Company and Commercial Law Review
IIC	International Review of Industrial Property and Copyright Law
IJL & IT	International Journal of Law and Information Technology
IHL	In-House Lawyer
Ill L Rev	Illinois Law Review
ILT	Irish Law Times
INTA	International Trade Association
Int T L R	International Trade Law and Regulation
Iowa L Rev	Iowa Law Review
IP News	Intellectual Property News
IPQ	Intellectual Property Quarterly
IPR	Intellectual Property Report

ITLQ	International Trade Law Quarterly
JBL	Journal of Business Law
J Intell Prop L	Journal of Intellectual Property Law
JL & Economics	Journal of Law and Economics
JIPLP	Journal of Intellectual Property Law
J Pat Off Soc'y	Japanese Patent Office Society
JPO	Japanese Patent Office
Law & Comtem Probs	Law and Contemporary Problems
Liverpool L R	Liverpool Law Review
LS	Legal Studies
Marq Intell Prop L Rev	Marquette Intellectual Property Law Review
MIP	Managing Intellectual Property
MLR	Modern Law Review
New Eng L Rev	New England Law Review
NLJ	National Law Journal
Nw J of Tech & Intell Prop	Northwestern Journal of Technology and Intellectual Property
OAMI	Spanish language for OHIM
OHIM	Office for Harmonisation in the Internal Market
Paniser IPB	Paisner Intellectual property Briefing
Paris Convention	The Paris Convention for the Protection of Industrial Property (of March 20, 1883)
Pharm LI	Pharmaceutical Law Insight
PLC	Practical Law Companies
Rev Litig	Review of Litigation
RPC	Reports of Patent Cases
Singapore Treaty	Singapore Treaty on the Law of Trademark
SJ	Solicitors Journal
SL Rev	Student Law Review
TLT	Trademark Law Treaty
TLR	Tulan Law Review
TM Bulletin	Trade Mark Bulletin
TMR	Trade Mark Reporter
TW	Trademark World
U Chi L Re	University of Chicago Law Review
U Dayton L Rev	University of Dayton Law Review
U Pa Int'l Econ L	University of Pennsylvania Journal of International Economic Law
USPTO	United States Patents and Trademarks Office
U W Ontario L Rev	University of Western Ontario Law Review
Vande L Rev	Vanderbilt Law Review
Vir L Rev	Virginia Law Review
Wake Forest L Rev	Wake Forest Law Review
Wash U J L & Pol'y	Washington University Journal of Law and Policy
WIPO	World Intellectual Property Organization

WIPR   World Intellectual Property Reporter
WLLR   World Licensing Law Report
WLR   Weekly Law Reports (UK)
WTLR   World Trademark Law Report
WTO   World Trade Organization
Yale L J   Yale Law Journal
YC & ML   Yearbook of Copyright and Media Law

List of Japanese terms

防護商標	*bogo-syohyo*	Defensive trademark
防護商標登録	*bogo-syohyo toroku*	Registration of defensive trademark
知的財産	*chiteki zaisan*	Intellectual property
知的財産法	*chiteki zaisan ho*	Intellectual Property Law
不正の目的	*fuseino mokuteki*	Unfair purposes
不正競争防止法	*fusei kyoso boshi ho*	Unfair Competition Law
漢字	*kanji*	Japanese kanji scripts
希釈化	*kisyakuka*	Dilution
混同	*kondo*	Confusion
混同のおそれ	*kondo no osore*	Likelihood of confusion
民法	*min po*	Civil Code
水際規制	*mizugiwa kisei*	Border control
識別力	*shikibetsu ryoku*	Distinctiveness
種苗法	*syobyo ho*	Plant Variety Protection Seed Act
商標	*syohyo*	Trademark
商標法	*syohyo ho*	Trademark Law
商標条例	*syohyo jyorei*	Old Trademark Ordinance
商標審査基準	*syhohyo shinsa kijyun*	Trademark Examination Guidelines
著名	*tyomei*	Famous
著名商標	*tyomei-syohyo*	Famous trademark
特許庁	*tokkyo cyo*	Patent Office

1 Well-known trade marks: background

1.1 Introduction

The main theme of this book is an exploration of well-known trade mark protection and, subsequently, the conceptualisation of well-known trade mark protection. Such an exploration contains two different limbs. The first is to look at well-known trade mark protection conceptually by exploring the conceptually comprehensive definition of well-known trade mark. The second is to examine the efficacy and credibility of well-known trade mark protection against 'dilution' in the EU and Japan.

This introductory chapter is divided into three parts. The first part provides essential background information to trade marks and well-known trade mark protection – that is, how trade marks and well-known trade marks are statutorily protected, and what the rationale for the protection is – followed by a brief introduction to the 'well-known trade mark'.

The second part looks at the dilution doctrine, outlining the development of the principle in the United States, the EU and Japan. The third part deals with other matters such as structure and terminology.

1.2 The life story of a well-known trade mark

The life of a well-known trade mark starts as an ordinary sign/symbol that is capable of distinguishing product A from others. Some of the ordinary marks, such as fanciful or coined marks (e.g. Kodak for photography products, Google for the internet search engine), are strongly distinctive at birth (inherent distinctiveness). Others, such as arbitrary marks (e.g. MANGO for clothing, Apple for computers), are not born as strongly distinctive as Kodak or Google, although they can obtain distinctiveness through intensive use (acquired distinctiveness). Furthermore, suggestive marks (e.g. Greyhound for buses, Jaguar for cars) are, yet again, not born as inherently distinctive as coined marks, but, like arbitrary marks, can acquire distinctiveness. The ordinary mark, irrespective of inborn distinctiveness, becomes well known when it obtains a certain degree of market recognition and further 'distinctiveness' (through use – see Figure 1.1 below). The transformation from an ordinary to a well-known and a well-known to a famous mark is illustrated in Figure 1.1 below.

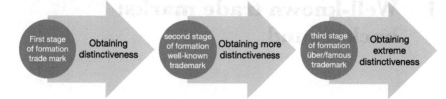

Figure 1.1 Formation of a well-known trade mark

The algorithm of the transformation here is from the most general to the most distinctive: trade mark → well-known trade mark → famous mark. Therefore, the passport to becoming a well-known trade mark is obtaining *a certain degree of distinctiveness*.

Although this book explores predominantly the second stage of formation, it is essential to explain the first stage at which the story of a well-known trade mark always begins.

1.3 Trade mark protection: briefing

Equipped with the trade mark taxonomy, this section serves as a brief introduction to the substance of trade marks and trade mark protection.

Trade marks are protected by law through registration (trade mark protection principle 1). The rationale of trade mark protection can be summarised as protection of the following functions. The trade mark is an indication of trade origin (i). Traders use their own mark to indicate the original producer and to differentiate their own product, to which the mark is attached, from others. As a result, consumers are given the (informed) choice to select the product for purchase. In the meantime, consumers may also have a certain degree of expectation as to the quality of the product that they have chosen to purchase. At this stage, the trade mark is working as a symbol of quality guarantee; this is known as the quality guarantee function of trade marks (ii). This does not mean that the product is of excellent quality; the trade mark operates to indicate an *equal* quality. Alongside these two functions, trade marks are also believed to disseminate a message and facilitate communication between the product to which the mark is attached and the consumer. This third function is known as the advertising function of trade marks (iii). It is understood that protecting these functions ultimately protects the interests of beneficiaries, including traders, consumers and the public as a whole.

In operation, the trade mark is protected through registration. Once the mark in question is registered, the registered trade mark acquires a bundle of exclusive monopolistic rights concerning the use of such a mark. One of these rights gives the trade mark proprietor a cause of action in trade mark infringement, where third parties attempt to register and/or use a mark that is identical or similar to the earlier registered trade mark in relation to identical or similar goods or services.

Trade mark protection operates on the principle that if such registration were allowed, this would be likely to cause confusion as to trade origin in the consumers/ public (beneficiaries), and the law aims to protect the beneficiaries from such confusion (trade mark protection principle 2).

The proprietor of the trade mark could claim that the mark is well known when it reaches the second stage (see Figure 1.1 above). Well-known trade mark protection departs from the original operation of trade mark protection in two ways (trade mark protection principles 1 and 2).

First, the protection given is not confined to registered marks; it can be given irrespective of whether or not the mark is registered (well-known trade mark protection principle 1). Therefore, it goes beyond the 'registration principle'. The proprietor of an unregistered well-known mark can enjoy protection against the situation in which the earlier mark is considered to be reproduced, imitated or translated by third parties, given that such use is likely to cause confusion in the relevant public. Second, one of the exclusive rights conferred on well-known trade mark proprietors is the right to prevent third parties from registering/using a mark that is identical or similar to the earlier well-known trade mark in relation to dissimilar goods or services. Well-known trade mark protection expands the scope of protection to situations in which there is no likelihood of confusion between the earlier well-known trade mark and the later mark in the relevant public, even though these two marks are used for dissimilar goods or services (well-known trade mark protection principle 2). Therefore, this goes beyond the second pillar of the trade mark protection principle – protecting trade marks as an indication of trade origin.

Comparing general/ordinary trade mark protection with well-known trade mark protection, it is obvious that the latter offers stronger protection and a broader scope of protection to well-known trade marks and empowers primarily the well-known trade mark proprietor. Placing the theory of well-known trade mark protection into a practical context, well-known trade mark proprietors would seek a way in which they could enjoy this extra layer of protection. So the first apparent hurdle for those wishing to have an extra layer of protection is to understand what a well-known trade mark consists of, and to learn the ways in which the mark can qualify as a 'well-known trade mark'. The next question therefore is 'What is a well-known trade mark?' This question is the starting point of this book and hereinafter will be referred as the key question.

In answering the key question, the first and main task is to explore the statutory definition of 'well-known trade mark' with a view to delineating and comprehending the conceptual definition of a well-known trade mark, which is found at the national (Japan), regional (the EU) and international level. The heart of my argument is that well-known trade mark protection has developed contextually, rather than conceptually. The contextualisation of well-known trade mark protection, as opposed to its conceptualisation, appears to cause uncertainty in determining the scope of well-known trade mark protection. The conceptuali- sation of well-known trade mark protection will be considered as a possibility for future development.

1.4 Well-known trade mark protection: legal framework

Now that the operation of well-known trade mark protection has been explained, this section will explore how an international notion of well-known trade mark protection was initiated and developed (more detailed treatment of the relevant international regimes may be found in Chapters 2 and 3).

The notion of establishing an international legal framework for well-known trade mark protection has developed gradually over decades.[1] The first relevant international instrument to embrace the general idea of protecting intellectual property rights, including trade marks, was the Paris Convention.[2] The first provision, which urged protection of the well-known mark, is contained in Article 6*bis* of the Paris Convention.

Debate and scrutiny of Article 6*bis* was undertaken during the 1920s in a series of meetings held by the Signatory States of the Paris Convention, and at The Hague conference in 1925[3] Article 6*bis* was introduced into the Paris Convention.[4] As a result, necessary amendments were made by signatory nations in order to be consistent with the Paris Convention.[5]

The trade mark provisions in the Paris Convention are based on a set of principles[6] to secure and protect trade mark rights, which ultimately aims to contribute to the development of international trade[7] and to offer future harmonisation of international trade mark law.[8]

Article 6*bis* is known as the first international provision that urged signatory nations to set up an infrastructure to promote protection of well-known trade

---

1 See WIPO, *Introduction to Intellectual Property: Theory and Practice*, London: Kluwer Law International, 1997.
2 Paris Convention for the Protection of Industrial Property.
3 See Japanese Patent Office, *Protection of Well-Known and Famous Trademarks*: Japan Patent Office Asia-Pacific Industrial Property Centre, 1999.
4 See Chapter 2, Section 2.3.1.1.
5 In fact, the Japanese Trademark Act was initially amended on this point in advance of the international change. In 1921, Section 2(1)(8) of the *Taisyo 10nen Syohyo ho* (the Trademark Act of 1921) introduced protection for unregistered well-known trade marks in Japan (Section 2(1)(5) of unregistered well-known mark protection). The Japanese trademark regime was then further amended in accordance with the Paris Convention in 1934 (by Act No. 15 of 1934). Please note that current protection of well-known trade marks in Japan is to be found in Article 4(1)(10) of the current law (Act No. 16 of 2008) and this section was itself introduced by an amendment in 1991 (Act No. 65 of 1991).
6 The Paris Convention requires signatory nations to implement the following: principle of territoriality (Articles 4, 4*bis*), the national treatment principle (Article 2), the principle of independence of rights (Articles 4*bis* and 6) and the *telle-quelle* principle (Article 6*quinquies* A(1)). The principle of territoriality means, for example, that Japan does not have to allow trade mark registration 'A' on the grounds that China has allowed trade mark registration 'A'. This principle of territoriality acknowledges the fact that national operation might differ from country to county and recognises that jurisdictions might have their own interpretation.
7 The Paris Convention requires signatory nations to implement the following: principle of territoriality (Articles 4, 4*bis*), the national treatment principle (Article 2), the principle of independence of rights (Articles 4*bis* and 6) and the *telle-quelle* principle (Article 6*quinquies* A(1)).
8 See, for example, J. Phillips, *Trade Marks at the Limit*, London: Edward Elgar Publishing, 2006.

marks.[9] Under Article 6*bis*, Signatory States of the Convention are required to protect well-known trade marks, irrespective of whether they were registered as national trade marks (well-known trade mark protection principle 1). However, Article 6*bis* has a limited application, affording protection to well-known trade marks only for unauthorised third-party use in relation to similar goods.[10] Therefore, well-known trade mark protection principle 2 did not yet come in force as a result of the Convention. Given that the Paris Convention provides the legal framework for well-known trade mark protection, the conceptual definition of the well-known mark is not provided. In other words, such a legal framework was established without having a clear conceptual definition of the well-known trade mark.

The second stage of international development in relation to well-known trade mark protection can be traced back to the introduction of Articles 16(1) and (2) GATT TRIPS,[11] which consolidated Article 6*bis*.[12] Yet again, the conceptual definition of the well-known trade mark is absent from GATT TRIPS. Although more thoroughly critiqued in Chapter 3, it can be noted here that Articles 16(1) and (2) collectively provide some guidance as to when a mark is 'well known' and extend Article 6*bis* to service marks and, in some circumstances, to unauthorised third-party use in relation to dissimilar goods and services (well-known trade mark protection principle 2).

Although the first meeting relating to the establishment of what later became GATT TRIPS is known to have taken place in March 1987, with GATT TRIPS finally coming into force in 1995 (see Chapter 2, Section 2.3.1.4, and Chapter 3, Section 3.2.2), it is interesting that there had been no perceived need (or opportunity) for the international community to revisit the issue of well-known trade marks in more than 60 years since the Paris Convention.

GATT TRIPS represents a further evolution of well-known trade mark protection. First, service trade marks are specifically recognised as a form of well-known trade mark (Article 16(2) of GATT TRIPS). Second, there is more detailed guidance provided, in the form of a knowledge requirement, for assessment as to whether a particular mark is well known or not (Article 16(3) of GATT TRIPS). Third, GATT TRIPS further extends the protection of registered well-known trade marks to goods or services that are not similar to those in respect of which the trademark has been registered, provided that its use would indicate a connection between those goods or services and the owner of the registered trade mark, and that the interests of the owner are likely to be damaged by such use (Articles 16(2) and (3) of GATT TRIPS). However, it should be noted here that, despite the introduction of these principles relating to the protection of well-known trade marks within these two international treaties,[13] there is no reference

9 For example, Phillips, *Trade Marks at the Limit*, 2006, p. 3.
10 A critical analysis of Article 6*bis* of the Paris Convention will be introduced in Chapter 3.
11 See Chapter 2, Section 2.3.1.4, and Chapter 3, Section 3.2.2.
12 See the full text of Article 6*bis* of the Paris Convention, Chapter 2, Section 2.3.1.1.
13 See Article 6*bis* of the Paris Convention and Article 15(1) of GATT TRIPS.

to *how* such marks should be protected at the local level, and nor, it is submitted, is there any clear and comprehensive definition of 'well-known trade mark' at the international level.[14]

The third and (to date) final stage in international development in relation to well-known trade mark protection was followed much more quickly by the soft law: the (non-binding[15]) WIPO Recommendation (the WIPO Joint Recommendation concerning Provisions on the Protection of Well-Known Marks).[16] Again, a fuller critique of this non-binding instrument can be found in Chapter 3, but it is sufficient to note here that the WIPO Recommendation sets out common principles and rules to assess the extent to which marks are 'well known'.

The WIPO Recommendation is considered to be a product of the recognition that well-known trade mark proprietors had been victims of counterfeiting,[17] and had suffered not only financial loss but also damage to face value as a result of the inappropriate use of well-known trade marks.[18] Having said that, it is disappointing to say that the conceptualisation of the definition of the well-known trade mark was not done therein; instead, contextualisation of the well-known trade mark seems to be evidenced.

In truth, an attempt to conceptualise the definition of 'well-known trade mark' has never materialised,[19] and the fluidity of its nature was accepted.[20] There is a strong school of thought that uncertainty (or at least fluidity) in the definition and regulation of well-known trade marks is somehow beneficial (or, at the very least, unproblematic).[21] As will be seen in the next section, the

---

14 See Chapter 3, Section 3.2.1, for the Paris Convention, and Chapter 3, Section 3.2.2, for GATT TRIPS.

15 The WIPO Joint Recommendation states that it is 'recommended that each Member State may consider the use of any of the provisions adopted by the Standing Committee on the Law of Trademarks, Industrial Designs and Geographical Indications (SCT) . . . as guidelines for the protection for well-known marks'. See the WIPO Recommendation, p. 3. Also, see J. Phillips, *Trade Mark Law: A Practical Anatomy*, Oxford: Oxford University Press, 2003, p. 413. Phillips explains that 'At present these recommendations are not enforceable propositions of law'.

16 See Chapter 3, Section 3.2.4 for the WIPO Joint Recommendation.

17 More detailed analysis will be provided in Chapter 5, Section 5.3.1. See, for example, C. Wadlow, '"Including Trade in Counterfeit Goods": The Origin of TRIPS as a GATT Anti-Counterfeiting Code' *Intellectual Property Quarterly*, 3, 2007, 350–402.

18 F. Mostert, 'Well-Known and Famous Marks: Is Harmony Possible in the Global Village?' *Trade Mark Reporter*, 86, 1996, 103–43.

19 For example, whilst the Paris Convention, which introduced the principle of the well-known trade mark to the international intellectual property regime (Article 1 of the Paris Convention), offers some principles relating to the special protection of well-known trade marks (see Article 6*bis* of the Paris Convention), it does not specify any measures for such protection. This is a recurrent theme in the international regulation of well-known trade marks: it is left to the individual signatory States to these various international agreements to develop their own measures to protect well-known trade marks.

20 One leading expert, Mostert, clearly stated in his article that 'the recognition and protection of well-known trade marks differ from country to country: the definitions and criteria in this area of trade mark law remain elusive'. See F. Mostert, 'When is a Mark "Well-Known"?', *Intellectual Property Quarterly*, 2, 1997, 377–83, p. 377.

21 See, for example, D. Tatham, 'WIPO Resolution on Well-Known Marks: A Small Step or a Giant Leap?', *Intellectual Property Quarterly*, 2, 2000, 127–37; A. Kur, 'Well-Known Marks, Highly Renowned Marks, and Marks Having a (High) Reputation – What's It All About?', *International*

'well-known trade mark' has been observed to be what 'we do not know; but we know when we see it'.[22]

Since the WIPO Recommendation was adopted in 1999, it is both surprising and contradictory that the law has not been revisited and that there have been no further significant international developments relating to the conceptualisation of the well-known trade mark.[23]

Certainly, technology that can be used to exploit such marks[24] has advanced,[25] and the environment in which (well-known) trade marks live has changed dramatically[26] and undoubtedly will continue to do so. In a similar vein, consumers themselves have also changed, becoming more sophisticated, educated, well informed and circumspect.[27]

This book therefore proposes, in accordance with changes in society, that the conceptualisation of well-known trade mark protection should be encouraged. The time has come to revisit and question the efficacy of the existing contextual approach to well-known trade mark protection. Re-examination of the law is required in order to provide sufficient scope of protection to the well-known trade mark in today's fast-moving society.

1.5 What is a 'well-known trade mark'?

What is a 'well-known trade mark'? . . . A well-known mark is . . . well, we can all recognise one when we see it, can't we? But can we verbalise that recognition? As St Augustine said: 'If no one asks me, I know what it is. But if I wish to explain it to him that asks me, I do not know.'[28]

Review of Intellectual Property and Competition Law, 23, 1992, 218–31; A. Kur, 'The WIPO Recommendations for the Protection of Well-Known Marks', *International Review of Intellectual Property and Competition Law*, 31, 2000, 824–45; A. Bertrand, 'French Trade Mark Law: From the Well-Known Brand to the Famous Brand', *European Intellectual Property Review*, 15, 1993, 142–5; M. Grinberg, 'The WIPO Joint Recommendation Protecting Well-Known Marks and the Forgotten Goodwill', *Chicago-Kent Journal of Intellectual Property*, 5, 2005, 1–11.

22 Tatham, 'WIPO Resolution on Well-Known Marks: A Small Step or a Giant Leap?', p. 129.

23 The WIPO Recommendation was adopted by the 34th series of meetings of the Assemblies of the Member States of WIPO, on 20–29 September 1999.

24 See, for example, J. Phillips, 'Information Overload and IP Practice', *Journal of Intellectual Property Law & Practice*, 4, 2009, 30.

25 For example, methods of communication have drastically changed in recent times with the mass use of social networking websites such as Facebook (see S. Sanghera, 'Facebook v Facetime: So What Do You Do?' *Times*, 23 August 2007). Facebook is said to have more than 1.23 billion active worldwide users in 2013 (statistics available online at www.facebook.com/facebook, accessed 4 November 2014). As this and other social networking sites can be a forum for both the marketing and abuse of well-known trade marks (see R. Bond, 'Business Trends in Virtual Worlds and Social Networks – An Overview of the Legal and Regulatory Issues Relating to Intellectual Property and Money Transactions', *Entertainment Law Review*, 20, 2009, 121–8), this relatively new medium of mass communication does pose some challenge to well-known trade mark protection.

26 See S. Maniatis, *The Communicative Aspects of Trade Marks: A Legal, Functional and Economic* Analysis, PhD thesis, University of London, 1998, p. 165.

27 Ibid.

28 Tatham, 'WIPO Resolution on Well-Known Marks: A Small Step or a Giant Leap?', p. 129.

As described in the previous section, there is no definition of a well-known trade mark provided in the international treaties, and therefore the most likely answer to the key question at this stage is 'we do not know, and the law does not define it'. A conceptual definition of well-known trade mark is not, *in fact*, established by national (Japanese) and regional (EU) laws. Equally importantly, there seems to be no interest in establishing it or any attempt to do so. It appears alarming that the legal framework was established by virtue of *not* having a clear definition of a well-known trade mark, and that the stronger protection has been offered without knowing what is to be protected.

This lack of conceptualising the definition of a well-known trade mark can be explained by the current accepted norm of well-known trade mark protection: well-known trade mark protection is 'not a matter of law; it is a matter of fact'.[29]

Under the current trade mark regime, a well-known trade mark is something to be assessed in its context (as opposed to something that is to be conceptually defined), and the author defines this method as the contextualisation of well-known trade mark protection as opposed to its conceptualisation. Until now, this contextual approach has not been challenged, and it looks as if it will remain unchallenged in the foreseeable future.

As a consequence of contextualisation, the courts make reference to fact-based criteria in order to *determine* whether a mark is well known, the scope of protection afforded to the well-known mark, and whether there is an infringement of the earlier well-known trademark or any other prohibited uses in the process of registration of the later mark. In other words, the courts put all the relevant factors into the particular context instead of using a conceptual definition of a well-known trade mark.

One possible benefit of the contextual approach to the well-known trade mark may well be flexibility and adaptability in the circumstances of a changing society. The determination of whether or not a mark in question is well known, and, if so, to what extent the exclusive rights conferred on the well-known trade mark can be exercised by its proprietor, is assessed on a case-by-case basis. As a result, changes in economy, society, culture and the financial markets can be reflected in the decision.

Contextualisation, however, might act as a double-edged sword. It looks too loosely defined and is likely to create ambiguity and uncertainty, which then leads to unpredictability in the application of the law. One of the most alarming consequences of contextualisation is that multiple ways of referring to 'well-known trade marks' have been generated – for example, famous marks, notorious marks, exceptionally well-known marks, highly reputed marks, highly renowned marks, marks of repute, marks with a (high) reputation, *marques de haut renommée*.[30] What is worse is that there is no means of testing whether these variations indicate the same concept as 'well-known trade mark'.

29 See Mostert, 'Well-Known and Famous Marks: Is Harmony Possible in the Global Village?'.
30 Tatham, 'WIPO Resolution on Well-Known Marks: A Small Step or a Giant Leap?', p. 128.

We will now look at the German approach to illustrate the point above. The author argues that the German approach is one exemplar of unwelcome diversity in interpretation resulting from the absence of a conceptual definition of the well-known trade mark. The following presents the indicative interpretation of 'well-known' and 'famous' trade marks:[31]

> *A Well-Known Mark* is a mark which is widely known in the country concerned, to at least *50% of the potential purchasers* of the goods or services for which it is known, and to at least *60% of the relevant trade circles.* Furthermore, *a well-known mark must be a registered mark* at least in its owner's home territory and have a value calculated by an internationally accepted method, of at least *$2000 million".* [Emphasis added]
> . . . *A Famous Mark* is a mark which is *extremely* widely known in the country concerned, to at least *80% of the potential purchasers* of the goods or services for which it is known, and to at least *90% of the relevant trade circles.* Furthermore, *a famous mark must be a registered mark* at least in its owner's home territory and have a value calculated by an internationally accepted method of at least *$4000 million.* [Emphasis added]

Two points in relation to the German approach to the well-known trade mark can be put forward, although it seems impossible to measure the credibility of the German system as there is no yardstick with which to compare and contrast. Overall, it could be argued that the German approach[32] provides a degree of improvement when compared with having no definition at all.

First, a clear distinction between a well-known and a famous mark is attempted, irrespective of whether or not such a distinction is agreeable. A famous mark can be seen – in the German context at least – to be a sub-category of the well-known trade mark. In addition, the threshold for famous marks seems to be set higher than that of well-known trade marks, since a higher percentage is required to qualify as a famous mark compared with the well-known trade mark. In consequence, there is apparently a degree of clarity in the requirements of well-known and famous marks. Second, the requirements of well-known and famous mark are provided, and these requirements place emphasis heavily on evidence- and fact-based criteria in assessing well-known and famous trade marks. For instance, evidence of the market domination and market value[33] of the mark plays a significant role in meeting the threshold of being 'well known'.

To summarise the German approach, the following points can be reiterated. The credibility of the German approach is questionable because there is no tool

---

31 Tatham, 'WIPO Resolution on Well-Known Marks: A Small Step or a Giant Leap?', p. 128.
32 This definition draws heavily on the WIPO Recommendation and actual figures, but does not capture all aspects of this Recommendation that are relevant to the definition of a 'well-known trade mark'. WIPO, Joint Recommendation Concerning Provisions on Protection of Well-Known Marks. Publication 833(E).
33 Tatham, 'WIPO Resolution on Well-Known Marks: A Small Step or a Giant Leap?', p. 128.

to test it. Furthermore, terminological confusion over the well-known/famous mark is evidenced, and the efficacy of the distinction between a well-known and a famous mark is in doubt, as the term 'famous mark' is not employed in the relevant international, EU or Japanese laws.

To conclude, we still do not know conceptually what constitutes a well-known trade mark, although there is an agreed consensus that it is not something to be conceptually defined, but that it ought to be assessed or determined.

Under the current trade mark regime, the law makes reference to a set of fact-based criteria[34] in order to determine the scope of protection afforded to the well-known trade mark, such as determining whether the rights conferred on the well-known trade mark proprietor are infringed. The scope of protection given to the well-known trade mark is determined without establishing a conceptual definition of 'well-known trade mark'. The author argues that in order to provide sufficient scope of protection to the well-known trade mark, we must understand what the well-known trade mark is. Further, it is submitted that sufficient scope of protection cannot be given unless we conceptually understand a definition of 'well-known trade mark'. If the law does not know what it is to protect, how can the law determine the scope of protection? In other words, how can the law provide a sufficient degree of protection if the subject matter requiring protection is not known?

This book challenges the unchallenged consensus that well-known trade mark protection is something to be contextualised, not conceptualised. The author argues that conceptualisation may bring innate certainty and consistency into the existing framework and lessen uncertainty and ambiguity surrounding well-known trade mark protection.

1.6 The conceptualisation of a 'well-known trade mark': a proposed definition

This book attempts to challenge the unchallenged: the norm that well-known trade mark protection is a question of facts and that there is therefore no need to conceptually define what a well-known trade mark is by law. As has already been stated, the lack of the conceptualisation of a well-known trade mark seems to be one of the causes of unclearness, uncertainty and incoherency surrounding well-known trade mark protection. This book also argues that the law will be incapable of providing a sufficient level and scope of well-known trade mark protection until the law is clear about what is to be protected.

I have argued that a conceptual definition of what constitutes a well-known trade mark should be proposed at the international level. The potential benefit of this is to provide a basic but solid foundation for the evolution of a

---

34 The accepted attitude towards the well-known trade mark protection is that it is 'not a matter of law; it is a matter of fact", See Mostert, 'Well-Known and Famous Marks: Is Harmony Possible in the Global Village?'

more harmonised approach to the protection of well-known trade marks at the local level.

A proposed definition contains a mixture of quite general criteria and more specific economic thresholds, and therefore provides a more conceptualised and comprehensive approach to the ambiguity of the well-known trade mark:

> A well-known trade mark is an *über* mark, which has acquired the highest level of distinctiveness in the mind of the relevant public through use in the course of trade.

This proposed definition focuses on the level of acquired distinctiveness, and it can be achieved only through use in the course of trade; the onus will be on the use of the well-known trade mark.

Whether a mark has obtained this high standard of acquired distinctiveness is to be determined in relation to a range of criteria including: the degree of knowledge or recognition of the mark in the relevant sector of the public;[35] the duration, extent and geographical area of any use of the mark;[36] any promotion of the mark (advertising or publicity and presentation);[37] any registration or trade mark applications;[38] the record of successful enforcement of rights in the mark;[39] and, finally, the value of the mark.[40]

1.7 What is 'dilution'?

A discussion of well-known trade mark protection cannot be fully appreciated without making reference to the 'dilution' theory, since this has a direct correlation with one of the characteristics of well-known trade mark protection.

As a reminder, the main features of well-known trade mark protection are (i) that the protection can be given irrespective of whether or not the mark is registered (well-known trade mark protection principle 1); and (ii) that one of the exclusive rights conferred on well-known trade mark proprietors is broadened to include the right to prevent third parties from registering/using a mark that is identical or similar to the earlier well-known trade mark in relation to *dissimilar* goods or services (well-known trade mark protection principle 2). The aim of principle 2 is to protect well-known/famous marks against dilution. This book does not challenge the legitimacy of the dilution theory; rather, it aims to examine its efficacy and credibility.

Well-known trade mark protection principle 2 can be further explained in the following manner: the trade mark proprietor can be entitled to an exclusive right

---

35 Derived from Article 2(1)(b)(1) of the WIPO Recommendation.
36 Ibid., derived from Article 2(1)(b)(2).
37 Ibid., derived from Article 2(1)(b)(3).
38 Ibid., derived from Article 2(1)(b)(4).
39 Ibid., derived from Article 2(1)(b)(5).
40 Ibid., derived from Article 2(1)(b)(6).

to prevent any unauthorised third-party use of the proprietor's mark, which has become well-known/famous, if this is likely to cause dilution by blurring or tarnishment, irrespective of actual or likely confusion.[41] Therefore, well-known trade mark protection principle 2 offers exclusive rights to well-known trade mark owners to prevent the following: (i) dilution by blurring when the distinctiveness of the earlier mark fades away as a result of the later use; (ii) dilution by tarnishment where the reputation of the earlier mark is damaged by the later use.[42]

By way of background, a sketch of the dilution theory will be briefly presented.

The theory of dilution was introduced by an eminent academic, Frank Schechter, in 1927;[43] indeed, Schechter himself became known as founder of the dilution theory. He recognised the importance of trade marks as financial assets and was already urging the necessity of protection in 1927. It is disappointing that the law did not pick up and develop this accordingly.

With his famous illustration of the German '*Odol*' case,[44] Schechter defined dilution as:

> the gradual whittling away or dispersion of the identity and hold upon the public mind of the mark or name by its use upon non-competing goods. The more distinctive or unique the mark, the deeper is its impress upon the public consciousness, and the greater its need for protection.[45]

Schechter originally suggested that it was necessary to prevent the use of protected marks on goods that were not identical or similar to those of the senior use – effectively all goods. However, he also indicated a limit in his application of the dilution theory to 'coined, arbitrary and fanciful' marks by virtue of his belief that only the mark that is 'unique' and 'original' should enjoy the stronger protection.[46]

The justification of giving stronger protection against dilution, explained by Schechter, was that the uniqueness of the trade mark should be protected because 'the value of the modern trademark lies in its selling power',[47] originating from the uniqueness and/or individuality of the mark, which was a vehicle of the creation and retention of custom,[48] and it is of paramount interest to the trade mark owner.

---

41 See 15 USC § 1125 (c) (1).
42 For example, in the US see 15 USC § 1125 (a) and (c). Further, the concept of dilution is quite broad in this jurisdiction: 15 USC § 1125 (c) provides that dilution can occur by 'blurring' and 'tarnishment' as follows: 'dilution by blurring' is association arising from the similarity between a mark or trade name and a famous mark that impairs the distinctiveness of the famous mark; and 'dilution by tarnishment' is association arising from the similarity between a mark or trade name and a famous mark that harms the reputation of the famous mark.
43 See F. Schechter, 'The Rational Basis of Trademark Protection', *Harvard Law Review*, 40, 1927, 813–33.
44 See Schechter, 'The Rational Basis of Trademark Protection', pp. 831–3.
45 Ibid., p. 825.
46 Ibid., p. 828.
47 Ibid., pp. 831–3.
48 Ibid., pp. 831–3, p. 822.

Although the legal concept of dilution has been described as 'exceedingly difficult to explain and understand. Misunderstanding is rampant',[49] the interpretation of dilution given by Schechter can be summarised in a simple manner: dilution is the gradual whittling away of the distinctiveness of the earlier coined famous mark by the later use of a similar or identical mark in relation to non-related goods or services.

At this stage, the author of this book argues that conceptualisation of the dilution theory, to a certain degree, has been undertaken, although it might not be as comprehensive as we would like. We can, at least, have a very brief concept of what dilution is.

1.7.1 The United States

This section will offer a very brief overview of the development of well-known trade mark protection against dilution initiated in US federal law. The US has a dual judicial system: state law and federal law. The former regulates the law at the state level and the latter governs the national level; the examination of state law is beyond the scope of this book.

As noted in the previous section, the US has been a key player and developer in relation to the study of dilution theory,[50] although it was only in 1995 that the US incorporated trademark protection against dilution into federal law. Surprisingly, prior to 1995 it was only state law that regulated dilution.

The first federal legislation, the Federal Trademark Dilution Act (the FTDA), which incorporated trade mark protection against dilution (well-known trade mark protection principle 2), came into force in 1996.[51] The life of the FTDA was not long. The FTDA was soon replaced, in accordance with case law,[52] by the current legislation, the Trademark Dilution Revision Act (TDRA), which came

---

49 See T. McCarthy, *McCarthy on Trademarks and Unfair Competition*, New York: Clark Boardman Callaghan 1995, § 24:67, and T. McCarthy, 'Proving a Trademark Has Been Diluted: Theories or Facts?', *Houston Law Review*, 41, 2004, 713–47, p. 726.

50 As a result, there has been significant analysis, resulting in a considerable literature, of dilution, particularly in the US. For example, see Schechter, 'The Rational Basis of Trademark Protection'; T. McCarthy, 'Dilution of a Trademark: European and United States Law Compared', *Trade Mark Reporter*, 94, 2004, 1163–81; B. Pattishall, 'The Dilution Rationale for Trademark–Trade Identity Protection, Its Progress and Prospects', *Trade Mark Reporter*, 67, 1997, 607–24; S.L. Burstein, S 'Dilution by Tarnishment: The New Cause of Action', *Trade Mark Reporter*, 98, 2008, 1189–252; G. Dinwoodie and M. Janis, 'Confusion over Use: Contextualism in Trademark Law', *Trade Mark Reporter*, 98, 2008, 1086–159. Outside US law, examples of dilution literature include T. Martino, *Trademark Dilution*, Oxford: Clarendon Press, 1996; I. Simon, *Trade Mark Dilution in Europe and The United States*, Oxford: Oxford University Press, 2012.

51 Codified.

52 *Moseley v V Secret Catalogue, Inc.*, 537 U.S. 418, 430, 123 S. Ct. 1115, 1123, 155 L. Ed. 2d 1, 65 U.S.P.Q.2d 1801 (2003). It was held that violation of the FTDA required a finding of actual dilution to the famous mark. The mark in question could not prove the actual dilution, and therefore the claim failed.

into force in 2006.[53] Hereinafter, reference will be made solely to the TDRA, as it entirely replaced the FTDA.

The TDRA provides an injunctive relief to famous mark proprietors against dilution:

> [T]he owner of *a famous mark* that is *distinctive, inherently or through acquired distinctiveness*, shall be entitled to an injunction against another person who, at any time after the owner's mark has become famous, commences use of a mark or trade name in commerce that is likely to cause dilution by blurring or dilution by tarnishment of the famous mark, *regardless of the presence or absence of* actual or likely confusion, of competition, or of *actual economic injury*.[54] [Emphasis added]

Further, the definition of a famous mark is provided as follows:

> [A] mark is famous if it is widely recognized by the general consuming public of the United States as a designation of source of the goods or services of the mark's owner. In determining whether a mark possesses the requisite degree of recognition . . .[55]

Although the main focus of this section stays within the analysis of the concept of dilution, it is of interest to share the US approach to the 'well-known trade mark' and its assessment criteria.

The first observation to be made by this author is that the term 'well-known mark' used in Article 6*bis* of the Paris Convention is not employed; instead, the term 'famous mark' is used.[56] Furthermore, the famous mark is defined as being an inherently or acquired distinctive mark. The famous mark is defined in two forms: as a mark that has acquired the requisite degree of recognition[57] and as a mark that is widely recognised by the general consuming public of the United States. Thus, the famous mark in the US can be interpreted as an inherently distinctive mark or a mark that has acquired distinctiveness, which possesses the requisite degree of recognition – that is, it is widely recognised by the general public of the US.

The second observation follows from the first point: the TDRA attempts to contextualise (not conceptualise[58]) the required degree of fame from two different

---

53 The TDRA is said to have been introduced in an attempt to solve concerns raised by the case of *Moseley v V Secret Catalogue, Inc.*

54 15 USC § 1125 (C)(1).

55 15 USC § 1125 (2)(A).

56 This is yet another example of inconsistency in the use of terminology across international borders.

57 15 USC § 1125 (2)(A).

58 X. Nguyen, 'New Wild West: Measuring and Proving Fame and Dilution under the Federal Trademark Dilution Act', *Albany Law Review*, 63, 2000, 201–40, pp. 209–12.

aspects: one is geographically based, and the other is knowledge-based (linking to the population).

The TDRA then provides a catalogue of the assessment criteria in determining the fame:

(i)   The duration, extent, and geographic reach of advertising and publicity of the mark, whether advertised or publicized by the owner or third parties;

(ii) The amount, volume, and geographic extent of sales of goods or services offered under the mark;

(iii) The extent of actual recognition of the mark;

(iv) Whether the mark was registered under the Act of March 3, 1881, or the Act of February 20, 1905, or on the principal register.[59]

At first glance, it appears very difficult and demanding to meet the criteria of 'fame'[60] under the TDRA, since the mark must be 'widely recognized by the general consuming public of the United States'[61] as a designation indicating a single source of goods or services.[62]

As a consequence of the rigour threshold, a mark that is famous only in a so-called niche market seems to be outside the scope of protection.[63] Thus, traders in a niche market, such as the supply of surgical components, seem likely to be disadvantaged due to the market size and targeted audience, even though it is certain that the mark would be well known within the medical profession.[64]

In contrast, there are some positives for the proprietors of famous marks. Under the FTDA, only the coined mark would qualify as a famous mark (a requirement that mirrors Schechter's proposal[65]), whilst the TDRA provides a remedy for a mark that is not innately distinctive. Moreover, the former FTDA required actual dilution of the mark – a likelihood of dilution was insufficient to meet the criteria – whereas the TDRA no longer requires actual dilution, and the likelihood is sufficient enough to obtain the injunctive relief.

On balance, the threshold to prove the mark of fame became higher, but the requirement to prove the dilution became more lenient. It can thus be summarised that the TDRA has broadened the scope of protection, but has limited the qualifying subject matter to a mark of fame.

This section now moves on to an exploration of the dilution concept. The TDRA provides an injunctive relief to famous trade mark owners where a third

59 15 USC § 1125 (2)(A)(i)–(iv).
60 See McCarthy, *McCarthy on Trademarks and Unfair Competition*, § 24:104.
61 15 USC § 1125 (2)(A).
62 See McCarthy, *McCarthy on Trademarks and Unfair Competition*, § 24:104.
63 Ibid., § 24:105.
64 Ibid.
65 See Schechter, 'The Rational Basis of Trademark Protection', p. 825.

party's use of the famous mark is likely to cause dilution by blurring or by tarnishment.[66]

Two forms of dilution are explained therein:

(i) 'dilution by blurring' is *association* arising from the *similarity* between a mark or trade name and a famous mark that impairs the *distinctiveness* of the famous mark;[67]

(ii) 'dilution by tarnishment' is *association arising from the similarity* between a mark or trade name and a famous mark *that harms the reputation* of the famous mark.[68] [Emphasis added]

Amongst a number of theoretical changes made in the TDRA, two are directly relevant to the concept of dilution. First, the TDRA departed from the original interpretation of dilution in the FTDA and introduced the new interpretation of dilution by blurring. Second, a list of the assessment criteria for dilution by blurring was, for the first time, included in law.

In the former law, the FTDA, dilution by blurring was 'the lessening of the capacity of a famous mark to identify and distinguish goods or services'[69] (mirroring the original Schechter definition[70]), whereas in the TDRA dilution by blurring is an association that impairs the distinctiveness of the famous mark because of the similarity of the two marks in question. 'Impairs the distinctiveness of the famous mark' appears to reflect Schechter's orthodox definition: 'lessening of the capacity of a famous mark to identify'. However, this lessening and impairment of the distinctiveness is predetermined in the TDRA to be caused solely by the association of two marks. In other words, the threshold has arguably become higher, as the proprietor must prove action-able association that is created by the similarity of the two marks. Another point is noteworthy here: the association is understood to be 'a real world state of mind that occurs in people's brains. It should be classified as a question of fact, not a question of law.'[71] Therefore, the assessment results in relying heavily on the survey-based evidence. This is yet another example of approving the contex-tualisation of well-known trade mark protection against dilution, as opposed to its conceptualisation.

Now, we shall look at the assessment criteria of dilution by blurring, bearing in mind that there are four limbs of dilution: association, similarity, impairment and distinctiveness.

---

66 15 USC § 1125 (C)(1).
67 15 USC § 1125 (B). This definition was significantly changed from FTDA. Under the previous legislation, FTDA defined dilution as 'the lessening of the capacity of a famous mark to identify and distinguish goods or services'.
68 15 USC § 1125 (C).
69 Lanham Act § 43(c)(1), 15 U.S.C.A. § 1125(c)(1):
70 See Schechter, 'The Rational Basis of Trademark Protection', p. 825.
71 See McCarthy, *McCarthy on Trademarks and Unfair Competition*, § 24:116.

(i) The degree of similarity between the mark or trade name and the famous mark. The 2006 Federal Antidilution Statute is silent on the crucial question of exactly how similar the conflicting marks must be to create the requisite 'association'.[72]

(ii) The degree of inherent or acquired distinctiveness of the famous mark. Although the TDRA does not exclude the non-inherently distinctive mark from the protectable subject matter, this criterion operates as a *de facto* control mechanism to see if the mark is inherently distinctive (i.e. coined marks). This is based on the assumption that the more distinctive the mark is, the more likely that dilution would occur.

(iii) The extent to which the owner of the famous mark is engaging in substantially exclusive use of the mark. This exercise aims to investigate any existing third party's use (i.e. quantity and types of use) of identical or similar marks in order to examine the exclusivity of the famous mark.

(iv) The degree of recognition of the famous mark. This duplicates the criterion of assessing the famousness of the mark (point (ii) above). This exercise examines how famous the mark is.

(v) Whether the user of the mark or trade name intended to create an association with the famous mark. This criterion, based I would suggest on bad faith, investigates whether the later owner had the intention of taking unfair advantage of the aura of the famous mark. This criterion was criticised as being 'misleading'[73] as it would give the misguided impression that the TDRA provides protection against free-riding (which the EU trade mark regime does).

(vi) Any actual association between the mark or trade name and the famous mark.[74] This criterion is explained as an introduction to any type of evidence of proof.[75] As has been explained, making an association between two marks is a state of mind; therefore, only evidence can prove whether a consumer has made an association between the two marks.

Although a list was a new, 'exciting' and forward-looking entry to the US legislation (pre-TDRA legislation, the list was not included in the statute and by the courts[76]), regrettably less enthusiastic feedback was received by the leading trade mark academic;[77] some of the criticisms have already been presented above. One of the

---

72 See McCarthy, *McCarthy on Trademarks and Unfair Competition*, § 24:119.
73 Ibid.
74 15 USC § 1125 (2)(B)(i)–(vi).
75 See McCarthy, *McCarthy on Trademarks and Unfair Competition*, § 24:119.
76 A list of six factors of blurring was established by Judge Sweet in the case of *Mead Data Cent., Inc. v Toyota Motor Sales, U.S.A., Inc.*, 875 F.2d 1026, 10 U.S.P.Q.2d 1961 (2d Cir. 1989). In 1999, the so-called Nabisco 10-factor test was also introduced by the case of *Nabisco, Inc. v PF Brands, Inc.*, 191 F.3d 208, 51 U.S.P.Q.2d 1882 (2d Cir. 1999).
77 McCarthy argued that the list of factors 'is both incomplete and misleading because none of the factors directs attention to the crucial issue: is there a likelihood that this defendant's mark is likely to be a use that "impairs the distinctiveness of the famous mark"?' See McCarthy, *McCarthy on Trademarks and Unfair Competition*, § 24:119.

most obvious points to note is the dearth of a list regarding dilution by tarnishment, irrespective of whether or not this is advantageous. Another heavily weighted criticism is that the TDRA appears to give an inaccurate impression that the law offers protection against free-riding within the TDRA. Taking into account all negative feedback to the list provided, there is, in the view of this author, some scope for appraisal. One development is that a new interpretation of dilution was put forward. This provides a certain degree of fluidity and flexibility in interpreting the theoretical framework of law, and presents the perspective that rigidity of the theoretical framework can be positively challenged. This is of significance as this author attempts to suggest a new approach to the theory of well-known trade mark protection; that is to say, the conceptualisation as opposed to contextualisation of well-known trade mark protection.

Overall, although the US dilution theory has been criticised as being difficult to understand,[78] it can be simply illustrated. When an ordinary mark 'possesses the requisite degree of recognition'[79] – that is to say, the mark is widely recognised by the general public – the proprietor of the famous mark is entitled to request an injunctive relief against a third party's use that 'causes dilution of the distinctive quality of the mark'.[80] In this book this is referred to as well-known trade mark protection principle 2.

The factors used to assess the mark of fame are: (i) the degree of advertising and publicity of the marks; (ii) how much the goods or services to which the mark is attached have been sold; (iii) evidence to show the actual recognition of the mark; (iv) whether the mark is registered. As has been explained, the higher threshold for the mark to be qualified as famous is self-evident. It is noteworthy that the interpretation of dilution by blurring was changed from that in the FDTA to that of the TDRA: an association arising from the similarity of the marks, which impairs the distinctiveness of the famous mark.

Following the new interpretation, a list of factors to assess whether there is an actionable dilution by blurring or not is, for the first time, set out: (i) the similarity of the two marks;[81] (ii) the degree of inherent distinctiveness of the marks;[82] (iii) the existing and concurrent use of the mark that is identical or similar to the famous mark;[83] (iv) degree of fame of the mark;[84] (v) the intention of the owner of the later mark to 'free-ride' on the aura of the famous mark;[85] (vi) evidence of the association of the two marks.[86]

---

78 It is said that 'because [dilution] is largely a theoretical and almost ephemeral concept, the legal theory of "dilution" is exceedingly difficult to explain and understand. Misunderstanding is rampant.' See McCarthy, *McCarthy on Trademarks and Unfair Competition*, pp.166–7.
79 15 USC § 1125 (2)(A).
80 Ibid.
81 15 USC § 1125 (2)(B)(i).
82 15 USC § 1125 (2)(B)(ii).
83 15 USC § 1125 (2)(B)(iii).
84 15 USC § 1125 (2)(B)(iv).
85 15 USC § 1125 (2)(B)(v).
86 15 USC § 1125 (2)(B)(vi).

On balance, well-known trade mark protection against dilution in the US appears to be theoretically grounded and the rationalisation of such concepts seems rather simple. I am in favour of raising the threshold for qualifying as a famous mark and expanding the scope of subject matter resulting from including marks that are not inherently distinctive. In contrast, the criteria to assess both the mark of fame and whether there is a dilution by blurring and tarnishment need to be revised, as the efficacy of some of the factors looks doubtful.

The following sections will examine the ways in which dilution theory[87] has been imported to the EU[88] and Japan[89] in contributing to the development of well-known trade mark protection.

1.7.2 The EU

The recognition and operation of well-known trade mark protection against dilution at the EU level seems to be more complex[90] than that of the US (federal law) or Japan. Although the root of dilution was recognised in the Benelux jurisprudence,[91] the EU seems to have shown hesitation in transplanting this US dilution concept and terminology into EU legislation.[92] Note that the term 'well-known mark' employed in Article 6*bis* of the Paris Convention is not used in the EU instrument either.

Instead of transplanting the dilution theory developed in the US, the EU demonstrates its own interpretation of dilution and its own methods of providing protection against dilution. For example, the principle of well-known trade mark protection set out by Article 6*bis* of the Paris Convention is transformed by the EU trade mark law as follows: the protection for a mark of repute against detrimental use of the distinctiveness/reputation of the mark and taking unfair advantage of the mark of repute or the distinctive mark.[93]

As can be noticed, a new form of dilution, which is intentionally excluded from the US legislation,[94] is included – dilution by free-riding. As a consequence, it is self-evident that the lack of uniformity and harmonised comprehension of trade

---

87 This theory has been discussed in detail by commentators from Frank Schechter onwards (Schechter can be said to have been a founding father of dilution theory in his famous illustration of '*Odol*'; see Schechter, 'The Rational Basis of Trademark Protection', pp. 831–3. Further, dilution has been a long-standing part of US law, the current provisions, following the Federal Trademark Dilution Act, being codified at 15 USC § 1125 (c)(1).

88 See Chapter 4, Section 4.4; B. Trimmer, 'An Increasingly Uneasy Relationship – the English Courts and the European Court of Justice in Trade Mark Disputes', *European Intellectual Property Review*, 30, 2008, 87–8; and Simon, *Trade Mark Dilution in Europe and the United States*, pp. 9–13.

89 Dilution has been a long-standing part of US law, the current provisions, following the Federal Trademark Dilution Act, being codified at 15 USC § 1125 (c)(1).

90 Simon, *Trade Mark Dilution in Europe and the United States*, pp. 9–13.

91 See Schechter, 'The Rational Basis of Trademark Protection', p. 825.

92 Ibid., p. 11.

93 See Article 4(4)(a) of the EU Trademark Directive/Article 8(5) of the CTMR.

94 As a reminder, the US interpretation of dilution was *association* arising from the similarity between a mark or trade name and a famous mark that impairs the *distinctiveness* of the famous mark and/or harms the reputation of the famous mark.

mark dilution has, yet again, brought another layer of inconsistency and confusion to protection against dilution.

The main legislation for (well-known) trade mark protection in the EU is the Trade Mark Directive (EU TMD).[95] Briefly, the following four different forms of actionable harm caused to the mark of repute (grounds for rejecting registration of a mark and trade mark infringement) are:

(i) detriment to the distinctive character of the earlier mark;
(ii) detriment to the reputation of the earlier mark;
(iii) unfair advantage of the distinctive character of the earlier mark;
(iii) unfair advantage of the repute of the earlier mark.

The first form is understood as dilution by blurring; the second is understood as dilution by tarnishment; the third and fourth are understood as free-riding.[96]

As noted above, the main difference between the US and the EU is that the EU recognises the extra form of dilution – that is, dilution by free-riding.

The EU system of well-known trade mark protection against dilution will be explored further in Chapter 4.

1.7.3 Japan[97]

The recognition of dilution theory in Japan was received in a less complex manner compared with the EU jurisdiction. The US-born concept was transferred to Japan and brought immediate influence to Japanese trademark scholars.[98]

The constitution of the US–German-born theory has never been substantially challenged; Japanese scholars and legislators accepted the developed concept and incorporated the notion into domestic law.[99] Therefore the concept of dilution in Japan shares the same characteristics as that of the originating sources. (Note that the US interpretation of dilution by blurring has been changed,[100] although the Japanese interpretation by legislation and academic scholars still follows the original FDTA interpretation.)

The concept of dilution amongst Japanese trademark scholars is therefore understood to be: the act that diminishes the power of the well-known trademark to attract consumers; acts that cause this commercial and economic value – the

---

95 The most current codified version is Directive 2008/95/EC of the European Parliament and of the Council of 22 October 2008 to approximate the laws of the Member States relating to trade marks (Codified version). Prior to this, First Council Directive 89/104/EEC of the Council, of 21 December 1988, to approximate the laws of the Member States relating to trade marks.

96 I. Simon, *Trade Mark Dilution in Europe and the United States*, at 17–18.

97 When discussing marks in a non-Japanese or general context, the term 'trade mark' (two words) is employed; the single word 'trademark' is used for the Japanese context.

98 See, for example, M. Ozaki, 'The Requirements of Fame in Trademark Dilution', *Patent*, 49, 1996, 46–65, p. 46.

99 Ibid., p. 65.

100 See 15 USC § 1125 (2)(B).

distinctiveness, good image and attractive force for consumers – to be diminished are regulated.[101]

Despite a smooth welcoming of dilution theory, the trademark legislature did not incorporate such protection into the legislation until the late 1990s. Prior to this, protection against dilution was first developed and undertaken under the unfair competition law in 1993, as a result of a new government strategic plan called 'Intellectual Property Strategy Outline [chisteki zaisansenryaku taiko]'. After one more source of external but implicit pressure to amend the trademark law – that is, the introduction of the EU Trade Mark Directive – protection against dilution was incrementally added into trademark law as Article 4(1)(19). As will be explained in Chapter 5, one of the main reasons for the slow development in trademark legislation was that such a protection was historically dealt with in the domain of unfair competition law.

Trademark law in Japan includes the following Article 4(1)(19): 'protection against dilution if such trademark is used for unfair purposes (referring to the purpose of gaining unfair profits, the purpose of causing damage to the other person, or any other unfair purposes, the same shall apply hereinafter)'. Like the EU Trade Mark Directive and the CTMR, the Japanese legislation does not employ the actual term 'dilution'. In Chapter 5, a detailed examination of well-known trade mark protection against dilution will be discussed.

1.8 Structure

A brief introduction of the structure of the book will give further insight into its main emphasis. This book explores the efficacy of well-known trade mark protection in the EU and Japan against dilution according to the law as at October 2014. Chapter 1 serves as an introductory chapter, providing an overview of the main theme, the rationale of the book and its methodology and structure. Chapter 2 explores the definition of 'trade mark', as background for the later analysis of the definition of 'well-known trade mark'. Definitions of 'well-known trade mark' at the international level are then critiqued in Chapter 3. In Chapter 4 there follows a critical analysis of the definition of 'mark of repute' and an examination of the credibility and efficacy of the protection afforded to marks of repute against dilution in the EU trade mark regime. The definition of '*syuchi-syohyo*' and the credibility and efficacy of the protection afforded to *syuchi-syohyo* against *dilution* in the Japanese Trademark Act will be examined in Chapter 5. Thereafter, a critical comparison of the findings in Chapters 4 and 5 will be undertaken in Chapter 6. Finally, Chapter 7, the concluding chapter, will offer some recommendations for reform.

The book attempts to provide a comprehensive and critical overview of trademark law in Japan, including the historical development of the law and the recent developments in case law and policy. It includes detailed coverage of the

---

101 See N. Koizumi, 'Dilution', *Jurist*, 1005, 1992, 29.

Japanese Unfair Competition Prevention Act, and contains the first systematic analysis of Japanese jurisprudence and legislative amendments of law in relation to well-known trade marks and unfair competition, in order to allow readers to get to grips with trademark law in this important jurisdiction. The book goes on to a comparative analysis of the Japanese trademark law alongside that of the European Community trade mark system, and covers both protection against dilution of the Trade Marks Directive and recent European case law in this area.

Furthermore, the book attempts to uncover the difficulties in comprehensively defining a 'well-known trade mark' in the relevant international trade mark instruments. It challenges the traditional approach to the definition of 'well-known trade mark' – that is, the contextualisation (as opposed to the conceptualisation) of the well-known trade mark: 'we do not know what it is, but we all know when we see it' – and sets out a new theoretical model for defining well-known trade mark protection against dilution in both the EU trade mark regime[102] and the Japanese trademark[103] systems.

The ambit of the book is based on a number of assumptions: (i) well-known trade marks are the purest or strongest category of 'trade mark', and therefore analysis and consideration of the latter can be used to infer the nature of the former; (ii) the essence or heart of what constitutes a trade mark is the criterion of distinctiveness and, thus, *acquired* distinctiveness both distinguishes a well-known trade mark from an ordinary trade mark and goes to the essence or heart of what constitutes a well-known trade mark;[104] and (iii), following from (i), developing a conceptualisation of the definition of 'trade mark' can assist in conceptualising the definition of 'well-known trade mark'. Further, the latter can be of assistance in critically interrogating selected aspects of the protection afforded to well-known trade marks.[105]

---

102 Directive 2008/95/EC of the European Parliament and of the Council of 22 October 2008, to approximate the laws of the Member States relating to trade marks (Codified version), which repealed the First Council Directive of 21 December 1988 to approximate the laws of the Member States relating to trade marks (89/104/EEC).

103 The correct term for 'trademark' in Japan is 商標 (this is transliterated as *syohyo*, and usually translated as 'trademark'). '*Syohyo*', and 'trademark' are the terms that will be used in this book in relation to Japanese trademarks. The Japanese trademark system consists of a national registration system, operated by the Japanese Patent Office (hereinafter known as the JPO) which is located in Tokyo, Japan, and is governed by the 商標法: (*Syohyo-ho*: the Japanese Trademark Act No. 127 of 1959, last amended by Act No. 84 of 2014): hereinafter known as the Japanese Trademark Act. A full text of the Act is available online at www.japaneselawtranslation.go.jp/law/detail/?ft=2&re=01&dn=1&yo=&ia=03&kn[]=%E3%81%97&_x=19&_y=19&ky=&page=50 (accessed 6 February 2015).

104 It should be noted here that there are two types of 'distinctiveness': inherent distinctiveness and acquired distinctiveness. It is also important to note that there is a relationship between distinctiveness and reputation (the latter being seen as dependent on acquired distinctiveness).

105 Under Articles 4(4)(a) and 5(2) of the EU TMD, the protection afforded to 'trade marks with a reputation' will be given where the following four conditions have been satisfied: (i) earlier registered trade mark with reputation in the relevant area; (ii) identity or similarity between the applied EU and the earlier trade marks; (iii) usage of the mark applied for must take an unfair advantage of or be detrimental to the distinctive character or the reputation of the earlier mark; and (iv) such use must be without due course.

1.9 Terminology

There is some terminological confusion relating to the use of the term 'well-known trade mark', and this needs further clarification and explanation.

The spelling 'trade mark' is used throughout this book to refer to trade marks in the EU, international and generic contexts. Hereinafter, the equivalent transliterated Japanese term *syohyo* (商標: the usual English translation of which is 'trademark') will be used when referring to trade marks in the Japanese context. Note that Article 4 of the CTMR[106] and Article 2 of the Japanese Trademark Act[107] provide the legal definitions of 'trade mark' and '*syohyo*', respectively. Similarly, the term 'well-known trade mark' is used in the generic and international contexts, but not in the EU context: here the equivalent EU term 'trade mark of repute' is used. The equivalent transliterated Japanese term is '*syuchi-syohyo*' (周知商標: the usual English translation of which is 'well-known trademark') and it is this Japanese transliteration – *syuchi-syohyo* – that will be used when referring to well-known trade marks in the Japanese context.

When the EU is considered, the terms 'detriment' and 'unfair advantage' are employed, and the same terms are used when these concepts are noted in a generic context. The equivalent transliterated Japanese term is '*fuseino mokuteki*' (不正の目的: usually translated as 'unfair purposes') and this will be the term used in the Japanese context. The reader will note that the use of Japanese transliterations is the preferred form, rather than translations, of key terms. These Japanese transliterations have been employed in the book as a means of ensuring a consistent approach to Japanese law. This consistency, it is submitted, lies in two aspects: richness and accuracy. First, a transliteration preserves more effectively the etymology and thus the richness of the implicit meaning(s) of Japanese terms to a non-Japanese speaker (please see Section 1.10 below); second, translation has a greater potential for introducing inaccuracy. Relating to this point on accuracy, it is submitted (and further argued in Chapter 2, Section 2.3.3) that the official (non-authoritative) English translation of the Japanese Trademark Act is inaccurate in parts. Referring to original Japanese phrases in a transliterated form avoids perpetuating mistranslations and inaccuracies, and appears to be the most effective linguistic basis for undertaking a comparative legal analysis in the English language.

1.10 Japanese etymology

An important note of Japanese etymology, in the sense of the implicit meaning found within Japanese law and written Japanese, needs to be made here. This is

---

106 Article 2 of the EU TMD can be paraphrased as follows: trade marks are any graphically representable signs being capable of distinguishing goods and services of one undertaking from those of another undertaking.
107 Article 2 of the Japanese Trademark Act can be paraphrased as follows: *syohyo* includes any characters, signs, three-dimensional marks or combinations of colours which are used for business purposes.

important in general because a failure to understand this is a considerable barrier to the non-Japanese speaker's ability to comprehend the meaning of Japanese law, and specifically because these linguistic niceties later play a role in the analysis.

Perhaps it would be helpful to explain the nature of Japanese writing a little more at this stage. There are three separate writing scripts in modern Japanese. These scripts are combined; indeed, a single Japanese sentence might be written utilising all three scripts. Of these three, *Hira-kana* and *Kata-kana* are alphabet-based (*Hira-kana* is used for native words and *Kata-kana* for words borrowed from other languages): in essence, these two scripts convey sounds to the reader. In contrast, the symbolic *kanji* script conveys both concepts and implicit meanings, and it is the consideration of key *kanji* symbols that forms part of the analysis of Japanese law.

The difficulties faced by non-Japanese-speaking readers in relation to *kanji* and English translations of *kanji* and the advantage of employing transliterated rather than translated Japanese terms can be illustrated by a simple non-legal example. The term 'work' in Japanese is represented by the *kanji* symbol 仕事.[108] This symbol combines two symbolic elements, the first – 仕 (*shi*) – meaning loyalty, and the second – 事 (*goto*) – meaning matters and/or business. Thus 仕事 may be translated as 'work', but, as well as this straightforward English translation, it also has an implicit meaning relating to professional allegiance: it is this implicit meaning that is obvious to a Japanese speaker but is missing in the English translation. Thus, utilising the transliteration *shi goto*, rather than the translation 'work', would both preserve (once it is explained) to the non-Japanese speaker the implicit richness of the Japanese *kanji* symbol and be more accurate than the English translation.

---

108 For completeness, it should be noted that *Hira-kana* or *Kata-kana* can also be used to convey how a *kanji* symbol should be pronounced – in relation to the *kanji* symbol for 'work', *Hira-kana* [しごと] would be employed.

2 Defining a 'trade mark'

2.1 Introduction

This chapter examines the definition of 'well-known trade mark' by referring back to 'trade mark' in substance, since exploring the definition of 'trade mark' is argued to assist in conceptualising the definition of 'well-known trade mark'.

This chapter is divided into two parts. The first part introduces the theoretical framework, the Definition Model, which breaks down the concept of 'well-known trade mark' into sub-categories. The Definition Model is a conceptualisation tool; the rationale for developing the model is to create a frame of reference for critical analysis of, first, the various definitions of 'trade mark' and, thereafter, 'well-known trade mark' to be found in the primary literature.

The second part considers the legal definition of 'trade mark' at the international level and relevant regional (EU) and national (Japan) levels,[1] utilising the Definition Model. Such an exercise is undertaken by first *mapping* elements of legal definitions of 'trade mark' (and then 'well-known trade mark') to be found in the international, EU and Japanese trade mark systems, and conceptualising these. A conceptualisation of 'well-known trade mark' cannot be completed without analysis and comparison of the respective definitions of 'trade mark' in this chapter and consideration and, thereafter, analysis and comparison of 'well-known trade mark' in Chapters 4, 5 and 6. The Definition Model enables this.

2.2 Conceptualisation of 'trade mark'

By way of background, a theoretical device – the Definition Model – to assist conceptualisation of '(well-known) trade mark' (see Figure 2.1 below) is explained.

---

1 It may be helpful at this stage to remind the reader of the point of terminology previously noted in Chapter 1, Section 1.10: in this book the word 'trade mark' is used to refer to trade marks in an EU or international context, or in general, whilst the equivalent transliterated Japanese term *syohyo* (商標; the usual English translation of which is 'trademark') is used when referring to trade marks in the Japanese context.

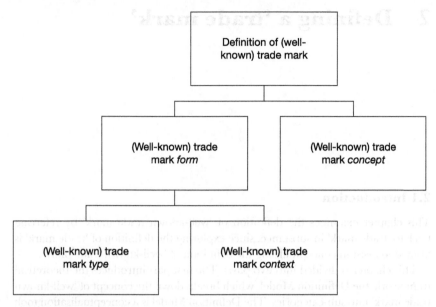

Figure 2.1 The Definition Model

The primary function of the Definition Model is to pragmatically encapsulate the 'legal reality'[2] of what constitutes a 'trade mark' (and also a 'well-known trade mark').

The first step taken by the Definition Model breaks down the components of '(well-known) trade mark' into sub-categories: quantitative (what *form* of signs are protected?) and qualitative categories or elements (*concept* – what *is* a trade mark?).

Form is then put into two sub-categories: *context* and *type*. Figure 2.1 illustrates the structural mechanism of the Definition Model. Figure 2.2 describes the dynamic of the Definition Model in operation, showing that legal regulation of trade mark *form* and *concept* is, *de facto,* interdependent and overlaps.[3]

Now that the theoretical rationale of the Definition Model has been explained, how the Definition Model can be applied to conceptualise '(well-known) trade mark' in practice will be demonstrated in Sections 2.2.1–2.2.3 below, with reference to two real-life well-known trade marks.

2 By being consistent with 'legal reality', it is implied that it is consistent with both the theoretical literature and the practical nexus of trade mark law.
3 See below Figure 2.2: The full Definition Model.

2.2.1 The form of 'trade mark': an illustration

Take the following well-known[4] trade marks:

(i) a representation of the word mark[5] 'Coca-Cola',[6] and
(ii) a representation of the logo[7] of Toyota.[8]

The *form* of the well-known trade marks at issue is as follows:

*   Coca-Cola:
    Type – it comprises a word mark and colour combination: the word 'Coca-Cola' has been represented in a stylised manner employing the colour red on a white background.
    Context – this is a trade mark for a product.
*   Toyota:
    Type – this is a logo comprising a figurative element (consisting of a two-dimensional, circular graphic representation of circles) and a colour (silver) element.[9]
    Context – this is a trade mark for a product.

When considering the examples of the Coca-Cola and Toyota marks, it should be noted that there are additional elements that have import for the Definition Model, but that do not appear to fit strictly in either *form* or *concept*. These additional elements are *graphic representation* (i.e. the ability to perceive the mark[10]) and

---

4 It is submitted that not only are these trade marks well known, but they are also part of very valuable brands. In the Interbrand 2014 survey Coca-Cola was the third most valuable brand, and Toyota was in eighth position overall. Evidence of these two trade marks being well known includes (i) the description of 'Coca-Cola' as a well-known mark in a WIPO publication (see WIPO, *Introduction to Intellectual Property: Theory and Practice*, p. 198) and (ii) the description of the Toyota logo as being a well-known trade mark by one of the lawyers involved in the Chinese case of *Toyota Motors v. Zhejiang Geely* (see Shi Yu-sheng, 'Trademark Infringement and Unfair Competition Case Study: Toyota Motors vs. Zhejiang Geely', *China Law & Practice* , 2003/04. Available online at www.chinalawandpractice.com/Article/1692947/Channel/9930/Trademark-Infringement-and-Unfair-Competition-Case-Study-Toyota-Motors-vs-Zhejiang-Geely.html (accessed 23 October 2014).
5 A word mark is usually a distinct text-only typographic treatment and thus comprises only text. For example, 'Coca-Cola', 'IBM', 'Google', 'Intel' and 'Microsoft' are categorised as word marks.
6 See Appendix 2: Illustrations of the Definition Model. 'Coca-Cola' is a registered trade mark under the CTM system (registration number 002091569) and in the JPO system it has been also registered as a defensive *syohyo* (registration number 106633).
7 A logo is a graphical mark and might comprise an ideogram, symbol, emblem or icon. Examples are the McDonald's logo and the Honda logo.
8 See Appendix 2: Illustrations of the Definition Model. The Toyota logo has been a registered trademark in Japan since 1997 (registration number 4039298). In the CTM system, the word mark 'Toyota' has been registered as a trade mark (registration number 00512780); however, the JPO does not provide any graphic image of this mark on the website.
9 Ibid.
10 There are, respectively, *visual recognition* (see Article 2 of the EU TMD; Article 2 of the Japanese Trademark Act) and *graphic representation* (see Article 2 of the EU TMD; Articles 2 and 5 of the Japanese Trademark Act) and criteria within the Japanese and EU definitions of 'trade mark'.

commercial use.[11] These two elements (*graphic representation* and *commercial use*) are clearly necessary and pragmatic preconditions to trade mark registration: they can be regarded as absolute preconditions to registration and thus within the context of the Definition Model enable both *form* and *concept*. *Graphic representation* and *commercial use* are not the same (unlike the absolute nature of *graphic representation* and *commercial use*,[12] *form* and *concept* have a more relative nature,[13] it is submitted) and they should not be incorporated within *form* and *concept*. Instead, they should be considered as being *preconditions* to registration, and in this way enable a mark to have *form* and *concept*.

Accounting for this, a full diagrammatic representation of the Definition Model is as follows (Figure 2.2).

As can be seen from the correlation between *form* and *concept* of '(well-known) trade mark' in Figure 2.1, although *form* and *concept* are separate elements, these two individual elements, *in practice*, closely interplay and overlap.[14] Figure 2.2 is presented in such a way to incorporate all the elements identified in Figures 2.1 and 2.2, and provides examples of each element. It is this version of the Definition Model that will be applied in this book hereinafter:

- *form* (*type*[15] and *context*[16]) and
- *concept*,[17] with
- the preconditions.[18]

---

11 *Commercial use* as a *precondition* of trade mark law taking the registration system is explicit within the Japanese Trademark Act (Article 2 of the Japanese Trademark Act), whereas it is somewhat implicit in the EU TMD (Article 3(3) of the EU TMD).

12 Absolute in the sense that trade mark systems require a minimum standard of *graphic representation* (e.g. in the EU Article 4 ('being represented graphically') and in Japan, Article 5(2) of the Japanese Trademark Act) and *commercial use* (e.g. in the EU TMD – see Articles 10(1) and 12(1)of the EU TMD; and in Japan – see Article 2 of the Japanese Trademark Act); the extent of such representation and use does not, in itself, affect the extent of trade mark protection, but is merely a precondition to registration.

13 It is submitted that these are relative in the sense that the wider the scope of *form* and *concept* (distinctiveness), the wider the scope of, and protection afforded by, registration (respectively, in relation to *form*, in the registration of more than one mark and the registration of marks in more classes and sub-classes, and, in relation to *concept*, ultimately in the recognition of well-known trade mark status, and protected in law accordingly).

14 So, for example, some *forms* of trade mark may possess more innate distinctiveness than others, something that is recognised by commentators. See, for example, R. Kojima, 'Rittai syohyo no toroku yoken: Maglight rittai syohyo jiken', *Chizai kanri*, 58, 2008, 25; and H. Aoki, 'Protection for three-dimensional Trademarks: an Examination of Maglight case', *CIPIC Journal*, 180, 2007, 20.

15 This includes signs, symbols, characters, letters, numbers, personal names, graphics, shapes of goods including two- and three-dimensional marks, packaging, colours and combination thereof, and perhaps so-called non-traditional trade marks (sound, olfactory and tactile marks) and so on.

16 This can include marks for goods (merchandising marks), service marks, domain names, business identifiers, retailers' marks, retailers' service marks, geographical indications, house marks, collective marks, grade marks, manufacturer marks, certification marks, family marks, coined marks, slogans, stock marks, trade names and so on.

17 A dominant element of the *concept* of 'trade mark' within the Definition Model is submitted to be distinctiveness. This Definition Model fits in the EU trade mark regime well since distinctiveness

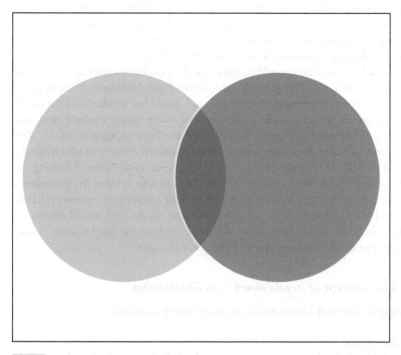

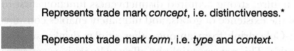

Represents trade mark *concept*, i.e. distinctiveness.*

Represents trade mark *form*, i.e. *type* and *context*.

Represents *preconditions* for trade mark registration, i.e. *graphic representation* and *commercian use*.

Figure 2.2 The full Definition Model

* It is submitted that mere distinctiveness is sufficient for 'trade mark' but that a high level of distinctiveness is required for 'well-known trade mark'.

A number of further observations on the Definition Model and the definition of 'trade mark' should be noted.

First, the scope of the Definition Model is considered. The scope of both *type* and *context* has broadened over time: for instance, three-dimensional marks are

as a *concept* of 'trade mark' is clearly explicit in the EU TMD; in the Japanese Trademark Act, on the other hand, it is not clearly explicit. It is submitted that the Definition Model is applicable for the Japanese Trademark Act by the following point: the Japanese term for 'trademark' is '*syohyo*', which contains the implicit meaning of a mark being distinctive; therefore, it is valid to argue that the Definition Model is still applicable for the Japanese Trademark Act and the *concept* of 'trade mark' is substantively distinctiveness. See Chapter 2, Section 2.3.3.

18 These are *graphic representation* and *commercial use*.

relatively newly included in *type* of trade mark,[19] whilst domain names are relatively newly included in *context* for trade marks.[20] Therefore, the scope of trade mark *form* is not permanently fixed and takes an incremental and thus flexible approach, allowing expansion. This feature invites flexibility in deciding the scope of trade mark *form* so that it could incorporate the possible increasing demands of sophisticated consumers[21] or unpredictable technological advances in the future.[22]

Second, a recent expansion of both *type* and *context* has resulted at least partly from changes in society, such as consumers being more sophisticated and technology being more advanced. Demand for the legal recognition of so-called non-traditional marks (including sound, olfactory and movement marks) might be regarded as indirect evidence of consumer recognition of the same (following the reasoning that what is commercially valuable must sustain its value from consumer demand). Additionally, technology now provides the platforms for commercial use of non-traditional marks (e.g. use of movement marks and sound marks on websites). In consequence, the scope of *form* of 'trade mark' has broadened over time in response to consumer and technological changes.

2.2.2 The concept of 'trade mark': an illustration

The *concept* of the well-known trade marks at issue is as follows:

- 'Coca-Cola'
  A highly distinctive nature: strong acquired distinctiveness functions first to inform consumers of the existence of goods, and ultimately enables consumers to select a Coca-Cola drink from among other similar drinks, such as Pepsi-Cola,[23] in practice. This process might be affected by various concerns of consumers. For example, when a consumer successfully identifies a Coca-Cola drink from among others including Pepsi-Cola (the guarantee of origin), 'Coca-Cola' brings other messages, which might inform the consumer of good quality (the guarantee of quality) and/or a positive and young image of the drink (the advertising function). A highly distinctive nature in 'Coca-Cola' may result from a combination of factors, including the (distinctive) attractive presentation (the combination of the colours of red and white)

---

19 For example, the Japanese Trademark Act introduced three-dimensional trademarks as a protectable trademark subject matter in 1996 (Act No. 68 of 1996).
20 It is important to note that domain names neatly illustrate the distinction drawn within the Definition Model between *type* and *concept*. Although domain names may have been explicitly protected as a new *form* of trade mark, the novelty lay in *context* (the use of trade marks in identifying web addresses), not *type* (a domain name is simply a word mark).
21 It is submitted that such consumers would be able to recognise new *types* of trade mark.
22 It is submitted that – just as the commercialisation of the internet led to the increased importance of, and subsequent explicit trade mark protection for, domain names – future technological developments may result in the recognition (and protection) of novel (commercially valuable) trade mark *forms*.
23 'Pepsi-Cola' is a registered trade mark under the CTM system (Registration Number 000563163) and in Japan (Registration Number 1353411).

of the words,[24] the extensive use of its marks in the market[25] (increasing distinctiveness) and/or the extensive advertising of Coca-Cola.[26]

• 'Toyota'

A highly distinctive nature: this strong acquired distinctiveness enables consumers to distinguish Toyota cars from those of competitors. The unique representation of the combination of the word mark 'Toyota' and the logo might have helped in establishing the highly distinctive nature of the logo, as may have intensive use and advertising. This can, again, be seen to lie in the distinctive nature of the logo, with factors such as the use of a simple logo and a combination of colours contributing to distinctiveness.

As a consequence of enjoying a (high) level of distinctiveness, a well-known trade mark strongly informs consumers as to the origin of the goods or services for which the mark is registered: this is known as the primary function of a trade mark.[27] More importantly, highly distinctive trade marks allow consumers to distinguish very effectively between goods of varying sources at the point of sale.[28] This might be regarded as the ultimate function of a trade mark. Although, as noted above, critical discussion of trade mark function is beyond the scope of this book, it is worth emphasising at this point the truism that without distinctiveness the existence and purposes of a trade mark becomes meaningless. Thus, not only is distinctiveness the *concept* of 'trade mark', but it is also the essential characteristic of any trade mark.

Nevertheless, the Toyota logo, in practice, might be less distinctive to general consumers than 'Coca-Cola'.[29] This suggestion might be supported by the observation that the Toyota logo *per se* is registered as a trade mark under the Japanese system, whilst the Toyota logo has been registered in combination with the 'Toyota' word mark under the CTM system. In Japan, the word mark and the logo have been registered individually,[30] whereas in the EU the word mark and

---

24 A graphic representation of 'Coca-Cola' is highly attractive to consumers. This may be because of the combination of use of such appealing colour and word font. See Appendix 2: Illustrations of the Definition Model.

25 For example, it is reported that Coca-Cola was first introduced in Japan around 1913 as it is evidenced that the word 'Coca-Cola' was quoted in a book published in 1914 (see K. Takamura, *Dotei*, Tokyo: Iwanami syoten, 1942, part 75). The word mark 'Coca-Cola' has been registered as a *syohyo* under the Japanese trademark system since 1964 (Registration Number 650399).

26 The estimated annual advertising expenditure of the Coca-Cola brand was $2.2 billion in 2007. See www.adbrands.net/us/cocacola_us.htm (accessed 14 June 2013).

27 See G. Tritton, *Intellectual Property in Europe*, London: Sweet & Maxwell, 2007, pp. 255–7 and 259; and A. Griffiths, 'The Impact of the Global Appreciation Approach on the Boundaries of Trade Mark Protection', *Intellectual Property Quarterly*, 4, 2001, 326–60, p. 329.

28 Tritton, *Intellectual Property in Europe*, p. 225.

29 The reason may be that although Toyota's logo is famous throughout the world, unlike Coca-Cola, a car is a high-end product: we do not buy a car on daily basis; therefore, in theory, the Toyota logo itself is unlikely to be seen on a daily basis. Therefore, the scope of a relevant sector of consumers seems to be narrower than that of daily products, such as Coca-Cola.

30 Ibid.

the logo have been registered in combination with each other[31] in relation to most of the trade mark classes except Classes 43,[32] 44[33] and 45.[34]

The suggestions as to relative distinctiveness in the paragraph above essentially relate to the submission that there is some correlation between *type* (with the suggestion that the word mark 'Coca-Cola' is more distinctive than the Toyota logo) and distinctiveness, and also the specifics of *context* (here, the nature of the goods – soft drinks and cars). This simply supports the Definition Model overlap between *form* and *concept*[35] and the assumption that the *concept* of 'trade mark' (i.e. distinctiveness) lies at the heart of what constitutes 'trade mark', whilst acquired distinctiveness lies at the heart of the 'well-known trade mark' *concept*.

2.3 Conceptualisation of 'trade mark' in law

The second part of this chapter considers the definitions of 'trade mark' at the international, regional (the EU/CTM) and national (Japan) levels, with reference to the Definition Model. The Definition Model, the conceptualisation tool, demonstrated that *form* and *concept* interconnect and that certain *preconditions* to registration also have to be present: the scope of (well-known) trade mark *form* remains flexible, whereas (well-known) trade mark *concept* has a more fixed and certain scope ('distinctiveness' for trade marks, 'a high level of distinctiveness' for well-known trade marks).

2.3.1 The international level

This section deals with the consideration of definitions of 'trade mark' at the international level. Trade mark law has been subject to international harmonisation over a considerable period of time.[36] International agreements relevant to trade mark law include the Paris Convention,[37] GATT TRIPS,[38] the Trademark

---

31 Ibid.
32 This refers to services providing food and drink; temporary accommodation.
33 This refers to medical services; veterinary services; hygiene and beauty care for human beings or animals; agriculture, horticulture and forestry services.
34 This refers to legal services; security services for the protection of property and individuals; personal and social services rendered by others to meet the needs of individuals.
35 See Figure 2.2: The full Definition Model.
36 See Mostert, 'When is a Mark "Well-Known"?'; Tatham, 'WIPO Resolution on Well Known Marks: A Small Step or a Giant Leap?'; M. Grabrucker, 'Marks For Retail Services – An Example for Harmonising Trade Mark Law', *International Review of Intellectual Property and Competition Law*, 34, 2003, 503–20.
37 The Paris Convention (the Paris Convention for the Protection of Industrial Property) was signed in Paris on 20 March 1883. It was one of the first intellectual property treaties. The provisions relating to trade mark subject matter are Articles 6*bis*, 6*ter*, 7*bis*, 8 and 9 of the Paris Convention. The Paris Convention came into force in 1884, signed by 14 States, and has been amended several times (the last amendment was in 1979). To date it has been ratified by 151 Member States. The Paris Convention is an international convention for promoting trade among the member countries, devised to facilitate protection of industrial property simultaneously in member countries without any loss in the priority date.
38 GATT TRIPS (the General Agreement on Tariffs and Trade, Agreement on Trade-Related Aspects of Intellectual Property Rights) was negotiated in the 1986–94 Uruguay Round and had

Law Treaty (TLT),[39] the Singapore Treaty,[40] the Nice Agreement[41] and the Madrid Protocol.

The first instrument to be considered here is the Paris Convention.[42] This is the earliest multilateral international intellectual property instrument, which, as part of this, addresses trade mark law.[43] Further, as the aim of the Paris Convention was to approximate national levels of intellectual property law to grant the same protection to signatory nations,[44] it is of obvious import to this

the effect of incorporating intellectual property directly into the legal regulation of the multilateral trading system for the first time. GATT TRIPS came into force, from 1 January 1995, in Marrakesh, Morocco, on 15 April 1994. It lays down minimum standards for protection and enforcement of intellectual property rights in member countries which are required to promote effective and adequate protection of intellectual property rights with a view to reducing distortions and impediments to international trade. The obligations under GATT TRIPS relate to provision of a minimum standard of protection within the member countries' legal systems and practices. Article 2(1) of GATT TRIPS requires Member States to comply with the substantive provisions of the Paris Convention. See, for example, G. Smith, 'Intellectual Property Rights, Developing Countries and TRIPS', *Journal of World Intellectual Property*, 6, 1999, 969–75, p. 967. Also, see D. Gervais, *The TRIPS Agreement: Drafting History and Analysis*, London: Sweet and Maxwell, 2008, Provisions in GATT TRIPS relating to trade mark subject matter can be found in Article 15(1). The full text is available online at www.wto.org/english/tratop_e/trips_e/t_agm2_e.htm (accessed 6 November 2014).

39 The Trademark Law Treaty (TLT) was adopted in Geneva on 27 October 1994. It was the first unified international trade mark law by the members of WIPO. The aim of the TLT is to harmonise trade mark law and simplify registration procedures. See *WIPO Handbook on Intellectual Property*, p.297. Available online at www.wipo.int/about-ip/en/iprm/pdf/ch5.pdf#tlt (accessed 23 October 2014).

40 The Singapore Treaty (the Singapore Treaty on the Law of Trademarks) is an international treaty on trademarks adopted on 28 March 2006. The Singapore Treaty deals mainly with procedural aspects of trademark registration and licensing. Furthermore, this treaty was built on the TLT to provide wider scope of application and addresses new developments in the field of communication technology. It also creates a dynamic regulatory framework for brand rights to introduce a new approach to securing investment in product differentiation. See, for example, WIPO Press Release 439 (Geneva/Singapore, 14 March 2006). The full text of the Singapore Treaty is available online at www.wipo.int/treaties/en/ip/singapore/singapore_treaty.html (accessed 23 October 2014). Articles relevant to trade mark subject matter are Articles 2(1) and (2) of the Singapore Treaty. However, the aim of this treaty is to facilitate administrative trade mark registration procedures and therefore further investigation of the international harmonisation of trade mark law is beyond the scope of this book.

41 The Nice Agreement (the Nice Agreement Concerning the International Classification of Goods and Services for the Purposes of the Registration of Marks) was adopted at Nice in June 1957 as revised and amended. It sets out an international classification of goods and services for the purposes of registering trade marks and service marks. The current edition of the Classification is the ninth, which entered into force on 1 January 2007. As the Nice Agreement does not pertain to the definition of trade mark, it does not merit further discussion in the context of this book.

42 The Paris Convention contains rules of substantive law, which guarantee a basic right, known as the right to national treatment (Articles 2 and 3); the avowed purpose of national treatment is to ensure that, in any Convention Member State, there is no difference in the treatment of national IP right holders (or applicants) and foreign IP right holders (or applicants).

43 Articles 6–9 of the Paris Convention.

44 WIPO, 'Summary of the Paris Convention for the Protection of industrial Property (1883)'. This summary is available online at www.wipo.int/treaties/en/ip/paris/summary_paris.html (accessed 23 October 2014).

book. An examination of GATT TRIPS,[45] the TLT[46] and the Singapore Treaty[47] will then follow.

2.3.1.1 The Paris Convention

The Paris Convention does not explicitly provide a definitive definition of 'trade mark'.[48] Therefore, the Definition Model is applied to relevant provisions of the Convention in order to summarise and critique the guidance that is provided (or that can be inferred) as to defining 'trade mark'. Despite the lack of an explicit comprehensive definition of 'trade mark', the Paris Convention indirectly speaks to aspects of *form* and *concept* of 'trade mark',[49] except *preconditions*, namely *graphic representation* or *commercial use*.

The first point to be made about the Paris Convention is that it makes clear[50] that the nexus of trade mark registrability is national (in this, it is therefore possible to conclude that the Convention can be seen as encouraging as paramount sovereignty and flexibility, and certainly allows for an expansionist approach to registrability at the local level). More specifically, *context in form* of 'trade mark' can thus be said to specifically include indications of source or appellations of origin,[51] well-known trade marks,[52] service marks,[53] collective marks[54] and trade names.[55] (The specific examples of *context in form* that are also listed[56] – state emblems,[57] official hallmarks[58] and emblems of intergovernmental organisations[59] – are beyond the scope of this book.) Aside from the mention of 'signs and indications',[60] the real guidance provided as to trade mark *types* of *form* is submitted to be Article 6(1): 'The conditions for the filing and registration of trademarks shall be determined in each country of the Union by its domestic legislation' – that is, the Convention is silent on *type*, and this is left for national law.

Whilst the Paris Convention does not provide a clear and explicit definition of the *concept* of 'trade mark', *concept* of 'trade mark' could be delineated by the

---

45 See Section 2.3.1.4.
46 See Section 2.3.1.2.
47 See Section 2.3.1.3.
48 Relevant Articles relating to protection of 'trade mark' and thus 'well-known trade mark' are 6*bis*, 6*ter*, 6*quinquies*, 6*sexies*, 7, 7*bis* and 8 of the Paris Convention.
49 See, for example, the protection afforded to service marks in Article 6*sexies*, collective marks in Article 7*bis*, and trade names in Article 8 of the Paris Convention.
50 Ibid., Article 6(1).
51 Ibid., Article 1(2).
52 Ibid., Article 6*bis*.
53 Ibid., Article 6*sexies*. Service marks are recognised, but there is no obligation to protect them.
54 Ibid., Article 7*bis*.
55 Ibid., Article 8.
56 It is assumed that these cannot be granted as registered trade marks on the grounds of public policy.
57 Article 6*ter*(1)(a) of the Paris Convention.
58 Ibid.
59 Ibid., Article 6*ter*(1)(b).
60 Ibid., Article 6*quinquies* B(ii).

instructive list of unregistrable categories of trade marks[61] (which themselves have an implicit connection with 'distinctiveness') and the following part of the Paris Convention:[62] marks that are 'devoid of any distinctive character'[63] and marks that 'consist exclusively of signs or indications which may serve, in trade, to designate the kind, quality, quantity, intended purpose, value, place of origin, of the goods, or the time of production, or have become customary in the current language'.[64] Thus it can be deduced that 'distinctiveness' is the *concept* of 'trade mark' within the Paris Convention.

To summarise, the Paris Convention addresses criteria that fall into both the *context* in *form* and *concept* elements of the Definition Model of 'trade mark'. Whereas *type* of *form* can be seen as largely being left for national law, the same might be said for the *preconditions*, *graphic representation* and *commercial use*, which are not explicitly present in the Paris Convention.[65]

2.3.1.2 The Trademark Law Treaty

There is a slightly different emphasis in the TLT,[66] wherein the following guidance of 'trade mark' is provided:

Article 2(1) [Nature of Marks]

(a) This Treaty shall apply to marks consisting of *visible signs,* provided that *only those Contracting Parties which accept for registration three-dimensional marks shall be obliged to apply this Treaty to such marks.*

(b) This Treaty shall *not apply to hologram marks and to marks not consisting of visible signs, in particular, sound marks and olfactory marks.*

(2) [Kinds of Marks]

(a) This Treaty *shall apply to marks relating to goods (trademarks) or services (service marks) or both goods and services.*

(b) This Treaty *shall not apply to collective marks, certification marks and guarantee marks.* [Emphasis added]

Again, this treaty does not offer a comprehensive definition of what a trade mark is. With reference to the Definition Model, *context* in *form* is explicit – that is to say, trade marks, which consist of marks relating to goods,[67] service marks,[68] but not

---

61 Ibid.
62 For an overview of the Paris Convention, see Appendix 1: Defining 'trade mark'.
63 Article 6*quinquies* B(ii) of the Paris Convention.
64 Ibid.
65 Ibid., Article 6(1).
66 It should be reiterated here that the main aim of the TLT is to approximate and streamline national and regional trade mark registration procedures.
67 Article 2(2)(a) of the TLT.
68 Ibid.

collective marks,[69] certification marks[70] and guarantee marks.[71] *Type* of trade mark *form* requires *visible* marks and also includes three-dimensional marks,[72] but excludes hologram marks, non-visible signs, sound marks and olfactory marks.[73] It should be highlighted that the TLT explicitly includes one of the *preconditions* of trade mark registration: that is visual representation within Article 2.[74] It is submitted that this term is synonymous with the term preferred within the Definition Model: *graphic representation*. Therefore, under the TLT the actual scope of trade mark registrability (in particularly, registrable *type* in *form*) is likely to be reduced *via* the criterion of *graphic* (visual) *representation*.

However, there is no explicit reference to *concept* of 'trade mark'. Thus it can be said that the TLT speaks mainly to *form* of 'trade mark' (although, as implied in the paragraph above, *graphic representation* may constitute a barrier to a generous and expansive approach to *type* in *form* to encompass so-called non-traditional marks) rather than detailed treatment of *concept*.

2.3.1.3 The Singapore Treaty

The Singapore Treaty takes rather a similar approach to the TLT, and sets out the following:

Article 2 *Marks to Which the Treaty Applies*

(1) [*Nature of Marks*] Any contracting party shall apply this Treaty to marks consisting of *signs* that can be registered as marks under its law.
(2) [*Kinds of Marks*]

   (a) This Treaty *shall apply to* marks relating to *goods (trademarks) or services (service marks)* or both goods and services.
   (b) This Treaty *shall not apply to collective marks, certification marks and guarantee marks.* [Emphasis added]

The guidance on what constitutes a trade mark provided in the Singapore Treaty primarily focuses on *form* of 'trade mark': for example, *context*, service marks are protected,[75] but collective marks, certification marks and guarantee marks are excluded from the ambit of the Treaty.[76] Unlike the approach taken by TLT,[77] the

69 Ibid.
70 Ibid.
71 Ibid.
72 Ibid.
73 Ibid.
74 See the wording of Article 2(1) of the TLT.
75 Article 16 of the Singapore Treaty.
76 The similarity between the TLT and the Singapore Treaty is pointed out within the WIPO's Standing Committee's document, 'Representation and Description of Non-Traditional Marks: Possible Areas of Convergence' (document SCT/19/2). The full text of this document is available online at www.wipo.int/edocs/mdocs/sct/en/sct_19/sct_19_2.pdf (accessed 23 October 2014).
77 Article 2(1) of the TLT.

Singapore Treaty is explicit in stating trade mark *type*, which includes signs that can be registered as marks[78] under national trade mark law (Article 2(1)).[79] As a result of this provision, the Singapore Treaty became the first international instrument[80] to positively recognise non-traditional marks[81] as a protectable *type* (part of *form*) of 'trade mark'. Such an expansionist (or, at least, flexible) approach of trade mark *type* in *form* shall be appropriated, as it is likely to enhance flexibility in law. Thus, it might well be said that potential at the international level for expansion of protectable trade mark *form* is inherent[82] in the Singapore Treaty, *via* the legal flexibility to be found in Article 2(1).

Given this, it is perhaps unsurprising that 'trade mark' under the Singapore Treaty is explicitly stated to include a wide variety of *forms* of 'trade mark' such as holograms, three-dimensional marks, colour, position and movement marks, sound, olfactory, gustatory and tactile marks.[83] The Singapore Treaty might thus be expected to have an impact on *form* of 'trade mark' at the national level,[84] in particular on those who are contracting parties of the Treaty.[85] The final point to be made here is that there is no explicit reference to any of the *preconditions*.

Overall, in the Singapore Treaty, similar to the TLT, the *form* of 'trade mark' seems to be the main concern, with no clear guidance of *concept* of 'trade

---

78 Article 2(1) of the Singapore Treaty.
79 This is of significance in relation to the international trade mark regime; the same principle is applied by the Paris Convention. The Singapore Treaty incorporates a more flexible concept of trade mark subject matter, largely because there is no requirement of *graphic representation* in the Singapore Treaty (Article 2(1) of the Singapore Treaty). Neither the Singapore Treaty nor the Paris Convention requires *graphic representations*; however, this is for different reasons. The aim of the Singapore Treaty is to provide the broader scope of trade mark subject matter; the Paris Convention does not attempt to provide the definition of trade mark. Also, collective marks, certification marks and guarantee marks are specifically excluded from the Singapore Treaty, whilst collective marks are specifically protected in Article 7*bis* of the Paris Convention. The Paris Convention contains rules of substantive law which guarantee a basic right to national treatment in each of the Member States, which sets up the minimum standard of harmonisation and gives the capacity to each nation to adapt; the Singapore Treaty, on the other hand, provides the maximum standard of trade mark protection followed by its own purpose.
80 As is noted in Section 2.3.1.2, the TLT is the first international instrument to note, albeit to exclude, sound and olfactory marks. See Article 2(1)(b) of the TLT.
81 Non-traditional trade marks are defined as a mark which cannot be graphically represented. See S. Sandri and S. Rizzo, 'Non-Conventional Trade Marks?', *Managing Intellectual Property*, 138, 2004, 8–10.
82 Ibid.
83 Ibid. See E. Barraclough, 'Introducing the Singapore Treaty', *Managing Intellectual Property*, 159, 2006, 16–18.
84 At its 18th meeting held in 2008, the WIPO Standing Committee on the Law of Trademarks, Industrial Designs and Geographical Indications (SCT) endorsed an agreement on areas of convergence on 'non-traditional marks', namely holograms and audio marks. Although the most recent meeting was held in June 2009, no major developments were made in relation to non-traditional trade marks. See WIPO 'Standing Committee on the Law of Trademarks, Industrial Designs and Geographical Indications, 21st Session Geneva June 22 to 26, 2009' (Document SCT/21/2).
85 Currently there are 36 contracting parties to the Singapore Treaty, but Japan is excluded. A list of the contracting parties is available online at www.wipo.int/treaties/en/ShowResults.jsp?lang=en&treaty_id=30 (accessed 23 October 2014).

mark' being explicitly present. However, the main aim of the Singapore Treaty cannot be said to be the provision of a conceptual definition of 'trade mark' (or, indeed, 'well-known trade mark'), so although deficient in terms of the Definition Model, the scope of the Singapore Treaty cannot be criticised in general terms. Nevertheless, together with the TLT, the Singapore Treaty has a role to play in establishing at the international level an expansionist approach to *form* of 'trade mark'.

2.3.1.4 GATT TRIPS

GATT TRIPS appears to provide a more detailed and instructive definition of 'trade mark',[86] compared with the international legal instruments considered thus far. The relevant Article in full is:

> Article 15(1) any *signs*, or any combination of signs, capable of *distinguishing* the goods or services of one undertaking from those of other undertakings, shall be capable of constituting a trademark. Such signs, in particular words including *personal names, letters, numerals, figurative elements and combinations of colours as well as any combinations of such signs*, shall be eligible for registration as trademarks. Where *signs are not inherently capable of distinguishing* the relevant goods or service, members may make registrability *depend on distinctiveness acquired through use*. Member may require, as a condition of registration, that *signs be visually perceptible*. [Emphasis added]

As can be seen in the extract above, attention is given to both *form* and *concept* (albeit in a slightly different manner from that used by the other international instruments[87]), and it stands out on its own in defining the scope of registered trade marks[88] in a fuller sense. What is more, GATT TRIPS provides a treatment to the *preconditions* of the Definition Model (see the explicit reference to visual perception (*graphic representation*)).[89]

---

86 See, for example, D. Gervais, 'The TRIPS Agreement: Interpretation and Implementation', *European Intellectual Property Review*, 21, 1999, 156–62, p. 158.

87 Articles 6*ter*, 6*sexies*, 7*bis* and 8 of the Paris Convention; Article 2 of the TLT; and Article 2 (1) of the Singapore Treaty.

88 W. Cornish and D. Llewelyn, *Intellectual Property: Patents, Copyright, Trade Marks and Allied Rights*, London: Sweet & Maxwell, 2007, p. 613; D. Rogers, 'The TRIPS Regime of Trademarks and Designs', *European Intellectual Property Review*, 29, 2007, 76–8; H. Rangel-Ortiz, 'Well-known Trademarks Under International Treaties: Part 1: Paris Convention and TRIPS', *Trademark World*, 94, 1997, 14–16; B. McGrady, 'TRIPS and Trademarks: The Case of Tobacco', *World of Trade Review*, 3, 2004, 53–82.

89 Article 15(1) of GATT TRIPS. As noted earlier, this term is regarded as being synonymous with *graphic representation*. It should also be noted that this is set out as an optional criterion for registration in GATT TRIPS. It might well be possible to infer that *commercial use* may well be implicit in Articles 15(2) and 15(3) of GATT TRIPS. It is conceded, however, that: (i) reference is made to mere 'use'; and (ii) Article 15(3) makes it clear that members *may* make registrability contingent on use.

Returning to other aspects of the Definition Model, the following can be noted: within trade mark *form*, trade mark *context* can be seen to include trade marks[90] and service marks;[91] geographical indication might also be included herein.[92] Also within trade mark *form*, trade mark *type* includes signs, words, personal names, letters, numbers and figurative marks, combination of colours and combination of signs.[93] The scope of *form type* thus appears to be sufficiently flexible to include non-traditional trade marks such as scents, as well as the more traditional trade mark examples explicitly listed.

The *concept* of 'trade mark' within the Definition Model is noted in the phrase 'signs, which are capable of *distinguishing*'. Notably, Article 15(1) distinguishes between what might be conceptualised as inherent distinctiveness ('capable of distinguishing') and acquired distinctiveness ('where signs are not inherently capable of distinguishing the relevant goods or service, members may make registrability depend on distinctiveness acquired through use'). GATT TRIPS clearly requires inherent distinctiveness, but gives the option for signatory States to recognise also acquired distinctiveness. The implications here for the Definition Model are not clear. Does the *mode* of distinctiveness (inherent or acquired) matter for the Definition Model? Should this be a distinction recognised in the Definition Model? The answer seems to be no. The mark with strong inherent distinctiveness (i.e. coined marks – e.g. Kodak, Google) is likely to have a head start compared with the mark with low inherent distinctiveness (i.e. arbitrary and suggestive marks); however, that acquired distinctiveness, where substantial, is submitted to be what distinguishes a well-known trade mark from a trade mark.

To conclude briefly, reference is made in GATT TRIPS to trade mark *form* and *concept*. Furthermore, it is submitted that GATT TRIPS appears to offer the most detailed guidance to both *form* and *concept* of 'trade mark'. Moreover, GATT TRIPS does address the *preconditions* (albeit that *graphic representation* is presented as an optional criterion for signatory States). GATT TRIPS must, it is submitted, be seen in a historical context, with both *form* and *concept* of 'trade mark' evolving from the position set out in the Paris Convention.[94] Although GATT TRIPS clearly provides more explicit guidance on both *form* and *concept* of 'trade mark', perhaps there is a little more guidance to distinctiveness (trade mark *concept*) in the Paris Convention,[95] where exemplars are provided. In terms of the *preconditions*, GATT TRIPS is clearly superior to the Paris Convention. Therefore, on balance, with reference to the Definition Model, GATT TRIPS seems to provide the clearest overall guidance as to the definition of 'trade mark'.

90 Ibid., Article 15(1).
91 The Paris Convention does not include service marks as a protectable trade mark *form*.
92 Article 22 of GATT TRIPS.
93 Ibid., Article 15(1).
94 See Section 2.3.1.1.
95 Article 6*quinquies* B(ii) of the Paris Convention.

2.3.1.5 Comparison

The application of the Definition Model to the relevant international instruments can be summarised as follows:

- *The Paris Convention.* Both an aspect of *form* and *concept* of 'trade mark' can be found, but the Convention would appear to be silent as to the *preconditions*. A trade mark appears to be a sign, which should not be devoid of distinctiveness (a negative definition, but one that is deemed to be synonymous with the Definition Model definition of *concept*: 'distinctiveness'). Exemplars of marks that are said not to be distinctive are helpfully provided and include description of mere information of the goods/services or a mark that is customarily used. Furthermore, there is implicit confirmation of *concept* in the statement that distinctiveness may be lost by a trade mark becoming customary to consumers. Within trade mark *form*, elements of *context* that are registrable include service marks, collective marks and trade names. In terms of trade mark *form*, guidance as to *type* is limited to 'signs and indications'; national law is presumably expected to regulate this area further. Exclusions from registration are noted, including marks that are contrary to morality or public order or are registered in bad faith: these, it is submitted, fall outside the Definition Model, being concerned with policy considerations rather than the definition of 'trade mark' *per se*. (Policy considerations similarly can explain the exclusion from registrability of state emblems, official hallmarks, emblems of intergovernmental organisations and so on.) Thus, the definition of 'trade mark' in the Paris Convention contains both *form* (with more detail on *context* than *type*) and *concept* elements from the Definition Model of 'trade mark', but not the *preconditions*.
- *The TLT.* Within the Definition Model, *form* of 'trade mark' is explicitly provided, and given reasonably detailed treatment, within the TLT, which states that a trade mark should be a visible[96] sign; sound marks, olfactory marks, marks not consisting of visible signs, hologram marks, collective marks, certification marks and guarantee marks are excluded. However, trade mark *concept* is absent; only *form* and one of the *preconditions* – *graphic representation* – are present in the definition of 'trade mark' offered in the TLT.
- *The Singapore Treaty.* Similar to the TLT, there is no explicit guidance on *concept* – here trade marks are said to be marks recognised under national law. (It might be argued that there is therefore an implicit recognition of *concept*, but that presupposes that all current and intended future Singapore Treaty signatory countries' national trade mark laws contain explicit mention of *concept*: a rather difficult argument to prove; therefore there is no implicit recognition of *concept* in the Singapore Treaty.) The *form* of 'trade mark' can be inferred in the Treaty, which explicitly excludes collective marks,

---

96 This explicitly reflects one of the *preconditions* of the Definition Model.

certification marks and guarantee marks. Like the TLT, not all elements of the Definition Model are present, with *concept* and *preconditions* here being absent, but there is some mention of *form*.[97]

- *GATT TRIPS*. Both *form* and *concept* of 'trade mark' are explicitly present, as is one of the *preconditions* (*graphic representation*). GATT TRIPS therefore addresses all elements identified in the full Definition Model (see Figure 2.2 above), and in this it exceeds the Paris Convention (see above). These elements can be found as follows. The first to note is *form*. Trade mark *type* is explicitly present, a trade mark being said to contain a sign including personal names, letters, numerals, figurative elements and combination of colour. Trade mark *context* is also explicit, registrable trade marks being said to include service marks and geographical indications. Second – *concept*: this is also explicitly addressed herein. A trade mark is a distinctive (*concept*) sign that is capable of being distinguished from the other competitors in the same sector. In addition, distinctiveness can be obtained through use of the mark. *Graphic representation*, as noted above, is also present (a *precondition*).

A basic comparison of these international treaties, it can be argued, shows that the Singapore Treaty provides the broadest (and therefore the most generous) interpretation as to *form* of 'trade mark', whereas GATT TRIPS provides the narrowest *form* of 'trade mark'. There are, thus, significant differences in the guidance as to what constitutes a trade mark in these international instruments. However, what is truly remarkable is the very different approaches taken in the treaties to defining trade mark *concept*. Whereas the Paris Convention and GATT TRIPS, for instance, do address trade mark *concept*,[98] the TLT and the Singapore Treaty concentrate on trade mark *form* and barely address trade mark *concept*.[99] Why this might be the case seems difficult to speculate, but it is interesting that no international agreement provides conceptualisation of the definition of 'trade mark': each of these international instruments shows a subtly different understanding of 'trade mark',[100] although these differences do not appear to be problematic in practice.[101]

---

97 Thus, here, not only has application of the Definition Model made it very clear that there are gaps in the definitions of 'trade mark' provided in the TLT and the Singapore Treaty, but it has allowed (it is hoped) for a relatively clear *conceptualisation of what is missing* from these definitions. For more detailed analysis of the relevant provisions of these treaties, see Section 2.3.1.2 for the TLT and Section 2.3.1.3 for the Singapore Treaty.

98 That is, providing conceptual guidance as to what constitutes a trade mark – e.g. *sign*, *distinctiveness*.

99 That is, focusing on trade mark subject matter – that is, service marks, collective marks and trade names are all permissible subject matter.

100 See each purpose of the international treaties in Sections 2.3.1.1–2.3.1.4.

101 See WIPO, *Introduction to Intellectual Property: Theory and Practice*, p. 423; V. von Bomhard, 'Dormant Trade Marks in the European Union – Swords of Damocles?', *Trademark Reporter*, 96, 2006, 1122–36; N. Caravalho, *The TRIPS Regime of Trademarks and Designs*, London: Kluwer Law International, 2006. In this book, it is pointed out that harmonisation of legal norms that is a consequence of GATT TRIPS places limitations on the legislation the members can adopt.

In summary, of these international instruments, the definition of trade mark to be found in GATT TRIPS is the most precise and clear; however, it should be noted here that the Paris Convention provides more concise guidance regarding *concept* (distinctiveness) *per se*.

Both the Paris Convention and GATT TRIPS address most of the criteria defined in the Definition Model, although GATT TRIPS provides the fuller treatment. Thus, a combination of the GATT TRIPS and Paris Convention trade mark definitions can be regarded as the most robust (although not the broadest) guidance at the international level as to the definition of 'trade mark', and conceptualisation can be expressed in terms of the Definition Model thus:

- trade mark *type* in *form*: signs and indications, including letters (including names), numerals, figurative elements and colour combinations, as well as any combinations of such signs;
- trade mark *context* in *form*: trade marks, service marks, well-known trade marks, trade names, geographical indications, collective marks and indications of source or appellations of origin;
- trade mark *concept*: distinctiveness; and
- the *preconditions*: *graphic representation* (and use, if not full *commercial use*).

In particular, it would appear that in trade mark *context* in *form*, collective marks, certification marks and guarantee marks are controversial subject matter, as under both the TLT[102] and the Singapore Treaty regime[103] they cannot be registered trade marks (although in GATT TRIPS they can be[104]). Interestingly, the Singapore Treaty, the most recent international trade mark legal instrument, does not address any visibility or *geographic representation* registration requirements (the *preconditions*), but there is some implication that protectable subject matter might become broader.

Above all, the definition of 'trade mark' in the international trade mark regime is less cohesive and comprehensive than might have been hoped. Nonetheless, the differing definitions of 'trade mark' offered can be seen as reflecting an evolving international consensus as to a broadening definition of 'trade mark'.

2.3.2 The regional level: the EU

Having outlined how 'trade mark' is defined at the international level, the focus of this section moves on to the regional level – the EU. In order to obtain the statutory trade mark rights in the EU, the trade mark proprietor can take the following routes: national registration *via* the national trade mark registry, EU registration (the CTM: community trade mark) *via* the OHIM (Office for Harmonisation in

---

102 Article 2(2)(b) of the TLT.
103 Article 2(2)(b) of the Singapore Treaty.
104 Article 15(1) of GATT TRIPS.

the Internal Market (Trade Marks and Designs)) and international registration *via* the Madrid Agreement.[105] The EU Member States, whose national trade mark systems continue to exist alongside the CTM, have largely ensured that their national trade mark laws are in line with the principle of the First Harmonisation Directive,[106] now replaced by the new Directive (hereinafter the EU TMD).[107] The focus of this book lies, however, with the EU, *not* the national or the CTM route to obtaining trade marks in Europe; therefore, all comments and analysis on EU trade mark law in this book are, hereinafter, confined to the CTM system unless specifically indicated otherwise.

The entry into force of the Community Trade Mark Regulation (the CTMR)[108] put the final seal on the establishment of a unified European trade mark system[109] and the establishment of dual national and EU routes to registering trade marks in the EU.[110]

A brief summary of the CTM route to trade mark registration would, at this stage, be helpful. Essentially, the outcome of the CTM application is that a single trade mark application can be made which, if successful, enables the trade mark owner to exercise its rights throughout the EU Member States.[111]

Hence, preliminary references made by national courts to the EU courts relating to the interpretation of the Directive may, it is submitted, also be useful in determining the approach of OHIM (Office for Harmonisation in the Internal Market (Trade Marks and Designs)), the General Court (previously known as the CFI (Court of First Instance)) and the Court of Justice (formally known as the European Court of Justice (ECJ)) to the CTM system (and vice versa). In short, although this book specifically excludes the national trade mark systems of each EU nation,[112] reference will be made to the EU courts' consideration of the EU TMD.

---

105 Madrid Agreement Concerning the International Registration of Marks of April 14, 1891 as amended. Detailed examination of the Madrid Agreement is beyond the scope of the book. The Madrid Agreement introduced so-called international trade mark registration, which could be effective throughout the globe. However, the signatory nations are too few for the Agreement to be effective.

106 First Council Directive of 21 December 1988 to approximate the laws of the Member States relating to Trade Marks (89/104/EEC) (OJ L 40, 11.2.1989).

107 Directive 2008/95/EC of the European Parliament and of the Council of 22 October 2008 to approximate the laws of the Member States relating to trade marks.

108 Council Regulation (EC) No. 40/94 of 20 December 1993 on the Community trade mark. Now amended as Council Regulation (EC) No. 207/2009 of 26 February 2009 on the Community trade mark (hereinafter 40/94/EEC refers to the CTMR as Regulation No. 207/2009/EC).

109 C. Gielen and B. Strowel, 'The Benelux Trademark Act: A Guide to Trademark Law In Europe', *Trademark Reporter*, 86, 1996, 543–75, p. 543.

110 The process of harmonisation of national trade mark laws in the EU states began in 1988 with the enactment of the EU Trade Mark Directive (First Council Directive of 21 December 1988 to approximate the laws of the Member States relating to Trade Marks (89/104/EEC) (OJ L 40, 11.2.1989). See G. Dinwoodie, 'The Integration of International and Domestic Intellectual Property Lawmaking', *Columbia-VLA Journal of Law and the Arts*, 23, 2000, 307–15, p. 307.

111 See Article 1(2) of the CTMR. See also W. Cornish, and D. Llewelyn, *Intellectual Property: Patents, Copyright, Trade Marks and Allied Rights*, p. 671.

112 There are some occasions where the national trade mark law, such as the UK, may be introduced as a point of reference. The UK national law is the Trade Marks Act 1994.

The conceptual definition of 'trade mark' in the EU TMD will now be examined. The EU TMD provides explicit guidance[113] here:

> Article 2 Signs of which a trade mark may consist
> A trade mark may consist of *any signs* capable *of being represented graphically,* particularly *words,* including *personal names, designs, letters, numerals, the shape of goods or of their packaging,* provided that such *signs are capable of distinguishing the goods or services of one undertaking from those of other undertakings.* [Emphasis added]

Applying the Definition Model, both *form* and *concept* are noticeably present here. Trade mark *type* in *form* in the EU TMD constitutes any signs, including symbols, logos, slogans, get-up, personal names, designs, letters, numerals and the shape of goods or of their packaging.[114] Trade mark *context* in *form* includes trade marks for goods and/or service marks, geographic marks[115] and certification marks.[116] An interesting observation of Article 2[117] is that it seems to take an incremental approach to the category of trade mark *form*, which would potentially allow the scope of *form* of 'trade mark' to be broadened over time[118] if necessary.[119] Trade mark *form* addressed in the EU TMD, Article 2, is therefore argued to be suggestive (to provide examples of both *type* and *context* in trade mark *form*,[120]) not definitive.[121]

---

113   Some similarities between the EU TMD and GATT TRIPS are as follows: 'trade mark' is defined both in the EU TMD and GATT TRIPS as a sign that is capable of being distinguished and being graphically represented, including personal names, designs, letters and colours.

114   In this respect, the EU TMD can be seen as being more innovative than international standards at the time of adoption. The TLT, which makes the first specific mention of three-dimensional marks, was adopted in 1994 (interestingly, there is no explicit mention of such marks in GATT TRIPS – see Section 2.3.1.4), whilst the first EU TMD was adopted in 1988.

115   Geographical indication can be protected by Council Regulation (EEC) No. 2081/92 of 14 July 1992 on the protection of geographical indications and designations of origin for agricultural products and foodstuffs (hereinafter the GIs). GIs are names associated with products from a specific place when the geographic origin of the product gives its specific characteristics and quality. See B. O'Connor, 'The EC Need Not Be Isolated on GIs', *European Intellectual Property Review,* 8, 2007, 303–6, p. 303. A general view of GIs is seen in D. Bainbridge, 'Changes to the Community Trade Mark', *Intellectual Property & Information Technology Law,* 9, 2004, 18–20.

116   J. Phillips, *Trade Mark Law: A Practical Anatomy,* p. 604.

117   A similar approach is taken by Article 15(1) of GATT TRIPS.

118   In time, the influence of the Singapore Treaty might be felt here – see Section 2.3.1.3. However, thus far the Court of Justice has taken a restrictive, rather than expansive, approach to the scope of trade mark *form* (see, for example, the decision in *Sieckmann* (*Sieckmann v. Deutsches Patent- Und Markenamt*: reported in [2003] RPC 38). In fact, under current EU jurisprudence, it is currently not possible to register two of the Article 2 exemplars of trade mark *form*: olfactory and gustatory marks.

119   Principally, S. Maniatis, *Trade Marks in Europe: A Practical Jurisprudence,* London: Sweet & Maxwell, 2009, p. 61.

120   Ibid.; see also S. Sandri and S. Rizzo, 'Non-Conventional Trade Marks?', *Managing Intellectual Property,* 13, 2004, 8–10.

121   As argued by, for example, S. Dunstan, 'Smells and Shapes in the United Kingdom: Continuing Pitfalls of Non-Traditional Trademarks', *Trademark World,* 197, 2007, 41–6; I. Hering, 'Pushing at the Boundaries of Protection', *Managing Intellectual Property,* 114, 2001, 23–32; A. Inglis, 'Registrability and Enforcement of Inherently Non-distinctive Trade Marks in the United Kingdom', *European Intellectual Property Review,* 19, 1997, 138–41.

Taking an incremental approach to trade mark *form* may well indicate a possibility of future expansion of trade mark *forms*.[122]

Concept of 'trade mark' can be found in the criterion of signs needing to be capable of *distinguishing* the goods or services of one undertaking from those of others – that is, trade mark *concept* is distinctiveness. As opposed to the incremental approach taken in trade mark *form*, trade mark *concept* gives an impression of being more rigid and fixed in nature, which, encouragingly, may invite more certainty and coherency.

Having explored Article 2, the second part of this section attempts to explore other provisions to seek for further conceptualisation of 'trade mark'. The implicit guidance of both *form* and *concept* of 'trade mark' can be found as part of the absolute grounds for refusal of registration:

Under Article 3(1), the following shall not be registered, or shall be declared invalid:

(a) signs which cannot constitute a trade mark;
(b) trade marks which are *devoid of any distinctive character*;
(c) trade marks which consist exclusively of signs or indications *which may serve, in trade, to designate the kind, quality, quantity, intended purpose, value, geographical origin or the time of production of the goods or of rendering of the service, or other characteristics of the goods or service*;
(d) trade marks which consist exclusively of signs or indications which have *become customary in the current language* or in the bona fide and established practices of the trade;
(e) signs which consist exclusively of: (i) the shape which *results from the nature of the goods themselves*; or (ii) the shape of goods *which is necessary to obtain a technical result*; or (iii) the shape *which gives substantial value to the goods* . . .

3. A trade mark shall *not* be refused registration or be declared invalid in accordance with paragraph 1(b), (c) or (d) if, before the date of application for registration and following the use which has been made of it, *it has acquired a distinctive character* . . . [Emphasis added]

So far, Article 3 (absolute grounds for refusal of trade mark registration) above seems to provide further guidance to trade mark *concept* by giving these (non-distinctive) exemplars (which are themselves similar to that found in the Paris Convention[123]). *Form* (*type* and *context*) of 'trade mark' is also implicitly present in Article 3, thus:[124]

122 Here, see J. Phillips, 'A Busy Year in Europe's Courts', *Managing Intellectual Property*, 79, 79–82, p. 82.
123 Article 6*quinquies* B(ii) of the Paris Convention.
124 Here, items that are related to morality are excluded from the extract quoted. It is considered that marks which fall within Articles 3(1)(f) and (g) of the EU TMD are excluded on public policy grounds, rather than true definitional grounds, and thus similar provisions will not be considered in the *context* of the Definition Model.

   (h)   trade marks which have not been authorized by the competent authorities
         and are to be refused pursuant to Article 6*ter* of the Paris Convention;

   (g)   trade marks which are of such a nature *as to deceive the public,* for instance
         as to *the nature, quality or geographical origin of the goods or service;*

   2(c) trade marks which include *badges, emblems or escutcheons other than those covered
   by Article 6ter of the Paris Convention* and which are of *particular public interest,*
   unless the consent of the appropriate authorities to their registration has
   been given in conformity with the legislation of the Member States. [Emphasis
   added]

Overall, trade mark *context* in *form* that are not registrable signs include geographical
origin of the goods or services.[125] Further, trade mark *types* in *form* that are not
registrable include signs or indications which may serve merely as an indication of
origins and description of the goods,[126] the shape which results from the nature
of the goods,[127] which is necessary to gain a technical result,[128] which gives
substantial value,[129] badges, emblems or escutcheons.[130] Regarding trade mark
preconditions, graphic representation is explicit in the EU TMD. The other *precondition
– commercial use –* is not explicitly present as a condition of registrability.[131]

   In short, Article 3 expands on Article 2 by setting out an explicit negative
definition of trade mark *form* (see the paragraph above), as well as implicit
guidance as to what is not distinctive (and, in this, guidance as to trade mark
concept): namely, signs that are not distinctive[132] are mere descriptions of the nature
of the products[133] and become common terms in the current language.[134]
Additionally, trade mark *concept* explicitly includes distinctiveness acquired
through use.[135] Thus, in the EU TMD, trade mark *concept* and *form* are present,
as is one of the *preconditions* for trade mark registration. Further, the EU TMD
provides a reasonably full treatment of both *form* and *concept,* with the former (at
least at surface reading, if not according to trade mark jurisprudence) allowing for
further expansion, and therefore almost all aspects of the full Definition Model
are positively addressed by the EU TMD.

   Similarities to aspects of the international regime can be seen: aspects of Article
2 of the EU TMD can be seen as being rather similar to the approach taken in
GATT TRIPS. There also appears to be a similar approach in the EU TMD in
terms of non-registrable *form* of 'trade mark' to that in the Paris Convention.

125 Ibid., Article 3(1)(g).
126 Article 3(1)(c) of the EU TMD.
127 Ibid., Article 3(1)(e)(i).
128 Ibid., Article 3(1)(e)(ii).
129 Ibid., Article 3(1)(e)(iii).
130 Ibid., Article 3(1).
131 For further comment and comparison on this point, see Section 2.3.4.1.
132 Ibid., Article 3(1)(b).
133 Ibid., Article 3(1)(c).
134 Ibid., Article 3(1)(d).
135 Ibid., Article 3(3).

2.3.3 The national level: Japan

Having discussed how 'trade mark' is defined at the international and regional level, this section moves on to the final part of three: the national level – Japan. Note that Japan has ratified both the Paris Convention[136] and GATT TRIPS,[137] but not yet the Singapore Treaty.

As a reminder, the structure of the EU TMD was: (i) the establishment of the definition of a registrable trade mark (Article 2); (ii) the introduction of absolute grounds for refusal, to establish what marks cannot be registered (Article 3); (iii) the introduction of relative grounds for refusal to establish in what circumstances the registration can be opposed (Article 4).

As will be seen, the Japanese Trademark Act takes a different approach to the structure of the law: (i) the establishment of a definition of a registrable trademark (Article 2); (ii) setting out the requirement of registered trade marks by providing a negative list of non-registrable trade marks (Article 3); (iii) the establishment of a non-registrable trade mark even if the mark is not barred by the second point. The EU TMD simply and more readily combines both the second and third stages of the Japanese approach into one absolute grounds for refusal.

The Cabinet Secretariat English translation[138] of the Japanese Trademark Act[139] defines *syohyo* as follows:

> Article 2 (Definitions, etc.)
>
> (1) 'Trademark' in this Act means *any character(s), figure(s), sign(s) or three-dimensional shape(s), or any combination thereof, or any combination thereof with colours* (hereinafter referred to as 'mark') which are:
>> (1) *used in connection with* the *goods* of a person who produces, certifies or assigns the goods as *a business*; or

---

136 Japan has been a signatory of the Paris Convention since 1899. The internationalisation of the Japanese Trademark Act began in 1899. See Y. Tamura, *Syohyo ho*, Tokyo: Kobun-do, 2004, p. 433.

137 The Japanese Trademark Act was amended in 1994 to sign the GATT TRIPS Agreement.

138 The Cabinet Secretariat English translation of Article 2 is considered to be the authorised translation of the Japanese Trademark Act. However, this is not the case for all provisions in the Japanese Trademark Act and there seems to be difficulty in giving the most accurate translation. For instance, an English translation of Article 2 does not use the term 'sign' in the same context as the international and the EU law. A 'sign' in Article 2 seems to be more like a symbol, since the scope of signs is broader than that of symbols. However, the sign in the international and EU context is implicit in the Japanese term *syohyo*. Understanding the Japanese etymology is important in order to examine the Japanese laws; lack of that understanding is likely to cause disadvantage to non-Japanese speakers, since they are incapable of reading the Japanese *kanji* scripts and comprehending all the implications of the Japanese characters. Therefore, a more detailed English translation of the law would be beneficial.

139 Act No. 127 of 1959 last amended by Act No. 84 of 2014. It is important to be clear here: only the original Japanese language version of the Trademark Act is official and considered to be legally binding; it is therefore this text that is analysed in this book. In deference to non-Japanese speakers, the unofficial Cabinet Secretariat translation will be introduced, but where this appears inaccurate or abbreviated the author's own translation will be provided.

(2)   *used in connection with* the *services* of a person who provides or certifies the services *as a business* (except those provided for in the preceding item). [Emphasis added]

The definition of '*syohyo*' in Japan is explicitly provided in the Act. Furthermore, the scope of trade mark *type* in *form* of '*syohyo*' to be found in the Act can be noted: characters, figures, signs, three-dimensional shapes or any combination thereof. It is noteworthy that a 'sign' is identified as the *only* trade mark *type* in trade mark *form* in the international and EU trade mark regimes, whereas in Japan this appears not to be the case; it seems as if 'sign' is just one among many such narrow *types*, according to the English translation of the Japanese Trademark Act.[140]

Trade mark *context* in *form* of '*syohyo*' can be summarised to include the mark that is attached to the goods and/or services. Comparison with the relevant international laws[141] and the EU TMD[142] shows the Japanese Trademark Act as providing a quite detailed explicit (if narrow) treatment of *form* of '*syohyo*'.

Regarding the scope of *syohyo form* as outlined in Article 2, it is apparent that *form* appears to be significantly narrower than that of equivalent provisions in the CTM system and also narrower than that set out in the (collective) international regime.

In order to seek further guidance as to conceptualisation of *syohyo form*, assistance is obtained from two different sources: the following article is one of those. Article 4 below sets out a negative list of *syohyo form*[143] as follows:

Article 4 (Unregistrable trademarks)

(1)   Notwithstanding the preceding Article, no trademark shall be registered if the trademark:
   (1)   is identical with, or similar to, the national flag, the imperial chrysanthemum crest, a decoration, a medal or a foreign national flag;
   (2)   is identical with, or similar to, the coats of arms or any other State emblems (except national flags of any country of the Union to the Paris Convention, member of the World Trade Organization or Contracting Party to the Trademark Law Treaty) of a country of the Union to the Paris Convention (refers to the Paris Convention

---

140   In fact, it is considered that the unofficial English translation of the Japanese Trademark Act is not entirely accurate. It is argued that the inclusion in this translated Act of 'sign' as one of the sub-categories of *type* is misleading. This view is supported when one considers 'sign' in a linguistic context. Etymological analysis of the Japanese symbol for 'trademark' reveals that the notion of 'sign' is implicit in *syohyo*. Thus, it appears that it would be more correct for 'sign' not to be regarded as one of the sub-categories of *syohyo* to be found in Article 2(1) of the Japanese Act.
141   See Section 2.3.1.1 for the Paris Convention; Section 2.3.1.4 for GATT TRIPS.
142   See Article 2 of the EU TMD and Section 2.3.2 for the further information regarding the EU TMD.
143   Here, items that are related to morality are not considered in the context of the Definition Model, as it is considered that the basis of the exclusion of marks that are listed in (f)–(k) stems from public policy reasons rather than from the definition of 'trade mark' *per se*. Similar exclusions founded on public policy can be found in the EU TMD.

for the Protection of Industrial Property of March 20, 1883, as revised at Brussels on December 14, 1900, at Washington on June 2, 1911, at the Hague on November 6, 1925, at London on June 2, 1934, at Lisbon on October 31, 1958, and at Stockholm on July 14, 1967; the same shall apply hereinafter), a member of the World Trade Organization or a Contracting Party to the Trademark Law Treaty designated by the Minister of Economy, Trade and Industry;

(3)   is identical with, or similar to, a mark indicating the United Nations or any other international organization which has been designated by the Minister of Economy, Trade and Industry;

(4)   is identical with, or similar to, the emblems or titles in Article 1 of the Act Concerning Restriction on the Use of Emblems and Titles of the Red Cross and Others (Act No. 159 of 1947) or the distinctive emblem in Article 158(1) of the Act Concerning Measures to Protect Japanese Citizens During Armed Attacks and Others (Act No. 112 of 2004);

(5)   is comprised of a mark identical with, or similar to, an official hallmark or sign indicating control or warranty by the national or a local government of Japan, a country of the Union to the Paris Convention, a member of the World Trade Organization or a Contracting Party to the Trademark Law Treaty which has been designated by the Minister of Economy, Trade and Industry, if such a trademark is used in connection with goods or services identical with, or similar to, the goods or services in connection with which the hallmark or sign is used;

(6)   is identical with, or similar to, a famous mark indicating the State, a local government, an agency thereof, a non-profit organization undertaking a business for public interest, or a non-profit enterprise undertaking a business for public interest;

(7)   is likely to cause damage to public policy;

(8)   contains the portrait of another person, or the name, famous pseudonym, professional name or pen name of another person, or famous abbreviation thereof (except those the registration of which has been approved by the person concerned).

Note that the subject matter of Article 4 is felt to stem mainly from public policy. The following mark will be excluded from:

(i)   trade mark *type* in *form*: the national flag, the imperial chrysanthemum crest, a decoration, a medal or a foreign national flag,[144] any State emblems;[145] marks indicating the United Nations or any other international organisation;[146] and

---

144 Article 4(1) of the Japanese Trademark Act.
145 Ibid., Article 4(2).
146 Ibid., Article 4(3).

the emblems or titles;[147] the portrait of another person, or the name, famous pseudonym, professional name or pen name of another person;[148]

(ii)   trade mark *context in form*: official hallmarks;[149] any famous signs of the State, a local government mark;[150] marks which are detrimental to public policy.[151]

The second source of assistance is the Trade Mark Registry Guidance,[152] which includes further examples of registrable trade marks. The section in the Guidance, supplement to Article 2, indicates the scope of *syohyo type* and *context in form*, and shows slightly wider scope than that indicated by Article 2 alone. For example, *syohyo type* is said to include character marks,[153] design marks,[154] symbol marks,[155] colour marks, three-dimensional marks,[156] combined marks with colours. *Syohyo context in form* of 'trade mark' is similarly broader, including merchandising marks,[157] service marks,[158] business marks,[159] collective marks,[160] grade marks,[161] manufacturer marks,[162] retailer marks,[163] house marks,[164]

---

147 Ibid., Article 4(4).
148 Ibid., Article 4(8).
149 Ibid., Article 4(6).
150 Ibid., Article 4(9).
151 Ibid., Article 4(7).
152 S. Ono, *Overview of Japanese Trademark Law*, Tokyo: Seirin-syoin, 2005, pp. 25–30.
153 文字商標 (*Moji-syohyo*); the author translates this as characters marks (e.g. 'Sony').
154 That is 図形商標 (*Zukei-syohyo*); the author translates this as referring to design marks (e.g. the Mitsubishi logo).
155 That is 記号商標 (*Kigo-syohyo*); the author translates this as referring to symbol marks (e.g. the Louis Vuitton symbol 'LV').
156 That is 立体商標 (*Rittai-syohyo*); the author translates this as referring to three-dimensional marks. Three-dimensional marks have been recognised as trademarks rather recently, although proving the distinctiveness in three-dimensional marks has become an obstacle for trademark registration in practice. Intellectual Property High Court, Heisei 17nen, (Gyo Ke) 10673. A three-dimensional shape of a chick was disputed. In the case, the Intellectual Property High Court concluded that the three-dimensional shape of a chick lacks the distinctiveness required to be a registered trademark. The official English translation of this case is not available; therefore, a brief summary of this case in English by the author is introduced. From this decision, it might be considered that distinctiveness, which is required in the Japanese Trademark Act, appears significantly high.
157 That is 商品商標 (*Syohin-syohyo*); the author translates this as referring to goods marks (e.g. the 'Shiseido' mark).
158 That is 役務商標 (*Yakumu-syohyo*); the author translates this as referring to service marks (e.g. 'JAL' or 'ANA').
159 That is 営業商標 (*Eigyo-syohyo*); a house mark is a part of a business mark; the author translates this as referring to business marks (e.g. 'Toshiba', 'Seiko' and 'Sony').
160 That is 団体商標 (*Dandai-syohyo*); collective marks, grade marks, certification marks and guarantee marks are protectable trademark subject matter whereas those are not in the TLT or the Singapore Treaty.
161 That is 等級商標 (*Tokyu-syohyo*); the author translates this as referring to grade marks (e.g. 'Nissan Gloria', 'Nissan Turismo', 'Nissan Custom' and 'Nissan Classic').
162 That is 製造標 (*Seizo-syohyo*); the author translates this as referring to manufacturer marks (e.g. the Muji logo).
163 That is 販売標 (*Hanbai-hyo*); the author translates this as referring to retailer marks (e.g. 'Uniqlo' or 'Muji'.)
164 That is 社標 (*Sya-hyo*); the author translates this as referring to house marks or company marks (e.g. 'Mitsubishi', 'Honda').

certification marks,[165] family marks,[166] coined marks,[167] stock marks[168] and promotional marks.[169]

Although the scope of *syohyo form* in Japanese law is somewhat broader than would first appear, it is submitted that it is still quite narrow in scope and that there are three substantial differences between Japanese law and that of the EU and (collectively) the international regime in relation to the Definition Model here. First, with respect to *syohyo form*, there is no explicit reference to 'sign' in a broad context: instead, reference is made to 'sign' in a narrower context, alongside concepts such as characters and figures. In contrast, in the EU TMD and GATT TRIPS,[170] the TLT[171] and the Singapore Treaty,[172] the broader *concept* of 'sign' appears to be explicit and the sole element of *syohyo form* within the Definition Model.

Although this might be seen as a significant difference, it is noted (and is explained in the etymological analysis of *syohyo* below) that 'sign' is in fact implicit in the Japanese symbols for 'trademark'.

Inadequate translation of Japanese to English is argued to be the reason for the explicit and misleading use of the word 'sign' in Article 2(1); to the Japanese reader it is linguistically implicit that the concept of 'sign' is broader than is indicated in the English-language translation of Article 2(1). Therefore, the differences between the Japanese and the EU (and international) approaches to trade mark *form* are not as marked as would first appear (although, as concluded below, the scope of *syohyo form* is clearly narrower than that of the EU trade mark *form*).

Before turning to *syohyo concept*, a few remarks on the treatment of *commercial use* (one of the *preconditions*)[173] will be noted. Interestingly, the Japanese trademark regime seems to have a stronger emphasis on *commercial use*[174] that that of the EU

---

165 That is 証明標 (*Syomei-hyo*); the author translates this as referring to certification marks (e.g. the 'JAS' mark).
166 That is ファミリーマーク; 派生商標 (family mark: *hasei-syohyo*); the author translates this as referring to family marks (e.g. 'Nintendo Wii' or 'Sony Vaio').
167 That is 造語商標 (*Zougo-syohyo*); the author translates this as referring to coined marks such as (e.g. 'Hello Kitty' and 'Sanrio').
168 That is 貯蔵商標 (*Vorratszeichen: Chozou-syohyo*); the author translates this as referring to marks not in current use.
169 That is 広告商標 (*Koukoku-syohyo*); the author translates this as referring to advertising marks (e.g. 'Touch! Generations' by 'Nintendo DS').
170 Article 15(1) of GATT TRIPS.
171 Article 1 of the TLT.
172 Article 2(1) of the Singapore Treaty.
173 Article 2 of the Japanese Trademark Act.
174 The requirement of *commercial use* is clearly present within Article 2(3) of the Japanese Trademark Act. Article 2(3) provides that: '(3) "Use" with respect to a mark as used in this Act means any of the following acts: (1) to affix a mark to goods or packages of goods; (2) to assign, deliver, display for the purpose of assignment or delivery, export, import or provide through an electric telecommunication line, goods or packages of goods to which a mark is affixed; (3) in the course of the provision of services, to affix a mark to articles to be used by a person who receives the said services (including articles to be assigned or loaned; the same shall apply hereinafter); (4) in the course of the provision of services, to provide the said services by using articles to which a mark

TMD[175] and international regimes,[176] where (in contrast) there is reference to use, but this is either not *required* as a *precondition* of registration (the international regime) or is more a matter for revocation (the EU regime[177]).

Regarding *graphic representation*, Article 2 does not explicitly require *graphic representation*[178] or visual perception[179] as a *precondition* for trade mark registration (here there is a direct contrast with Article 2 of the EU TMD[180] and Article 15(1) of GATT TRIPS[181]). However, it is generally understood that a mark must be displayed visually in a plane or three-dimensional form with respect to goods or services in Japan[182] – that is, graphic representation is an *implicit* requirement, so in practice the Japanese law here is similar to both the EU requirements[183] and the requirements found at the international level.[184] This implicit legal requirement is bolstered by administrative requirements in the Japanese system (Article 5(2) requires submission of an application form, upon which the *syohyo* for which registration is sought is to be shown[185]). As a consequence of the implicit criterion of *graphic representation* in Japan, sound, light, taste or smell marks cannot be registered as *syohyo*[186] (this policy is under consideration for reform[187]), and thus

is affixed and which are to be used by a person who receives the said services; (5) for the purpose of providing services, to display articles to be used for the provision of the services (including articles to be used by a person who receives the services in the course of the provision of services; the same shall apply hereinafter) to which a mark is affixed; (6) in the course of the provision of services, to affix a mark to articles pertaining to the provision of the said services belonging to a person who receives the services; (7) in the course of the provision of services through an image viewer, by using an electromagnetic device (an electromagnetic device shall refer to any electronic, magnetic or other method that is not recognizable by human perception; the same shall apply in the following item), to provide the said services by displaying a mark on the image viewer; or (8) to display or distribute advertisement materials, price lists or transaction documents relating to goods or services to which a mark is affixed, or to provide information on such content, to which a mark is affixed by an electromagnetic device.'

175 See Article 10 of the EU TMD. See also Section 2.3.2 above.
176 See Article 10 of the EU TMD. See also Section 2.3.2 above.
177 See Article 12 of the EU TMD.
178 Ibid., Article 4.
179 Article 15(1) of GATT TRIPS and Article 2(1) of the TLT.
180 See Section 2.3.2.
181 See Section 2.3.1.4.
182 Article 5(2) of the Japanese Trademark Act.
183 Article 42 of the EU TMD.
184 Article 15(1) of GATT TRIPS and Article 2(1) of the TLT.
185 'Article 5: (Application for trademark registration): (1) Any person who desires to register a trademark shall *submit an application* to the Commissioner of the Patent Office accompanied by the required documents. The application *shall state* the following matters: (1) the name and the domicile or residence of the applicant for trademark registration; (2) *the trademark for which registration is sought*; and (3) the designated goods or designated services and the class of goods or services provided by Cabinet Order as provided for in Article 6(2).' [Emphasis added]
186 Sound trademarks are recognised under the Unfair Competition Prevention Act in Japan but are not approved as registered trademarks in the Japanese Trademark Act. Remarkably, the sound of 'Harley-Davidson' (motor bikes) was regarded as a distinctive mark in the Unfair Competition Prevention Act (Tokyo District Court, *Syowa 55nen 1gatsu 28 nichi, Mutaishi-shu 5562go* at 42).
187 A very important recent development in relation to future expansion of the scope of *syohyo type* in *form* needs to be made here. In June 2009, the JPO officially announced a consideration of broadening the trademark subject matter to non-traditional trademarks – that is, movement

the *graphic representation* requirement is both legally and administratively implicit[188] in the Japanese regime.

Regarding *concept* of '*syohyo*', there is no explicit *concept* of '*syohyo*', and the Japanese Act would appear to both contradict the Definition Model and contrast sharply with the international[189] and EU[190] trade mark regimes on this point. In other words, there is no explicit reference to a criterion of distinctiveness within Article 2 of the Japanese Trademark Act (which is itself equivalent to Article 2 of the EU TMD[191] and Article 15(1) of GATT TRIPS[192]). Such a myth of missing the trade mark *concept* can be solved by utilising the etymological approach to the law and by looking beyond Article 2.

First, by using the etymological approach, the trade mark *concept* distinctiveness is clearly found in the Japanese Trademark Act. This is because the requirement of distinctiveness is conceptually implicit[193] in the written Japanese symbol of 'trademark'. The etymological mechanics of the *kanji* symbols for 'trademark' is that '商標' (trademark, or *syohyo*) consists of two *kanji* symbols: (i) 商 (*syo*) and (ii) 標 (*hyo*). The first symbol, *syo*, implies *business*, trade and commerce,[194] and the second symbol, *hyo*, represents signs, symbols, marks or indications,[195] and also implies distinctiveness.[196] Japanese speakers are therefore automatically able to read '*syohyo*' not only as 'trademark' but also as referring to distinctive signs used in a business (and/or commercial) context. Thus, not only does use of etymological methodology clarify that there is an implicit distinctiveness criterion in the Japanese trademark regime, but it also reveals that: (i) the concept of 'sign' is implicitly used in a broad sense in the Japanese system (as well as the explicit, confusing and incorrect reference to 'sign' in a narrow context in Article 2(1)); and (ii) there is implicit (as well as explicit) reference to commercial use.

The second means by which to solve the disappearance of trade mark *concept* is through a careful consideration of Article 3 of the Japanese Trademark Act. Article 3 may support the argument that there is an implicit notion of distinctiveness in the Japanese regime. Article 3 provides a requirement of registered trade mark including a negative list of items that cannot be granted

marks and sound marks. See the JPO press release '*Sangyo kozo shingikai ni working group wo secchishi, ugoki oto tou wo riyoushita atarashii type no syohyo nitsuite kennto wo kaishi shimashita*': here, the JPO announced that it has started consideration of new types of trademarks, including movement marks and sound marks, by setting up a working group under the industrial structure committee' (press release no longer available on website).
188 Article 5 of the Japanese Trademark Act.
189 See Section 2.3.1.
190 See Section 2.3.2.
191 See Section 2.3.2.
192 See Section 2.3.1.4.
193 See Chapter 1, Section 1.10, for a brief explanation of written Japanese.
194 I. Shinnmura, *Koji-en*, Tokyo: Iwanami-syoten, 1998, p. 1298. *Koji-en* is regarded as the most authoritative dictionary amongst Japanese citizens.
195 Ibid., p. 2274.
196 Ibid., p. 1298.

a registration.[197] The unofficial translation of the relevant part of this Article provides that:

Article 3 (Requirements for trademark registration)

(1)   Any trademark to be used in connection with goods or services pertaining to the business of an applicant may be registered, *unless the trademark*:
   (1)   consists solely of a mark *indicating, in a common manner, the common name of the goods or services*;
   (2)   is *customarily used* in connection with the goods or services;
   (3)   consists solely of a mark i*ndicating, in a common manner*, in the case of goods, *the place of origin, place of sale, quality, raw materials, efficacy, intended purpose, quantity, shape (including shape of packages), price, the method or time of production or use, or, in the case of services, the location of provision, quality, articles to be used in such provision, efficacy, intended purpose, quantity, modes, price or method or time of provision*;
   (4)   consists solely of a mark *indicating, in a common manner, a common surname or name of a juridical person*;
   (5)   consists solely of *a very simple and common mark*; or
   (6)   is in addition to those listed in each of the preceding items, a trademark by *which consumers are not able to recognize the goods or services as those pertaining to a business of a particular person*. [Emphasis added]

In summary, the following can be excluded from qualifying a registered *syohyo*: a mark that is used in a common manner;[198] one used ordinarily to present the goods/services;[199] a mark that is merely a description of the product information including the place of origin, price, quality, quantity, material, and intended purpose;[200] a mark that consists of common surname or common name;[201] and very simple and common marks.[202] The common theme running through Article 3(1)(i)–(vi) is that these are all examples of marks that lack distinctiveness. Thus (in addition to the earlier arguments as to linguistic implicitness), Article 3(1)(i)–(vi) itself alludes to an implicit criterion of distinctiveness.

---

197   The function of Article 3 of the Japanese Trademark Act is equivalent, it is submitted, to that of Article 3 of the EU TMD (which concerns the absolute grounds for refusal).
198   Article 3(1) of the Japanese Trademark Act.
199   Ibid., Article 3(2).
200   Ibid., Article 3(1)(3).
201   Ibid., Article 3(1)(4).
202   Ibid., Article 3(1)(6). Linguistic context is also important here. The Japanese symbols used in the official version of the Law here are 'あ り ふれた' [which transliterates as *arifureta* and translates as 'simple/commonly used'] and/or '普通' [the transliteration of which is *futsu* and the translation 'common']. These terms, which are employed in this context to represent one of the situations in which a mark will not be registrable, are also used as a synonym of not being distinctive in Japan (please note that authority for this point can be found in most Japanese–English Dictionaries, e.g. Shinnmura, *Koji-en*, pp. 1947 and 1974). Thus, there is also a linguistic basis within Article 3(1)(4) for concluding that there is an implicit criterion of distinctiveness in the Japanese Act.

Overall, both *form* and *concept* of '*syohyo*' can be found in the Japanese Trademark Act, but the latter is implicitly, rather than explicitly, present. The Japanese approach to the definition of *syohyo* can therefore be summarised as follows. Although *concept* of '*syohyo*' is not explicitly stated in the law *per se*, it is implicitly present within the Japanese *kanji* symbols (商標) for *syohyo*: distinctiveness. There is further implicit guidance as to *concept* in Article 3, where exemplars of non-distinctive marks are set out. *Syohyo type* in *form* is very developed in the Act, if not particularly broad in scope. It is explicitly set out in Article 2 (which at Article 2(1) specifies character(s), figure(s), sign(s) or three-dimensional shape(s), or any combination thereof, or any combination thereof with colours), and this is further supplemented by Trade Mark Registry guidance, which includes examples of registrable trade marks (here, in addition to the subject matter found in Article 2: design marks, symbol marks and colour marks). *Syohyo context* in *form* is found in explicit form in Article 2 (here, trade marks or goods marks with a trade mark attached to the goods, and service marks), and this is further supplemented by Trade Mark Registry guidance, which includes additional examples of registrable trade marks (here, in addition to the subject matter of Article 2: merchandising marks, business marks, collective marks, grade marks, manufacturer marks, retailer marks, house marks, certification marks, family marks, coined marks, stock marks, promotional marks). Although there is some confusion, in the English translation of the Act, as to the scope of 'sign', this can be resolved, as has been submitted, with reference to Japanese etymology.

Of the Definition Model *preconditions*, *commercial use* is not only explicitly present in the Act but is heavily emphasised. In contrast, *graphic representation* is not explicitly present, but is legally and administratively implicit.

Thus all elements of the Definition Model are present in the Japanese system. Further, the merits of preferring transliterations to translations of key Japanese terms (and of understanding of Japanese etymology)[203] have been illustrated in this section of the book: placing the Act in the correct *linguistic* context is, it is submitted, essential.

It is also helpful to note the *legislative* context of *syohyo* protection: it should be made clear that, in practice, the Japanese Trademark Act very much operates with the Japanese Unfair Competition Prevention Act (discussed in Chapter 5).[204] In fact, it would be fair to observe that the Unfair Competition Prevention Act both complements and supplements the Japanese Trademark Act, and that the scope of the former is substantively broad.[205]

---

203 See Chapter 1, Section 1.10.
204 Unfair Competition Prevention Act (Law No. 14 of 1934 last amended by Law No. 30 of 2009). An unofficial translation of the law made by the Japanese Cabinet Secretariat is available online at www.japaneselawtranslation.go.jp/law/detail/?ft=2&re=01&dn=1&yo=&ia=03&kn[]=%E3%81%B5&_x=16&_y=18&ky=&page=4 (accessed 6 February 2015).
205 Y. Tamura, *Fusei kyoso boshi ho*, Tokyo: Iwanami-syoten, 2003, p. 56. See one example of the protectable subject matter in the Unfair Competition Act: J.A. Thessensohn and S. Yamamoto, 'Japan: Unfair Competition – Pharmaceuticals – Trade Dress', 2007, 29 *European Intellectual Property Review*, N43–44.

In brief, according to the Definition Model, *syohyo form* seems to be broader than that of the Trademark Act; for instance, an extra level of protection is provided for three-dimensional marks.[206] The same can be said of *syohyo context* in trade mark *form*: the Unfair Competition Prevention Act appears to provide some protection for trade dress,[207] and specifically protects domain names[208] and business reputation.[209] Thus, although there is a restricted notion of '*form*' in Article 2 of the Japanese Trademark Act, the regulation of *marks* (i.e. the combined regulation of the Japanese Trademark Act and the Unfair Competition Prevention Act) is broader. It should be noted here that the scope of this book is confined to (well-known) trade marks, the *form* of which is relatively narrowly drawn in Japanese law, but it cannot be ignored that some less traditional *forms* of mark are afforded protection in Japan in practice via a different route: the Unfair Competition Prevention Act.

Thus placing the Trademark Act in its *legislative* context leads us to the conclusion that a wider range of *syohyo form* can be protected in general Japanese law (using both the Trademark Act and the Unfair Competition Prevention Act) than is immediately apparent, but it must be conceded that this is *still* narrower than in the EU system.

2.3.4 Comparison

A comparison of the conceptualisation of the various definitions of 'trade mark' to be found within international, EU and Japanese laws will now be undertaken.

To provide an overview of both *form* and *concept* of 'trade mark', as variously defined, a basic comparison of the international treaties seems to show that the Singapore Treaty provides the broadest (and therefore the most generous) definition regarding *form* of 'trade mark', whereas GATT TRIPS has what is regarded as being the neatest representation of *form* of 'trade mark'. There are significant differences in the international guidance as to *concept* of 'trade mark'. Some (e.g. GATT TRIPS and the Paris Convention) focus on both *form* and *concept* guidance,[210] whereas others (e.g. the TLT and the Singapore Treaty) take a more *form*-oriented approach[211] – that is, there is a lack of consistency in both the detail and mention of *concept* of 'trade mark' in these international treaties. As should be clear to the reader, although the definitions of 'trade mark' found within each of these international instruments are different, this inconsistency does not appear to be problematic in practice.[212]

---

206 Articles 2(1), (2), (3) and (13) of the Japanese Unfair Competition Prevention Act.
207 Ibid., Articles 2(1), (2), (3) and (13) and 2(3).
208 Ibid., Article 2(12).
209 Ibid., Article 2(14).
210 That is, providing conceptual guidance to what constitutes a trade mark – e.g. *sign, distinctiveness.*
211 That is, focusing on trade mark subject matter – that is, service marks, collective marks and trade names are all permissible subject matter.
212 Perhaps due to the differing purpose of the international treaties; see Section 2.3.1.

Of these international instruments, the most precise and clear overall treatment of *form* and *concept* and the *preconditions* is to be found in GATT TRIPS, which also manages to provide relatively equal weight to both *form* and *concept* of 'trade mark'. In addition, GATT TRIPS also mentions the *preconditions*. Although GATT TRIPS nearly fully addresses the Definition Model (as illustrated in Figure 2.2), there are still deficiencies in the scope of the definition offered. Although combining the GATT TRIPS and Paris Convention definitions, as undertaken above, results in a slightly broader definition, other international instruments go still further. Noticeably, the Singapore Treaty takes an incremental approach to *form* of 'trade mark'. Although there is no guidance as to *concept* of 'trade mark', nor remarks of *graphic representation* and *commercial use*,[213] this does appear to represent a high-water mark as to *form* of 'trade mark'.

If one 'mosaics' or combines all the material on *form* and *concept* of 'trade mark' from the international instruments, 'trade mark', at the international level, can be summarised as constituting certain *signs* including service marks, trade names and three-dimensional marks that are capable of being *graphically represented*, and used (if not *commercially used*), and of *distinguishing* the goods of one undertaking from those of other undertakings.[214] This proposed definition of 'trade mark' contains both *form* and *concept* of 'trade mark' and at least one of the *preconditions*.

There *has* been a degree of innovation *vis-à-vis* the scope of both *type* and *context* in *form* of 'trade mark' in recent times — particularly at the national level.[215] At the international level, although the Singapore Treaty and the TLT do not fall into the Definition Model in a full sense, the Singapore Treaty, in particular, gives a generous impression regarding *types* in *form* of 'trade mark'. This is because this treaty affords protection for non-traditional marks such as sound marks, colour, position and movement marks, olfactory, gustatory and tactile (known as 'feel') marks.[216] It is presumed that this expansion might be caused by the increase in the sophistication of both consumers and trade mark proprietors. At the international level, the scope of *context* in *form* of 'trade mark' is variable; for example, collective marks, certification mark and guarantee marks appear to be controversial in the *context* in *form* of 'trade mark'; under both the TLT[217] and the Singapore Treaty regime[218] they cannot be registered trade marks, whilst in GATT TRIPS they can be.[219]

213 If the provisions of the Singapore Treaty were replicated at the national level, the lack of a *concept* of 'trade mark' (in particular the absence of a visibility criterion) would have the effect of increasing the scope of marks that could be registered. Thus, reducing the concept of 'trade mark' *increases* the scope of trade mark protection, whereas reducing the form (type and context) of 'trade mark' *decreases* the scope of trade mark protection.
214 Section 1(1)(a) of the WIPO Model Law for Developing Countries on Marks, Trade Names and Acts of Unfair Competition of 1967. WIPO Publication No 805 (E) (1967).
215 S. Ono, *Syohyo ho*, Tokyo: Seirin-syoin, 2005.
216 Article 2(1) of the Singapore Treaty.
217 Article 2(2)(b) of the TLT.
218 Article 2(2)(b) of the Singapore Treaty.
219 Article 15(1) of GATT TRIPS.

According to the EU TMD, with reference to the Definition Model, 'trade mark' is *a sign* that is capable of distinguishing the goods of one undertaking from those of other undertakings and of being represented graphically.

Concept of 'trade mark' according to this definition is somewhat explicit – that is, distinctiveness. In addition, it is helpful that *graphic representation*, one of the *preconditions*, is explicit within the EU TMD. Under the EU regime (see Section 2.3.2), certain signs are said to constitute *type* in *form* of 'trade mark', with examples of signs given including symbols, logos, slogans, get-ups, personal names, designs, letters, numerals and the shape of goods or of their packaging, and *context* of 'trade mark' may include service marks, collective marks and so on.[220] However, these forms of 'trade mark' in the EU TMD seem to be a simplified version of Article 15(1) of GATT TRIPS.[221] Therefore, the EU trade mark system can similarly be seen to address nearly all aspects of the Definition Model. Although many so-called non-traditional trade marks[222] are explicitly included in the examples of *form* of 'trade mark' in the EU TMD,[223] in practice it remains difficult to register some non-traditional trade marks; this appears to be an issue of particular concern amongst legal academics[224] and the difficulties experienced here are invariably due to the strict interpretation of the *precondition* of *graphic representation*.[225] 'Distinctiveness' as a *concept* of 'trade mark' seems to have great importance within the treatment of 'trade mark' within the EU TMD.

In contrast, the *concept* of '*syuchi-syohyo*' in Japan is implicit, not explicit (distinctiveness being implicit in the Japanese *kanji* symbols 商標: *syohyo* or trademark). Even if this implication was missed by non-Japanese speakers, the Japanese law includes another independent article,[226] which also implies 'distinctiveness' (although this term is not used in this article). Therefore, the Japanese law falls into the Definition Model; moreover, it is submitted that the concept of 'trade mark' is reasonably comprehensively, if implicitly, addressed. Also, there is explicit inclusion of one *precondition* for trade mark registration, but here it is business use (equivalent to *commercial use*). The crucial difference in the EU trade mark system lies in the *form* of 'trade mark': this is rather narrowly interpreted by the law,[227] although the JPO Guidelines[228] provide slightly more generous guidance as to the scope of *form* of '*syuchi-syohyo*'.

---

220 Article 2 of the EU TMD.
221 Article 15(1) of GATT TRIPS.
222 Conventional trade marks are known as letters, words and pictures or drawings, and the range of non-conventional trade marks are: (i) slogans; (ii) three-dimensional signs (shapes); (iii) colours; (iv) sound signs, taste signs and scent signs; (v) action signs and holograms. The criteria for registering non-conventional trade marks are known to be established by a case called *Sieckmann* (*Ralf Sieckmann v Deutsches Patent- und Markenamt* (C-273/00) [2003] RPC 38).
223 Article 2 of the EU TMD.
224 See, for example, S. Maniatis and A. Sander, 'A Consumer Trade Mark: Protection Based on Origin and Quality', *European Intellectual Property Review*, 15, 1993, 406–51.
225 Article 15(1) of GATT TRIPS; Article 2 of the EU TMD. See also *Sieckmann* [2003] RPC 38.
226 Article 3 of the Japanese Trademark Act.
227 Ibid., Article 2.
228 Item 4 of Part 2: Principal Paragraph of Article 3(1) of the CTM Guidelines.

Here, an additional point relating to 'distinctiveness' in the EU and Japanese regimes can be made: acquired distinctiveness through use is explicitly allowed in both the Japanese[229] and EU[230] systems. In this respect, trade mark *concept* has a similar scope in both jurisdictions.

Although both the EU system and the Japanese trademark system do provide definitions of 'trade mark' and '*syuchi-syohyo*', these definitions are not complete (in terms of the Definition Model), and there could be further guidance provided as to how the existing definitions are to be interpreted. In this regard, perhaps the Japanese system is slightly better. First, the JPO Guidelines to the Japanese Trademark Act[231] indicate a still wider scope of *type* in *form* of 'trade mark' (stating that it includes any characters, figures, signs (symbols) or three-dimensional shapes, or any combination thereof, or any combination thereof with colours). Second, Japanese legal scholars categorise trade marks from a functional perspective,[232] and this gives a good 'flavour' of the actual scope of *context* in *form* of 'trade mark' in Japan. Japanese academics would thus categorise *types* in *form* of 'trade mark' as including character marks, design marks, symbol marks, colour marks, three-dimensional marks, combined marks; and *context* in *form* of 'trade mark' as including merchandising marks, service marks, business marks, collective marks, geographical indications, grade marks, manufacturer marks, retailer marks, certification marks, family marks, coined marks, stock marks and promotional marks.[233] Nevertheless, the actual scope of *form* of 'trade mark' is narrower in the Japanese Trademark Act than it is in the EU regime, with the Japanese Trademark Act appearing to be both more proscriptive and more restrictive than the EU *vis-à-vis* the scope of *form* (i.e. *type*) of 'trade mark'.

2.4 Conclusion

The main purpose of Chapter 2 has been to critically conceptualise the definitions of 'trade mark' in the international, the EU and the Japanese trade mark regimes

---

229 Article 3(2) of the Japanese Trademark Act.
230 Article 3(3) of the EU TMD.
231 See, for example, Chapter I: Article 3(1) Part 2: Principal Paragraph of Article 3(1) of the JPO Guidelines. The functional definitions of trademarks in Japan are generally accepted by legal academics. See also M. Amino, *Syohyo-ho*, Tokyo: Yuhi-kaku, 2004, p. 23; and Ono, *Syohyo ho*.
232 See Ono, *Syohyo ho*.
233 Trade mark subject matters are narrowly indicated in the Japanese law whilst the future expansion of trade mark subject matter in the EU regime is implicit in Article 2 of the EU TMD. The non-traditional trade marks are highly unlikely to be protected. See also Item 4 of Part 2: Principal Paragraph of Article 3(1) of the Guidelines. In Japan, the functional aspects of trade marks can have an impact on the classification of trade marks. The legal aspect of trade marks is seen in the statutory definition of 'trade mark' such as signs, symbols, characters; see Article 2 of the Japanese Trademark Act. The functional aspect can be classified as character marks, design marks, symbol marks, colour marks, three-dimensional marks, combined marks with related to merchandising marks, service marks, business marks, collective marks, geographical indications, grade marks, manufacturer marks, retailer marks, certification marks, family marks, coined marks, stock marks, and promotional marks. In the EU regime, on the other hand, the lesser categorisation of 'trade mark' can be seen.

with reference to the Definition Model and to make a comparison of those in order to delineate the conceptual definition of 'trade mark'. It was explained that a 'well-known trade mark' (the focus of this book) can be regarded as being stronger than a trade mark; thus, this exploration of 'trade mark' can be seen as a helpful first step in defining what constitutes a 'well-known trade mark'.

As has been seen, the various definitions of 'trade mark' in the international agreements differ in both scope and detail, with varying attention being paid to *form* and *concept* of 'trade mark'.[234] These differences seem to depend on the purpose and, to a certain extent, the age of the laws in question. The fact that there is not a consistent definition of 'trade mark' to be found in all these agreements does not appear to be problematic in practice.

As can be seen, in the EU TMD, both *concept*[235] and generously defined *form*[236] elements can be explicitly found in the definition of 'trade mark' offered. However, in Japan (at least to a non-Japanese speaker) there is only explicit reference to very narrowly defined scope of *form*[237] of 'trade mark'. As noted above, however, *concept* of 'trade mark' is, in fact, *implicit* in the native language of the Japanese Act.[238] Therefore, it might be fair to say that the EU definition of 'trade mark' appears to have an equal balance between *form* and *concept* of 'trade mark', whereas the Japanese version of 'trade mark' seems to put more explicit emphasis on *form* of 'trade mark' than of *concept*. Both in the EU TMD and the Japanese Trademark Act, *concept* of 'trade mark' is present. It is summarised that the emphasis on *concept* in the Definition Model is supported by the analysis, in this chapter, of the definitions of 'trade mark'.

234 For example, Article 15(1) of GATT TRIPS, Article 2(1)(a) of the TLT, and Article 2(1) of the Singapore Treaty can be seen as relating to a *concept-oriented* definition. Articles 6*bis*, 6*ter* and 6*sexies* of the Paris Convention, Article 15(1) of GATT TRIPS, Articles 2(1)(b), 2(2) of the TLT, and Article 2(2) of the Singapore Treaty can be regarded as *form-oriented* definitions.
235 'Distinctiveness' is categorised as a *concept* of 'trade mark', and 'graphically represented' is categorised as one of *preconditions* of trade mark registration in Article 2 of the EU TMD.
236 Personal names, designs, letters, numerals, the shape of goods or of their packaging are regarded as *types* of trade mark *form* in Article 2 of the EU TMD.
237 Any characters, figures, signs or three-dimensional shapes, or any combination thereof, or any combination thereof with colours, are seen as *types* of trade mark *form* in Article 2 of the Japanese Trademark Act.
238 Japanese *kanji* symbols for trade marks refer to '商標' (*syohyo*). '商標' (*syohyo*) implies one of the *concepts* of 'trade mark' (distinctiveness) and one of *preconditions* for trade mark registration (*commercial use*).

3 'Well-known trade mark' at the international level

3.1 Introduction

This chapter undertakes the task of a critical conceptualisation and comparison of the definitions of 'well-known trade mark' in the relevant international treaties (the Paris Convention, GATT TRIPS) and instruments (the WIPO Joint Recommendation (hereinafter the WIPO Recommendation)),[1] utilising the Definition Model.

3.2 Conceptualisation of a 'well-known trade mark'

By way of background, the following points are to be noted: (i) there have been no recent major international developments relating to well-known trade mark protection in the legislative context;[2] and (ii) overall, relatively little academic legal

---

1 The World Intellectual Property Organization (WIPO) is an international organisation dedicated to promoting the use and protection of works of the human spirit. These works – intellectual property – are expanding the bounds of science and technology and enriching the world of the arts. Through its work, WIPO plays an important role in enhancing the quality and enjoyment of life, as well as creating real wealth for nations. The WIPO has published 'A Joint Recommendation Concerning Provisions on the Protection of Well-Known Marks adopted by the Assembly of the Paris Union for the Protection of Industrial Property and the General Assembly of the World Intellectual Property Organization (WIPO) at the Thirty-Fourth Series of Meetings of the Assemblies of the Member States of WIPO September 20 to 29, 1999 World Intellectual Property Organization Geneva 2000', according to which consideration is to be given not only to the trade mark's degree of prominence in the relevant consumer circles of the country of protection but also to other parameters. The WIPO Recommendation, nonetheless, is not binding. Apart from the WIPO Recommendation, there has been one further attempt to create a definition of well-known marks. At its Executive Committee Meeting in Barcelona in 1990, the AIPPI (International Association for the Protection of Industrial Property) defined a well-known mark as 'a mark which is known to a large part of the public, being associated with the article or service in the mind of the public as indicating their origin'.
2 There is the WIPO Recommendation, but this instrument does not have binding force and it would be helpful to have modern treaty provisions (or an entire treaty) concerned with the comprehensive definition of and protection of 'well-known trade marks'. The view here of the import of *binding* international law is not supported in the secondary literature, where some commentators are much more enthusiastic about the role and utility of the Recommendations. For example: 'I believe that we now have in our hands, at last and for the first time, an authoritative statement of how to define a well-known mark and the rights which an owner of it can claim.

research has been undertaken in relation to the conceptualisation of well-known trade mark protection at the international level[3] and secondary material is therefore limited.

The key condition needs to be repeated here: in Chapter 1, the following formula[4] was proposed: trade mark → well-known trade mark → famous mark (a transformation of a mark from the most general to more distinctive to the most distinctive). Therefore, the passport to becoming a well-known trade mark *concept* is obtaining *a certain degree of distinctiveness*.

3.2.1 The Paris Convention

As was explained in the previous two chapters, Article 6*bis* of the Paris Convention was the first international legal instrument[5] to establish the principle of well-known trade mark protection[6] and to set out the minimum standard of protection.[7] Part of the limitation of the Paris Convention lies in its non-self-executing nature; for example, Article 6*bis* does not provide an independent cause of action at the national level. Further, it is a well-understood principle that the protection afforded to trade marks that are well known was primarily for jurisdictions that do not otherwise afford protection to unregistered trade marks.[8]

A critical examination of the Paris Convention as a threshold of the definition of 'well-known trade mark' is vital to this chapter. Thus, the conceptualisation of 'well-known trade mark' in the Paris Convention with reference to the Definition Model will now be undertaken.

This comes 74 years after the introduction of Article 6*bis* into the Paris Convention and 41 years since it was last revised, but a mere five years since GATT TRIPS last extended' (Tatham, 'WIPO Resolution on Well-Known Marks: A Small Step or a Giant Leap?', p.137). In the course of this chapter, it will be argued that, along with the other relevant international treaties (which, in the main, cannot be expected to provide comprehensive and detailed provisions as their purpose is to provide a minimum standard of IP protection that signatory States are expected to meet – see, for example, the purpose of the Paris Convention, Chapter 2, Section 2.3.1.1), this 'authoritative statement' is not comprehensive.

3 See, for example, Kur, 'The WIPO Recommendations for the Protection of Well-Known Marks'; Grinberg, 'The WIPO Joint Recommendation Protecting Well-Known Marks and the Forgotten Goodwill'.

4 See Chapter 1, Section 1.2, Figure 1.1: Formation of well-known trade mark.

5 It is generally known that the beginning of the developed system of international intellectual property law can be found in the 1880s, with the conclusion of the Paris Convention and the Berne Convention. These treaties were built around two basic positions. First, signatory States had to provide minimum levels of intellectual property protection – so-called substantive *minima* in their domestic law. Second, as a general rule, a signatory State was obliged to offer protection to nationals of other signatory States that matched the protection it afforded its own nationals. This is the principle of national treatment.

6 See WIPO, *Introduction to Intellectual Property: Theory and Practice*; and Kur, 'Well-Known Marks, Highly Renowned Marks, and Marks Having a (High) Reputation – What's It All About?', p. 219. Kur argues that the contribution made by the Paris Convention to the protection of well-known trade marks is rather minor.

7 WIPO, *Introduction to Intellectual Property: Theory and Practice*, pp. 359–84.

8 Tritton, *Intellectual Property in Europe*, p. 231.

The article in full is as follows:

Article 6*bis*:
the countries of the Union undertake, *ex officio* if their legislation so permits, or *at the request of an interested party*, to *refuse or to cancel the registration, and to prohibit the use, of a trademark which constitutes a reproduction, an imitation, or a translation, liable to create confusion*, of a mark considered by the competent authority of the country of registration or *use to be well known in that country* as being already the mark of a person entitled to the benefits of this Convention and used *for identical or similar goods*. These provisions shall also apply when the essential part of the mark constitutes a reproduction of any such well-known mark or an *imitation liable to create confusion therewith*. [Emphasis added]

As was briefly noted in Chapter 1, Article 6*bis* does not offer a conceptual definition of 'well-known trade mark';[9] this simply establishes that the well-known trade mark proprietors shall enjoy the exclusive legal rights irrespective of registration (well-known trade mark protection principle 1) where the later mark, which is identical to the earlier mark, upon its registration, is used for identical or similar goods where such a registration is likely to cause confusion.

In order to embark on conceptualisation of 'well-known trade mark' with reference to the Definition Model, attention will first turn to 'well-known trade mark' *form* (both *type* and *context*). No explicit reference is made to 'well-known trade mark' *form*, although we can infer the form of 'well-known trade mark' from the *form* of 'trade mark'[10] by referring back to the original form of 'well-known trade mark' – 'trade mark'.

Therefore, (well-known) trade mark *context* in *form* can be held to include service marks,[11] collective marks[12] and trade names,[13] but exclude hallmarks[14] and marks contrary to morality or public order[15] and those registered in bad faith.[16] 'Well-known trade mark' *type* in *form* can be held to specifically exclude State emblems, armorial bearings, marks of intergovernmental organisations and so on, without authorisation.[17] Thus, in terms of *form*, the Paris Convention can be seen as providing some guidance as to *context*, but only providing examples of what are *not* to be regarded as acceptable *form*.

---

9 Ibid., p. 230.
10 Here, see Chapter 2, Sections 2.3.1.5 and 2.3.4, for a comparison overview of 'trade mark' at the international level. See also Appendix 1: Defining 'trade mark'.
11 Article 6*sexies* of the Paris Convention; however, the Union countries are not required to provide for the registration of such marks.
12 Ibid., Article 7*bis*.
13 Ibid., Article 8.
14 Ibid., Article 6*ter*.
15 Ibid., Article 6*ter* (3)(7).
16 Ibid., Article 6*quinquies* B(iii).
17 Ibid., Article 6*ter*.

Second, the *concept* of 'well-known trade mark' is to be examined. It has already been noted[18] that the *concept* of 'trade mark' could be delineated in the Paris Convention; however, there are no such provisions on *concept* that are particular to 'well-known trade marks'. Again, exercising the assumption that one can infer what constitutes a 'well-known trade mark' from what constitutes a 'trade mark', it can be submitted that (well-known) trade mark *concept* is a distinctive character,[19] and that such distinctive character needs (at least) to be national in nature.[20] No conceptual definition of a distinctive character in relation to 'trade mark' is provided, but certain things are listed as *not* possessing such character – for example, signs or indications that are customary. This list gives us negative examples of signs or indications that *do not* have distinctive character (in the context of 'trade mark'), but does not tell us what it *is* (either in relation to trade marks or well-known trade marks).

Thus, the Paris Convention can be seen to provide implicit guidance (on the basis of the assumption that one can infer what constitutes a 'well-known trade mark' from what constitutes a 'trade mark') on *form*. There is no explicit guidance as to *concept*, although some guidance can be (tentatively) inferred, largely from that relevant to 'trade mark'. The same applies to *preconditions*: the Paris Convention does not specify any of the *preconditions*: '. . . the conditions for the filing and registration of trademarks shall be determined in each country of the Union by its domestic legislation'.[21]

By now, it has become noticeable that although the Paris Convention requires Member States to provide protection for well-known trade marks,[22] it is – in effect – silent as to the definition of such marks, and the only real guidance as to the definition of 'well-known trade mark' is that this can be inferred from the definition of 'trade mark'. Article 6*bis* therefore seems to encourage individual interpretation of what constitutes a 'well-known trade mark' by each of the Union countries.[23]

---

18 See Chapter 2, Section 2.3.1.
19 Article 6*quinquies* B(ii) of the Paris Convention. Again, to clarify, this provision relates to the definition of 'trade mark'. It can be expected that the *concept* of a 'well-known trade mark' would be more developed than that of 'trade mark' (here, distinctive character), so it is tentatively suggested that – at least – *concept* of 'well-known trade mark' in the Paris Convention might be inferred and assumed to be a 'highly distinctive character'. It should also be noted that there is not a substantive difference between the (Paris Convention) term 'distinctive character' and the terminology used in the Definition Model ('distinctiveness').
20 Ibid., Article 6*bis*(1).
21 Ibid., Article 6.
22 Ibid., Article 6*bis*. Here it is stated that protection must be provided (concerning registered marks or well-known marks) against reproduction, imitation or translations liable to create confusion where used for identical or similar goods. It is also specifically stated that Article 6*bis* also applies where a well-known mark is reproduced in its essential parts, or is imitated, or is liable to create confusion.
23 Ibid., Article 2. It is stated that: '(1) Nationals of any country of the Union shall, as regards the protection of industrial property, enjoy in all the other countries of the Union the advantages that their respective laws now grant, or may hereafter grant, to nationals; all without prejudice to the rights specially provided for by this Convention. Consequently, they shall have the same protection as the latter, and the same legal remedy against any infringement of their rights, provided that the

Against its intention, it can be submitted that the Paris Convention could have gone beyond merely requiring that signatory States protect well-known trade marks against certain actions. To be more precise, the Paris Convention could have undertaken a task of conceptualisation and provided a conceptual *definition* of 'well-known trade marks' and an indication of *how* such trade marks are to be protected in national law.

An alternative mechanism for well-known trade mark protection in the Paris Convention can be found in the unfair competition clause.[24] Although unfair competition law[25] is beyond the scope of this book, a short comment on this Paris Convention provision would be helpful. Clearly Article 10*bis* protects more than trade marks (and well-known trade marks) as it applies to any act of unfair competition. Nonetheless, Article 10*bis*[26] would apply to *particular manners of use* of trade marks, including: (i) allegations and indications used in the course of trade; (ii) those that might cause confusion; and (iii) those that might mislead the public. Thus the scope of protection provided by Article 10*bis* can be seen as being at once more general (in that it extends beyond trade marks) than Article 6*bis* and having some similarities (inasmuch as both Articles 6*bis* and 10*bis* refer to protection against confusion).

With relation to unfair competition issues, signposts are given by Article 10*bis*: 'well-known trade mark' may well include allegations and indications used in the course of trade, which might cause confusion and mislead the public. Both trade mark *form* and *concept* of 'well-known trade mark' might be seen. The former includes allegations and indications used in the course of trade; the latter includes those that might cause confusion and mislead the public. However, it is submitted that this definition by Article 10*bis* seems to be that of 'trade mark' rather than that of 'well-known trade mark'.

conditions and formalities imposed upon nationals are complied with. (2) However, no requirement as to domicile or establishment in the country where protection is claimed may be imposed upon nationals of countries of the Union for the enjoyment of any industrial property rights. (3) The provisions of the laws of each of the countries of the Union relating to judicial and administrative procedure and to jurisdiction, and to the designation of an address for service or the appointment of an agent, which may be required by the laws on industrial property are expressly reserved.' See G. Dinwoodie 'Trademarks and Territory: Detaching Trademark Law from the Nation-State', *Houston Law Review*, 41, 2004, 885–974.

24 Article 10*bis*: '(1) The countries of the Union are bound to assure to nationals of such countries effective protection against unfair competition; (2) Any act of competition contrary to honest practices in industrial or commercial matters constitutes an act of unfair competition; (3) The following in particular shall be prohibited: (i) all acts of such a nature *as to create confusion* by any means whatever with the establishment, the goods, or the industrial or commercial activities, of a competitor; (ii) *false allegations in the course of trade* of such a nature as to discredit the establishment, the goods, or the industrial or commercial activities, of a competitor; (iii) *indications or allegations* the use of which in the course of trade is liable to mislead the public as to the nature, the manufacturing process, the characteristics, the suitability for their purpose, or the quantity, of the goods.'

25 The Unfair Competition Prevention Act will be introduced again in Chapter 5.

26 Kur, 'The WIPO Recommendations for the Protection of Well-Known Marks', p. 828.

3.2.2 GATT TRIPS

This section will now examine the conceptualisation of 'well-known trade mark' within GATT TRIPS[27] in conjunction with the Definition Model.

GATT TRIPS builds upon the well-known trade mark protection proposed in the Paris Convention, and reinforces a stronger and wider scope of protection[28] to well-known trade marks than that offered by the Paris Convention.[29] For instance, the scope of protection was expanded to include dissimilar goods under certain circumstances (see below: Article 16(3)) (well-known trade mark protection principle 2 is embedded here), whilst the Paris Convention is applicable only to identical or similar goods.

There seems to be more guidance provided here than in the Paris Convention as to the definition of 'well-known trade mark', and this provides an interesting contrast to the Paris Convention,[30] although conceptualisation of 'well-known trade mark'[31] is not one of the purposes of the GATT TRIPS.

The relevant article of GATT TRIPS[32] is:

Article 16 *Rights Conferred*

2. Article 6*bis* of the Paris Convention (1967) shall apply, *mutatis mutandis*, to services. *In determining whether a trademark is well-known, Members shall take account of the knowledge of the trademark in the relevant sector of the public, including knowledge in the Member concerned which has been obtained as a result of the promotion of the trademark.*

3. Article 6*bis* of the Paris Convention (1967) shall apply, *mutatis mutandis*, to goods or services *which are not similar to those in respect of which a trademark is registered,* provided that use of that trademark in relation to those goods or services would *indicate a connection between those goods or services and the owner of the registered trademark and provided that the interests of the owner of the registered trademark are likely to be damaged by such use.* [Emphasis added]

---

27 Further information regarding GATT TRIPS and other international instruments is to be found in Chapter 2, Sections 2.3.1.1–2.3.1.4.

28 Other notable features of GATT TRIPS can be described as follows. GATT TRIPS emphasises enforcement both internally and at national borders, taking into account the widespread nature of infringement of intellectual property rights (Article 51). GATT TRIPS further provides that enforcement procedures should be meaningful (Article 41). The enforcement procedures must be fair and equitable, and not unnecessarily complicated or costly. They should not entail unreasonable time limits or unwarranted delays. In so doing, the enforcement mechanisms in GATT TRIPS may be more effective than those found in the Paris Convention.

29 See, for example, B. Malkawi, 'Well-Known Marks in Jordan: Protection and Enforcement', *Communications Law*, 12, 2007, 119–24.

30 It is submitted that the definition of 'well-known trade mark' in the Paris Convention implies a mark that is well known in that country, including unregistered trade marks. See Chapter 2, Section 2.3.1.1.

31 See Gervais, *The TRIPS Agreement: Drafting History and Analysis*, p. 170. See also the aims of GATT TRIPS in Chapter 2, Section 2.3.1.4.

32 GATT TRIPS is the Marrakesh Agreement Establishing the World Trade Organization, signed in Marrakesh, Morocco, on 15 April 1994.

With reference to the Definition Model, part of trade mark *form* is present: an explicit reference was made only to *context* – that is, the service mark was, for the first time, included in well-known trade mark *context* in Article 16(2).[33]

Article 16(2) is not helpful in obtaining nore detailed conceptualisation of 'well-known trade mark' as it merely explains that 'well-known trade mark is something to be assessed'.

Bearing in mind the transformation of trade mark to famous mark[34] and the assumption that the trade mark *concept* is distinctiveness, a well-known trade mark is a mark that has obtained a certain degree of distinctiveness. A degree of acquired distinctiveness is considered to be equated with a degree of well-knownness, and therefore the concept of well-known trade mark can be considered to be a certain degree of distinctiveness. In this respect, there is some explicit guidance as to assessing the degree of distinctiveness,[35] which is where the contextualisation of well-known trade mark is evident.

One of the criteria to assess a degree of well-knownness is the degree of the *knowledge* of trade marks in the relevant sector of the public, which has been obtained through the promotion of the mark.[36] Two points can be learnt from this: one is that the main concept of distinctiveness for well-known trade mark is an acquired one, and another is the means by which such distinctiveness can be obtained – that is, through promoting the mark. These two points help to solve the inherent and acquired distinctiveness dichotomy: the question posed in Chapter 1 as to whether the *mode* of distinctiveness (inherent or acquired) matters for the Definition Model.[37] The answer with regard to conceptualising 'trade mark' was no, whilst the answer with regard to conceptualising 'well-known trade mark' seems to be yes: it is acquired distinctiveness that distinguishes a well-known trade mark from a trade mark. In consequence, the well-known trade mark *concept* in the Definition Model can be re-engineered from distinctiveness to acquired distinctiveness and the amended formula is: trade mark → well-known trade mark → famous mark (trade mark *concept*: from the most general inherent distinctiveness to more acquired distinctiveness to the most acquired distinctiveness).

33 Although there is some recognition of service marks in the Paris Convention, it is only here in GATT TRIPS that we see the full recognition of service marks specifically as a *form* of 'well-known trade mark'.

34 A proposed transformation of trade mark to well-known/famous mark – a mark from the most general to more distinctive to the most distinctive: trade mark → well-known trade mark → famous mark.

35 The Paris Convention does not provide the assessment criteria and this lack has been criticised; see, for example, Tritton, *Intellectual Property in Europe*, p. 230.

36 Article 16(2) of GATT TRIPS. It also submitted that the term 'knowledge of the trade mark' can be seen from the two different aspects: the extent to which the mark is known to consumers and the geographical extent of the mark (for example, how many Member States recognise the trade mark in question) – see L. Rahanasto, *Intellectual Property Right, External Effect, and Anti-Trust Law: Leveraging IPRs in the Communications Industry*, Oxford: Oxford University Press, 2003, p. 35.

37 See Chapter 1, Figure 1.1.

Equally importantly, GATT TRIPS is explicit that the well-known trade mark concept – acquired distinctiveness – is knowledge-based, and the promotion of the mark is the main vehicle of obtaining such knowledge.[38] It is, though, still unclear as to what extent of acquired distinctiveness ought to be demonstrated for the purpose of a trade mark to be well known.

It should not be forgotten that the Definition Model also has *preconditions*. One of these does appear to be present in GATT TRIPS,[39] although the term used is 'visual perception' rather than *graphic representation*. It should be noted that *commercial use* (the other *precondition*) is not present.

To sum up, the following aspects of GATT TRIPS can be appreciated: (i) well-known trade mark protection principle 2 is established (going beyond the indication of trade origin principle);[40] (ii) contextualisation of well-known trade mark is evidenced; and (iii) with reference to the Definition Model, further guidance on trade mark *concept* is provided: distinctiveness is acquired through promoting the trade mark.

In terms of *context* within *form*, it is clear that in addition to the guidance provided by the Paris Convention, service marks are specifically included in GATT TRIPS in relation to 'well-known trade marks'.

3.2.3 A comparison: the Paris Convention and GATT TRIPS

Before moving on to the next relevant international instrument, the WIPO Recommendation, it will be helpful to undertake a very brief comparative analysis of the Paris Convention and GATT TRIPS with regard to the definitions provided of 'well-known trade mark'.

A summary of the comparison between these two treaties, using the Definition Model, is as follows:

- *The Paris Convention*: 'well-known trade mark' is a trade mark that is well known in the country of registration or use. Thus, there is no explicit guidance as to *form* or *concept*.

---

38 It is submitted that this might be one of the conceptual differences between 'trade mark' and 'well-known trade mark', as alluded to in Chapter 2, Section 2.2.3, where it was noted that the *concept* of the well-known trade mark 'Coca-Cola' relied on acquired distinctiveness. In this line of reasoning, 'trade mark' *concept* could be innate and/or acquired, but to achieve the level of distinctiveness (or knowledge) required of a well-known trade mark, a very significant amount of distinctiveness must be acquired (whether the mark was originally innately distinctive or not). This line of reasoning does not, it is submitted, substantively affect the Definition Model, but it is a refinement worth noting.

39 Article 15(1) of GATT TRIPS.

40 Another point of similarity between the two instruments (although further discussion of this is precluded by the scope of this book) lies in unfair competition. Similarly to Article 10*bis* of the Paris Convention, an alternative route to well-known trade mark protection could be provided by the unfair competition provision under Article 39 of GATT TRIPS. Article 39 is clearly based on the equivalent Paris Convention provision (it is stated in Article 39 that the purpose here is to ensure effective protection against unfair competition as provided in Article 10*bis* of the Paris Convention).

- *GATT TRIPS*: a 'well-known trade mark' is a trade mark (including a service mark (*context* in *form*) that has acquired a degree of distinctiveness through promoting the trade mark; the *concept* of acquired distinctiveness lies here in knowledge (*knownness*) amongst the relevant sector of the public.

Placing these two definitions together does not provide much more in the way of guidance: collectively from these two treaties it can be said that a well-known trade mark is a trade mark or service mark that is well known (in the sense of there being sufficient knowledge in the relevant sector of the public in the country of registration or use).

It is submitted that GATT TRIPS has the broader definition[41] of 'well-known trade mark' *context*, as in terms of *form* it is clear that service marks are included.[42] Neither, however, explicitly provides for 'well-known trade mark' *type*. The other difference between the Paris Convention and GATT TRIPS is that the latter does give some guidance as to *concept*,[43] explicitly providing that there has to be sufficient knowledge and awareness of the trade mark in the relevant part of the public, including knowledge obtained as a result of a trade mark being promoted.[44]

Overall, 'well-known trade mark' *context* in *form* is addressed to some degree in these two treaties, but what *level* of knowledge is required for a trade mark to be 'well known'[45] is not explicitly set out, so 'well-known trade mark' *concept* is not set out fully. There are also deficiencies relating to form, as *context* is only lightly dealt with and there is no explicit guidance as to *types* of well-known trade mark.

3.2.4 The WIPO Recommendation

This section considers the definition provided by WIPO Recommendation[46] and applies the Definition Model to this. The main focus remains the conceptualisation

41 It can be said that it also has the broader scope of well-known trade mark protection since protection is extended to dissimilar goods (see Article 16(2) of GATT TRIPS).
42 Article 16(2) of GATT TRIPS.
43 A fact recognised, albeit not using the terminology of the Definition Model, in G. Wurtenberger, 'Risk of Confusion and Criteria to Determine the Same in European Community Trade Mark Law', *European Intellectual Property Review*, 24, 2000, 20–9, p. 27.
44 See Article 16(2) of GATT TRIPS.
45 GATT TRIPS is aimed at providing the additional legal standards for the recognition and protection of well-known marks, although the aim of both the Paris Convention and GATT TRIPS is to provide the minimum standard of IP protection. See Chapter 2, Section 2.3. See also M. Handler, 'Trade Marks Dilution in Australia?', *European Intellectual Property Review*, 29, 2007, 307–18, p. 308.
46 See the Preamble of the WIPO Recommendation and document A/32/2-WO/BC/18/2 at 86 and 'Main Program 09 WIPO Program and Budget for the biennium 1998–99, which comes under Main Program 09' document A/32/2-WO/BC/18/2 at 86. It seeks to provide more flexibility into the legal context as follows: 'Given the practical imperative for accelerated development and implementation of certain international harmonised common principles and rules in industrial property law, the future strategy for this main program includes consideration of ways to complement the treaty-based approach … If Member States judge it to be in their interests so to proceed, a more flexible approach may be taken towards the harmonisation of industrial property principles and rules …'

of 'well-known trade mark'[47] suggested by the WIPO Recommendation, and does not explore the historical development[48] or consideration of the administrative aspects[49] of WIPO as an institution.

The purpose of the WIPO Recommendation is to actively promote, at the international level, a harmonised approach to common principles for well-known trade mark protection and rules for assessing whether a mark is well known.[50]

The WIPO Recommendation is, sadly, not a binding legal instrument,[51] but its importance for both pragmatic and legal reasons could be argued. First, pragmatism: the WIPO Recommendation, by virtue of being one of the few international guides in this area, seems to be the main model for the regulation of well-known trade marks at the national level.[52] Second, law: in the introductory part of the Recommendation there is a specific recommendation that Member States of WIPO and signatories of the Paris Convention ought to bring the Recommendation to the attention of regional trade mark organisations.[53] If or

---

47 Apart from the WIPO Recommendation, it has been noted that Tatham has proposed a definition of both famous and well-known trade marks (see Chapter 1, Section 1.2). There is an attempt to create a definition of 'well-known mark' at the international level: the AIPPI (International Association for the Protection of Industrial Property, at its Executive Committee Meeting in Barcelona, 30 September–5 October 1990), defined a well-known mark as 'a mark which is known to a large part of the public, being associated with the article or service in the mind of the public as indicating their origin'. See AIPPI Yearbook 1991/I 'Question 100 Protection of unregistered but well-known trademarks (Art. 6*bis* Paris Convention and protection of highly renowned trademarks', pp. 295–7). The author submits that this constitutes a very general description rather than a definition of 'well-known marks' and, as such, has elected not to critically analyse this further.

48 The predecessor of the WIPO was the BIRPI (*Bureaux Internationaux Réunis pour la Protection de la Propriété Intellectuelle*: French acronym for United International Bureau for the Protection of Intellectual Property), which was set up in 1893 to administer the Berne Convention (Berne Convention for the Protection of Literary and Artistic Works) and the Paris Convention for the Protection of Industrial Property in 1883. It should be noted here that the Paris Convention is administered by the WIPO. See WIPO website, 'WIPO-Administered Treaties'. Also, a full text of the Berne Convention may be found online at www.wipo.int/treaties/en/ip/berne/trtdocs_wo001.html (accessed 4 November 2014).

49 The role of WIPO in relation to trade marks and trade mark law can be set out as follows: (i) *normative activities*, involving the setting of norms and standards for the protection and enforcement of trade marks (and other intellectual property rights) through the conclusion of international treaties and instruments (the WIPO Recommendation can be categorised under (i)); (ii) *program activities*, involving legal technical assistance to States in the field of intellectual property; (iii) *international classification* and standardisation activities, involving cooperation among industrial property offices concerning patents, trade marks and industrial design documentation (the Nice Classification of trade marks can be categorised as (iii)); and (iv) registration activities, involving services related to international applications for patents for inventions and for *the registration of international marks* and industrial designs (the TLT and the Singapore Treaty can be categorised as (iv)).

50 See the third paragraph of the Preamble of the WIPO Recommendation.

51 The non-binding nature of the WIPO Recommendation can be read from the third paragraph of the Preamble of the WIPO Recommendation. It is clearly stated that 'each Member State may consider the use of any of the provisions adopted by the Standing Committee on the Law of Trademarks, Industrial Designs and Geographical Indications (SCT)'.

52 Indeed, it is said that the WIPO Recommendation has influenced the contents of the JPO Guidelines.

53 See the third paragraph of the Preamble of the WIPO Recommendation.

where such regional organisations have noted the Recommendation, this could influence the development of regional (and national) trade mark law. Thus, by an unofficial route, the Recommendation could attain a *quasi*-official character at the local level.

The WIPO Recommendation does not handle well-known trade mark protection from a conceptual perspective – it does so from a contextual perspective – and therefore there is no conceptual definition of well-known trade mark in the WIPO Recommendation. Based on the contextual approach, an exhaustive list of fact-based assessment criteria in determining whether a trade mark[54] is well known is proactively provided.

Having said that, the Definition Model will be applied to the WIPO Recommendation, to assist conceptualisation of the WIPO version of 'well-known trade mark' below.

First, *form* (*type* and *context*) of 'well-known trade mark'. *Type* and *context* of 'well-known trade mark' *form* are explicitly present: *forms* include logos (*type*), trade names and other business identifiers and internet domain names (*context*).

In addition, the WIPO Recommendation specifically includes the subject matter set out in the Paris Convention;[55] thus, all the implicit guidance as to what constitutes a 'well-known trade mark' set out in Section 3.2.1 should apply equally to the Recommendation.

Furthermore, self-evidently, 'well-known trade mark' *context* in *form* takes an incremental approach and allows the scope of *form* not to be rigid and therefore be able to reflect changes in society.[56] 'Well-known trade mark' *context* in *form* now includes business identifiers[57] and domain names,[58] which are newly recognised as part of trade mark *form*. In other words, any definition of *context* must, as a result, be indicative (albeit, it is submitted, detailed), rather than definitive. In a similar

---

54 See Article 2 of the WIPO Recommendation.
55 See the WIPO Recommendation at 4. It is stated: 'taking *into account* the provisions of the Paris Convention for the Protection of Industrial Property relative to the protection of well-known marks . . .'.
56 See, for example, Chapter 2, Section 2.3.2.
57 The definition of 'business identifier' is to be found at Article 1(iv) of the WIPO Recommendation as follows: 'business identifier' means any sign used to identify a business of a natural person, a legal person, an organisation or an association. The former are further explained in the Recommendation as being 'signs which *identify* businesses as such, and not the products or services offered by the business, the latter feature constituting a pure trademark function. Signs that may constitute business identifiers are, for example, *trade names, business symbols, emblems or logos*. Some confusion as regards the functions of marks and business identifiers stems from the fact that, sometimes, the name of a company, i.e., its business identifier, is identical with one of the company's trademarks' [emphasis added].
58 The definition of domain name is to be found at Article 1(v) of the WIPO Recommendation as follows: 'domain name' means an alphanumeric string that corresponds to a numerical address on the Internet. With relation to 'domain name', the following definition is provided: 'can be described as user-friendly substitutes for numerical Internet addresses. A numerical Internet address (also referred to as "Internet Protocol address" or "IP address") is *a numeric code which enables identification of* a given computer connected to the Internet. The domain name is a mnemonic substitute for such an address which, if typed into the computer, is automatically converted into the numeric address' [emphasis added].

vein, flexibility should also apply to 'well-known trade mark' *type*: again, the scope of trade mark *type* can be expected to expand over time,[59] and therefore any definitions offered of *form* of 'well-known trade mark' should accommodate some level of flexibility.

The 'well-known trade mark' *concept* will now be examined. In the application of the Definition Model, acquired distinctiveness is claimed to be at the heart of the 'well-known trade mark' *concept*,[60] and acquired distinctiveness equates with a degree of well-knownness.

As the WIPO Recommendation takes the contextual approach to 'well-known trade mark',[61] Article 2(1)(b) offers the list of factors – all, some or none[62] of which can be used in inferring that the mark is well known as follows:

Article 2 (1)

(b)   In particular, the competent authority *shall consider information* submitted to it with respect to *factors* from which it may be inferred that the mark is, or is not, well known, *including, but not limited to, information* concerning the following:

1.   the *degree of knowledge* or *recognition of the mark in the relevant sector of the public*;

2.   the *duration, extent and geographical area* of any *use of the mark*;

3.   the duration, extent and geographical area of *any promotion of the mark, including advertising or publicity and the presentation, at fairs or exhibitions,* of the goods and/or services to which the mark applies;

4.   the duration and geographical area of *any registrations, and/or any applications for registration, of the mark,* to the extent that they reflect use or recognition of the mark;

5.   the *record of successful enforcement of rights in the mark*, in particular, the extent to which the mark was recognized as well known by competent authorities;

6.   the *value associated with the mark.* [Emphasis added]

Those six non-exhaustive factors can be used in attempting to infer the *concept* (acquired distinctiveness) of a well-known trade mark. Two different forms of the criteria can be identified: knowledge-based and value-based.

Nevertheless, it is submitted that if *concept* were clearly conceptualised in the Recommendation as part of a conceptualisation of the definition of 'well-known

---

59 See the demand for registrability of non-traditional trade marks in the TLT (Chapter 2, Section 2.3.1.2) and the Singapore Treaty (Chapter 2, Section 2.3.1.3).
60 See Chapter 2, Section 2.2.2.
61 See Article 2(1)(a) of the WIPO Recommendation, which states that 'the competent authority shall take into account any circumstances from which it may be inferred that the mark is well-known'.
62 See Article 2(1)(c) of the WIPO Recommendation. As is made very clear, again, in item 2.10 of the Explanatory Notes, these factors are *not* exhaustive.

trade mark' (rather than just having indicative factors that may be used in a case-by-case factual enquiry), this would lead to greater understanding and certainty as to what a 'well-known trade mark' *is*.

The first factor relates to *knowledge* or *recognition of the mark in the relevant sector of the public*.[63] It has already been submitted[64] that, in this context, acquired distinctiveness is assessed by knowledge of the mark (see GATT TRIPS). It is also submitted that 'recognition' of the mark is synonymous with knowledge. The second factor relates to the *duration, extent and geographical area* of any *use of the mark*.[65] It is submitted that temporal and geographic considerations (and extent of use) are parameters to examine a degree of knowledge and therefore acquired distinctiveness.[66] The third factor relates to the duration, extent and geographical area of *any promotion of the mark, including advertising or publicity and the presentation, at fairs or exhibitions*, of the goods and/or services to which the mark applies.[67] Again, these are parameters to examine a degree of knowledge and thus acquired distinctiveness.[68] The fourth factor relates to the duration and geographical area of *any registrations, and/or any applications for registration, of the mark*, to the extent that they reflect use or recognition of the mark.[69] This follows the reasoning set out

---

63 See the Explanatory Note: 2.3 No. 1: 'The degree of knowledge or recognition of a mark can be determined through consumer surveys and opinion polls. The point under consideration recognizes such methods, without setting any standards for methods to be used or quantitative results to be obtained.'

64 This argument has already been made in Section 3.2.2.

65 See the Explanatory Note: 2.4 No. 2: 'The duration, extent and geographical area of any use of the mark are highly relevant indicators as to the determination whether or not a mark is well known by the relevant sector of the public. Attention is drawn to Article 2(3)(a)(i), providing that actual use of a mark in the State in which it is to be protected as a well-known mark cannot be required. However, use of the mark in neighbouring territories, in territories in which the same language or languages are spoken, in territories which are covered by the same media (television or printed press) or in territories which have close trade relations may be relevant for establishing the knowledge of that mark in a given State.'

66 In the context of the Paris Convention, it has already been seen that *duration* of use may be a factor in relation to protection being afforded to trade marks (see Article 6*quinquies*C(1) of the Paris Convention).

67 See the Explanatory Note: 2.6 No. 3: 'Although "promotion of a mark" may well be considered to constitute use, it is included as a separate criterion for determining whether a mark is well known. This is mainly done in order to avoid any argument as to whether or not promotion of a mark can be considered to be use of the mark. Where an ever increasing number of competing goods and/or services are on the market, knowledge among the public of a given mark, especially as regards new goods and/or services, could be primarily due to the promotion of that mark. Advertising, for example, in print or electronic media (including the Internet), is one form of promotion. Another example of promotion would be the exhibiting of goods and/or services at fairs or exhibitions. Because the visitors at an exhibition may come from different countries (even if the access as exhibitors is limited to nationals from one country, for example, in the case of a national fair or exhibition), "promotion" in the sense of No. 3 is not limited to international fairs or exhibitions.'

68 In the context of the Paris Convention, it has already been seen that *duration* of use may be a factor in relation to protection being afforded to trade marks (see Article 6*quinquies*C(1) of the Paris Convention).

69 See the Explanatory Note: 2.7 No. 4: 'The number of registrations of a mark obtained worldwide and the duration of those registrations may be an indicator as to whether such a mark can be considered to be well known. Where the number of registrations obtained worldwide is held relevant, it should not be required that those registrations are in the name of the same person,

above, that these are parameters to examine a degree of knowledge and therefore acquired distinctiveness.

The fifth factor relates to the *record of successful enforcement of rights in the mark* – in particular, the extent to which the mark was recognised as well known by competent authorities.[70] This knowledge, it is suggested, is a form of informal mutual recognition – that is, if one State has recognised a mark as being well known, then others might consider doing so. Combined with other factors, this might usefully contribute some indication of whether a mark is well known. The last factor relates to the '*value associated with the mark*'.[71] This points to a valuable mark, rather than a well-known mark. Because of the possible confusion between valuable and well-known marks,[72] it is submitted that value is not an appropriate indicator of degree of knowledge. Therefore, the last criterion is not knowledge-based, but is more (financial) value-based. Despite all those criteria, the term 'well-known' can be extremely broadly interpreted. For example, if the mark is known (not well known[73]) in a relevant sector of the public, then the mark may be considered to be a well-known trade mark.[74]

The WIPO Recommendation also provides some interpretation as to the relevant sector[75] and that includes: (i) *actual and/or potential consumers* of the type of goods and/or services to which the mark applies;[76] (ii) *persons involved in channels of distribution* of the type of goods and/or services to which the mark applies;[77] (iii) *business circles* dealing with the type of goods and/or services to which the mark applies.[78]

With reference to the Definition Model, 'well-known trade mark' in the WIPO Recommendation can be summarised as follows: both *form* and *concept* of 'well-known trade mark' can be found herein.[79] More guidance as to 'well-known trade mark' *form* (*context*) can be noticed as domain names and business identifiers are

since in many cases a mark is owned in different countries by different companies belonging to the same group. Registrations are relevant only to the extent that they reflect use or recognition of the mark, for example, if the mark is actually used in the country for which it was registered, or was registered with a *bona fide* intention of using it.'

70 See the Explanatory Note: 2.8 No. 5: 'Due to the principle of territoriality, well-known marks are enforced on a national basis. Evidence of successful enforcement of the right to a well-known mark or of the recognition of a given mark as being well known, for example, in neighbouring countries, may serve as an indicator as to whether a mark is well known in a particular State. Enforcement is intended to be construed broadly, also covering opposition procedures in which the owner of a well-known mark has prevented the registration of a conflicting mark.'

71 See the Explanatory Note: 2.9 No. 6: 'There exists a considerable variety of methods for trademark evaluation. This criterion does not suggest the use of any particular method. It merely recognizes that the value associated with a mark may be an indicator as to whether or not that mark is well known.'

72 See Chapter 1, Section 1.3.

73 Article 2(2)(b) of the WIPO Recommendation.

74 Ibid., Article 2(2)(c).

75 Ibid., Article 2(2)(a).

76 Ibid., Article 2(2)(a)(i).

77 Ibid., Article 2(2)(a)(ii).

78 Ibid., Article 2(2)(a)(iii) of the WIPO Recommendation.

79 Ibid., Articles 2(3)(i) and (ii).

now included.[80] However, there is no clear and explicit elucidation of 'well-known trade mark' *concept*, although a range of factors can be used jointly or individually (or not at all) to infer well-known status (i.e. acquired distinctiveness). Of these factors, two different formats of the criteria, knowledge-based[81] and value-based,[82] are identified. The first[83] and third[84] are knowledge-based factors, which seem to be directly derived from GATT TRIPS,[85] with consolidation and confirmation that the relevant sectors include actual and potential consumers,[86] including particular business traders[87] in particular business circles.[88]

In addition to this, a mark ought to be well known[89] – *known* can be sufficient[90] – in at least one relevant sector of the public,[91] but it is not necessary to be well known by the public at large;[92] well known in at least one (or more) jurisdiction(s) is sufficient to qualify as a well-known trade mark.[93]

Concluding this application of the Definition Model, none of the *preconditions* appears to be present in the Recommendation.

So the original Definition Model can now be improved to:

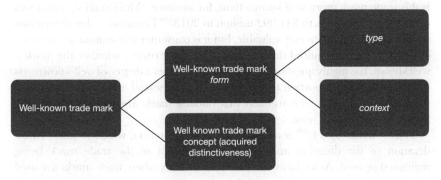

Figure 3.1 Definition Model: well-known trade mark

This section will now move on to critique of the WIPO Recommendation to identify its deficits, leading therefore to a proposal for future reform.

---

80 Ibid., Article 3(1).
81 Ibid., Articles 2(1)(b)(1), (2), (3), (4) and (5).
82 Ibid., Article 2(1)(b)(6).
83 Ibid., Article 2(1)(b)(1).
84 Ibid., Article 2(1)(b)(3).
85 See Article 16(1) of GATT TRIPS. See Kur, 'The WIPO Recommendations for the Protection of Well-Known Marks', p. 828.
86 Article 2(2)(a)(i) of the WIPO Recommendation.
87 Ibid., Article 2(2)(a)(ii).
88 Ibid., Article 2(2)(a)(iii).
89 Ibid., Article 2(2)(b).
90 Ibid., Article 2(2)(c).
91 Ibid., Article 2(2)(b).
92 Ibid., Article 2(3)(iii).
93 Ibid., Article 2(3)(b).

First, whilst the implicit guidance as to *concept* in the Recommendation could appear to encapsulate the heart of 'well-known trade mark' *concept* – acquired distinctiveness – there is no explicit indication of 'well-known trade mark' *concept* contained therein.

Second, there are some unconvincing provisions that pertain to (implicit) 'well-known trade mark' *concept*. The criteria suggested herein can be divided into two parts according to the differences in emphasis; one is on knowledge, and the other is on value. Given that the concept of well-known trade mark is acquired distinctiveness, the efficacy of value-based criteria is questionable, as there seems no clear correlation between the market and financial value of the mark and acquired distinctiveness of the mark. As a result, the WIPO Recommendation seems to muddle 'valuable marks'[94] and 'well-known trade marks'[95] altogether, without providing a clear account of the term 'the value associated with the mark'.[96] The example below attempts to illustrate this point more fully: the trade mark 'GE' was ranked as one of the top ten *most valuable marks* in 2014;[97] the market value of the 'GE' mark has been estimated at $46.947 million.[98] However, is this trade mark more well known than, for instance, 'McDonald's', which was estimated as being worth $41.992 million in 2013?[99] Economic value determines whether a mark is financially valuable, but it is consumer recognition (at the heart of which must be acquired distinctiveness) that determines whether the mark is well known. It is highly questionable, however, whether a degree of well-knownness of the mark is in proportion to the degree of commercial and financial value of the mark, and therefore it is arguable that valuable marks are not the same as well-known marks and *vice versa*.

Third, Article 1(b)(4)[100] is a knowledge-based criterion, which requires consideration of the duration and geographical extent of the trade mark being registered or used. As to duration of use, particularly where trade marks are used

---

94 See Article 2(1)(b)(6) of the WIPO Recommendation. Regrettably, no further explanation is given with relation to 'valuable mark' in the Explanatory Notes.

95 See the legal recognition of valuable trade marks; M. Blakeney, 'Trade Marks and the Promotion of Trade', *International Trade Law and Regulation*, 5, 1999, 140–6, p. 140. See F. Mostert and L. Aplozon, *From Edison to iPod: Protect Your Ideas and Make Money*, New York: DK Publishing, 2007, pp. 88–9.

96 See Article 2(1)(b)(6) of the WIPO Recommendation.

97 Interbrand reported that the top ten of the most valuable international brands between 2011 and 2014 were as follows: Apple (US); Google (US); Coca-Cola (US); IBM (US); Microsoft (US); GE (US); Samsung (South Korea); Toyota (Japan); McDonald's (US); and Mercedes (Germany). An interesting change can be observed: the mark 'Apple' was ranked 17th in 2010, 8th in 2011, and 2nd in 2012. An evaluation of the legitimacy of the Interbrand survey is beyond the scope of this book. The Interbrand survey is used *as one of the exemplars* to see how a trade mark can be commercially valuable in practice.. Available online at bestglobalbrands.com/2014/ranking (accessed 23 October 2014). The methodology employed by the Interbrand survey is based on a financial analysis. Note that there are different surveys such as BrandZ.

98 Interbrand survey.

99 Ibid.

100 Article 1(b)(4) of the WIPO Recommendation.

in the context of the internet,[101] it is conceivable that a trade mark could now become 'well known' in a very short period of time. Admittedly, duration is just one of the factors that can be used in determining to what extent a mark is well known (well-knownness), but there is an argument that, at least in some contexts (e.g. domain name use), the duration guidance provided should indicate that very short periods of use can be sufficient. As to geographic extent of use, there is also, it is submitted, rather old-fashioned guidance: it is stated that a mark shall be assumed to be well known *within the country of protection* if it satisfies the relevant criteria. However, as noted by a number of legal scholars,[102] trade marks are no longer merely national assets and now exist in a very international and, in some respects, borderless world. That a more modern approach to geographic extent of use of well-known trade marks is necessary has already been conceded by WIPO,[103] but this view is not reflected in the Recommendation itself.

On balance, the Recommendation is insufficiently helpful in this regard, and it is tentatively submitted that if the Recommendation were to include an explicit definition of 'well-known trade mark' that fully addressed both concept and form, the mention of famous marks here would be less problematic.

3.3 Conclusion

This chapter has sought a definition of 'well-known trade mark' within the relevant international framework (the Paris Convention,[104] GATT TRIPS[105] and the WIPO Recommendation[106]) and has critiqued the same, utilising the Definition Model[107] in this process.

Here it is helpful to set out a dual composite definition of 'well-known trade mark' by combining the guidance on this to be found in the Paris Convention[108] and GATT TRIPS,[109] and framing this within the basic binary definition within the Definition Model (*form* and *concept*), as follows:

- 'well-known trade mark' *form*: a mark includes a 'trade mark' defined under the Paris Convention and includes, as *per* GATT TRIPS, service marks;

101 Social networking sites can be a forum for both the marketing and abuse of well-known trade marks (see R. Bond, 'Business Trends in Virtual Worlds and Social Networks – An Overview of the Legal and Regulatory Issues Relating to Intellectual Property and Money Transactions'). This relatively new medium of mass communication does pose some challenge to well-known trade mark protection.
102 See Mostert, 'Well-Known and Famous Marks: Is Harmony Possible in the Global Village?'
103 It has been argued that that the WIPO Recommendation should be amended to protect well-known trade marks in territories of their goodwill, and not within Members State's national boundaries. See WIPO, 'Compare Protection of Well-Known Marks', pp. 8–9, Document SCT/1/3/ (14 May 1998).
104 See Article 6*bis* of the Paris Convention.
105 See Articles 15 and 16 of GATT TRIPS.
106 See mainly Article 2 of the WIPO Recommendation.
107 See Chapter 2, Section 2.2, for the application of the Definition Model.
108 See Section 3.2.1 above.
109 See Section 3.2.2 above.

- '**well-known trade mark**' *concept*: a mark being well known in a number of States and being held in the knowledge of the relevant public, in which the promotion of trade marks needs to be taken into consideration in assessing whether a mark is well known or not.

The additional elements brought by the WIPO Recommendation with reference to the Definition Model, are as follows.

Both *form* (*type* and *context*) and *concept* of 'well-known trade mark' are explicitly expanded upon: the former contains business identifiers, and the latter comprises the detailed guidelines or tests of determining whether a mark is a 'well-known trade mark'. Business identifiers and domain names are recognised as falling within the *form* of 'well-known trade mark'. As to the *concept* of 'trade mark', the WIPO Recommendation does not really add, it is submitted, to the jurisprudence in this area, although the *means* of determining whether marks are well known are set out. The following knowledge- and value-based factors are to be considered in determining whether a mark is well known: the degree of knowledge or recognition of the mark in the relevant sector of the public;[110] the duration, extent and geographical area of any use of the mark;[111] any promotion of the mark (advertising or publicity and its presentation);[112] any registration or trade mark applications;[113] the record of successful enforcement of rights in the mark;[114] and, finally, the value of the mark.[115]

Considering all three instruments within the Definition Model, a composite international definition of 'well-known trade mark' can be composed as follows:

> 'Well-known trade mark' *form* explicitly includes registrable trade marks, service marks, business identifiers and domain names. 'Well-known trade mark' *concept* lies in the consideration of to what extent a mark is well known (well-knownness), which is submitted to relate to distinctiveness. Factors that may be used in assessing whether a mark is well known or not include: the degree of knowledge or recognition of the mark in the relevant sector of the public; the duration, extent and geographical area of any use of the mark; promotion of the mark; trade mark registration or applications; a record of successful enforcement of rights in the mark; and the value of the mark.

Having concluded that the definitions of 'well-known trade mark' provided at the international level are not particularly clear or comprehensive, and speculated on

---

110 Article 2(1)(b)(1) of the WIPO Recommendation.
111 Ibid., Article 2(1)(b)(3).
112 Ibid., Article 2(1)(b)(2).
113 Ibid., Article 2(1)(b)(3).
114 Ibid., Article 2(1)(b)(4).
115 Ibid., Article 2(1)(b)(6).

the centrality of *concept* in a successful definition of 'well-known trade mark', it is time to turn to the main part of this book: the consideration of the definitions of the concepts analogous to 'well-known trade mark' in the EU and Japanese trade mark systems, and the consideration of the extent of protection afforded to such trade marks against dilution.

4　'Trade mark of repute' in the EU

4.1 Introduction

The purpose of this chapter is to critically assess the effectiveness and credibility of the protection of 'trade mark of repute' (a concept analogous to 'well-known trade mark') against detriment and unfair advantage (a concept analogous to dilution and, arguably, free-riding) in the EU. This will be approached in two stages: the first attempts to conceptualise 'trade mark of repute' with reference to the Definition Model, and the second looks at 'trade mark of repute' in the context of dilution.

This chapter divides into three parts: in the first part, an overview of the EU trade mark system, including the Community trade mark system, will be reiterated in more detail;[1] the second part will consist of critical conceptualisation of the definition of 'trade mark of repute' in the EU trade mark regime; and the third part will be a critical consideration of the protection of trade mark of repute against dilution (detriment and taking unfair advantage) in the EU trade mark sphere, with particular reference to whether the scope of such protection is uncertain (Section 4.4, below).

4.2 Background

The basic historical background of the EU trademark system, including the Community trade mark system, will be set out.

4.2.1 European harmonisation of national trade mark law

Harmonisation of trade mark law in Europe was first contemplated in the 1960s, although it was not until the late 1980s that the first substantial step was taken. The First Council Trade Mark Directive to approximate the laws of the Member States relating to trade marks[2] was adopted in 1988, and is now codified as

---

1 See also Chapter 2, Section 2.3.2.
2 First Directive 89/104/EEC of the Council, of 21 December 1988, to approximate the laws of the Member States relating to trade marks. Council Directive 89/104/EEC, 1988 OJ (L40)1.

Directive 2008/95/EC of the European Parliament and of the Council of 22 October 2008 to approximate the laws of the Member States relating to trade marks (hereinafter 89/104/EEC refers to EU TMD Directive 2008/95/EC).[3] Alongside the original 89/104/EEC Directive, the Community Trade Mark Regulation[4] was introduced in 1993, now amended as Council Regulation (EC) No. 207/2009 of 26 February 2009 on the Community trade mark (hereinafter 40/94/EEC refers to the CTMR as Regulation No. 207/2009/EC). To understand why trade mark harmonisation was desired in the EU, it is necessary to state the obvious: trade mark rights are exclusive[5] and territorial;[6] in other words, national trade mark registrations can be used as obstacles to cross-border trade between national markets within the EU.[7]

The EU Trade Mark Directive (TMD) introduced a number of changes to the national trade mark laws of each EU Member State in the following areas:[8] (i) types of trade marks that can be registered;[9] (ii) grounds for opposition;[10] (iii) rights granted;[11] and (iv) sanction for non-use and acquiescence.[12] The EU TMD, and its implementation at the national level, is just one part of the EU trade mark regime: the Community trade mark (CTM) system, as governed by the Regulation, was introduced in order to further reduce territorial trade barriers between EU Member States.[13]

The EU TMD itself sets out detailed provisions on registrability and scope of protection, which must be incorporated into national laws.[14] It is also stated in the Recitals that Member States are not to be deprived 'of the right to continue to protect local unregistered trade marks acquired through use; however, they are taken into account . . . in regard to the relationship between them and registered trade marks'.[15] It is further stressed in the Recitals that the EU TMD 'does not exclude the application (of other national laws) to trade marks . . . such as . . . provisions relating to unfair competition, civil liability, or consumer protection'.[16]

---

3 Directive 2008/95/EC of the European Parliament and of the Council of 22 October 2008 to approximate the laws of the Member States relating to trade marks (Codified version).
4 Council Regulation 40/94/EEC, 1994 OJ (L11) 1.
5 See, for example, Article 9 of the CTMR.
6 See, for example, Article 2 of the Paris Convention.
7 See A. Muhlendahl, 'Community Trade Mark Riddles: Territoriality and Unitary Character', *European Intellectual Property Review*, 30, 2008, 66–70.
8 A well-defined summary of the EU Trade Mark Directive can be seen in C. Roche and J. Rosini, 'Trade Marks in Europe 1992 and Beyond', *European Intellectual Property Review*, 13, 1991, 404–12, p. 407.
9 Article 2 of the EU TMD. It is stated that: 'A trade mark may consist of any sign capable of being represented graphically, particularly words, including personal names, designs, letters, numerals, the shape of goods or of their packaging, provided that such signs are capable of distinguishing the goods or services of one undertaking from those of other undertakings.'
10 Ibid., Articles 3 and 4.
11 Ibid., Article 5.
12 Ibid., Article 1.
13 Roche and Rosini, 'Trade Marks in Europe 1992 and Beyond', p. 404.
14 Articles 3–15 of the EU TMD.
15 Ibid., Recitals.
16 Ibid.

Somewhere in the middle lie provisions that are optional for Member States to adopt.

4.2.2 The Community trade mark (CTM) system

In 1980 an EU Commission Proposal for a CTM system[17] was approved in a first reading by the European Parliament, subject to several recommendations for amendment.[18] In 1984 the Commission promulgated an amended proposal, incorporating the Parliament's recommendations.[19] As of July 1991 that amended proposal was before the European Council of Ministers for debate; once a common position on the issues was formed, the proposal was sent to the European Parliament for a second reading.[20] As a consequence, the Community Trade Mark Regulation (the CTMR (40/94/EEC))[21] came into force in 1994 with several amendments being made under the administration of the OHIM (the Office for Harmonisation in the Internal Market (Trade Marks and Designs))[22]

---

17 The effort to establish a CTM system has a long legislative history. In 1976 the EC Commission proposed a Draft Regulation to establish a CTM system. See 'Memorandum on the Creation of an EEC Trade Mark', *Bull. Eur. Communities* (Supp. August 1976). A Draft Council Regulation on the Community Trademark, Doc. COM(78) 753, was circulated in July 1978. In 1980 the Commission promulgated another proposal for a Regulation on the Community Trade Mark. Doc. COM(80) 635 final; 23 OJ [1980] C351, 31 December 1980 (known as the 1980 CTM Proposal). The Commission amended this proposal in 1984. See: Amended Proposal for a Council Regulation on the Community Trade Mark, Doc. COM(84) 470 final; 27 OJ [1984] C230, 31 August 1984 (known as the 1984 CTM Proposal). The proposal continues to be amended, and the most recent publicly available proposal was published in May 1988. See: Amended Proposal for a Regulation on the Community Trade Mark, Doc. COM(88) 5865 draft (IP/36), 11 May 1988 (known as the 1988 CTM Proposal). Although additional amendments continue to be debated, this article comments on the proposed CTMR as embodied in the 1988 CTM Proposal. See Roche and Rosini, 'Trade Marks in Europe 1992 and Beyond'.
18 Ibid.
19 Ibid.
20 Ibid.
21 Council Regulation 40/94/EEC, 1994 OJ (L11) 1.
22 A few amendments are as follows: first, Council Regulation (EC) No. 422/2004 of 19 February 2004 amending Regulation (EC) No. 40/94 on the Community trade mark; second, Council Regulation (EC) No. 1992/2003 of 27 October 2003 amending Regulation (EC) No. 40/94 on the Community trade mark to give effect to the accession of the European Community to the Protocol relating to the Madrid Agreement concerning the international registration of marks adopted at Madrid on 27 June 1989; third, Council Regulation (EC) No. 1653/2003 of 18 June 2003 amending Regulation (EC) No. 40/94 on the Community trade mark (Article 118a) (Article 136), in force since 1 October 2003; fourth, Incorporation of Article 142a to Regulation (EC) No. 40/94 on the Community trade mark according to Annex II (4. Company law – C. Industrial property rights) of the Act of Accession, in force since 1 May 2004; fifth, Council Regulation (EC) No. 807/2003 of 14 April 2003 adapting to Decision 1999/468/EC the provisions relating to committees which assist the Commission in the exercise of implementing powers laid down in Council instruments adopted in accordance with the consultation procedure (unanimity) – amendment of Article 141 of Council Regulation (EC) No. 49/94 on the Community trade mark, in force since 5 June 2003; and, most currently, Council Regulation (EC) No. 3288/94 of 22 December 1994 amending Regulation (EC) No. 40/94 on the Community trade mark for the implementation of the agreements concluded in the framework of the Uruguay Round, in force since 1 January 1995.

and is codified by No. 207/2009.[23] A number of the substantive provisions of the Regulation mirror those in the EU TMD,[24] and, indeed, one of the reasons for the EU TMD was to pave the way for the CTMR, by ensuring that Member States' national trade mark laws accord in key respects with the CTM regime (so that neither system should be markedly inferior to the other).[25] Note that the EU Commission recently submitted and adopted a proposal for a revision of the EU TMD and the CTMR.[26]

The CTM system[27] created a unified regional trade mark registration system in Europe,[28] whereby one registration provides protection in all Member States of the EU.

Therefore, the CTM proprietor can, in principle, enjoy exclusive rights throughout the Member States. One of the most symbolic characteristics of the CTM system is that it is *unitary* in character.[29] In other words, the CTM operates alongside Member States' national trade mark registration systems. Although an objection against a CTM application in any Member State can defeat the entire CTM application, a CTM registration is enforceable in all Member States.[30]

---

23 Council Regulation (EC) No. 207/2009 of 26 February 2009 on the Community trade mark.
24 For example, Article 2 of the EU TMD and Article 4 of the CTMR are identically termed; Article 3 of the EU TMD and Article 7 of the CTMR are also rather similarly termed.
25 It is questionable whether each of the EU Member States speaks the same language as a result of the EU TMD, particularly given the difference between common and civil law approaches.
26 Proposal for a Regulation of the European Parliament and of the Council amending Council Regulation (EC) No, 207/2009 on the Community trade mark (COM/2013/0161 final – 2013/0088 (COD)) and Proposal for a Directive of the European Parliament and of the Council to approximate the laws of the Member States relating to trade marks (Recast) (COM/2013/0162 final – 2013/0089 (COD)). The purposes of these proposals are to upgrade, streamline and modernise the current legislation in order to make the trade mark registration systems throughout the Union more accessible and efficient for businesses in terms of lower costs and complexity, increased speed, greater predictability and legal security.
27 The motive of establishing the community trade mark system (CTM) and concepts are known to stem from the single market theory, since it was clear that the common single market required a single industrial property right. Although the CTM was set out by a Commission proposal in the 1970s, it still took another 13 years to acquire approval of the Member States. However, the CTM became a reality as from 20 December 1993, when the Commission regulation was adopted, entered into force on 15 March 1994, and, following the OHIM (Office of Harmonisation for the Internal Market), began to operate in Alicante, Spain.
28 A great number of articles in relation to the CTM system and CTMR have been written. See, for example, B. Pretnar, 'Is the Future Enlargement of the European Union an Immediate Issue for the Community Trade Mark System?', *European Intellectual Property Review*, 14, 1997, 185–7; C. Gielen, 'Harmonisation of Trade Mark Law in Europe: The First Trade Mark Harmonisation Directive of the European Council', *European Intellectual Property Review*, 14, 1992, 262–9.
29 See Paragraph 2 of Article 1 of the CTMR: '2. A Community trade mark shall have a unitary character. It shall have equal effect throughout the Community: it shall not be registered, transferred or surrendered or be the subject of a decision revoking the rights of the proprietor or declaring it invalid, nor shall its use be prohibited, save in respect of the whole Community. This principle shall apply unless otherwise provided in this Regulation.' For an example of critics, see A. Muhedahl, 'Community Trade Mark Riddles: Territoriality and Unitary Character'.
30 See R. Mallinson, 'Trade Marks in the EU: One Right, One Law, One Decision – or Not?', *European Intellectual Property Review*, 29, 2007, 432–7, p. 432.

Nevertheless, these developments and the popularity[31] of the CTM suggest that a *supra*-national EU law seems welcomed by the Member States and may well play an important role of the future of Europe,[32] including further enlargement of the EU. Aside from this, it should be noted that not only the advantage but also the potential disadvantage to a CTM applicant is that a CTM will stand or fall as a single unit.[33]

On the whole, the majority of legal scholars are in favour of the principle of the CTM system,[34] with the main advantage being that the CTM system is considered to be the system of seniority[35] (as provided in Articles 34 and 35 of the CTMR[36] and Rules 9 and 28[37]). The potential for conflict between *national* trade mark rights and the establishment of a common market without national frontiers has already been noted, and the CTM system goes some way to addressing this.[38]

Armed with this brief background knowledge of the EU trade mark regime and the advantages of the CTM system, we will now begin to explore the conceptual definition of 'well-known trade mark' in the EU.

4.3 Conceptualisation of 'trade mark of repute': the regional level

The second part of this chapter undertakes the task of conceptualisation of the definitions of 'well-known trade mark' in the EU, given that the actual term 'well-known trade mark' is not employed as the language of the EU instrument.[39] The term 'trade mark of repute' is alternatively employed as analogous to 'well-known trade mark', and therefore this section explores the definition of 'trade mark of repute'. Before starting the conceptualisation of 'trade mark of repute', the confusion in terminology of 'well-known mark' and 'trade mark of repute' needs to be resolved.

31 An increase in a number of CTM trade mark applications has occurred over a decade. For example, in 2001 the number of the CTM trade mark application was reported to be 49,606, whilst by 2013 (the most current statistic reported by the OHIM) the number of applications reached 114,427. Available online at pmd.oami.europa.eu.edgesuite.net/Annual-Report/FINAL/ohim/en/trademarks.html (accessed 6 August 2014).
32 A. Brown, 'Post Harmonisation Europe – United, Divided or Unimportant?', *Intellectual Property Quarterly*, 3, 2001, 275–86.
33 Ibid.
34 Ibid.; A. Muhlendahl, 'Community Trade Mark Riddles: Territoriality and Unitary Character'.
35 See D. Tatham and F. Gervers, 'The Continuing Story of the Examination of Seniority Claims by the OHIM in Alicante', *European Intellectual Property Review*, 21, 1999, 228–35; G. Ghidini, 'European Trends in Trade Mark Law', *European Competition Law Review*, 12, 1991, 122–5.
36 See Council Regulation (EC) No. 40/94 on Community trade mark.
37 See Commission Regulation (EC) No. 2868/95 of 13 December 1995 implementing Council Regulation (EC) No. 40/94 on Community trade mark.
38 Maniatis, 'Arsenal & Davidoff: The Creative Disorder Stage', *Marques Intellectual Property Law Review*, 7, 2003, 99–148, p. 99.
39 It should be noted here, however, that Article 4(2)(d) imported 'well-known trade mark' cited in the Paris Convention. According to this Article, the EU TMD seems to offer protection to 'well-known trade mark' within the meaning of the Paris Convention. However, as was argued in Chapter 2, Section 2.3.1.1, and Chapter 3, Section 3.2.1, the utility of this seems doubtful, as the Paris Convention provides no comprehensive definition of 'well-known trade mark'.

4.3.1 'Well-known trade mark' v 'trade mark of repute': are they the same?

Although EU jurisprudence highlights the insufficiently defined nature of well-known trade mark protection,[40] the court in *General Motors*[41] made a clear distinction between 'well-known trade mark' in Article 6*bis* and 'trade mark of repute' in Article 4(4)(a) and 5(2) of the EU TMD.[42] However, one question can be posed: since the Paris Convention does not clearly define 'well-known trade mark', to what extent can the EU say 'well-known trade mark' and 'trade mark of repute' are different? For example, in the ruling of *General Motors*, the court plainly distinguishes 'well-known trade mark' in Article 6*bis* of the Paris Convention from 'trade mark with reputation' in Article 5(2) of the EU TMD,[43] which has led to considerable confusion as to the true meaning of the term 'reputation'.[44]

According to Advocate General Jacobs in *General Motors*,[45] a mark with a 'reputation' need not be as well known as a well-known mark.[46] In other words, this seems to indicate that 'well-known trade mark' and 'trade mark of repute' are in some ways different, even though the principle of well-known trade mark in the Paris Convention is not sufficiently defined.

A possible point of confusion, which might be caused by the linguistic differences in interpreting 'trade mark with reputation' based on the different national languages of the EU Member States, was also highlighted; for instance, Jacobs AG observed that[47] the German, Dutch and Swedish versions of the Regulation used words closer to the first term without indicating the extent of knowledge required, whereas the other versions used expressions close to 'reputation', implying 'at a quantitative level a certain degree of knowledge amongst the public'.[48] This situation poses the question whether it is even appropriate to speak of 'trade mark with a reputation' in a CTM context when there is linguistic variation amongst EU Member States.

The question above emphasises the necessity of clarity as to terminology ('trade mark of repute' or 'well-known trade mark') *and* definition of 'trade mark of repute' in order to avoid linguistic confusion.

---

40 This is something that is clearly distinguished from a 'well-known' mark referred to in Article 6*bis* of the Paris Convention at 19.

41 *General Motors Corporation v Yplon SA* (Case C-375/97) [1999] ETMR 122 (The Opinion of Advocate General Francis Jacobs).

42 *General Motors Corporation v Yplon SA* (C-375/97) [1998] ETMR 950 at 19.

43 See Chapter 1, Section 1.2, and see Section 4.3.3 and *infra* note 726. For example, the variety of the English term 'a mark with reputation'; the words '*er renommeret*' in the Danish version of that provision; '*bekannt ist*' in the German version; '*Εχει φημη*' in the Greek version; '*goce de renombre*' in the Spanish version; '*jouit d'une renommée*' in the French version; '*godo di notorieta*' in the Italian version; '*bekend is*' in the Dutch version; '*goze de prestigio*' in the Portuguese version; '*laajalti tunnettu*' in the Finnish version; '*är känt*' in the Swedish version.

44 In paragraphs 34–36 of the Opinion of Advocate General Jacobs in *General Motors*.

45 *General Motors* [1999] ETMR 122 (The Opinion of Advocate General Francis Jacobs).

46 Ibid., para 37.

47 Ibid.

48 Ibid., paras 36–7.

The following question can then be posed: does the replacement of the original interpretation of 'well-known trade mark' with the term 'trade mark of repute' serve to describe more accurately the distinction between mere trade marks and well-known trade marks? In other words, is the term 'trade mark of repute' a more accurate term than 'well-known trade mark'?

Does the term 'trade mark of repute' more accurately describe the nature of a well-known trade mark – that such marks are not only more distinctive than mere trade marks, but that the distinctiveness has to be sufficient to amount to a reputation? These suggestions are entirely speculative as to the purpose of employing the term 'trade mark of repute' rather than 'well-known trade mark', but further consideration of this issue is outside the ambit of this book, and it has been settled that the term 'trade mark of repute' is analogous to well-known trade mark.

In other words, it could be argued that, at a basic level, the definition of 'trade mark of repute' is indeed close to what is understood by 'well-known trade mark' according to international norms. *How* close is more difficult to indicate, simply because there is not, as argued throughout this book, a clear definition of what constitutes a well-known trade mark. It should also be noted that the similarities to be found within the definitions of 'trade mark' and 'trade mark of repute' in the EU trade mark regime support another assumption made in this book, which is that 'well-known trade mark' is the purest form of 'trade mark'.[49]

In Chapter 2, the Definition Model for conceptualisation of 'trade mark' was illustrated (see Figure 4.1 below).

In the above model, distinctiveness is submitted to be trade mark *concept*. In an ordinary trade mark sense, distinctiveness can be considered to be a capacity that can distinguish the goods or services of one undertaking from those of another undertaking.

In Chapter 3, one element of the Definition Model for conceptualisation of 'well-known trade mark' was slightly amended: well-known trade mark *concept* is changed from mere distinctiveness to acquired distinctiveness (see Figure 4.2 below).

The following case attempted to interpret acquired distinctiveness, and it is of interest to observe the attempt of such a judicial interpretation. *Windsurfing Chiemsee Produktions-und Vertriebs GmbH v Boots- und Segelzubehör Walter Huber and Franz Attenberger* (hereinafter *Windsurfing Chiemsee*) is the first case to be brought to the Court of Justice involving discussion of the scope of Article 3(1)(c) of the EU TMD[50] – acquired distinctiveness with relation to a geographical indication.[51]

---

49 See Chapter 1, Section 1.9, for the assumption that 'well-known trade mark' is the purest form of 'trade mark'.

50 Article 3(1)(c) of the EU TMD refuses the registration of 'trade marks which consist exclusively of signs or indications which may serve, in trade, to designate the kind, quality, quantity, intended purpose, value, geographical origin, or the time of production of the goods or of rendering of the service, or other characteristics of the goods or services'.

51 Note that this case also stressed the public policy nature of the provisions (*Windsurfing Chiemsee* [1999] ETMR 585, paras 26 and 27): it confines the scope of protection by ensuring descriptive

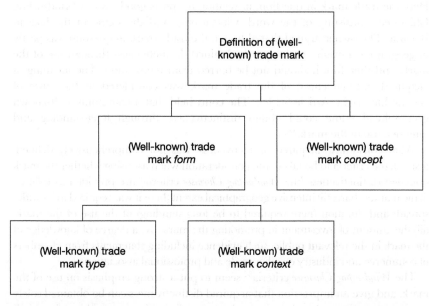

Figure 4.1 The Definition Model

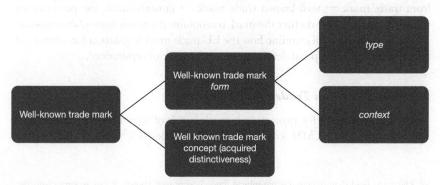

Figure 4.2 The Definition Model – well-known trade mark

signs might be freely used by all. The Court of Justice made plain that: 'Article 3(1)(c) of the Directive pursues an aim which is in the public interest, namely that descriptive signs or indications relating to the categories of goods or services in respect of which registration is applied for may be freely used by all, including as collective marks or as part of complex or graphic marks. Article 3(1)(c) therefore prevents such signs and indications from being reserved to one undertaking alone because they have been registered as trade marks' (Ibid., para 25).

Here the trade mark in question, in relation to sports goods, was a 'windsurfing Chiemsee' consisting of the word 'windsurfing' and the name of the lake in Bavaria. The owner argued that although the trade mark in question was partly of geographical origin, such a mark obtained distinctiveness through use of the mark, and therefore it should not be barred from registration. The meaning of 'acquired distinctiveness' of the trade mark was considered in the sense of geographic origin (Article 3(1)(c)). The court held that a commonly well-known geographical name could obtain distinctiveness through long-standing and intensive use of the mark.[52]

What constitutes 'acquired distinctiveness' was not comprehensively defined; instead, the criteria to be taken into consideration when assessing whether the mark obtained distinctiveness (the *Windsurfing Chiemsee* criteria) are provided as follows: (i) the market share; (ii) intensive geographical extent (here it was required to be widespread) and duration (here required to be long-standing) of the use of the mark; (iii) the amount of investment in promoting the mark; (iv) a degree of knowledge of the mark in the relevant public, such evidence including statements from chambers of commerce and industry or other trade and professional associations.[53]

The *Windsurfing Chiemsee* criteria[54] seem to put a strong emphasis on use of the mark, and give an impression that acquired distinctiveness can be obtained solely through use. Thus the close nexus between distinctiveness and use is noted, and this supports the algorithm submitted in Chapter 1 of the transformation from trade mark → well-known trade mark → famous mark, the passport for transformation being whether the mark has obtained *a certain degree of distinctiveness*.

The next section will examine how the EU trade mark legislation has attempted to delineate the conceptual definition of 'trade mark of reputation'.

4.3.2 The European Trade Mark Directive

The relevant Articles for protecting a 'trade mark of repute' are Articles 4(4)(a) and 5(2) of the EU TMD (corresponding to Articles 8(5)[55] and 9(1)(c)[56] of the

---

52 The court held that: 'where a geographical name is very well known, it can acquire distinctive character under Article 3(3) of the Directive *only if there has been long-standing and intensive use of the mark* by the undertaking applying for registration . . . an undertaking applying for registration of the name in respect of goods in that category *must show that the use of the mark – both long-standing and intensive –* is particularly well established' (*Windsurfing Chiemsee* [1999] ETMR 585, paras 50 and 54).

53 *Windsurfing Chiemsee* [1999] ETMR 585, para 51.

54 Ibid., paras 49–51 and 54.

55 Article 8(5) states as follows: 'Furthermore, upon opposition by the proprietor of an earlier trade mark within the meaning of paragraph 2, the trade mark applied for shall not be registered where it is identical with or similar to the earlier trade mark and is to be registered for goods or services which are not similar to those for which the earlier trade mark is registered, where in the case of an earlier Community trade mark the *trade mark has a reputation in the Community* and, in the case of an earlier national trade mark, *the trade mark has a reputation in the Member State* concerned and where the use without due cause of the trade mark applied for would *take unfair advantage of,* or *be detrimental to, the distinctive character or the repute of the earlier trade mark*' [emphasis added].

56 A parallel provision of the CTMR concerning infringement of such marks is as follows: 'Article 91. A Community trade mark shall confer on the proprietor exclusive rights therein. The proprietor

CTMR). The focus will remain on Article 4(4)(a), which is one of the relative grounds for refusal at the registration level.

Article 4(4)(a) sets out:

> Any Member State may, in addition, provide that a trade mark shall not be registered or, if registered, shall be liable to be declared invalid where, and to the extent that:
>
> (a) the trade mark is identical with, or similar to, an earlier national trade mark within the meaning of paragraph 2 and is to be, or has been, registered for goods or services which are not similar to those for which the earlier trade mark is registered, where the earlier *trade mark has a reputation in the Member State concerned* and where the use of the later trade mark without due cause would *take unfair advantage of, or be detrimental to, the distinctive character or the repute of the earlier trade mark.* [Emphasis added]

As was explained in Chapter 1, Article 4(4)(a) is of essence in two ways: (i) to establish protection for trade mark of repute (well-known trade mark protection principle 1); and (ii) to set out occasions where a mark of repute is protected against a third party's registration as part of the relative grounds for refusal[57] (well-known trade mark protection principle 2). First, this section attempts to conceptualise 'trade mark of repute' with application to the Definition Model.

In relation to the *form* of 'trade mark of repute', trade mark *type* in *form* in the EU TMD[58] constitutes any signs, including symbols, logos, slogans, get-up, personal names, designs, letters, numerals and the shape of goods or of their packaging; *context* in *form* includes trade marks, service marks, geographic marks[59] and certification marks,[60] Community trade marks,[61] marks being registered under the Benelux Trade Mark Office[62] and international instruments,[63] and well-known marks stated in the Paris Convention.[64]

EU trade marks include signs under Article 2 of the EU TMD, but excluded under Article 3 is subject matter such as mere description of the indications of

shall be entitled to prevent all third parties not having his consent from using in the course of trade: (c) any sign which is identical with or similar to the Community trade mark in relation to goods or services which are not similar to those for which the Community trade mark is registered, where the *latter has a reputation in the Community* and where use of that sign without due cause takes unfair advantage of, or is detrimental to, *the distinctive character* or *the repute of the Community trade mark'* [emphasis added].
57 Article 4 of the EU TMD.
58 Ibid., Article 2.
59 Geographical indication can be protected by Council Regulation (EEC) No. 2081/92 of 14 July 1992 on the protection of geographical indications and designations of origin for agricultural products and foodstuffs.
60 Phillips, *Trade Mark Law: A Practical Anatomy*, p. 604.
61 Article 4(2)(a)(i) of the EU TMD.
62 Ibid., Article 4(1) and (2)(a)(ii).
63 Ibid., Article 4(2)(a)(iii).
64 Ibid., Article 4(2)(d).

trade origin or goods,[65] a mark which has become common,[66] inevitable shapes of the goods for technical results[67] or substantive value,[68] emblems or national escutcheons[69] and geographical indication.[70]

Plainly speaking, 'trade mark of repute' *type* and *form* are the same as those for ordinary trade marks (see Chapter 2, Section 2.3.2) and more detailed than for well-known trade marks at the international level (see Chapter 3).

In the previous chapter, well-known trade mark *concept* was argued to be acquired distinctiveness, which equates with well-knownness. That is to say, well-known trade mark *concept* = acquired distinctiveness = a degree of well-knownness. This formula can now be transformed to: well-known trade mark (= mark of repute?) *concept* = acquired distinctiveness = degree of *reputation*?

In applying the Definition Model, *concept* of 'trade mark of repute' can be said to constitute a degree of reputation in the *Member States*. This very much emphasises geographical area, and therefore the well-known trade mark *concept* – acquired distinctiveness – is based on geographic area, unlike GATT TRIPS, which is knowledge-based.

Finally, one aspect of the Definition Model – namely, *preconditions* – is also present (in part). It is clear from Article 4(4)(a) that *graphic representation* is required for trade mark registration. It appears possible to infer that the same is the case for the registration of a well-known trade mark.[71] Although Article 4(4)(a) (correspondingly 5(2) for trade mark infringement) does speak to 'use in the course of trade', this is not a term used in the Definition Model, and in any case Article 5(2) relates to the scope of protection of trade marks, not the definition of (well-known) trade marks; it is submitted therefore that there is no explicit requirement of *commercial use* in the Regulation.

Overall, *form* appears to be the same as that for 'trade mark' in the EU TMD. Having inferred both the *form* and *concept* of 'well-known trade mark' in the EU trade mark regime from analysis of the EU TMD, further clarification as to what constitutes a trade mark of repute is now sought by critical consideration of the CTM Guidelines (Section 4.3.2) and EU jurisprudence (Section 4.3.3), respectively. It might sound odd to refer to the 'CTM Guidelines' for conceptualisation of the mark of repute in the EU, when the main focus of the book is not on the analysis of the CTMR. However, the CTM Examination Guidelines provide rather useful instruction, which helps conceptualisation of 'trade mark of repute'. Therefore, we will refer to the CTM Examination Guidelines.

65 Ibid., Article 4(1)(c).
66 Ibid., Article 4(1)(a) and (d).
67 Ibid., Article 4(1)(e)(ii).
68 Ibid., Article 4(1)(e)(iii).
69 Ibid., Article 4(2)(c).
70 Ibid., Article 4(1)(g).
71 Whether this is also required, *de jure*, of well-known trade marks that are not registered is not possible to say.

4.3.3 The CTM Guidelines

The Community Trade Mark Opposition Examination Guidelines (the CTM Guidelines) provide a sufficient amount of information as to 'trade mark of repute' (here the actual term employed is 'trade mark with reputation')[72] with reference to case law. Although the function of the Guidelines is a supplementary one[73] to the CTMR in practical contexts,[74] further exploration of the Guidelines will be of benefit in facilitating conceptualisation of a mark of repute, since the Guidelines work closely with the Regulation,[75] and therefore the EU TMD. Note that a set of new Guidelines came into force in August 2014,[76] with the intention of replacing the old Guidelines.[77]

We will now seek further guidance from both the old and updated versions of the Guidelines to help conceptualise the definition of 'trade mark of repute' in the EU trade mark regime. The old Guidelines offer rather instructive and indicative explanation and summary and still appear to function as a point of reference.

Before starting the conceptualisation, an attempt will be made to solve a degree of taxonomical concern with regard to the replacement of the term 'well-known trade mark' with the term 'trade mark of repute', as addressed in the previous section. This concern includes whether the terms 'well-known trade mark' and 'trade mark of repute' are taxonomically equivalent to each other. The EU court in the case of *General Motors*[78] attempted to answer the question and held that:

> [T]hus, it will not be unusual for a mark which has acquired well-known character, to have also reached the threshold laid down by the Court in *General*

72 In addition to these Guidelines, there is a Trade Mark Manual called 'The Manual concerning proceedings before the Office for Harmonization in the Internal Market (Trade Marks and Designs)'; an examination of the CTM Manual, however, is not of relevance to this book. The wording of the CTM Manual is almost identical to that of the CTM Guidelines in order to combine the parts of the existing CTM Guidelines which remain unchanged since the last revision, with amendments reflecting current trade mark practice. See the editorial notes of the Manual. It is advised that: 'From a practical point of view, the Manual should be the first point of reference for users of the Community trade mark system and professional advisors who wish to make sure they are using the latest information.'
73 The CTM Guidelines provide a significant amount of explanatory comment regarding 'trade mark of repute' in a different structure of reference to the JPO Guidelines (a comparative analysis will be further explored in Chapter 6). Nonetheless, they seem not to be as helpful as hoped.
74 It is clearly stated that these CTM Guidelines are not legislative texts. See the second paragraph of the General Introduction. The JPO Guidelines and the Japanese Trademark Act are conceptually similar. See Chapter 5, Section 5.3.2.
75 The purpose of the CTM Guidelines is to outline the practical guidelines as to the interpretation of the CTMR.
76 One part of the new Guidelines was adopted by the President on 4 December 2013 (Decision No. EX-13–5) and another set of Guidelines was adopted by the President on 13 June 2014 (Decision No. EX-14–1). These documents reflect the law, case law, practice and amendments of OHIM's current practice. Available online at oami.europa.eu/ohimportal/en/manual-of-trade-mark-practice (accessed 30 October 2014).
77 The old Guidelines are available online at oami.europa.eu/ohimportal/en/guidelines-community-trade-mark (accessed 30 October 2014).
78 See the CTM Guidelines, Part 5, Article 8(5) CTMR at 6 and *General Motors* [1998] ETMR 950. *General Motors* is cited as a significant exemplar; other relevant cases will be examined in the next chapter.

Motors as regards marks with reputation, given that in both cases the assessment is principally based on quantitative consideration as regarding the degree of knowledge of the mark among the public, and the thresholds required for each case are expressed in quite similar terms ('known or well-known in the relevant sector of the public' for well-known marks as against 'known by a significant part of the relevant public' as regards marks with reputation).[79]

The court held that both terms are expressed in quite similar ways, and therefore the mark that meets the threshold for a well-known trade mark also meets the threshold for a mark with reputation. In other words, it is likely that, although 'well-known trade mark' and 'mark with reputation' do not have identical meanings, both are so similar that the differences are not noteworthy. Therefore, the legitimacy of the transformation suggested above – that is, well-known trade mark = trade mark of repute, and such a *concept* = acquired distinctiveness = degree of *reputation* – is justified and the formula seems not to be incorrect. Another crucial point that can be delineated from *General Motors* is that the evidence of contextual approach (as opposed to conceptual approach) to trade marks of repute and of the degree of reputation (= acquired distinctiveness) seems knowledge-based, like GATT TRIP. The court explicitly states that assessment is based on quantitative consideration based on the degree of knowledge of the mark.

Now that some assumptions are proven valid and the dominant approach to the trade mark of repute is the contextual one, the conceptualisation of a trade mark of repute under the CTM Guidelines with reference to the Definition Model will be undertaken. Note that in relation to the explanation of trade mark of repute, there seem no major differences between the old and new Guidelines.

First, 'trade mark of repute' *form*. No further assistance is found, although *form* can be inferred from the *form* of 'trade mark' herein. In this sense, the EU law seems to show, at first glance, the *narrowest*[80] but the most precise and concise *form* of 'well-known trade mark' at all levels considered.[81]

Part of the *concept* of 'well-known trade mark' was already noted earlier: that although 'well-known trade mark' (traditionally used in Article 6*bis* of the Paris Convention) and 'trade mark with reputation' denote distinct legal concepts, there is a substantial overlap between them as shown by a comparison of the way well-known marks are determined[82] in the WIPO Recommendation. At first

---

79 Ibid.
80 Although the legislation seems to show the narrowest scope of trade mark *form*, this is incorrect – the Japanese Trademark Act shows the narrowest form, for instance, non-traditional marks in Japan are not registrable signs. A comparative analysis will be undertaken in Chapter 6.
81 As Chapter 5 will introduce the Japanese Trademark Act, unregistered marks are included as the protectable well-known trademark subject matter in Japan. A critical comparison of the EU and Japan is to be found in Chapter 6.
82 It is important to note there that the Guidelines employ the word 'defined' instead of 'determined'. It is stressed in Chapter 3 that the WIPO Recommendation provides a way of determining

glance, the influence of the WIPO Recommendation (non-binding in nature[83]) does not seem significant, and hence *form* and *concept* of 'well-known trade mark' composed in the WIPO Recommendation[84] may well not be applicable here to the EU regime.

Finally, the Guidelines do not seem to contain any specific reference to the *preconditions* found in the Definition Model.

A fuller treatment of the relevant jurisprudence is undertaken in outline in Section 4.3.3 below, although the Guidelines themselves do make some reference to the case law in this area.

4.3.4 Jurisprudence

So far, neither the CTMR[85] nor the Guidelines have been of much help in delineating what conceptually constitutes 'trade mark of repute' within the meaning of Article 8(5). Hence, a final attempt to seek a conceptual definition of 'trade mark of repute' follows in the examination of CTM jurisprudence – the Court of Justice of the European Union (CJEU, previously known as ECJ),[86] the Board of Appeal (BoA)[87] and the General Court (previously known as CFI) – with application to the Definition Model. The preliminary rulings are particularly important, as they provide interpretation of the EU TMD.[88] In this section, a number of the relevant cases will be examined in order to seek guidance on the conceptualisation of 'trade mark of repute'. Although the cases that will be utilised here address more than one issue, the main focus will remain the conceptualisation of the definition of 'trade mark of repute'.

The first case to be introduced is *General Motors*.[89] This case plays a fundamentally important role in helping to conceptualise 'trade mark of repute', as follows. First,

---

'well-known trade mark', *not* of defining it. See the old CTM Guidelines, Part 5, Article 8(5) CTMR at 6, and New CTM Guidelines Part C, Article 8(5) CTMR at 10–11.

83 See the old CTM Guidelines, Part 5, Article 8(5) CTMR at 6. See *General Motors Corporation v Yplon SA* (C-375/97) [1998] ETMR 950.

84 See the composite definition of 'well-known trade mark' at the international level in Chapter 3.

85 See Articles 4(4)(a) and 5(2) of the EU TMD. So far, the delineation of 'trade mark has a reputation' is: trade marks, which include 'well-known trade mark' in the Paris Convention and 'trade mark has a reputation' within the Member States concerned.

86 The term 'Court of Justice' will be applied to indicate both the European Court of Justice (ECJ) and the Court of Justice of the European Union (CJEU) in order to avoid any further terminological confusion.

87 It can be noted that the decisions of the BoA are still limited in number, and, of these, relatively few have dealt with the interpretation of Article 8(5) of the CTMR thoroughly (see the CTM Guidelines, Part 5, Article 8(5) CTMR at 4, and new Guidelines Part C, Article 8(5) CTMR at 10).

88 Directive 2008/95/EC of the European Parliament and of the Council of 22 October 2008 to approximate the laws of the Member States relating to trade marks (Codified version).

89 See the case comment, S. Brevetti, 'European Community: Trade Marks – Just How Well Known Must a Well-Known Trade Mark Be? – the "Chevy" Case Question Answered', *European Intellectual Property Review*, 22, 2002, N46–7. The facts of this case can be summarised as follows: General Motors holds the trade mark 'Chevy' for motor vehicles and asked for an injunction against Yplon's use of the same mark for dissimilar goods – that is, cleaning products. The main focus of this was whether reputation within one of the Benelux countries or part thereof would be sufficient. CTM Guidelines, Part 5, Article 8(5) CTMR at 4.

it made a clear distinction between 'well-known mark' referred to in the Paris Convention and 'trade mark with reputation'.[90] It made clear that well-known trade marks and marks of repute do not mirror each other. This is where the institutional failure of establishing a conceptually unified definition of 'well-known trade mark' is yet again evidenced. Second, an interpretation of a trade mark with reputation is proposed.[91] The condition for a trade mark with reputation is achieved where the mark is known by a significant part of the relevant public (without any given percentage being proposed by the court[92]) concerned with the products or services covered by that trade mark. Third, the contextual approach to the trade mark of repute is again evidenced, and the ways (see below) in which the trade mark of repute can be delineated are provided:[93] (i) the market share; (ii) intensity, geographical extent, duration of the use of the mark; (iii) the size of the investment in promoting the mark. In addition, if a mark has strong inherent distinctiveness, this makes the process of establishing detrimental use (in terms of the establishment of dilution) easier than for the mark with weak inherent distinctiveness.[94]

With application of the Definition Model, we will first focus on well-known trade mark *concept* – acquired distinctiveness – and look at how it is interpreted by the EU jurisprudence. So far, the well-known trade mark *concept* is argued to be a degree of acquired distinctiveness, which makes a general trade mark well known – that is, capable of obtaining the extra layer of protection. The ways in which the EU courts have interpreted such a well-known trade mark *concept* (a degree of acquired distinctiveness) will be now examined in more detail.

General Motors appears instructive in delineating the well-known trade mark *concept* and the requirements for obtaining a 'mark of repute' status.[95] The court held that '"a trade mark with a reputation" should be understood as meaning a trade mark having a reputation with the public concerned [the mark in question was a Benelux trade mark]'.[96] Therefore, well-known trade mark *concept* – acquired

90 *General Motors Corporation v Yplon SA* [1999] ETMR 950 at 19.
91 Ibid., at 21, 25 and 26.
92 See *Lloyd Schuhfabrik Meyer & Co. GmbH v Klijsen Handel BV* (C-342/97) [2000] FSR 77, para 25. The German approach (the use of a percentage to assess whether a mark is well known) was rejected as an EU approach as in *Lloyd*: 'it is not possible to state in general terms, for example by referring to given percentages relating to the degree of recognition attained by the mark within the relevant section of the public, when a mark has a strong distinctive character' (para 25). Instead: 'In making that assessment, account should be taken, in particular, of the inherent characteristics of the mark, including the fact that it does or does not contain an element descriptive of the goods or services for which it has been registered; the market share held by the mark; how intensive, geographically widespread and long-standing use of the mark has been; the amount invested by the undertaking in promoting the mark; the proportion of the relevant section of the public which, because of the mark, identifies the goods or services as originating from a particular undertaking; and statements from chambers of commerce and industry or other trade and professional associations' (para 24).
93 *General Motors Corporation v Yplon SA* [1999] ETMR 950 at 21, 22 and 27.
94 Ibid., at 30.
95 Maniatis, *Trade Marks in Europe: A Practical Jurisprudence*, p. 370.
96 *General Motors Corporation v Yplon SA* [1999] ETMR 950 at 19.

distinctiveness – is understood as being equated with a degree of having a reputation. Further guidance on the degree of having a reputation is provided and the mark is qualified when the mark acquires a certain degree of knowledge (knowledge-based)[97] – that is to say, a trade mark obtains a certain degree of reputation when the mark is *known* by a significant part of the relevant public considering the nature of the goods and/or services to which the mark is attached.[98] It can thus be observed that *General Motors* suggested that a degree of reputation can be assessed from two different perspectives: one is the knowledge of the public (knowledge-based) and the other is a geographical area in which the mark is known (geographic-area-based), given that the court declines to give an exact percentage.[99]

Having established the interpretation of trade mark of repute, the court then took the contextual approach to 'having a reputation' by referring to the German, French and Norwegian jurisdictions and making an assessment based on the factual evidence. It was suggested that the following quantitative factors[100] should be taken into consideration: (i) market share; (ii) intensity, geographical extent, duration of the use of the mark; (iii) the size of the investment in promoting the mark. In addition, if a mark has strong inherent distinctiveness, this makes the process of establishing detrimental use (in terms of the establishment of dilution) easier than for the mark with weak inherent distinctiveness.[101] In addition, the court made references to geographic-area-based criteria that the mark is not required to be known throughout the entire Benelux territory.[102]

By reference to the Definition Model, it can be inferred that no guidance as to *form* of 'trade mark of repute' is to be found in *General Motors*.[103] Instead, there is some degree of guidance as to what constitutes *concept* of 'trade mark of repute', in the sense that factors indicative of repute are noted. *General Motors* explicitly states the prerequisite that marks have to be known by a significant part of the relevant sectors of the public and the assessment criteria include: the *degree of knowledge or recognition of the mark* in the relevant sectors of the public; the duration, extent and geographical area of use of the mark; and the scale and scope of investment in promoting the mark. However, the court refused to provide any

97 Ibid., paras 22 and 26.
98 *General Motors* [1999] ETMR 950, para. 26.
99 See opinion of General Advocate General Jacobs that: '. . . it is difficult to give a general definition and it is essential that national courts should proceed on a case-by-case basis without using fixed criteria which may prove arbitrary in their application to specific cases. For example, the practice of using fixed percentages of the relevant public is now widely criticised, and may be inadequate if taken alone.' *General Motors* [1999] ETMR 122 (The Opinion of Advocate General Francis Jacobs), para 40.
100 Ibid., para 27.
101 This approach was followed by a number of cases, such as *Canon Kabushiki Kaisha v Metro Goldwyn Mayer Inc* (Case C-39/97) [1999] ETMR 1 (dismissal of referring to the given percentages as evidence of reputation); *El Corte Ingles SA v Office for Harmonisation in the Internal Market (Trade Marks and Designs)*.
102 See *General Motors Corporation v Yplon SA* [1999] ETMR 950 at 19.
103 Ibid.

given percentage to indicate the trade mark of repute status.[104] The correlation between acquired distinctiveness of a mark and reputation of a mark can be seen above, and thus it can be argued that 'trade mark of repute' *concept* is acquired distinctiveness. Furthermore, it may well be inferred from those criteria above that 'trade mark of repute' *concept* (acquired distinctiveness) is closely related to knowledge-based (similar to the approach by GATT TRIPS[105]) and geographical-area-based notions.

With regard to the quantitative factors that are taken into consideration, some degree of similarity between *General Motors* and Article 15(2) of the GATT TRIPS[106] can be identified. As in GATT TRIPS, the *General Motors* guidance does seem to present a criterion of value (which may be appropriate for defining or identifying a 'valuable trade mark', but is not a useful indicator of distinctiveness) as being indicative of the status of 'trade mark of repute' (in GATT TRIPS the status of 'well-known trade mark').

It is thus acknowledged that the stronger the mark's distinctive character and reputation, the easier it will be to accept that detriment has been caused to it.[107] It is thus possible to show an interconnection between distinctiveness and 'trade mark of repute' (distinctiveness has already been shown to be important to the *concept* of 'well-known trade mark'). However, there is also the statement that 'well-known trade mark' under the Paris Convention and 'trade mark of repute' under the EU TMD differ in terms of the level of what is here called 'well-knownness' (to what extent a mark is well known) – perhaps, it is submitted, a reflection of the use of the term 'of repute' rather than 'well-known'.

In summary, with reference to the Definition Model, the EU jurisprudence seems silent in terms of trade mark *form* as well as *preconditions*, and says little about trade mark *concept*. It is argued that the term 'trade mark of reputation' implies a higher level of *distinctiveness* than 'well-known trade mark': a knowledge threshold that is reached when a trade mark is known by a significant part of public concerned with the products or services covered by the mark, in a substantial number of the relevant Member States.[108] Therefore, it is very interesting to observe that in the EU context, unlike the Japanese context, trade mark *concept* is related to the knowledge-oriented *concept*, whilst that of Japan is the geographically defined *concept*. Therefore, it can be concluded that the requirement could not be specified more precisely – for example, in terms of a given percentage of the

104 *Canon* (dismissal of referring to the given percentages as evidence of reputation) was also followed, for instance, in *El Corte Ingles SA v Office for Harmonisation in the Internal Market (Trade Marks and Designs)*. It was held that: 'There is, however, no requirement for that mark to be known by a given percentage of the relevant public or for its reputation to cover all the territory concerned, so long as that reputation exists' (*El Corte Ingles SA* [2007] ETMR 81, para 107).
105 See Chapter 3, Section 3.2.2.
106 See Chapter 3, Section 3.2.2. It has been argued that there is a similarity in wordings between GATT TRIPS and the WIPO Recommendation (see Chapter 3, Section 3.2.4).
107 *General Motors* [1999] ETMR 122 (The Opinion of Advocate General Francis Jacobs), para 30.
108 *Intel Corporation Inc. v CPM United Kingdom Limited* (Case C-252/07) [2009] ETMR 13 para 23; Advocate General Sharpston summarised *General Motors* in his opinion.

relevant public. It seems that not relying on a given percentage does provide a greater amount of both flexibility and discretion to the court and trade mark examiners. However, this might well operate less consistently and less clearly. It seems correct therefore to say that 'trade mark of repute' is not conceptually defined but assessed on a case-by-case basis.

So far, conceptualisation of 'trade mark', 'well-known trade mark' and 'trade mark of repute' has been considered by looking solely at the mark itself. We will now look at the trade mark as it is found in real life (the product, to which the trade mark is attached, and the mark) in seeking further guidance on the *concept* of 'trade mark of repute'. *Dior v Evora*[109] provides an interesting insight into the *concept* of 'trade mark of repute' and the situations in which the rights of trade mark of repute are exploited (in the context of parallel import (Article 7(2) of the EU TMD).[110]

The court paid more attention to the nature of the goods and/or services to which the mark is attached, and put an emphasis on the possible impact that the nature of the goods/services can bring to the 'trade mark' itself.

In *Dior v Evora*, the trade mark in question was used in relation to perfumes, which the court described as prestigious, luxury goods.[111] The case was brought by Dior, the trade mark owner of the Dior Perfume lines, including Eau Sauvage, Poison, Fahrenheit and Dune. The defendant here was Evora, who attempted to resell the Dior perfume products, which were obtained by parallel import. In order to resell, Evora produced their own advertising and brochures, which Dior argued were of inferior quality. Dior also alleged that Evora's use of Dior's marks impaired the allure, prestigious image and aura of luxury of the goods, and

---

109 *Parfums Christian Dior SA and Another v Evora BV* (C-337/95) [1998] ETMR 26. The facts of the case are as follows: Christian Dior is the proprietor of a number of trade marks for luxurious perfumes, such as Poison, Fahrenheit and Dune. Despite the fact that Evora, the Dutch company, is not an authorised dealer of Christian Dior in the Netherlands, Evora obtained the Dior products through parallel imports by Evora's subsidiaries. Evora then used those products and displayed them for advertising purposes. Dior claimed that the defendant's use harmed the prestige and image of the Dior trade marks. The Court of Justice gave a preliminary ruling and held that where goods bearing a registered trade mark had been put on the market in the EU by the legitimate trade mark owners or with his/her consent, a reseller is free to make use of the trade mark in order to attract the consumer's attention to the further commercialisation of those goods. Therefore, the trade mark proprietor could not oppose the use of those articles by a reseller where the proprietor was itself involved in the sale and marketing of those goods in that jurisdiction. See B. Isaac, 'European Court of Justice: Trade Marks – Trade Mark Infringement in Relation to the Advertising of Parallel Products', *European Intellectual Property Review*, 20, 1998, 13–14; G.-J. Van de Kamp, 'Protection of Trade Marks: The New Regime – Beyond Origin?', *European Intellectual Property Review*, 20, 1998, 364–70, p. 366.
110 *Dior* [1998] ETMR 26, para 43. It was held that: 'The damage done to the reputation of a trade mark may, in principle, be a legitimate reason, within the meaning of Article 7(2) of the Directive, allowing the proprietor to oppose further commercialisation of goods which have been put on the market in the Community by him or with his consent.'
111 *Dior* [1998] ETMR 26, para 45: 'As regards the instant case, which *concerns prestigious, luxury goods*, the reseller must not act unfairly in relation to the legitimate interests of the trade mark owner. He must therefore endeavour to prevent his advertising from affecting the value of the trade mark by detracting from the *allure and prestigious image of the goods* in question and from their *aura of luxury*' (emphasis added).

resulted in the impairment of the 'mental condition' of the goods – that is to say, the allure, prestigious image and aura of luxury surrounding the goods.[112]

The product in question was perfume, which is considered one of the special categories of goods or services that transmits allure, prestigious image and an aura of luxury. Where the 'mental condition' (allure, prestigious image and an aura of luxury) of the goods, resulting from the trade mark owner's effort in promoting and advertising, is impaired, the value and reputation of the trade mark itself could also be impaired.[113]

It can thus be speculated that allure and prestigious image of the mark and the aura of luxury are linked not only by the value of 'trade mark of repute' *per se*, but also by the 'mental condition' of the specific category of the goods or services. As a result, the reseller 'must . . . endeavour to prevent his advertising from *affecting the value of the trade mark* by detracting from the *allure and prestigious image of the goods* in question and from their aura of luxury'[114] [emphasis added].

It is clear that the substance of 'repute' depends not only on the *concept* of 'trade mark of repute', but also on the category of goods or services that the mark represents. It appears that the court implicitly distinguished commonly consumed goods and/or services (an example here being dairy products or a loaf of bread) from luxurious and prestigious goods or services (in this case, perfume).[115] *Dior v Evora* seems to provide more questions than answers. For example, can this mean that the court implicitly accepts the fact that a mark attached to a so-called product of luxury is more likely to have a positive and prestigious reputation, and thus attracts protection more easily, than that of the commonly consumed products? Is the mark of repute in relation to the luxurious goods in a better position than that of the commonly consumed products to receive stronger protection? For instance, does the luxurious line in the lower-end products, such as the bread, represent the same degree of an aura of luxury as that in the high-end products, such as luxurious cars? It is quite plain that the kind of aura of luxury that attaches to the mark varies depending on the class of goods and/or services. Unfortunately, the questions posed above remain unanswered.

On balance, a new condition of the *concept* of trade mark of repute can now be added into the existing framework: that knowledge-based and geographic-area-based acquired distinctiveness can be influenced by which goods or services the mark is used for.

One of the points made in *Dior v Evora* – that the trade mark's value included the 'prestigious image of the goods in question' and 'their aura of luxury'[116] – was mentioned by *Hollywood*,[117] and the correlation of the value of trade mark of

---

112 B. Isaac, 'European Court of Justice: Trade Marks – Trade Mark Infringement in Relation to the Advertising of Parallel Products', *European Intellectual Property Review*, 20, 1998, 13–14.
113 *Dior* [1998] ETMR 26, paras 45 and 46.
114 Ibid., para 45:
115 Ibid., para 45:
116 *Hollywood SAS v Souza Cruz SA* (Case R 283/1999–3) [2002] ETMR 64 at 66.
117 *Hollywood* [2002] ETMR 64. A brief outline of the facts of the case is as follows: Hollywood was the trade mark proprietor of the mark 'HOLLYWOOD' for chewing gum. Hollywood objected

repute and image in the context of dilution was explored further therein. The court went on to mention that the value of the image of the mark is that:

> [T]he trade mark . . . is also *a vehicle for communicating a message to the public, and itself represents financial value. This message is incorporated* into the trade mark *through use*, essentially for advertising purposes, which enables the trade mark to assume the message itself, whether informatively or symbolically. The message may refer to *the product's qualities*, or indeed to *intangible values such as luxury, lifestyle, exclusivity, adventure, youth, etc.* It may result from the qualities of the product or service for which it is used, but also from its proprietor's reputation or other elements, such as the particular presentation of the product or service or on the exclusivity of sales networks.[118] [Emphasis added]

In order to explain an extra qualitative element (*concept* in the Definition Model) of 'trade mark of repute', which is a main vehicle of assessing detriment and unfair advantage, the court returned to explain the legitimate function of the trade mark by making a reference to *Dior*.

> [T]he trade mark is not only a sign affixed to a product to indicate its business origin, but is also a vehicle for communicating a message to the public, and itself represents financial value. This message is incorporated into the trade mark through use, essentially for advertising purposes, which enables the trade mark to assume the message itself, whether informatively or symbolically. The message may refer to the product's qualities, or indeed to intangible values such as luxury, lifestyle, exclusivity, adventure, youth, etc. It may result from the qualities of the product or service for which it is used, but also from its proprietor's reputation or other elements, such as the particular presentation of the product or service or on the exclusivity of sales networks.[119]

Hollywood v Souza pointed out disparity in the current method of examining the mark of repute (in the context of Article 5(2) of the EU TMD) – that is, a mark must be 'known by a significant part of the public concerned by the products or services covered by that trade mark'[120] – and indicated that the current method might not sufficiently encapsulate the significance of reputation of the mark in

the contestant's community trade mark registration for the word mark 'HOLLYWOOD' for cigarettes, tobacco products, lighters and matches. Since such an objection was rejected, Hollywood appealed against the decision, alleging that the appellant's mark established an association with youth and health, and such an association would be damaged to the detriment of the use of the contestant's mark under Article 8(5) of the CTMR.

118 *Hollywood* [2002] ETMR 64 at 67.
119 *Parfums Christian Dior SA v Evora BV* (C-337/95) [1998] ETMR 26.
120 See *General Motors* para 26.

the sense of 'reputation' and 'image' of the mark.[121] Although the power of the message and/or image that the trade mark conveys cannot be ignored, in order for it to be protected within the meaning of Article 8(5) CTMR, this image must have acquired a level of reputation,[122] and the owner of the mark of repute must provide the evidence to prove the existence of an image association with the trade mark possessing this reputation. Therefore 'the evidence to be adduced must focus specifically on the existence of this image association with the trade mark which possesses the reputation'.[123]

Returning to the Definition Model, *form* (*type* and *context*) of 'trade mark of repute' appears to be the same as that for 'trade mark' defined under Article 2 of the EU TMD.[124] Concerning the *concept* of 'trade mark of repute', this can be implied to be a very high level of acquired distinctiveness, which can possibly contain 'image'. The examples of 'image' that can be included in acquired distinctiveness are the 'prestigious image of the goods in question' and 'their aura of luxury',[125] which also relates to the goods or services to which the mark is attached. It is also held that the mark can convey a particular type of message in the mark, but, in order to argue that image is the reputation of the mark, the trade mark owner must submit evidence to prove that relevance.[126] Hence, the trade mark may also serve as a 'medium for a message associated with it which must be protected along with it'.[127] Evidence of the existence of image, which includes the allure/prestigious/luxurious image of the mark, is required by the proprietor of the alleged trade mark of repute. Therefore, the *concept* of trade mark of repute under the Definition Model can be amended as follows: a degree of reputation (= acquired distinctiveness), which might be affected by the allure/prestigious/ luxurious image of the mark. The mark of repute can therefore be said to be the mark having reputation, such as including the positive image of allure, prestige and luxury. This approach implies a possibility that certain types of trade marks, which are known yet do not possess any such 'positive image', can be excluded from being 'trade mark of repute'.

The application of the Definition Model in the EU is shown in Figure 4.3 below.

---

121 *Hollywood* [2002] ETMR 64, para 61: 'The Board of Appeal considers that the fact that a trade mark has a reputation simply means that it is known by a significant part of the relevant public. On the other hand, a trade mark's reputation in the sense of recognition of the sign does not decide in advance the particular significance this reputation may have, in the sense of "repute", or "image", to which registration of the contested trade mark would be detrimental.'
122 *Hollywood* [2002] ETMR 64 at 68.
123 Ibid., para 68.
124 See Chapter 2, Section 2.3.2.
125 *Dior* [1998] ETMR 26, para 45.
126 Ibid., para 68.
127 Ibid., para 66.

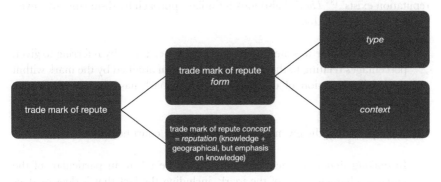

Figure 4.3 Application of the Definition Model – EU

4.3.5 Assessment of 'trade mark of repute'

In the previous section, we looked at conceptualisation of the mark of repute, and the emphasis was on the *concept* of the trade mark of repute. *General Motors* provided the quantitative assessment of the mark of repute, which was a combination of the knowledge-based and the geographical-area-based criteria. As a brief reminder of the *General Motors* criteria, it is held that 'an earlier mark is known by a *significant part of the public concerned by the products or services* covered by the trade mark'[128] – that is to say, 'depending on the product or service marketed, either the public at large or a more specialised public, for example traders in a specific sector':[129] this might be seen as beneficial, and provides considerable flexibility for consideration of the scope of Article(s) 4(4)(a) (and 5(2)) of the EU TMD. It is clear that 'significant' does not mean that the earlier mark has to be known in one or more countries: in the *General Motors* decision itself, part of one of the Benelux countries was recognised as 'a significant part of the public concerned'.[130] Although quantitative-based, *General Motors* was reluctant to indicate any figures to suggest the percentage required to meet the criteria of the mark being known in the substantial part of the relevant public concerning the goods and/or services.[131] Such a stance taken by *General Motors* (dismissal of referring to a given percentage as evidence of reputation) was also followed by, for instance, *El Corte Ingles*,[132] which held that: 'There is, however, no requirement for that mark to be known by a given percentage of the relevant public or for its reputation to cover all the territory concerned, so long as that

---

128 *General Motors* [1999] ETMR 950, para 26.
129 Ibid., para 24.
130 Ibid., para 31.
131 *General Motors* [1999] ETMR 950 at 25.
132 *El Corte Ingles SA v Office for Harmonisation in the Internal Market (Trade Marks and Designs)* [2007] ETMR 81, para 107.

reputation exists'.[133] *Lloyd*[134] also took a similar approach by dismissing the given percentage and held that:

> [I]t is not possible to state in general terms, for example by referring to given percentages relating to the degree of recognition attained by the mark within the relevant section of the public, when a mark has a strong distinctive character.[135]

Instead of providing the given fixed percentage, the court held that:

> In making that assessment, account should be taken, in particular, of the inherent characteristics of the mark, including the fact that it does or does not contain an element descriptive of the goods or services for which it has been registered; the market share held by the mark; how intensive, geographically widespread and long-standing use of the mark has been; the amount invested by the undertaking in promoting the mark; the proportion of the relevant section of the public which, because of the mark, identifies the goods or services as originating from a particular undertaking; and statements from chambers of commerce and industry or other trade and professional associations.[136]

Given that the court is reluctant to suggest any given percentage, and suggests determining the status of trade mark of repute case by case, the EU trade mark jurisprudence *de facto* relies on the evidence to assess whether or not the mark is of repute. This is an expected and inevitable consequence of well-known trade mark protection being a matter of fact, not law, and therefore the conceptualisation of the mark of repute is paramount. *General Motors* suggests looking at the assessment of reputation from two different perspectives, one of which is more dominant than the other: one is based on knowledge, the other on geographical area.

In *Nieto Nuno v Monlleo Franquet*,[137] being well known in one part of Spain, which accounts for 10 per cent of the Spanish population, was *not* considered to be well known in the Spanish territory.[138] On the other hand, in one of the other cases involving the Benelux countries, the mark in question was known only in the part of Benelux where only Dutch is spoken,[139] and it was sufficient to be considered as being known by the substantial part of the relevant public. Another case

---

133 Ibid.
134 *Lloyd Schuhfabrik Meyer & Co. GmbH v Klijsen Handel BV* (C-342/97) [2000] FSR 77.
135 Ibid., para 25.
136 Ibid., para 24.
137 *Nieto Nuno v Monlleo Franquet* (Case C-328/06) [2008] ETMR 12.
138 Ibid., para 18: 'However, the customary meaning of the words used in the expression "in a Member State" preclude the application of that expression to a situation where the fact of being well known is limited to a city and to its surrounding area which, together, do not constitute a substantial part of the Member State.'
139 *Bovemij Verzekeringen NV v Benelux-Merkenbureau* (C-108/05) [2007] ETMR 29.

involving the Benelux territory is 'SPA-FINDERS'[140] (note that Spa is a city in Belgium). This case caused surprise as the 'reputation' of the word mark 'Spa' is not approved,[141] and it was held that having a 'reputation' in the Benelux nations is not sufficient to be considered well known in this case.[142] It was established that only the Benelux SPA mark had a reputation, and detriment to the distinctive character of this mark could not be inferred from the link that the public would make between Spa and the applied-for mark 'SPA-FINDERS'. The existence of such a link was insufficient to demonstrate the risk of detriment to distinctive character, which was limited in any event owing to the fact that Spa was the name of a Belgian town.[143] Therefore, the assessment of acquired distinctiveness, despite the indicative criteria, is still determined on a case-by-case basis: nothing is conceptually defined.[144]

Clearly the geographic extent of 'knownness', whilst it has to be significant, does not have to follow territorial boundaries: 'knownness' in smaller geographically defined populations may suffice, as may groups defined by language or profession within or across EU Member States. The reference to average consumers was made by *Nasdaq*.[145] It was argued that that:

(1) the reputation was to be determined in relation to the perception of a specialised public, which was especially well informed and highly attentive, and the term 'nasdaq' identified, in the eyes of the European public, a pre-eminent provider of recognised financial market indices.[146]

4.3.5.1 Proving 'trade mark of repute'

The *Intel*-type[147] of stricter reasoning in relation to the proof of acquired distinctiveness and reputation can be seen in the earlier EU jurisprudence in relation to the proof of acquired distinctiveness and reputation.

---

140 Another example is *SIGLA SA v Office for Harmonisation in the Internal Market (Trade Marks and Designs) (OHIM)* (T-215/03) [2007] ETMR 79.
141 *Spa Monopole, compagnie fermière de Spa SA/NV v Office for Harmonisation in the Internal Market, Spa-Finders Travel Arrangements Ltd Intervening* (T-67/04) [2005] ETMR 109.
142 It is identified that this case can be of reference as it was clearly stated that 'the purpose of Art. 8(5) is *not* to prevent the registration of every mark that is identical or similar to a mark with a reputation. Instead, it is limited to preventing the registration of marks which are likely to be detrimental to the repute or distinctive character of the earlier mark or which are likely to take unfair advantage of them' (ibid. at 4). This case confirmed three points as follows: first, that the marks at issue are identical or similar; second, that the earlier mark cited in opposition has a reputation; and, third, that there is a risk that the use without due cause of the trade mark applied for would take unfair advantage of, or be detrimental to, the distinctive character or the repute of the earlier trade mark. Those conditions are cumulative and failure to satisfy one of them is sufficient to render that provision inapplicable.
143 *Spa Monopole* [2005] ETMR 109.
144 See the judgments of *El Corte Ingles SA v Office for Harmonisation in the Internal Market* (T-443/05) [2007] ETMR 81.
145 *Antarctica Srl v Office for Harmonisation in the Internal Market (Trade Marks and Designs)* (T-47/06) [2007] ETMR 77.
146 Ibid.
147 *Intel v CPM* [2009] ETMR 13.

For instance, it is held in *Flexi Air*[148] that 'the result would be that where the earlier mark has only a weak distinctive character a likelihood of confusion would exist only where there was a complete reproduction of that mark by the mark applied for'.[149] In *Sergio Rossi*,[150] the earlier marks were, in fact, not highly distinctive.[151] 'Therefore, it need only be examined whether the similarities between the marks are sufficient to outweigh the differences between the goods in question and to give rise to a likelihood of confusion on the part of target public.'[152] Finally, in *Picasso*,[153] it can be concluded that where a name such as Picasso is used in a completely different way to its original context, it will not automatically carry with it its distinctiveness; without use, it is doubtful whether the name conveys information regarding the source of products.[154] It can thus be summarised that there seems to be a difference in approach between current and acquired distinctiveness; more reputation is needed for a less inherently distinctive trade mark than for a trade mark that is more inherently distinctive.

In *Mango Sport System*,[155] the degree of reputation was proved by submitting several items of survey evidence, including revenue statistics, expenditure on advertising and promoting the trade mark in well-known fashion magazines, promotional statements made in well-known Spanish financial newspapers and other magazines that attested to the revenues achieved in the previous years, and a record and the map of a number of the existing outlet shops in Spain, to prove physical domination throughout the territory of Spain.[156] However, we can pose the question with regard to the admissibility and efficacy of evidence: to what extent can the court rely on the evidence which is submitted by the parties? The issue of legitimacy and reliability of evidence was discussed in length in the case of *Interflora*.[157] The claimant, Interflora, submitted the evidence of witnesses who were selected by two separate witness-gathering pilot surveys, where the defendant, M&S, did not intend to rely on the same sort of evidence. Admissibility

---

148 *L'Oréal SA v Office for Harmonisation in the Internal Market (Trade Marks and Designs)* (C-235/05 P) [2005] ECR II-949.
149 Ibid., para 61.
150 *Sergio Rossi v Office for Harmonisation in the Internal Market (Trade Marks and Designs)* (T-169/03) [2005] ECR II-68.
151 See Maniatis, *Trade Marks in Europe: A Practical Jurisprudence*, p. 99.
152 *Sergio Rossi* [2005] ECR II-68.
153 *Claude Ruiz-Picasso v Office for Harmonisation in the Internal Market (Trade Marks and Designs)* (C-361/04 P) [2006] ETMR 29.
154 See Maniatis, *Trade Marks in Europe: A Practical Jurisprudence* , p. 350.
155 *Mango Sport System S.R.L. Socio Unico Mangone Antonio Vincenzo v Diknah S.L.* (R 308/2003–1) [2005] ETMR 5.
156 Ibid., para 13: 'The applicant was wrong to argue that only a luxury mark can attract customers and be the subject of infringement under Art. 8(5). An earlier mark can be attractive to the consumer and yet enjoy a reputation for everyday goods (such as the fashion goods in this case) that are not luxury goods' (see at 15).
157 See *Interflora Inc v Marks and Spencer Plc* [2012] EWHC 1722 (Ch). After the preliminary rulings by the Court of Justice, the case was returned for trial before Arnold J. Permission was given to Interflora to undertake two of the pilot surveys, against which M&S appealed (see *Marks & Spencer Plc v Interflora* [2012] EWCA Civ 1501).

of the evidence was discussed and the UK Court of Appeal provided guidance on this matter.[158]

It seems that not relying on a given percentage does provide a great amount of flexibility and discretion to the court and trade mark examiners. This might, however, operate less consistently and less clearly.

Above all, the test for a registered 'trade mark of repute' is that it shall be known by a significant part of public; this is known as the knowledge-based requirement. Furthermore, significance may be defined geographically – that is, concerning a substantial part of a territory – but it could also be defined by linguistic considerations or by profession. All the relevant factors need to be considered, including the market share of the trade mark, the intensity, geographical extent and length of its use, and the size of the investment in promotion of the trade mark.

However, at a fundamental level, this adds very little to an understanding of the conceptualisation of 'trade mark of repute'. In other words, it appears that the courts have not yet approached this question from a conceptual perspective. Therefore, two sets of question to determine whether Article 4(4)(a) is applicable need to be established: one is to deal with the mark with distinctiveness and the other is to deal with the mark with repute. It is plain that the former focuses more on the attractive force of the mark, whereas the latter focuses more on the positive image of the mark. Although there are some conceptual similarities between the mark with distinctiveness and the mark with repute, these are in fact different and some of the differences can be found in the difference in the assessment criteria.

Overall, conceptualisation of a trade mark of repute can be observed as follows: the purpose of the law seems not to define what a 'trade mark of repute' is, but to determine the appropriate scope of protection for the same. Protection afforded to 'trade mark of repute' is approached primarily by assessing the situations where use of the sign applied for is capable of taking an unfair advantage of or being detrimental to the distinctiveness or the repute of the earlier mark (such use must be without due cause). It is argued that a conceptual definition of 'trade mark of repute' might provide more help in delineating the scope of 'trade mark of repute' protection.

Thus, as implied above, the process of determining how 'trade mark of repute' is defined requires a reliance on implicit, rather than overt, guidance as to what constitutes a 'trade mark of repute'. Further, the court has simplified the test of reputation, as compared with what was often needed in the past for accepting that marks enjoyed reputation.[159] It has already been examined, in relation to the 'mosaicing' guidance as to what constitutes a 'trade mark of repute', that the noted criteria (see above) relate to the commercial value of the mark.[160] If there

158 *Interflora Inc v Marks and Spencer Plc* [2012] EWCA Civ 1501.
159 2333–2000 Telefonica on line/t-online (EN).
160 Griffiths, 'The Impact of the Global Appreciation Approach on the Boundaries of Trade Mark Protection', p. 346.

was an overriding factor in the list, that might help in conceptually defining 'trade mark of repute'.

4.3.6 Summary

Yet again, the conceptualisation of 'trade mark of repute' provided by the primary materials seems not to have been achieved. Even applying the Definition Model, no explicit comprehensive conceptual definition of 'trade mark of repute' has been found in either the EU TMD or the cases.

There is some (implicit) guidance as to *form* (*type* and *context*) of 'trade mark of repute' in the EU TMD, but little guidance is provided by the cases. Where the cases do contribute to the jurisprudence is in developing fact-based criteria to assess 'trade mark of repute' status: thus, in this sense, the cases do provide some indication (if not an explicit definition) of *concept*. In order to assess whether a trade mark is a mark of repute, a certain degree of knowledge on behalf of the relevant public must be achieved, with the factual criteria outlined in *General Motors*[161] being indicative (but not conclusive) of this. Similarities between these criteria and those of the WIPO Recommendation may be noted, and thus many of the same criticisms apply to the EU approach (see Chapter 3, Section 3.2.4). From this, *concept* of 'trade mark of repute' includes notions of distinctiveness, although value, which can be incorrectly defined, also appears to be relevant.

Not only can the EU trade mark regime be criticised for failing to provide a full conceptualised definition of 'trade mark of repute' according to the Definition Model, but there are – as noted earlier – issues as to the clarity of the guidance provided for determining well-known trade mark status. It is submitted that these requirements should be specified more precisely. That is to say, why should there not be a fixed percentage of the public which must recognise the mark, and why should the national court be directed to take into consideration all the relevant factors of the case (in addition to the *General Motors* criteria)? The result of this lack of clarity is that 'trade mark of repute' is bound to be variously interpreted due to the unspecified parameters of the fact-based assessments. It is this uncertainty that also accounts for the approaches employed in the cases at the Court of Justice, the General Courts and the BoA.[162] Not only is there scope for variation in defining and recognising 'trade mark of repute' at the national level, but there is also similar scope within the EU regime system itself. For example, in the EU context, trade mark *concept* is mainly defined by the consumer-knowledge-defined approach, as opposed to the geographically defined approach.

---

161 *General Motors* [1998] ETMR 950.
162 See the recent examples of cases in terms of Article 5(2) of the EU Trade Mark Directive. *Nieto Nuno v Monlleo Franquet* (Case C-328/06) [2008] ETMR 12. *Crunch Fitness International Inc v Société des Produits Nestle SA*, (Case R-52/2005–4) [2008] ETMR 18; *L'Oreal SA v Bellure NV* (Case C-487/07) [2009] ETMR 55; M. Walmsley, 'Trade Mark Dilution – Court of Appeal Waters Down Trade Mark Owners' Rights', *European Intellectual Property Review*, 30, 2008, 109–11; *Intel* [2009] ETMR 13; *Riemann & Co v Linco Care Ltd* [2007] ECC 23; *Antarctica Srl v Office for Harmonisation in the Internal Market* (T-47/06/2007) [2007] ETMR 77.

Discretion and flexibility at both the national and regional levels on this issue hinder the development of a consistent and certain approach to both defining and identifying 'trade marks of repute'. In this author's view, law should always be consistent, concise and certain, and there is no reason why this should not be so in the case of the definition and identification of 'trade mark of repute'.

It is submitted that an additional layer of uncertainty is provided by language: the terms employed to describe 'trade mark of repute' in the different EU languages[163] are not fully equivalent to each other, which must contribute to uncertainty as to the true meaning of the term 'trade mark of repute'.[164] Also, more fundamentally, it is argued that there is a difference between 'well-known trade mark' in Article 6*bis* of the Paris Convention and 'trade mark of repute' in the EU TMD.[165] The nature of any such difference is not clear and no attempt has been made to provide any conceptual definition of 'reputation'.[166]

The loosely defined concept of 'well-known trade mark' at the international level[167] could pose advantages and disadvantages for the EU and Japanese trade mark laws. An advantage might be the scope for flexibility in the regional and national regulation of well-known trade marks, whilst a disadvantage might be confusion, inconsistency and uncertainty in the protection afforded to well-known trade marks. Indeed, a consequence of the international approach to well-known trade mark protection is that the EU has (to some extent) taken its own route here – for example, in introducing the term 'trade mark of repute' rather than using 'well-known trade mark'. However, there also appears to be implicit recognition of the benefits of a harmonised approach to this issue, inasmuch as the fact-based criteria to test whether a mark is a 'trade mark of repute' draw heavily on international norms. It is, therefore, not clear how, at the international level, an appropriate balance between flexibility and consistency/certainty can be struck. However, there is evidence of a lack of clarity as to the definition of, and means of determining, 'trade mark of repute' in the EU trade mark regime. Whether there is a causal connection between the lack of clarity on this issue earlier identified at the international level and at the EU level as to the definition of 'well-known trade mark'/'trade mark of repute' is not something that can be objectively evidenced in this book – although such a causal link can be positively suggested.

4.4 'Trade mark of repute' against detriment and unfair advantage

We will now move on to the third limb of the book: a critical examination of protection for a mark of repute (equivalent to well-known trade mark) against

---

163 *General Motors* [1998] ETMR 950, para 20.
164 *General Motors* [1999] ETMR 122 (The Opinion of Advocate General Francis Jacobs), paras 34–6.
165 *General Motors* [1998] ETMR 950, para 19.
166 For example, it has been clearly stated that 'the Directive itself makes no attempt at a definition'. See *General Motors* [1999] ETMR 122 (The Opinion of Advocate General Francis Jacobs), para 2.
167 See Chapter 3, Section 3.2.1, for the Paris Convention.

dilution – that is, detrimental or unauthorised use where such use would take unfair advantage of the mark of repute. In this part, the focus will be shifted to the examination of 'dilution'.

The rationale for this is linked with the second element of the principle of well-known trade mark protection: (i) well-known trade mark protection principle 1 – protection can be given irrespective of whether or not the mark is registered; and (ii) well-known trade mark protection principle 2[168] – a broader scope of protection is conferred, including the right to prevent third parties from register-ing/using the mark, which is identical or similar to the earlier well-known trade mark, in relation to the *dissimilar* goods or services where such a use causes dilution of the earlier well-known trade mark.[169]

In other words, the well-known trade mark owners ought to enjoy exercising the broader scope of the exclusive rights given where the dilution occurs. Therefore, completion of the examination of the efficacy of well-known trade mark protection seems impossible without placing the well-known trade mark in the dilution context.

A similar structure to that employed in Section 4.3 will be followed: first, the statutory definition of 'dilution' in the EU TMD (and the CTMR) will be explored, before moving on to the CTM Guidelines and relevant jurisprudence.

Having considered the conceptual definition of and conceptualisation of 'trade mark of repute', difficulties in clearly defining what constitutes a trade mark of repute have been identified. As a result, the following questions are posed and comprise the central discussion for third part of the book:

(i)   How far is the law able to provide protection against dilution, where there is no conceptualisation of a mark of repute?
(ii) How far is the law able to determine the scope of protection where there is so-called dilution without conceptually establishing what it is the law protects?

The main focus of this part of the book is to explore ways in which the trade mark of repute is protected, and the efficacy of the scope of protection given to the mark of repute. The author argues that the credibility of the scope of protection given to the mark of repute, without any conceptual definition, is doubtful.

4.4.1 Background

By way of background, the inconsistency and absence of uniformity of the language being applied in the laws of individual nations needs to be noted again (this was addressed in Chapter 1).

---

168   The rationale of well-known trade mark protection principle 2 lies in the recognition and appreciation of the well-known trade mark being an important commercial asset and an attractive force, which brings custom, and being a victim of wrongdoers who intend to misuse such a power. Ways in which such a misappropriation occurs is submitted to be dilution by law.
169   See Chapter 1, Section 1.3.

Unsurprisingly, the EU has not imported the US term and the approach taken by the US into the EU law; the theme of well-known trade mark protection against dilution therefore needs to be placed in the EU trade mark context. The EU trade mark regime offers protection to the trade mark of repute where there is detrimental use of the distinctiveness/reputation of the mark and/or an act of taking unfair advantage of the distinctiveness/reputation of the mark.

4.4.2 The European Trade Mark Directive

The EU TMD regulates the occurrence of dilution at two different points of time: the first at the point of registration and the second at the point of trade mark infringement. The former is regulated by Article 4(4)(a) of the EU TMD[170] (Article 8(5) of the CTMR), whilst the latter is regulated by Article 5(2) of the EU TMD (Article 9(1)(c) of the CMTR[171]). The central discussion here is at the registration level.

Articles 4(4)(a) and 5(2) recognise three different forms of actionable harm caused to the mark of repute at the point of the third party's registration: (i) detriment to the distinctive character of the earlier mark (known as dilution by blurring); (ii) detriment to the reputation of the earlier mark (known as dilution by tarnishment); (iii) unfair advantage of the distinctive character/reputation of the earlier mark (known as free-riding). Furthermore, an identity with or similarity of the earlier and the later marks is required. Needless to say, it has been a difficult task to conceptualise what the trade mark of repute is, whilst conceptualisation of 'dilution' might be not as challenging as that of the mark of repute. In exploring further, additional assistance will be sought from the CTMR Guidelines below.

4.4.3 The CTM Guidelines

Whilst establishing a conceptual definition of 'taking unfair advantage' or 'detrimental to' seems to be beyond the scope of the CTM Opposition

---

170 The wording of Article 8(5) of the CTMR and of Article 4(3) of the EU Directive mirror each other. Article 4(3) of the EU Directive is as follows: 'A trade mark shall furthermore not be registered or, if registered, shall be liable to be declared invalid if it is identical with, or similar to, an earlier Community trade mark within the meaning of paragraph 2 and is to be, or has been, registered for goods or services which are not similar to those for which the earlier Community trade mark is registered, where the earlier Community trade mark has a reputation in the Community and where the use of the later trade mark without due cause would take unfair advantage of, or be detrimental to, the distinctive character or the repute of the earlier Community trade mark.'

171 'Article 9 Rights conferred by a Community trade mark: 1. A Community trade mark shall confer on the proprietor exclusive rights therein. The proprietor shall be entitled to prevent all third parties not having his consent from using in the course of trade: (c) any sign which is identical with, or similar to, the Community trade mark in relation to goods or services which are not similar to those for which the Community trade mark is registered, where the latter has a reputation in the Community and where use of that sign without due *cause takes unfair advantage of, or is detrimental to, the distinctive character or the repute of the Community trade mark.*' [Emphasis added]

Guidelines,[172] the Guidelines appear helpful in delineating an overall picture of 'detrimental use' and the act of 'taking unfair advantage of'. The Guidelines provide rather useful contextual explanations of the above, and the umbrella term to describe the recognisable harm under Articles 8(5) and 9(1)(c) of the CTMR corresponding to 4(4)(a) and 5(2) of the EU TMD – encroachment of the reputation – was introduced.

As previously stated, the newly updated CTM Guidelines came into force in August 2014.[173] In comparison with the old Guidelines,[174] the new Guidelines appear to simplify the explanation of Article 8(5) (Article 4(4)(a)) and provide more instruction with the practical illustration of case law – in particular, instruction of the harms under Article 8(5) of the CTMR (Article 4(4)(a) of the EU TMD). Given that the old Guidelines are, in the view of the author, very instructive, occasional reference to the old Guidelines will be made.

Instead of conceptualising 'detriment' or 'unfair advantage', the old Guidelines provided a number of occasions where 'detriment' and 'unfair advantage' can be recognised and possible harm can be caused to the proprietors of the earlier trade mark of repute. The new Guidelines refer to an overarching term to describe 'detriment' and 'taking unfair advantage' – encroachment (see Figure 4.4 below).

Three different types of actionable harms – encroachment – are recognised: (i) detriment to the distinctive character of the earlier mark (known as dilution

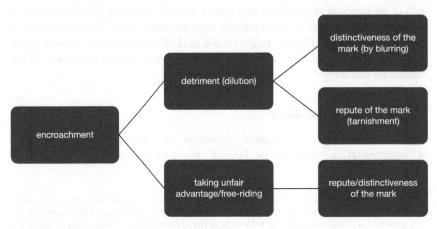

Figure 4.4 Mapping 'detriment' and taking unfair advantage

172 See the old CTM Guidelines, Part 5, Article 8(5) CTMR.
173 The Guidelines state that: 'As case-law is evolving constantly, the Guidelines will also evolve. They will be adapted to reflect developments in Office practice on a yearly basis by means of an ongoing revision exercise.' See the CTM Guidelines, Editor's Note and Introduction, p. 3. The Guidelines are available online at oami.europa.eu/tunnel-web/secure/webdav/guest/document_library/contentPdfs/law_and_practice/trade_marks_practice_manual/wp_2_2014/00_editors_note_and_general_introduction_2014_en.pdf (accessed 26 October 2014).
174 The old Guidelines are to be found online at oami.europa.eu/ohimportal/en/guidelines-community-trade-mark (accessed 26 October 2014).

by blurring); (ii) detriment to the reputation of the earlier mark (known as dilution by tarnishment); (iii) unfair advantage of the distinctive character/ reputation of the earlier mark (known as free-riding).[175] The old Guidelines, on the other hand, explained four types of harm: (a) cause unfair detriment to the distinctiveness, (b) cause unfair detriment to the repute, (c) take unfair advantage of the distinctiveness of the earlier mark or (d) take unfair advantage of the repute of the earlier mark.[176]

Further explanation can be found in the old Guidelines: the notion of unfair detriment extends to all cases where the use of the application is likely to have an *adverse effect on the earlier mark* in the sense that it would *diminish its attractiveness* (detriment to distinctiveness) or would devalue the image it has acquired among the public (detriment to repute), whereas the notion of unfair advantage covers cases where use of the opposed mark is likely to result in a misappropriation of its attractive powers (unfair advantage of distinctiveness) or an exploitation of its image and prestige (unfair advantage of repute).[177]

Therefore, it seems that the Guidelines do not *conceptualise* but *contextualise* Article 8(5), and therefore the concept of 'encroachment'. We will examine how sufficient such a contextualisation is and how helpful it is in conceptualising the purposes of Article 4(4)(a) of the EU TMD in the context of Article 8(5) of the CTMR.

The first step is to look at the phrase 'cause unfair detriment to the distinctive-ness'. The Guidelines suggest that 'detriment to distinctiveness' equates with 'dilution by blurring' and occurs when the trade mark is no longer capable of evoking in the mind of the public an immediate association with the products it covers;[178] in other words, 'if the public ceases to associate the earlier mark with a given range of goods or services originating from a single source and starts associating it with different goods, having distinct origins, then "detriment to distinctiveness occurs"'.[179]

Moreover, the consequence of dilution by blurring 'is likely to diminish its capacity to stimulate the desire of the public to buy the products for which it is registered'; this also 'leads to an erosion of distinctive character caused by the proliferation of "parasitic" marks which, although not debasing the original trade mark, are so numerous that they may deprive the trade mark of its distinctive character and hence of its attractiveness'.[180]

The second step is to look at 'cause unfair detriment to the repute'. The Guidelines explain this as 'dilution by tarnishing' – that is to say, *to devalue the image or the prestige* that a mark with reputation has acquired among the public.[181] As a consequence, the reputation of the earlier trade mark may be tainted or debased.[182]

175 See the new CTM Guidelines Part C, Article 8(5) CTMR at 49.
176 See the old CTM Guidelines, Part 5, Article 8(5) CTMR at 37
177 Ibid., p. 35.
178 Ibid. and the New CTM Guidelines Part C, Article 8(5) CTMR at 57.
179 See the Old CTM Guidelines, Part 5, Article 8(5) CTMR at 35.
180 Ibid.
181 See the New CTM Guidelines Part C, Article 8(5) CTMR at 51.
182 See the Old CTM Guidelines, Part 5, Article 8(5) CTMR at 38.

Here we could find some indication as to conceptualisation of trade mark of repute. The Guidelines could be read to include the image or the prestige of the mark in the definition of repute. If this is the case, conceptualisation of 'trade mark or repute' would take a massive step forward. If not, it would pose another interesting question: does the definition of repute, in fact, equate with the reputation? Either way, conceptualisation of trade mark of repute will make significant progress.

The third and fourth steps look at the terms 'taking unfair advantage of the distinctiveness' and 'taking unfair advantage of repute'. The new Guidelines do not make any distinction between 'taking unfair advantage of the distinctiveness of the mark' and 'taking unfair advantage of repute', whereas the old Guidelines did.[183] 'Taking unfair advantage' is described as misappropriation of the *attractive powers and advertising value* of the earlier mark, as an act of 'commercial parasitism' and as 'free-riding on the investment of the opponent in promoting and building up a goodwill for his mark'.[184] Under the old Guidelines, 'taking unfair advantage of repute' was explained, but was less clear.[185] Taking unfair advantage gives rise to the situation where the quality image of the mark, or good or special reputation, image of excellence, reliability or quality, or some other positive message is exploited. Therefore, it gives a flavour of free-riding. The difference between 'taking unfair advantage of distinctiveness' and 'taking unfair advantage of repute' is that the former focuses more on the fact of the mark being an attractive force, whilst the latter does so more on the fact of the mark representing quality image and/or good or special reputation. This is where the law differentiates the mark that carries the so-called 'luxurious' status from the mark that is famous but does not hold such a status.

The Guidelines make an interesting and intriguing grouping of the trade mark of repute; we will now be able to move the conceptualisation of trade mark of repute forward. The summary of such a categorisation is illustrated by Figures 4.5 and 4.6 below.

Distinctive characters of trade mark of repute include either (i) distinctiveness and distinctive quality of the mark or (ii) the image and prestige of the mark.

The mark with reputation includes either (i) the attractive power and advertising value of the mark or (ii) the good quality, special relationship, quality of excellence, reliability, and positive message of the mark.

Therefore, it can be inferred that the one of the components that distinguishes mainly the mark of distinctiveness from the mark of repute is the presence of a degree of luxury, such as luxurious image or good quality – so-called quality of excellence.

In addition, the issue of which part of the pie becomes relevant is in accordance with the kind of act in question – for example, if the third party's use is either the

---

183 See the Old CTM Guidelines, Part 5, Article 8(5) CTMR at 40 and 41.
184 See the Old CTM Guidelines, Part 5, Article 8(5) CTMR at 40, and the New CTM Guidelines Part C, Article 8(5) CTMR at 48.
185 See the Old CTM Guidelines, Part 5, Article 8(5) CTMR at 41.

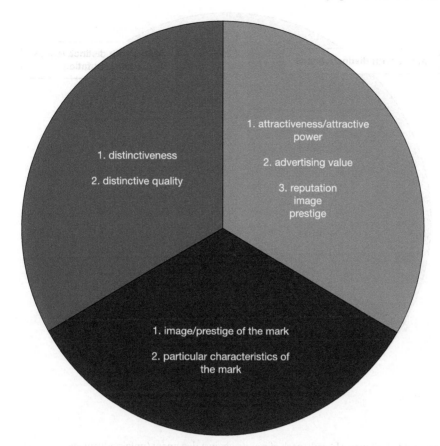

1. attractiveness/attractive
power

2. advertising value

3. reputation
image
prestige

1. distinctiveness

2. distinctive quality

1. image/prestige of the mark

2. particular characteristics of
the mark

Figure 4.5 Trade mark of repute – mapping

act of detriment or the act of taking unfair advantage. One final point is that there should not be any discrimination against the mark of distinctiveness and the mark of repute: Article 8(5) does not seem to make any differentiation in legal treatment conferred on the two different groups of mark.

This exploration of the Guidelines greatly encourages the conceptualisation of the mark of repute to move forward, and the following was achieved with supplementary reading of the Old and New CTM Guidelines.

There are three types of actionable harm (i.e. encroachment) recognised in the EU trade mark law. Detrimental use occurs where the distinctiveness or repute of the mark is either blurred (not being capable of evoking an immediate association in the mind of the public) or tarnished (the image or prestige of the earlier mark is devalued). Taking unfair advantage occurs where either the attractive powers and advertising value of the earlier mark are misappropriated and are being free-ridden or the quality image of the marks or image of excellence are exploited.

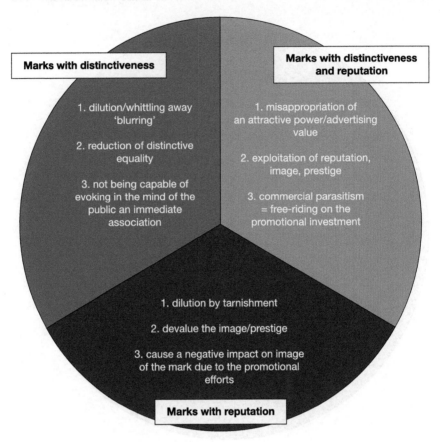

Figure 4.6 Full map of 'trademark of repute against detriment/unfair advantage'

It can be observed that the Guidelines show a thorough contextualisation of 'detriment' and 'unfair advantage', and situations where such prohibited acts can be evidenced. As a result of contextualisation, the conceptualisation as a whole is moved forward. It is very interesting that Articles 4(4)(a) and 8(5) seems to recognise four types of harm, and those types receive the same treatment, yet those four different types of harm cause a different level of disadvantage to the relevant proprietors. It could be argued yet again that providing the extra layer of protection to the mark of repute would work well only if the conceptualisation of the mark of repute, and therefore comprehension of what the mark of repute constitutes, was present. It is also very clear that Articles 4(4)(a) and 8(5) recognise two different types of well-known trade mark – the mark of distinctiveness and the mark of repute, and those are not conceptually defined.

The Guidelines make a useful distinction between 'distinctiveness' and 'repute': the former includes the attractive power or advertising value; the latter refers more to the quality image or image of excellence. Therefore, it can be said that a difference between those two marks is that the latter holds a special image – that is to say, image of excellence. In other words, they can be differentiated by asking what type of image the mark holds. This poses the question: does Article 4(4)(a) serve the main purpose that Article 10*bis* of the Paris Convention intended to achieve – that is, to provide protection to the mark of repute?

It seems that the EU trade mark regime has muddied the water between two different marks by putting those into the same box and attempting to deal with them as if they are the same.

So far, the EU TMD and the CTMR have been examined in considering the test for, and scope of, dilution. Three types of actionable harm caused to the mark of repute have been identified, yet it cannot be said that these comprise sufficient guidance as to delineate the conceptual definition of dilution. Similarly, although guidance as to the scope of protection against dilution is provided, there has not yet been the opportunity to consider whether that scope is appropriate. Lastly, no clear distinction has yet been drawn between how marks of distinctiveness and how marks of repute benefit from the protection against dilution. Therefore, further examination of the cases addressed in the CTM Guidelines will be undertaken in order to obtain further guidance as how to delineate 'dilution'.

4.4.4 Jurisprudence

Since establishing a conceptual definition of the mark of repute in the context of detriment and unfair advantage does not appear to be the intention of the EU TMD, it is necessary to examine the relevant jurisprudence[186] for further guidance as to the scope of dilution and correlation with the mark of repute, to then allow investigation as to what is the extent of protection provided for marks of repute against dilution. It is important to note that Article 4(4)(a) does *not* protect the 'reputation' (of a mark) *per se*; it prohibits four occasions where the earlier mark of 'repute' is being misused; these are: (i) detriment to distinctiveness; (ii) detriment to repute; (iii) taking unfair advantage of distinctiveness; and (iv) taking unfair advantage of repute. Although it is clear that 'distinctiveness' and 'repute' are different, without a complete conceptualisation of what exactly the mark of repute is, it seems impossible to come to any conclusion.

Hereinafter, we will observe a carefully selected number of influential judicial interpretations of 'detriment' and 'taking unfair advantage of', with a view to shaping as sufficiently as possible the scope of protection afforded to the trade mark of repute.

This section is divided into two parts: the first part will look into pre-*Bellure* cases (mainly *Intel*[187]) and the second part will consider post-*Bellure* cases,[188] as the

---

186 See, for example, N. Prentoulis, 'The Omega Ruling: Trade Mark Co-Existence Agreements in the Tension Between "Public" and "Private" Trade Mark Law', *European Intellectual Property Review*, 30, 2008, 202–5.

187 *Intel* [2009] ETMR 13.

188 The majority are related to AdWords. The opening sentence of Mr Justice Arnold's judgment in *Interflora, Inc. Interflora British Unit v Marks and Spencer PLC Flowers Direct Online Limited* [2009] EWHC

author argues that *Bellure* could possibly shape the future protection of trade mark of repute against dilution.

4.4.4.1 *Pre*-Bellure

This section will pay an attention only to cases held before the delivery of *Bellure* – that is, *Dior*,[189] *Hollywood*,[190] *Intel*[191] and *Bellure*[192] respectively – in order to discover the ways in which the pre-*Bellure* jurisprudence interpreted the link between the mark of repute and the determination of its scope against dilution at the registration level.

First, we will revisit the decision of *Hollywood*,[193] although the focus here will be on interpreting the scope of dilution by tarnishment (detrimental to repute of the mark). Here the claimant argued that the later use of the identical mark for dissimilar goods would be detrimental to the image and repute of the earlier trade mark:[194] 'a sign which is detrimental to the image of the earlier mark'.

In order to apply 'detrimental to the repute of the mark', the owner of the earlier mark of repute must prove that the later use would cause *inappropriate or at least negative mental association*, or *conflict with the image that the mark of repute obtains*.[195] In the decision of *Hollywood*, the court recognised the negative image and connotation of tobacco, and the possible harm caused by this association.[196]

The approach undertaken by *Hollywood*, though this was a pre-*Intel* decision, identified, to a certain extent, a possible occasion where detriment is recognised, and put some new input into Figure 4.6: that the detriment to the repute/image of the mark (known as blurring by tarnishment) occurs due to the negative or inappropriate association between two marks being made in the mind of the public and that causes it to be 'sullied or debated by its association with something inappropriate'.[197]

1095 (Ch) was; 'This is another case about Google AdWords and registered trade marks. It is one of a considerable number of cases around Europe in which trade mark owners are complaining that the sale of keywords by Google to third parties infringes their rights. Such cases have been brought against both Google itself and against advertisers' (para 1).

189 *Dior* [1998] ETMR 26.

190 *Hollywood* [2002] ETMR 64.

191 *Intel* [2009] ETMR 13.

192 *Bellure* [2009] ETMR 55.

193 *Hollywood SAS v Souza Cruz SA* (Case R 283/1999–3) [2002] ETMR 64. The facts of *Hollywood* are as follows: the applicant wished to register the word mark 'Hollywood' for cigarettes, tobacco products, lighters and matches. The opponent, who was a proprietor of the word mark 'Hollywood' in France for chewing gum, argued, inter alia, that the applicant's registration of the mark amounted to taking unfair advantage of, of being detrimental to, the reputation which the earlier mark enjoyed in France.

194 *Hollywood v Souza Cruz* [2002] ETMR 64, para 10.

195 Ibid., para 87.

196 It was held: 'It must, therefore, be shown that the trade mark is sullied or debased by its association with something inappropriate. This could happen when the trade mark is used, on the one hand, in an unpleasant, obscene or degrading context or, on the other hand, in a context which is not inherently unpleasant but which proves to be incompatible with the trade mark's image and what is known in English as dilution by tarnishment' (*Hollywood v Souza Cruz* [2002] ETMR 64, para 85).

197 Ibid., para 85.

Furthermore, the relationship between distinctiveness (previously identified as being the *concept* of a well-known trade mark and, by inference, also a trade mark of repute) and detriment can be observed, as evidenced by the statement that 'the proprietor of the earlier trade mark must show that use of the applicant's trade mark would prompt inappropriate or at least negative mental associations with the opponent's trade mark, or associations conflicting with its image, which would be detrimental to it'.[198] In other words, there does appear to be a clear recognition in the EU jurisprudence that part of the conceptual *definition* of a trade mark of repute (*concept*) has import for the scope of protection of trade marks (including marks of repute) against dilution. The key to the conceptualisation of the mark of repute, which can be gathered from *Hollywood*, is 'inappropriate, negative mental association, conflicting image against the intention of the proprietor of the trade mark of repute'.

The court found that Article 8(5) shall become applicable when the relevant public makes inappropriate and negative association between the earlier mark, which contains a special symbolic or informative message, and later marks due to the similarity of those marks. What does appear to be clear is that well-known trade mark *concept* (distinctiveness) does determine the scope of protection of such marks – in the EU trade marks of repute – against detriment/unfair advantage.

The next cases to be considered are *Intel*[199] and *Bellure*.[200]

Intel[201] is of importance in interpreting the scope of dilution by blurring (detrimental to the distinctive character of the mark), as this has the direct interference of the 'detriment to the distinctive character'[202] (see Figure 4.5). It is also hoped that analysis of the *Intel* judgment will help to achieve completion of the pie chart in Figure 4.5. *Intel* is known to be the first case in which the Court of Justice instructed detriment to the distinctive character. Some might argue that the significance of an analysis of pre-*Intel* cases might be diminished, although it is important to look at such cases to trace the footsteps of the EU jurisprudence.

The earlier mark in question was 'Intel', which was alleged to have a huge reputation for computers and computer-related products. The contestant had a mark 'Intelmark' as a registered trade mark for marketing and telemarketing. The claimant, Intel, sought a declaration of invalidity of the contestant's mark, claiming that the contestant's use of the mark amounted to being *detrimental to the distinctiveness* of the earlier 'Intel' mark. The main argument submitted by the claimant was that, for the purpose of finding for detriment to distinctive character, a link that the average consumer might make between the two marks could constitute any kind of mental association, including a mere bringing to their

198 Ibid., para 87.
199 *Intel* [2009] ETMR 13.
200 *Bellure* [2009] ETMR 55.
201 *Intel* [2009] ETMR 13.
202 I. Simon, 'Dilution by Blurring – A conceptual Roadmap', *Intellectual Property Quarterly*, 1, 2010, 44–87.

mind. The Court of Appeal of England and Wales[203] asked the Court of Justice for a preliminary ruling[204] in determining what is required to prove a 'link' and the existence of unfair advantage or detriment for the purposes of Article 4(4)(a) of the EU TRD. The Court of Justice gave a preliminary ruling on the questions referred by the UK Court of Appeal.

The Court of Justice delivered the preliminary rulings on the following points. In applying for Article 4(4)(a) of the EU TMD, the proprietor of the earlier trade mark must show a link between the earlier mark and later mark (mental association between the two marks). In assessing whether there is such a link, this must be assessed globally[205] by taking into account criteria[206] such as degree of the similarity of the two marks, the nature of the goods or services, the relevant sector in the public, the degree of reputation of the earlier mark, the degree of distinctiveness of the mark and the likelihood of confusion. In assessing whether the unfair advantage or detriment is present, the proprietor of the mark of repute must prove that serious harm was caused to the proprietor by demonstrating the change in the economic behaviour of the average consumer of the relevant goods or service or serious likelihood that such a change would occur in the future.[207]

On first reading the judgment, there seems little guidance to enhance the pie chart in Figure 4.6 and outline the 'mark of repute' in the context of dilution and free-riding, whilst there is some guidance in the opinion of General Advocate Sharpston, who reiterated the concept of dilution by blurring and by tarnishment,[208] and reaffirmed the rationale of such protection.

She then introduced the new element of Article 4(4)(a) – free-riding. Furthermore, the General Advocate referred to the term 'best known mark';[209] such a mark is capable of presenting a strong marketing message, such as a powerful image of quality, exclusivity, youth, fun, luxury, adventure, glamour or other reputedly desirable lifestyle attribute.[210] Therefore, it could be argued that the protectable subject matter against free-riding is the trade mark working as a communicating tool, carrying a broader marketing message[211] (than just a mere indication of origin), whereas that against dilution by blurring or tarnishment focuses more on the trade mark working as an indication of origin.

In summary, the Court of Justice provided the instructive interpretation of 'detrimental to the distinctive character' and made a useful note for unfair advantage.

First, the concept of 'unfair advantage' focuses on benefit to the later mark rather than harm to the earlier mark. What must be established is some sort

203 *Intel* (Court of Appeal) [2007] ETMR 59.
204 *Intel* (C-252/07) [2009] ETMR 13.
205 Ibid. at 41.
206 Ibid. at 42.
207 Ibid. at 77.
208 Ibid. at AG9.
209 Ibid. at AG8.
210 Ibid. at AG8.
211 Ibid. at AG13.

of boost given to the later mark by its link with the earlier mark. If, despite its reputation, the connotations of the earlier mark have a dampening or even merely neutral effect on the performance of the later mark, unfair advantage seems less likely.[212]

Second, as a prerequisite for free-riding, the earlier mark should have a reputation and the later mark should bring the earlier mark to mind for the average consumer. There seems to be no necessity for the goods or services covered by the two marks to meet any particular standard of similarity or dissimilarity. Nor can it be concluded simply from the fact that the earlier mark is unique that the later mark takes unfair advantage of it.[213]

Third, that said, it seems clear that as the reputation and distinctiveness of the earlier mark, and the similarity between the goods or services covered by the two marks, increase, so will the likelihood that the later mark will derive advantage from any link established between the two in the mind of the public.[214] The fact that, for the average consumer, who is reasonably well informed, observant and circumspect, the later mark called to mind the earlier mark with a reputation was tantamount to the existence of such a link between the conflicting marks.

Fourth, more is needed. If the later mark is to derive unfair advantage, the association of the earlier mark must be such as to enhance the performance of the later mark in the use that is made of it. A relevant factor to consider, therefore, will be the relationship between the prestigious connotations of the earlier mark and the context in which the later mark is used. Any unfair advantage may well be greater if the earlier mark is unique, but there is nothing in the legislation to suggest that protection against free-riding can vary according to the extent of the unfair advantage derived.[215]

Fifth, if the later mark has already been registered and used (as in the main proceedings), or if it is a sign whose use is sought to be prevented under Article 5(2), it may well be possible to provide consumer survey evidence indicating whether there has been any boosting or enhancing effect on the later mark as a result of the existence of the earlier mark. If, under Article 4(4)(a), it is a question of preventing the registration of a mark that has not yet been used, such evidence may be less easy to obtain, and inferences may have to be drawn from all the circumstances of the case as to the likely effect.[216]

Finally, Article 4(4)(a) of the EU Trade Mark Directive (thus Article 8(c) of the CTMR) was to be interpreted as meaning that: (i) the use of the later mark could be detrimental to the distinctive character of the earlier mark with a reputation, even if that mark was not unique; (ii) a first use of the later mark could suffice to be determined to be detrimental to the distinctive character of the earlier mark; and (iii) proof that the use of the later mark was or would be detrimental to the

212 Ibid., para 62.
213 Ibid., para 64.
214 Ibid., para 65.
215 Ibid., para 66.
216 Ibid., para 67.

distinctive character of the earlier mark required evidence of a change in the economic behaviour of the average consumer of the goods or services for which the earlier mark was registered consequent on the use of the later mark, or a serious likelihood that such a change would occur in the future.

Above all, *Intel*[217] appears to establish authority for the proposition that protection of trade marks of repute against *detriment* should be drawn narrowly.[218] What is interesting about *Intel*-type reasoning is the insistence that proprietors of marks of repute must provide evidence of serious harm (the change in the economic behaviour of the average consumer in the relevant public[219]) in the context of dilution. Applying *Intel*-type reasoning, the proprietor needs to prove there was a link and a change in the economic behaviour of the average consumer of the earlier goods or services as a consequence of the use of the later mark, or some likelihood that such a change would occur in the future.[220] Thus, it may be inferred that *Intel* provides additional support for the proposition that the proprietors of marks of repute must provide *evidence* of dilution and free-riding of marks of repute, where evidence of damage is required. Further, *Intel* could be seen as an indication that the Court of Justice may be moving to a stricter position under Article 5(2) on protection of marks of repute *per se* in the context of dilution.

Against the prediction above, a contrasting proposal[221] seems to have put forward by *Bellure*,[222] which offered a generous approach under Article 5(2) on

217 Primarily concerning Article 4(4)(a) of the Directive, a brief summary of the facts of the case is as follows. Intel had a large number of trade marks including the word mark 'Intel'. Its 'Intel Inside' advertising campaign had made it a household name. The respondent was CPM United Kingdom Ltd (hereinafter CPM), a specialist in field marketing and telemarketing. It had a registered trade mark consisting of the word 'Intelmark', short for Integrated Telephone Marketing. The decision turned on whether the appellant's earlier mark ('Intel') had a large reputation, whether the earlier mark was unique, and whether the earlier mark would be brought to the mind of the average consumer when he or she encountered the later mark ('Intelmark').

218 For example, as with proving 'detriment to the distinctive character', evidence is required to show the following: a change in the economic behaviour of the average consumer of the earlier goods or services as a consequence of the use of the later mark, or some likelihood that such a change will occur in the future.

219 *Intel* (C-252/07) [2009] ETMR 13 at 77.

220 Ibid.

221 Primarily concerning Article 5(2) of the Directive, a brief summary of the facts of the case is as follows. L'Oréal SA, Lancôme parfums et beauté and Laboratoire Garnier are members of the L'Oréal group, which produces and markets luxury fragrances. They are proprietors of the well-known trade marks 'Trésor', 'Miracle', 'Anaïs-Anaïs' and 'Noa'. In the United Kingdom, Malaika and Starion market imitations of those fragrances, which are produced by Bellure. The bottles and packaging used to market those imitations are generally similar in appearance to those used by L'Oréal, which are protected by word and figurative trade marks. Malaika and Starion also use comparison lists, which are provided to retailers and which indicate the word mark of the luxury fragrance of which the perfume being marketed is an imitation. L'Oréal brought an action against Bellure, Malaika and Starion, alleging infringement of their trade mark rights.

222 *Bellure* [2009] ETMR 55. There is a significant body of secondary literature in relation to this decision: A. Blythe, 'Attempting to Define Unfair Advantage: An Evaluation of the Current Law in Light of the Recent European Decisions', *European Intellectual Property Review*, 11, 2012, 754–61; H. Onishi 'Revisiting the Japanese Unfair Competition Law: Post-Bellure', *European Intellectual Property Review*, 33, 2011, 363–74; and A. Horton, 'The Implications of L'Oréal v Bellure – A Retrospective and a Looking Forward: The Essential Functions of a Trade Mark and When is an Advantage Unfair?', *European Intellectual Property Review*, 33, 2011, 550–8.

protection of marks of repute against free-riding.[223] *Bellure* considered not only the further exploration of the judicial interpretation of 'detriment' and 'unfair advantage', but also the role of image of the mark of repute in protecting marks of repute in the context of Article 5(2) of the EU TMD. In consequence, different treatment might be applied, depending on which type of actionable harm the proprietor claims,[224] with the effect of causing unnecessary inconsistency within Article 5(2).

Now we will look at *Bellure*. The claimant, L'Oréal, was a well-known manufacturer of expensive and luxurious perfumes, and owned a number of registered trade marks for the relevant perfume products in the UK. These registered trade marks covered both the names and packaging of the products. The defendant sold and marketed 'smell-alike' perfume products in the UK, and advertised their products coupled with photographic images of the claimant's products. The claimant sued the defendant for trade mark infringement, alleging that the defendant's use of the claimant's mark would be detrimental to the distinctive character of the earlier trade mark of repute, and took unfair advantage. Jacob LJ at the Court of Appeal of England and Wales[225] referred a number of questions to the Court of Justice for a preliminary ruling:[226] (i) Were the circumstances of this case sufficient for the necessary link to come into play? (ii) If not, what factors would allow a national court to find such a link? (iii) What is required to find detriment to the distinctive character of the mark of repute? (iv) Would there be unfair advantage under Article 5(2) without (a) confusion and (b) detriment to the earlier mark?

The answer to the first question was that in order to apply for the injury caused by taking unfair advantage (free-riding) under Article 5(2), the proprietor of the mark of repute does not need to prove either a likelihood of confusion or detriment; it is sufficient to demonstrate there is a link between two marks in the mind of the public. *Bellure* reaffirmed the global assessment and indicative criteria suggested by *Intel* in assessing the existence of the actionable link between two marks. A list of the indicative criteria includes the strength of the mark's reputation and the degree of distinctive character of the mark, the degree of similarity between the marks at issue, and the nature and degree of proximity of the goods or services concerned.[227] The strong nexus between the strength of the distinctiveness of the mark and ease of proving the presence of detriment[228] is

---

223 See Section 4.4.2.
224 *L'Oréal* has been applied and followed in subsequent cases: *Coty Germany GmbH v eBay International AG* [2012] ETMR 29 (Berlin); *Beko Plc v Socks World International Ltd* [2011] RPC 11; *Portakabin Ltd v Primakabin BV* (C-558/08) [2010] ETMR 52; *Google France Sarl v Louis Vuitton Malletier SA* (C-236/08) [2010] ETMR 30; *Adam Opel GmbH v Autec* (I ZR 88/08) [2010] ETMR 50 (GER); and followed by *Kingspan Group Plc v Rockwool Ltd* [2011] EWHC 250 (Ch).
225 *L'Oréal SA v Bellure NV* Court of Appeal (Civil Division) [2008] ETMR 1. After the preliminary ruling delivered by the ECJ, the case was referred back to the UK court [2010] ETMR 47. It was held for the claimant.
226 *Bellure* [2009] ETMR 55.
227 Ibid., para 44.
228 Ibid., para 44.

positively recognised. It is also clear from the case law that the more immediately and strongly the mark is brought to mind by the sign, the greater the likelihood that the current or future use of the sign is taking, or will take, unfair advantage of the distinctive character or the repute of the mark, or is, or will be, detrimental to it.[229]

The answer to the second question is that in order to apply for one of the injuries under Article 5(2), the essential function of the trade mark – that is, the indication of the origin – does not need to be harmed; it is sufficient to show that one of the functions was harmed. In particular, there will be unfair advantage where 'by reason of a transfer of the image of the mark or of the characteristics which it projects to the goods identified by the identical or similar sign, there is clear exploitation on the coat-tails of the mark with a reputation'.[230]

Bellure reaffirms the interpretation of dilution and hence helps to improve the completion of the pie chart in Figure 4.6 as follows:

(i) The interpretation of detriment to the distinctive character of the mark, referred to as 'dilution', 'whittling away' or 'blurring'. Such detriment is caused when the mark's ability to identify the goods or services for which it is registered is weakened, since use of an identical or similar sign by a third party leads to dispersion of the identity and hold upon the public mind of the earlier mark. That is particularly the case when the mark, which at one time aroused immediate association with the goods or services for which it is registered, is no longer capable of doing so.[231]

(ii) The interpretation of detriment to the repute of the mark, also referred to as 'tarnishment' or 'degradation'. Such detriment is caused when the goods or services for which the identical or similar sign is used by the third party may be perceived by the public in such a way that the trade mark's power of attraction is reduced. The likelihood of such detriment may arise in particular from the fact that the goods or services offered by the third party possess a characteristic or a quality that is liable to have a negative impact on the image of the mark.[232]

(iii) The interpretation of 'taking unfair advantage of the distinctive character or the repute of the trade mark', also referred to as 'parasitism" or 'free-riding'. This concept relates not to the detriment caused to the mark but to the advantage taken by the third party as a result of the use of the identical or similar sign. It covers, in particular, cases where, by reason of a transfer of the image of the mark or of the characteristics which it projects to the goods identified by the identical or similar sign, there is clear exploitation on the coat-tails of the mark with a reputation.[233]

229 Ibid.
230 Ibid., para 50.
231 Ibid., para 39.
232 Ibid., para 40.
233 Ibid., para 41.

The significance of *Bellure* in the context of conceptualisation of the mark of repute in the context of dilution is three-fold. First, and specifically, it appears to clarify that 'detriment' and 'unfair advantage' can be a flexible vehicle in applying Article 5(2) for protecting the marks of repute. Second, and more generally, given that *Bellure* concerned different provisions (Article 5(2) of the EU TMD and Article 3(a) of the 84/450) to *Intel* (Article 4(4)(a) of the EU TMD) and could be distinguished on this basis, it does seem to take a more generous position on protection of marks of repute *per se*, and be representative of a new and stronger position on marks of repute, which may affect future legal developments in this area (see Chapter 7). Third (and included only for reference as it is not as germane to this book), *Bellure* makes it clear that, in the context of dilution (Article 5(2)), unfair advantage does not require there to be proved a likelihood of detriment to the earlier mark as well as unfair advantage or a confusion (i.e. the proprietor of the trade mark of repute, *de facto*, can, in my opinion, cherry-pick which type of injuries is the least troublesome to prove): this has some significance for this book as this is a more generous (and more accurate) interpretation of Article 5(2) of the Directive and, again, is indicative of the more generous position on marks of repute postulated in the points above.

Overall, the approach taken by the Court of Justice on Article 5(2) of the EU TMD must be interpreted as meaning that the taking of unfair advantage of the distinctive character or the repute of a mark *does not require* that there be *a likelihood of detriment to the distinctive character or the repute of the mark* or, more generally, to its proprietor. The advantage arises where a third party uses a sign similar to a mark of repute or distinctive character in order to: (i) benefit from the power of attraction, the reputation and the prestige of that mark; and (ii) to exploit, without paying any financial compensation, the marketing effort expended by the proprietor of the mark in order to create and maintain the mark's image.

Obviously, Article 5(2) does not require a likelihood of confusion to be present; however, what is striking is that the court held that there was no need to prove a likelihood of detriment to either the distinctiveness of the character or the repute of the mark. Therefore, the unfair advantage or the detriment to the distinctive character of the mark *prima facie* arises where the third party uses the earlier mark of repute or distinctive character, without paying any financial compensation.

This ultimately demonstrates that the existence of detriment or unfair advantage, *prima facie*, is established when the third party does not pay any financial contribution. This approach seems to be rather immaturely thought out and results in muddied water between unfair competition and trade mark law.[234]

---

234 See Onishi, 'Revisiting the Japanese Unfair Competition Law: Post-Bellure', pp. 373–4; Horton, 'The Implications of L'Oréal v Bellure – A Retrospective and a Looking Forward: The Essential Functions of a Trade Mark and When is an Advantage Unfair?', p. 558.

Above all, the Court of Justice has taken a parallel path[235] to interpret both *Intel*[236] and *Bellure*.[237] Since the two different approaches seem hard to reconcile and are far from being consistent and rationalised, it is of great interest to examine the post-*Bellure* cases to analyse the implications of these cases.[238]

4.4.4.2 Post-Bellure

So far, we have looked at the cases prior to the influential rulings of *Intel* and *Bellure*. This part will consider the aftermath of *Intel* and *Bellure*, in order to investigate how the EU jurisprudence has handled the protection of the mark of repute in the context of dilution and free-riding. The continued attempt to seek a fuller completion of the conceptualisation of the mark of repute and the pie chart in Figure 4.6 will, of course, be made.

The first of these cases is *Google v Louis Vuitton*[239] (one of the three joint cases[240]). Note that the main concern of *Google v Louis Vuitton* and *Interflora*[241] goes slightly beyond the scope of this book; of interest here is whether the use of AdWords[242] that contain a registered trade mark (of repute) can amount to a trade mark

---

235 See, for example, Blythe, 'Attempting to Define Unfair Advantage: An Evaluation of the Current Law in Light of the Recent European Decisions', pp. 756–7.

236 *Intel* [2009] ETMR 13.

237 *Bellure* [2009] ETMR 55.

238 Pre-*Bellure*: *Antarctica Srl v Office for Harmonisation in the Internal Market (Trade Marks and Designs) (OHIM) (C-320/07 P)* [2009] ETMR 47; *Maurer + Wirtz GmbH & Co KG v Office for Harmonisation in the Internal Market (Trade Marks and Designs) (OHIM) (T-63/07)* [2010] ETMR 40; *Nute Partecipazioni SpA (formerly Gruppo La Perla SpA) v Office for Harmonisation in the Internal Market (Trade Marks and Designs) (OHIM) (T-59/08)* [2011] ETMR 19; *Environmental Manufacturing LLP v Office for Harmonisation in the Internal Market (Trade Marks and Designs) (OHIM) (T-570/10)* [2012] ETMR 54; *IG Communications Ltd v Office for Harmonisation in the Internal Market (Trade Marks and Designs) (OHIM) (T-301/09)* [2013] ETMR 17; *El Corte Ingles SA v Office for Harmonisation in the Internal Market (Trade Marks and Designs) (OHIM) (T-39/10)* [2013] ETMR 3; *Kraft Foods Schweiz Holding GmbH v Office for Harmonisation in the Internal Market (Trade Marks and Designs) (OHIM) (T-357/10)* [2012] ETMR 51; the UK national case, *Red Bull GmbH v Sun Mark Ltd* [2012] EWHC 1929 (Ch).

239 *Google France Sarl v Louis Vuitton Malletier SA* (C-236/08) [2010] ETMR 30.

240 Other co-joined cases are: *Google France Sarl v Centre National de Recherche en Relations Humaines (CNRRH) Sarl* (C-238/08), and *Google France Sarl v Viaticum SA* (C-237/08).

241 *Interflora Inc and Interflora British Unit v Marks & Spencer plc and Flowers Direct Online Limited* (Case C-323/09). Mr Justice Arnold asked the Court of European Union for a preliminary rulings from the High Court of Justice of England and Wales ([2009] EWHC 1095 (Ch)). The case then returned for trial before Arnold J at [2012] EWHC 1722 (Ch).

242 The AdWords program is operated by Google and comprises 98 per cent of their revenue. AdWords works as follows: Google sells keywords, known as 'AdWords', as links to websites, where the advertisers are entitled to choose their wanted keywords. The company purchase so-called 'key words'. Whenever users of Google enter the keyword, the advertiser's website will come up as a sponsored link at the top of the search results. If that sponsored link is clicked by the users, a fee payable to Google will be incurred by the advertiser. One of the acute legal issues arising from this AdWords system is whether Google shall be held liable in trade mark infringement by not preventing the unauthorised use of a registered trade mark as keywords which are incorporated into the advertisements of unauthorised third parties. For further explanation, see S. Blakeney, 'Adverse to AdWords? An Overview of the Recent Cases Relating to Google AdWords', *Computer and Telecommunications Law Review*, 13, 2007, 83–87 at 83; and S. Blakeney, 'Google AdWords: Searching for More Answers', *Computer and Telecommunications Law Review*, 16, 2010, 152–5.

infringement under Article 5(2) of the EU TMD. However, some useful application of Article 4(4)(a) and the interpretation of 'detriment' and 'unfair advantage' can be sought.

The claimants were the proprietors of the trade mark 'Louis Vuitton'. The defendant was the internet search engine provider Google, operating the system called Google AdWords. Louis Vuitton alleged that Google had allowed advertisers, who were in competition with the claimant and sold the counterfeited goods of Louis Vuitton, to reserve keywords in which some elements of Louis Vuitton's trade marks are present. As a consequence, internet users were guided to those advertisers' websites through sponsored links. The claimants argued that such use by the defendant had amounted to a trade mark infringement under Article 5(2) of the EU TMD.

The UK national court asked the Court of Justice for a preliminary ruling in providing the answers to three questions, one of which is relevant to the interpretation of 'detriment' and 'unfair advantage'. The question is whether the proprietor of the mark of repute is allowed to oppose such use (here, the trade mark 'Louis Vuitton' being used/included in AdWords) under Article 5(2) of the EU TMD (and thus Article 9(1)(c) of the CTMR).[243]

The Court of Justice applied the *Bellure*-type of reasoning, as opposed to the *Intel*-type, interlinking with the legitimate functions of a trade mark,[244] and held that Article 5(2) offers the proprietor of the trade mark of repute special protection to prohibit a third party from using, without the proprietor's consent, a sign identical to its trade mark in relation to goods or services that are identical to those for which that trade mark is registered, in the case where that use adversely affects the proprietor's use of its mark as *a factor in sales promotion* or as *an instrument of commercial strategy*.[245]

In terms of application of Article 5(2), the court reaffirmed *Bellure*[246] and stated that:

> [W]here a third party attempts . . . to ride on *the coat-tails of that mark* in order to benefit from *its power of attraction, its reputation and its prestige*, and to exploit, *without paying any financial compensation* and without being required to make efforts of its own in that regard, the marketing effort expended by the proprietor of that mark in order to create and maintain *the image of that mark, the advantage* resulting from such use must be considered to *be an advantage that has been unfairly taken* of the distinctive character or the repute of that mark.[247]
> [Emphasis added]

---

243 *Interflora Inc v Marks & Spencer Plc* [2009] EWHC 1095 (Ch) at 67, 70 and 73. .
244 Two functions can be found: one is to promote innovation and commercial investment; another is to create incentive for further innovation and investment (see para 96).
245 *Google v Louis Vuitton* [2010] ETMR 30, para 92.
246 *Bellure* [2009] ETMR 55, para [49].
247 *Google v Louis Vuitton* [2010] ETMR 30, para 102.

To grasp the flavour of the approach of *Google* to the taking the unfair advantage, and add this to the pie chart in Figure 4.6, we can say that free-riding is an attempt to ride on the coat-tails of the mark (power of attraction, reputation, prestige) where no financial compensation was made to the owner, and to exploit their marketing effort to create and maintain the image and thus the advantage of the mark.

Therefore, under the 'taking unfair advantage' heading, it seems to make a difference if the mark is of distinctive character or of repute. Moreover, unfair advantage will arise where the image of the mark is harmed so that the mark does not serve to promote innovation and investment. This is classic *Bellure*-type reasoning, which focuses on the financial (future) gain that the image of the mark of repute can generate. This can provide a broader scope of the interpretation of free-riding 'unfair advantage', since future loss of investment is included and no proof of actual harm is required.

To summarise, the judicial explanation of the correlation between this particular function and 'unfair advantage (free-riding)' is, in the view of this author, reasonably drawn. The proprietor of a trade mark of repute is entitled to prevent any third parties from using any mark that is identical or similar to the earlier mark, where one of the legitimate functions of the trade mark, including the function to promote innovation and commercial investment, is harmed. Further to this, the unfair advantage could be related to the (potential) financial loss to the proprietor of the mark of repute. This confirms the point made earlier that the third function of the trade mark, as a communication and promotional tool, is the main focus of the issues concerning free-riding. In other words, the essential function of the trade mark – the indication of the trade origin – is likely to be put aside and become less powerful in determining whether there is free-riding in the context of Article 5(2). In this sense, the trade mark of repute can be *über* on the grounds that the trade mark works as a powerful promotional and commercial vehicle. It could then be concluded, with reference to the pie chart in Figure 4.6, that the protectable subject matter of trade mark with distinctive character and that with reputation, under the heading of 'taking unfair advantage', seems to show a great deal of overlap, irrespective of the status of the mark (being of distinctive character or of repute). It can thus be inferred for either the mark of distinctive character or the mark of repute, that so long as the function of the trade mark as the commercial, promotional and advertising tool is adverse, the taking the unfair advantage ought to be established. If this is the case, where does the distinction between the mark of distinctive character and that of repute come into play? Does such a distinction ultimately not matter?

The feeling of puzzlement might be cleared and the question posed above answered by looking at *Interflora*.[248] The heart of *Interflora* is similar to that

---

248 *Interflora* [2012] ETMR 1. Mr Justice Arnold asked the Court of Justice of the European Union for a preliminary ruling from the High Court of Justice of England and Wales ([2009] EWHC 1095 (Ch)). The case was then returned for trial before Arnold J at [2012] EWHC 1722 (Ch)).

of *Google v Vuitton*:[249] the unauthorised use of (part of) a trade mark of repute as (part of) AdWords. Marks & Spencer, a competitor of the claimant's company, Interflora, purchased the keyword 'interflora' from the Google AdWords service, so that when customers type 'interflora' into a Google search, customers would find the advertisement for Marks & Spencer at the top of the sponsored links. Interflora brought proceedings against Marks & Spencer in order to stop Marks & Spencer from using the word 'interflora' as a key word. The UK national court[250] referred a number of questions[251] to the Court of Justice for a preliminary ruling.

The same exercise done previously in the analysis of *Google* will be undertaken: first, an attempt to seek for conceptualisation of the mark of repute and for further guidance to complete the mapping of dilution and free-riding.

First, the opinion of Advocate General Jääskinen will be considered, as some helpful overall observations of trade mark protection against dilution were made herein.[252] Also, the rationalisation of 'trade mark dilution' (made with analogy to the functions of a trade mark[253]) is rather persuasive and its summary is as follows.

The purpose of protecting against dilution in the context of Article 5(2) is to protect (i) the efforts and investments made by the proprietor of the mark of repute and (ii) the independent value (goodwill) of the mark *per se*.[254]

Dilution by blurring was explained to be a stricter sense of the dilution, since, because of the use of a sign identical or similar to a trade mark of repute,[255] the distinctiveness of the trade mark of repute is watered down, which leads to the mark of repute becoming commonplace.[256]

---

249 *Google v Louis Vuitton* [2010] ETMR 30.
250 Mr Justice Arnold asked the Court of Justice of the European Union for a preliminary ruling from the High Court of Justice of England and Wales ([2009] EWHC 1095 (Ch)). The case was then returned for trial before Arnold J at [2012] EWHC 1722 (Ch).
251 There were ten questions asked by Mr Justice Arnold. See [2012] ETMR 1, para 20. One of the main issues was whether Interflora should be allowed to call the evidence of witnesses who were identified by means of two separate witness-gathering exercises, where the proprietor of the allegedly infringed trade mark does not intend to rely on the survey or questionnaire by means of which those witnesses were identified.
252 Opinion of Advocate General Jääskinen at AG1 to AG107 in *Interflora Inc and Interflora British Unit v Marks & Spencer plc and Flowers Direct Online Limited* [2012] ETMR 1.
253 This 'property-based' approach to trade marks differs from the 'deception-based' idea that trade mark law primarily protects the origin function with a view to preventing consumers and other end users from erring as to the commercial origin of goods and services. The property-based approach also protects the communication, advertising and investment functions of trade marks with a view to creating a brand with *a positive image and independent economic value (brand equity or good will)*. Consequently, the trade mark can be used for various goods and services having nothing in common apart from being under the control of the trade mark proprietor. The origin and quality functions would be protected as factors contributing to the value of the brand. In the judgment, the court referred to three categories of the functions of a trade mark: (i) function of indicating origin; (ii) advertising function; (iii) investment function. The second and third functions are explained as follows: the advertising function serves as the opportunity of using the mark effectively to inform and win over consumers and to intensify advertising in order to maintain or enhance its profile with consumers; and a trade mark may also be used by its proprietor to acquire or preserve a reputation capable of attracting consumers and retaining their loyalty.
254 *Interflora* [2012] ETMR 1, para AG50.
255 Ibid., para AG80.
256 Ibid., para AG 81.

By referring to *Bellure*,[257] dilution by tarnishment is interpreted to occur when, because of the use of a sign identical or similar to a trade mark of repute, *the image of the trade mark*, which contains *the power of attraction*, is reduced or causes negative impact on the image of the mark.[258] Given that *Bellure* was referred, *Bellure*-type reasoning is expected.

By making a causal link with unfair advantage and putting the notion of free-riding into the context, free-riding was explained to occur where, through the use of a sign identical with or similar to the mark of repute, a third party intends to ride on the *coat-tails of that mark in order to benefit from its power of attraction, its reputation and its prestige*, and *to exploit, without paying any financial compensation and without being required to make efforts of his own in that regard.*[259] In other words, free-riding happens when the third party takes, without paying any compensation, unfair advantage of the efforts or goodwill that has been made/established by the proprietor of the mark of repute in order to establish the reputation of the mark.

The ruling of the Court of Justice added some extra guidance, with reference to the essential function of the trade mark, in explaining dilution by blurring: at the end of the process of dilution, the trade mark is no longer capable of creating an immediate association, in the minds of consumers, with a specific commercial origin,[260] given that the ongoing (as opposed to the completed) process of reducing the distinctiveness of the mark being reduced is sufficient to be recognised as dilution by blurring.[261]

Second, the court emphasised the difference between dilution by blurring and tarnishment, and it is the trade mark's power of attraction that is reduced, not the distinctiveness of the mark.[262]

Third, the court, with reference to *Bellure*, distinguishes dilution from free-riding, which relates to the mark but to the advantage taken by the third party, such as a *clear exploitation on the coat-tails of the mark with a reputation* as a result of the use of the identical or similar sign.[263]

Concerning the interpretation of the trade mark of repute, in *Google v Louis Vuitton*[264] it was summarised that the protectable subject matter of the trade mark of repute in the context of Article 5(2) is the element of the mark being the powerful force to attract promotion in innovation and investment, whilst in *Interflora* its scope is broader: the protectable subject matter of the trade mark of repute in the context of Article 5(2) is the element of protection of trade mark of repute to protect the efforts and investment made by the proprietor and the intrinsic value of the mark itself. In other words, a trade mark of repute comes

257 *Bellure* [2009] ETMR 55.
258 *Interflora* [2012] ETMR 1, para AG92.
259 Ibid., para AG 93.
260 Ibid., para 76.
261 Ibid., para 77.
262 Ibid., para 73.
263 Ibid., para 74.
264 Ibid.

with a positive image and independent economic value (known as brand equity or goodwill).[265]

Post-*Bellure*, there is a noticeable tendency for the court to become proactively vocal in recognising the importance of the mark of repute working as a communication and commercial tool, and the court no longer hesitates to import business terms such as 'brand equity'[266] into the legal domain. Such a term was employed to explain the causal link between trade mark of repute and financial commodity. In other words, the court attempts to recognise the mark of repute in terms of being a commodity, a (potential) financial asset and (future) profit generator. The 'repute' as a profit generator has now become a stand-alone protectable subject matter and appears to have taken its own journey.

The third reference is made to *Rubinstein and L'Oréal v OHIM*.[267] This, together with the case below, shows a different path to Article 5(2), which is to follow more *Intel*-type reasoning as opposed to *Bellure*-type reasoning. The Court of Justice upheld the decision delivered by the General Court,[268] holding that the General Court did not make any errors in concluding that L'Oréal's mark for Botocyl and Helena Rubinstein's mark for Botolist took advantage of the distinctive character and reputation of Hollywood's anti-aging cocktail of choice, Botox. The General Court held that the marks of Helena Rubinstein and L'Oréal were intended to take advantage of the distinctive character and repute acquired by Botox for the treatment of wrinkles, which would have the effect of decreasing the value of the mark. The claimant appealed the General Court's decision, alleging that an error had been made.

The Court of Justice held that Allergan's mark 'Botox' was also well known in the healthcare profession, given significant media coverage for the general public of the 'Botox' products, and at the filing date of the Rubinstein and L'Oréal trade mark applications, the trade mark 'Botox' had a reputation in the UK for 'pharmaceutical preparations for the treatment of wrinkles' within Class 5. Moreover, it was held that:

> The General Court had been right to hold that the proprietor of an earlier mark was not required to demonstrate actual and present harm to its mark but had only to adduce *prima facie* evidence of a future risk of unfair advantage or detriment. Such a conclusion might be established on the basis of logical deductions made from an analysis of the probabilities and by taking account of the normal practice in the relevant commercial sector as well as all the other circumstances of the case.[269]

---

265 Ibid., at [AG50].
266 Ibid.
267 *Helena Rubinstein SNC and L'Oréal SA v Office for Harmonisation in the Internal Market (Trade Marks and Designs) (OHIM)*. (C-100/11 P) [2012] ETMR 40.
268 *Rubinstein and L'Oréal v OHIM* (T-345/08) (unreported).
269 *Helena Rubinstein* [2012] ETMR 40, at [95].

Endorsing *Intel*-type reasoning,[270] the court found the likelihood of harm as well as the association of the link. On the contrary, if the court had followed *Bellure*-type reasoning, the advantage would have arisen where the use by a third party of a sign similar to a mark of repute or distinctive character in order to (i) benefit from the power of attraction, the reputation and the prestige of that mark and (ii) to exploit, without paying any financial compensation, the marketing effort expended by the proprietor of the mark in order to create and maintain the mark's image, the outcome of the case might have been different. In *Bellure*-type reasoning, the establishment of an unfair advantage hugely depends on the degree of the *image* of the mark (of repute), irrespective of the mark being of distinctive character or of repute. This gives an impression that the proprietor has the option of selecting the status of their mark at their convenience.

The inconsistent approach taken by *Bellure* and *Intel*, and the conclusion that can be drawn from this, is that free-riding is easier to establish than dilution. The latter needs to prove a link between the two marks and serious harm caused by changes in consumers' behaviour in the relevant public. Such a finding seems, to this author, to create a place for forum shopping under Article 5(2). Frankly, it would be the obvious choice for the proprietor whose mark of repute works as a communication and commercial tool, containing a strong market message of positive image and prestige (even more appropriate), to down the free-riding route rather than that of dilution by tarnishment, as the former is easier to prove. Therefore, *Rubinstein* might be interpreted to have put a stop to such forum shopping.

The fourth and final reference is made to *Environmental Manufacturing LLP v OHIM*,[271] in which the Court of Justice affirmed *Intel* and confirmed that evidence of change in the economic behaviour of the average consumer is required in order to prove trade mark dilution under Article 8(5). The applicant, Environmental Manufacturing, had applied to register pictorial marks representing a wolf-like canine head in relation to professional wood and green-waste processing machines. The opponent, Société Elmar Wolf, is the proprietor of the earlier French and international figurative marks consisting of a wolf's head and the words 'WOLF Jardin' or 'Outils WOLF', in relation to garden machinery and tools. The opposition was filed on the basis that such a registration would cause the likelihood of confusion and detriment to the distinctive character of the earlier marks. The Opposition Division of the OHIM found no likelihood of confusion and no evidence of detriment or unfair advantage. The BoA, on the contrary, established the existence of unfair advantage being taken from the distinctive character or the reputation of the earlier trade mark.[272] The applicant

---

270 Ibid. See Opinion of General Advocate P. Mengozzi, para 32.
271 *Environmental Manufacturing LLP v OHIM* (C- 383/12 P). (unreported). The General Court decision is T-570/10. *Environmental Manufacturing LLP v Office for Harmonisation in the Internal Market (Trade Marks and Designs) (OHIM), Société Elmar Wolf* [2012] ETMR 54.
272 T-570/10. *Environmental Manufacturing LLP v Office for Harmonisation in the Internal Market (Trade Marks and Designs) (OHIM), Société Elmar Wolf* [2012] ETMR 54.

proceeded the claim to the Court of Justice,[273] which annulled the decision of the General Court.

The Court of Justice made reference to *Intel* and held that, without adducing evidence that that condition is met, the detriment or the risk of detriment to the distinctive character of the earlier mark provided for in Article 8(5) cannot be established.[274] The court also endorsed the requirement of the higher standard of proof in finding the dilution within the meaning of Article 8(5) and 5(2), which was established by *Intel*.[275]

Environmental Manufacturing appears to imply that there are two different types of standard being demanded under Article 5(2). The higher standard of proof is required for applying dilution by blurring or tarnishment, whilst the lower standard is required for applying free-riding. This seems, in the view of this author, to encourage, yet again, the undesirable forum shopping by the proprietor of the trade mark of repute. As the pie chart in Figure 5.6 demonstrates, the differences in the protectable subject matters in the four parts of the chart are extremely subtle and overlap a great deal. The outcome of the case will be shaped depending on how the proprietor intends to play the dilution game. What I have found is that the interpretation of the mark of repute is very loose and flexible – depending and based on what type of harm the proprietor of the mark of repute is claiming against, the meaning of the mark of repute will be transformed.

4.4.5 Summary

In Section 4.4, we have looked at the protection of trade mark of repute in the context of detriment and dilution. The EU trade mark regime does not offer the natural, stand-alone right to the trade mark of repute: the proprietor of the trade mark of repute can exercise the statutory exclusive right against detrimental use of or taking unfair advantage of distinctive character and/or reputation of the mark (Articles 4(4)(2) and 5(2) of the EU TMD). The author has attempted to conceptualise the protection of trade mark of repute in the context of detriment and dilution, and the following can be found.

There are three different types of actionable harm (encroachment) caused to the mark of repute: (i) dilution by blurring; (ii) dilution by tarnishment; and (iii) free-riding.

The conceptualisation of detrimental use and taking unfair advantage has created the synergetic effect of obtaining more support for conceptualisation of the mark of repute.

Returning to the Definition Model, 'trade mark of repute' *concept* was argued to be acquired distinctiveness. The following *concepts* of 'trade mark of repute' are legitimately recognised and protected against detriment and taking unfair

273 *Environmental Manufacturing LLP v OHIM* (C-383/12 P) (unreported).
274 At 36.
275 At 40.

advantage (see the pie chart in Figure 4.5) and become also part of acquired distinctiveness, which varies depending on the type of encroachment: attractiveness/attractive power, advertising value, reputation/image/prestige, particular characteristics, distinctiveness, distinctive quality. Above all, it could be argued that conceptualisation, if not complete, can be evidenced.

4.5 Conclusion

The main purpose of this chapter has been to explore the EU framework of protecting trade marks of repute against detriment/taking unfair advantage and to assess the certainty of the same.

The lack of clarity found, both in this chapter and in Chapter 3, in the definition and identification of trade marks of repute/well-known trade marks justifies the time taken in earlier chapters to address the foundation question of 'What constitutes a well-known trade mark?' by reference to the definition of 'trade mark' in Chapter 2. It has been highlighted that the term 'well-known' is not employed in the EU trade mark regime, with the term 'trade mark of repute' being preferred instead.

In this chapter, the EU TMD and relevant jurisprudence have been investigated in an attempt to define both 'trade mark of repute' (Section 4.3) and 'detriment' and 'unfair advantage' (Sections 4.4.1–4.4.4 above). It has been found that there is no conceptualisation or clear comprehensive definition of either of these terms.

Due to the dearth of conceptualisation, reference was made to the Definition Model in analysing 'trade mark of repute' (Section 4.3 above). It has been concluded that there is limited, implicit guidance as to *form* (*type* and *context*) of 'trade mark of repute' in the EU TMD, but that no further guidance is provided by the cases. The cases do contribute a range of fact-based criteria to assess 'trade mark of repute' status, and, from this, it has been inferred that *concept* of 'trade mark of repute' includes notions of distinctiveness and (unhelpfully) value.

The result of this lack of clarity is that not only is 'trade mark of repute' bound to be subject to various interpretations due to the unspecified parameters of the fact-based assessments, but 'detriment' and 'unfair advantage' have the same fate. This means that the scope of protection of marks of repute against detriment and unfair advantage in the EU system appears inherently unclear and incoherent.

In relation to detriment and taking unfair advantage, three types of actionable harm (encroachment) have been identified: dilution by blurring (detrimental to the distinctiveness of the mark), dilution by tarnishment (detrimental to the reputation of the mark) and taking unfair advantage of the distinctiveness and/or reputation of the mark (free-riding). This is, in the view of the author, where some attempt at conceptualisation of the protection against encroachment has been evidenced.

When considering the international context of well-known trade marks, in Chapter 3, it was noted that a loose definition of 'well-known trade mark' could be advantageous, with the advantage of flexibility compensating for uncertainty. On the basis of evidence considered, it seems unlikely that it is possible to come to a definitive conclusion that the lack of clarity on what constitutes a mark of repute in the EU system is disadvantageous. However, it is viewed that more clarity here would be helpful to proprietors of trade marks of repute in cases where the mark of repute faces an identical or similar mark for identical or similar goods and services, and, if only on this basis, this author would argue for the introduction of greater clarity.

The exploration of the EU framework leads to the conclusion that the protection of marks of repute in the EU system against detriment and unfair advantage is *not* sufficiently conceptualised. The contextualisation of those notions in the EU may be a causal factor of uncertainty, but it is submitted that the key reasons for this uncertainty are:

(i)   the absence of conceptualisation of the protection of marks of repute against detriment and unfair advantage (see Sections 4.3 and 4.4);
(ii) the emphasis on non-exclusive factors to determine when a mark is a mark of repute (see Section 4.3.5); and
(iii) the emphasis on the factual contexts to determine when (any) trade mark is subject to detriment and unfair advantage (see Section 4.4.).

The next chapter will undertake an examination of well-known trade mark protection at the national level, considering the definition of '*syuchi-syohyo*' (well-known trademark) in Japanese law and the protection of the same against detriment/taking unfair advantage. It is hoped the reader will be interested to see how the concept of 'well-known trade mark' within the meaning of the Paris Convention[276] has been imported to this non-English-speaking national trade mark regime.

---

276 Article 6*bis* of the Paris Convention.

5   'Syuchi-syohyo' in Japan

5.1 Introduction

The purpose of this chapter is to critically assess the effectiveness and credibility of the protection of '*syuchi-syohyo*' (a concept analogous to 'well-known trade mark') against *fuseino mokuteki* (a concept analogous to dilution and, arguably, free-riding) within the Japanese trademark system. This chapter divides into four parts. First, an overview of the Japanese legal and trademark system will be provided. Second, the conceptualisation of the definition of '*syuchi-syohyo*' in the Japanese Trademark Act will be undertaken, utilising the Definition Model. Third, the efficacy and credibility of the protection of '*syuchi-syohyo*' against *fuseino mokuteki* will be critically examined. Fourth, alternative ways in which the '*syuchi-syohyo*' can be protected will be introduced. Together, these will give a complete and exhaustive picture of 'well-known trade mark' protection in Japan.

5.2 Background

This section attempts to equip readers with background knowledge of the Japanese legal system and trademark system.

In order to retain accuracy and not lose the nuances and authenticity of the Japanese language,[1] it is preferable to employ the transliterated Japanese trademark terms. A list of the transliterated Japanese trademark terms[2] employed in this book and their English translation is shown below.

5.2.1 Introduction to the Japanese legal system

Japan is a civil law jurisdiction,[3] and its constitution is codified.[4] The Constitution of Japan (hereinafter the Constitution) was promulgated in 1946, came into force

---

1 See Chapter 1, Section 1.4. 2.
2 Ibid.
3 See, for example, K. Doi, *Chiteki Zaisan Ho Nyumon*, Tokyo: Tyuokeizai-sha, 2005.
4 The Constitution of Japan, 3 November 1946. The Constitution was promulgated on 3 November 1946 and came into force on 3 May 1947. Since the Constitution was established, it has not been

Table 5.1 Japanese trademark terms

Japanese transliteration	Translation of Japanese term	EU equivalent
Syohyo	Trademark[5]	Trade mark
Syuchi-syohyo	Well-known trademark	Mark with distinctive character
Tyomei-syohyo	Famous trademark	Mark of repute
Bogo-syohyo	Defensive trademark	N/A
Kisyaku ka	Dilution	Dilution
Fuseino mokuteki	Unfair purposes	Unfair advantages

in 1947 and to date has never been amended. The Constitution sits at the top of the hierarchy of laws in Japan, holding the ultimate legal authority,[6] and provides the fundamental (human) rights afforded to Japanese citizens.

In relation to trademark law, the claimant can bring a claim in trademark infringement under the Civil Code of Japan (the Civil Code).[7] Article 709 of the Civil Code is the main provision for general actions in tort,[8] civil liabilities and remedies. The main remedy available for civil wrongs – that is, damages (pecuniary remedies)[9] – and some guidance in determining the amount of damages[10] is also provided in Article 709. The pecuniary and non-pecuniary remedies available for actions in trademark infringements are set out in Articles 38[11] and 36[12] respectively.

amended. The full English text of the Constitution of Japan is available online at www.japaneselawtranslation.go.jp/law/detail/?ft=2&re=01&dn=1&yo=%E6%86%B2%E6%B3%95&x=0&y=0&ky=&page=1 (accessed 6 November 2014).

5 When discussing marks in a non-Japanese context, the term 'trade mark' (two words) is employed.
6 Article 98 of the Constitution states that 'this Constitution shall be the supreme law of the nation and no law, ordinance, imperial rescript or other act of government or part thereof, contrary to the provisions hereof, shall have legal force or validity'.
7 The Civil Code (Parts I, II and III). Act No. 85 of 1896 last amended by Act No. 61 of 2011. The Civil Code is divided into two parts: the first consists of Parts I, II and III; the second consists of Parts IV and V. The full text of the first part of the Civil Code in English is available online at www.japaneselawtranslation.go.jp/law/detail/?ft=2&re=01&dn=1&yo=&kn[]=%E3%81%BF&x=14&y=23&ky=&page=9 (accessed 6 November 2014).
8 Ibid. Article 709 states: 'A person who has intentionally or negligently infringed any right of others, or legally protected interest of others, shall be liable to compensate any damages resulting in consequence.'
9 Ibid., Article 41. It states: 'Unless other intention is manifested, the amount of the damages shall be determined with reference to monetary value.'
10 Ibid., Article 722(2). It sets out: 'If a victim is negligent, the court may determine the amount of compensation for costs. All such judges shall receive, at regular stated intervals, adequate compensation which shall not be decreased during their terms of office compensation by taking that factor into consideration.'
11 Ibid., Article 710. It states: 'Persons liable for damages under the provision of the preceding must also compensate for damages other than those to property, regardless of whether the body, liberty or reputation of others has been infringed, or property rights of others have been infringed.'
12 Ibid., Article 723. It states: 'The court may, at the request of the victim, order a person who defamed others, to effect appropriate measures the reputation of the victim in lieu of, in addition to, damages.'

5.2.1.1 Court procedure

The Japanese judicial system takes a three-tier appeal system, where an individual has a guaranteed constitutional right[13] to make an appeal against the same decision three times. Generally speaking, the first instance will begin at the District Court, the second instance will be at the High Court, and the third will be at the final appeal court, the Supreme Court. The Japanese language distinguishes between the terms used when an appeal is made to the lower court and when it is made to the highest court, the Supreme Court. The former is presented as 'kouso [控訴: kouso]' in the *kanji* form; the latter is presented as 'jyokoku [上告: jyoukoku]'. Therefore, it is explicit in the Japanese literature as to which court an appeal has been made.

The Supreme Court of Japan (hereinafter the Supreme Court) is the highest appeal court for both civil and criminal matters. Although Japan is not a common law jurisdiction, the legal principle of *precedent* seems to be present; the lower courts are likely to follow the higher court's decision for reasons of legal consistency and stability. The lowest courts include the summary court, family courts and district courts; the lower court is the High Court; and the final appeal court is the Supreme Court of Japan.

5.2.1.1.1 THE SUPREME COURT OF JAPAN

Although an individual can, in principle, take any matter to the Supreme Court, there are limitations as to when this appeal is allowed: (i) an error in the interpretation of the Constitution; (ii) an error in the interpretation of case law from the Supreme Court or High Court; (iii) an appeal filed against a ruling in a civil case or a domestic relations case either on the grounds of violation of the Constitution or with the permission of the High Court that may be given in a case that the court deems to involve an important issue concerning the construction of laws and regulations; and (iv) a special appeal filed against an order or direction in a criminal case to which no ordinary appeal is permitted in the Code of Criminal Procedure, or an appeal filed against an order, *inter alia*, of an intermediate appellate court in a juvenile case, on the grounds of violation of the Constitution or for the reason of a conflict with judicial precedents.

5.2.1.1.2 HIGH COURT AND INTELLECTUAL PROPERTY HIGH COURT

High Courts generally serve as the court of second instance, and there are eight such courts throughout Japan. While appeals in criminal cases originating in summary courts come directly to High Courts, appeals in civil cases originating in summary courts are usually brought first to district courts and then final

13 This right is guaranteed in Article 32 of the Constitution.

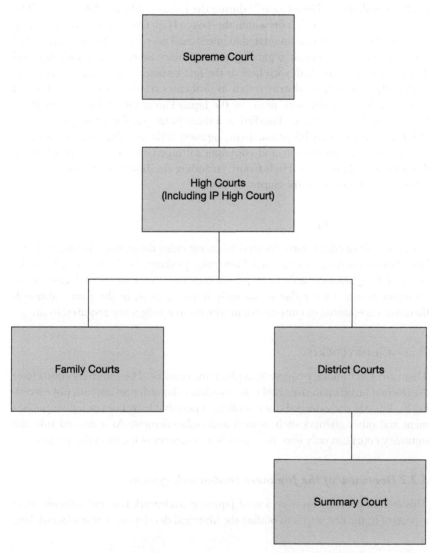

Figure 5.1 The Japanese court structure

appeals are lodged with High Courts. In addition, the High Court has original jurisdiction over administrative cases on election, insurrection cases and so on. The Tokyo High Court also has exclusive original jurisdiction over cases to revoke determinations of such *quasi*-judicial agencies as the Japan Marine Accident Tribunal.

The Intellectual Property High Court (*Chiteki zaisan koto saiban syo*) was established in 2005 by the implementation of the 'Act for Establishment of the

Intellectual Property High Court'[14] during the *Koizumi* Cabinet (2001–2005). The function of this court, which sits within the Tokyo High Court, is to provide a more specialised court for litigation related to intellectual property. All cases against trial decisions and civil appeals regarding patent, utility model, semiconductor and digital copyrights are dealt with here as the first instance. Furthermore, the court deals with appeals from district courts in civil cases relating to patent rights and actions against trial decisions made by the Japan Patent Office (hereinafter JPO). Cases in the High Court are handled by a three-judge panel in principle.

Intellectual property litigation, involving most IPRs including registered trademarks, patent infringements and copyright infringements, may be heard in the district court, then in the High Court, including the Intellectual Property High Court, and ultimately in the Supreme Court.

5.2.1.1.3 DISTRICT COURTS

There are 50 district courts, located in major cities throughout Japan, and 203 branches are currently operational. Generally speaking, district courts serve as the court of first instance and have jurisdiction over appeals in civil cases from summary courts. One judge is normally required to sit in the court, although there are exceptional circumstances in which three judges are required to sit.

5.2.1.1.4 SUMMARY COURTS

There are 438 summary courts throughout the country. The summary courts have the original jurisdiction over civil cases involving claims for an amount not exceeding ¥1,400,000 and criminal cases of offences punishable by fines or lighter punishment and other offences such as theft and embezzlement. As a general rule, the summary court can only issue fines or prison sentences of less than three years.

5.2.2 Overview of the Japanese trademark system

This section provides an overview of Japanese trademark law and administrative aspects of it; the first step is to outline the historical development of trademark law.

5.2.2.1 Historical development of the Japanese Trademark Act

The Japanese Trademark Act and its registration systems have a long-established history in comparison with the relatively new CTM system.[15]

---

14 Act for Establishment of the Intellectual Property High Court. Act No. 119 of 2004 as amended. An English translation of the Act is available online at www.japaneselawtranslation.go.jp/law/detail/?ft=2&re=01&dn=1&yo=&ia=03&kn[]=%E3%81%A1&_x=19&_y=12&ky=&page=3 (accessed 7 February 2015).
15 See Chapter 4, Section 4.4.2. It is submitted that an examination of the long-established Japanese trademark system and the newly established CTM system makes an interesting comparative study.

The first Trademark Act (known as 商標条例 – the *Syohyo jyorei*, or the Trademark Ordinance) was implemented in 1884,[16] during the *Meiji* era (1868–1912).[17] This statute consisted of 24 main Articles and additional Rules.

The 24 Articles of the Trademark Ordinance 1884 included all of the most essential aspects of the framework of trademark protection, such as the registration system, the first-to-file system, right to the prior use, one application for one trademark registration, the term of protection, the renewable nature of the registration, and recognition of the different classifications. Since then, the Japanese Trademark Act has been revised and amended on an almost annual basis in order to reflect social and economic changes.[18]

However, it has been noted[19] that the major revisions have tended to occur when Japan has ratified various international treaties[20] such as the Paris Convention,[21] the Nice Agreement,[22] the TLT[23] and the Madrid Protocol,[24] and also upon accession to GATT TRIPS.[25]

Although the fundamentals of the modern trademark framework were established in 1922,[26] the most significant period of evolution of the Act was probably the period following accession to the Paris Convention[27] in 1889.

16 The first patent law was introduced in 1885. The Trademark Act of 1884 is often described as being simplistic (e.g. T. Doi, *Chiteki Zaisan Ho Nyumon*, Tokyo: Tyuokeizai-sha, 2005, pp. 45–6); however, it is accepted (e.g. Ono, *Syohyo ho*, pp. 28–9) that the 1884 Law contained all the fundamental elements that have helped to shape the modern Japanese Trademark Act including: the first-to-file system, first use, one trademark/one application and publication, an effective period (15 years) of registration, an application for the renewal of registered trademarks and the classification of goods by type. The Trademark Act of 1884 required the applicant to submit an application to the Ministry for Agriculture and Commerce through a local agency; however, after an 1888 amendment, the applicant was allowed to send the application directly to the Minister of Agriculture and Commerce.
17 The Trademark Ordinance was first enacted in 7 June 1884 and implemented in 1 October 1884. This is one year earlier than the establishment of the Japanese Patent Law. See Ono, *Syohyo ho*, pp. 29–30; and JPO, 'History of Industrial Property Rights'. Available online at www.jpo.go.jp/ seido_e/rekishi_e/rekisie.htm (accessed 14 June 2013). During the *Edo* era (1603–1868), it is accepted that the *Edo bakudu* (the *Edo* Government) announced a law called '新規法度 (*Shinki hatto*): a new law for any new inventions' (unofficial translation). Therefore, it might be suspected that the Trademark Act was established before the patent law. See M. Toyokaki, 'Takahashi korekiyo to syohyo jyorei', *Gakisyuin University Law Journal*, 8, 1973, 187–239, p. 190.
18 The latest amendment occurred in April 2008 and came into force in June 2008.
19 See Y. Inoue, 'Syohyo ho saisei to kongo nokadai', *IPR Forum*, 23, 2002; M. Terushima, 'Syohyo to brand – konogoro no jyokyo', *Patent*, 57, 2004, 72–5.
20 Japan has not yet ratified the Singapore Treaty.
21 Japan has been a signatory nation of the Paris Convention since 15 July 1899.
22 Japan ratified the Nice Agreement in 1990; it came into force 1 April 1992.
23 Japan submitted a ratification instrument to the office in 1 January 1996, which came into force in 1 April 1997.
24 Japan signed the Madrid Protocol in 14 April 1891.
25 Japan became a signatory member of GATT TRIPS in 15 April 1994 in Marrakesh, Morocco.
26 Protection for *syuchi-syohyo* and a system for cancellation of trademarks in non-use were introduced in this amendment.
27 See Chapter 2, Section 2.3.1.1, for the Paris Convention. Articles that are related to trade marks and well-known trade marks, respectively, are Articles 6*bis*, 6*ter*, 6*quineuies*, 6*sexies*, 7*bis*, 8 of the Paris Convention.

In 1889, following ratification of the Paris Convention, the Act was required to make a number of amendments in order to be consistent with the Paris Convention and was amended by the 1909 Act.[28]

After the 1909 Act came into force, the Japanese economy showed a remarkable recovery and improvement, which led to a staggering increase in the number of trademark registrations. In order to reflect changes in the economy and society, the 1922 Act, known as the Old Trademark Act, was introduced.[29] Between the 1922 Act and the current 1959 Act, minor amendments were implemented in 1929, 1934, 1938, 1947, 1948, 1949 and 1951. The most current Trademark Act was formed in 1959.[30] The main characteristic of the 1959 Act is that the definitions of 'trademarks', 'registrable trademarks', 'signs' and 'trademark use' were explicitly set out. Since the 1959 Act came into force, minor changes appear to have been made almost on an annual basis: in 1975,[31] 1991,[32] 1994,[33] 1996,[34] 1998,[35] 1999,[36] 2002,[37] 2005,[38] 2008,[39] 2011[40] and 2014.[41]

---

28 Key elements of this amendment can be summarised as follows: (i) introduced associated trademark system; (ii) allowed divisional transfer of a Trademark Act; (iii) added a provision calling for a trademark to be 'distinctive' in order to be registered.

29 Today, the Trademark Act of 1921 is still well known as 'the former law' and is compared with the present law. See Ono, *Syohyo ho*, pp. 6–7. The followings were introduced: (i) 'application Publication System'; (ii) collective mark system; (iii) incorporation of a trial for the cancellation of a trademark application; and (iv) a change in the definition of an infringement from an offence prosecutable on complaint to an offence prosecutable without complaint.

30 The following were introduced: (i) a term of protection for a trademark right set at ten years from the date of registration; (ii) all forms of transfer being allowed; (iii) abolition of the collective mark system; (iv) the right to license the use of a registered trademark; and (v) introduction of the defensive mark system.

31 The following were introduced: (i) a requirement of indicating 'Business of Applicant' in an trademark application; (ii) adding a provision concerning examination of the status of use at the time of a renewal of the term of a registered trademark; and (iii) a placement of burden of proof in case of a trial for the cancellation of a registered trademark on its owner.

32 The followings were introduced: (i) service marks system; (ii) adoption of the international classification under the Nice Agreement.

33 New provisions were added and revisions made to comply with requirements under GATT TRIPS.

34 The Amendment of 1996 consisted of many substantive changes as follows: (i) a multi-class application system was introduced to bring Japan into compliance with the TLT; (2) the requirement that an applicant enter his type of business in the application was removed; (iii) the 'associated mark' system was abolished in an effort to tackle the problem of unused trademarks; (iv) a system that allowed objections to be raised after a trademark was registered was established (this change was implemented to respond to the demand for the time-efficient granting of trademark rights); (v) a standard lettering system was implemented; (vi) the filing of applications with fraudulent intent was forbidden in an effort to protect famous trademarks; (vii) the three-dimensional trademark system in Japan was created; (viii) a collective trademarks system was adopted; (ix) the system for explaining the designated goods was revised.

35 The following were introduced: (i) review of the method of calculating the amount of indemnity for damages caused by infringements; and (ii) the certification of trademark registration and the defensive mark registration certificate.

36 The following were introduced: (i) establishment of the pecuniary right of a claim based on a trademark prior to the registration; (ii) implementation of the Madrid Protocol; (iii) establishment of a prompt publication system for trademark registration applications; (iv) acceptance

5.2.2.2 Role of the Japanese Patent Office (JPO)

The JPO is one of the central government agencies and comes under the Ministry of Economy, Trade and Industry (METI) located in Kasumigaseki, Tokyo. The first trademark registry office was established in 1884, and the first Director General was Korekiyo Takahashi.[42]

The main function of the JPO is as follows: (i) granting intellectual property rights appropriately; (ii) design, planning and organising matters relating to industrial property rights; (iii) harmonisation of national and international law to promote industrial property rights; (iv) assisting SMEs (small and medium-sized enterprises) and universities in maintaining the infrastructure of industrial property rights protection; (v) reforming the structure of industrial property rights protection; and (vi) appropriate dissemination of information relating to industrial property rights.

The overriding function of the JPO, in fact, is examination and assessment of patents, utility models, designs and trademark applications. In addition, the JPO engages in international activities – for example, to assist developing countries in Asia in drafting an intellectual property law.

5.2.2.3 Obtaining trademark rights in Japan

This section explains the procedure that trademark owners take in order to obtain trademark rights in Japan.

Japan has a first-to-file registration system, administered by the JPO: whoever files the application for the registration first will be the holder of the trademark rights. Once the trademark is registered, the rights conferred to the mark have an immediate effect throughout Japan. Furthermore, the Japanese trademark system offers defensive trademark registration, whereby the proprietor of well-known or famous registered trademarks can obtain an additional layer of protection by registering the mark for a defensive trademark. The registered trademark is valid for ten years (Article 19(1)), subject to renewal (Article 19(2)).

The registration procedure is laid out in Article 5 of the Japanese Trademark Act and the examination process is laid out in Articles 14–17. The following shows how the trademark registration system proceeds (see also Figure 5.2):

(i) File application: the application form must be filled in and submitted to the JPO. Online application for trademark registration can be made via the JPO

of the restrictions and corrections related to classification at the time of payment of the registration fees.
37 In this amendment, the meaning of 'trademark in use' was defined.
38 Introduction of the protection of collective trademarks.
39 Act No. 127 of 1959 amended by Act No. 84 of 2014.
40 Amended by Act No. 74 of 2011.
41 Act No. 84 of 2014.
42 Ono, *Syohyo ho*, pp. 28–9.

website. After the application has been filed, the JPO will publish the contents of the unexamined application in the Official Trademark Gazette.

(ii) Examination: the first examination is to ensure that the procedural requirements in the Act have been met. If necessary, an applicant may correct any mistakes and amend the application. When the first stage is passed, the application will move on to the next stage of examination, which is more substantive. The second examination considers the application and whether any of the absolute grounds for refusal apply (Articles 4 and 5).

Note that the Japanese Trademark Act does not recognise so-called absolute and relative grounds for refusal, as the EU TMD does.[43] The Japanese trademark regime seems to provide a negative list of marks, which are not registrable as trademarks due to either lack of distinctiveness (Article 3) or public policy considerations (Article 4). The trademark examiners fully examine both grounds, and therefore these seem to be equivalent to the absolute grounds for refusal in the EU trade mark regime.

(iii) Acceptance/refusal (opposition): if the application seems to have met the criteria above, the application is accepted. If not, the notification of refusal will be sent to the applicant. The applicant will then be given an opportunity to correct any mistakes and amend the application and/or to file an opposition for the decision of refusal.

(iv) Decision of registration/refusal: the final decision is made at this stage.

(v) Appeal: the applicant may appeal against the decision of refusal; an appeal examination will be held by a body of examiners.

(vi) Registration: when the application has been accepted and payment of the registration fee has been made, the registration of the applied trademarks will be completed and the trademark rights will become effective.

(vii) Publication: the mark will be published in the Official Trademark Gazette.

(viii) Opposition: under Section 43(2), any person may lodge their opposition within two months of the date of publication. The grounds of opposition for invalidation of the marks must be submitted in writing to the Registrar of the JPO. If the decision made by the Registrar is unsatisfactory, the applicant may appeal to the Intellectual Property High Court. See Figure 5.2 below.

5.2.2.4 Criminal sanctions

Primary and secondary infringers of trademark rights are subject to criminal sanction,[44] together with civil action in seeking damages.[45] Up to ten years' imprisonment may be imposed for infringement of trademarks.[46] Proprietary rights to prohibit the act of importing products that infringe the trademark

---

43 Article 3 of the EU TMD.
44 Articles 78–85 of the Trademark Act.
45 Article 38 of the Trademark Act.
46 This sanction was made stricter by the amendment in 2006, Act No. 55 of 2006.

Procedures for Obtaining a Trademark Right

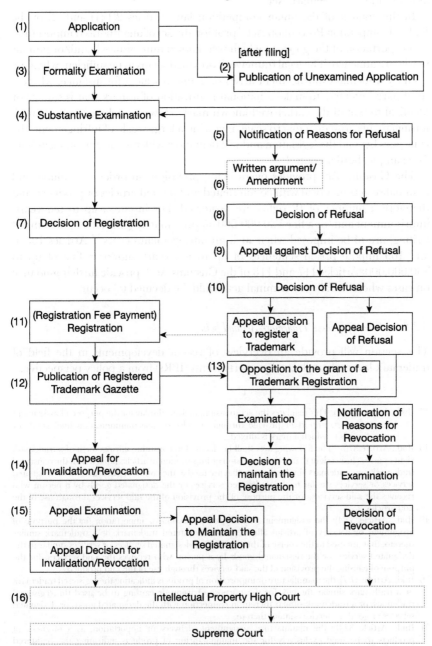

Figure 5.2 Procedures for obtaining a trademark right

proprietor's exclusive rights are conferred by Articles 2(3)(2),[47] 37(3),[48] (4),[49] (7)[50] and (8)[51] of the Trademark Act.

In the context of the unfair competition law, Articles 2(1)(1) and (2) of the Unfair Competition Prevention Act[52] prohibit the act of unauthorised importation and exportation of the goods to which well-known (unregistered) and/or famous marks are attached. The legal framework provided seems to be sufficient when the primary trademark infringement arises on a micro scale – for instance, where a third party attempts to make a national registration of a mark that is similar or identical to that of the earlier well-known mark. However, where the trademark infringements arise on a macro scale, involving a larger scale of infringement, the issue goes beyond the legislation and will demand a wider involvement, including, for example, border control.

The Customs Act provides overarching provisions in order to prohibit and criminalise acts that deal with counterfeited and pirated articles or products, and therefore a number of IP rights are protected. For instance, up to ten years' imprisonment and/or a fine ¥30,000,000 (approximately £164,000 at the time of writing) are to be imposed when such an infringement occurs.[53] Articles 108(4) and 109 impose prison sentences of up to ten years and/or a fine of up to ¥30,000,000; Articles 117 and 118 of the Customs Act[54] provide further guidance on cases where the alleged criminal act would (be deemed to) occur.

5.2.2.5 Modern Japanese Trademark Act and policy

This section will provide an overview of recent developments in the field of trademark law and intellectual property rights (IPRs) from a policy perspective.

---

47 Ibid., Article 2(3)(2). This regulates the act to assign, deliver, display for the purpose of assignment or delivery, export, import or provide through an electric telecommunication line, goods or packages of goods to which a mark is affixed.

48 Ibid., Article 37(3). The following acts shall be deemed to constitute infringement of a trademark right or an exclusive right to use: the possession or importation of articles affixed with the registered trademark or a trademark similar thereto, that are used in the course of the provision of designated services or services similar to the designated services or the designated goods by a person who receives the said services, for the purpose of the provision of the said services through use of the said articles.

49 Ibid., Article 37(4): the assignment, delivery, or possession or importation for the purpose of assignment or delivery of articles affixed with a registered trademark or a trademark similar thereto, that are used in the course of the provision of designated services or services similar to the designated services or the designated goods by a person who receives the said services, for the purpose of causing the provision of the said services through use of the said services.

50 Ibid., Article 37(7): the manufacture or importation of products indicating the registered trademark or a trademark similar thereto, for the purpose of using or causing to be used the registered trademark or a trademark similar thereto in connection with the designated goods or designated services or goods or services similar thereto.

51 Ibid., Article 37(8): the manufacture, assignment, delivery or importation, as a business, of products to be used exclusively for the manufacturing of products indicating the registered trademark or a trademark similar thereto.

52 Unfair Competition Prevention Act, Act No. 47 of 1993, last amended by Act No. 12 of 2012.

53 Articles 108(4) and 109, 117 and 118 of the Customs Act.

54 Trademark Act, Act No. 61 of 1954 last amended by Act No. 84 of 2014.

The IPRs and laws have become highly policy-driven and such a policy has had tremendous impact on determining the direction the Japanese legislatures and judiciary have taken.

This section can be divided into two parts: the first is pre-2002, and the second is post-2002 when the Koizumi Cabinet became the government in Japan.

The major legislation amendments that strengthened protection for *syuchi-syohyo* in trademark law, in particular, occurred between 1996 and 1999. In 1996, Article 4(1)(19) (known as the protection for *syuchi-syohyo*) was introduced to reflect the protection provided by Article 4(4)(a) of the EU TMD (and, correspondingly, Article 8(5) of the CTMR).[55] Article 4(1)(19) of the Japanese Trademark Act, and Articles 8(5) and 9(1)(c) of the CTMR may, as a consequence, offer the same level of protection, and '*syuchi-syohyo*' can be equated with 'trade mark of repute'. Accordingly, in 1999, important amendments were made to strengthen protection for *syuchi-syohyo*. There were two important developments for *syuchi-syohyo* protection: (i) amendment of the JPO Guidelines regarding Articles 4(1)(10), (11), (15) and (16); and (ii) the introduction of the principle that a *syohyo* application in which the applied-for mark is combined with a *syuchi-syohyo* shall be refused.

Post-2002, the re-establishment and reinforcement of Japan as a pro-IP nation was initiated during the Koizumi[56] Cabinet between 2001 and 2006 in order to enhance the international competitiveness of Japanese industries and revitalise the national economy.[57] In 2002, the Prime Minister at the time, Koizumi, called for a meeting to discuss plans for Japan to become a pro-IP nation. Four areas of focus were: (i) creation of IPs; (ii) protection of IPRs; (iii) utilisation of IPRs; and (iv) education and recruitment of human resources. As a consequence, the 'Intellectual Property Strategic Charter (*chitekizaisan taikou*)'[58] was established as part of the national IP policy (*chitekizaisan suishin keikaku*)[59] and an Intellectual Property Strategy Headquarters (*chiteki zaisan senryaku honbu*)[60] was formed. Following the Charter, the following tasks were completed: implementation of

55 See Ono, *Syohyo ho*, p. 448.
56 The former Japanese Prime Minster, Koizumi, announced that he would set as one of Japan's national goals the strategic protection and use of the results of research activities and creative endeavours as intellectual property so as to enhance the international competitiveness of Japanese industries'; see '2002 Policy Statement by Prime Minister Koizumi'. He also proposed an international treaty related to the prevention of counterfeiting products at the G8 summit in 2003.
57 The former Prime Minister Koizumi announced 'the Prime Minister's Decision; concerning the Strategic Council on Intellectual Property' in 2005.
58 This Charter was established in July 2002 by the Strategic Council on Intellectual Properties. It sets out the principles for IP protection in four main areas: creation, protection and utilisation of IP rights, and recruitment and education of the required professionals. So far, under this regime, law, Intellectual Property Strategy Headquarters and the Intellectual Property High Court have been created.
59 Article 23 of the Intellectual Property Basic Act sets out the fundamental framework for this. The fundamental IP policy, called 'the Intellectual Property Strategic Plan (hereinafter the Strategic Plan)', is set out annually by Intellectual Property Strategy Headquarters. In *kanji* script – 知的財産推進計画: *chitekizaisan suishin keikaku*.
60 In *kanji* script – 知的財産戦略本部: *chiteki zaisan senryaku honbu*. It was established in March 2003.

the Intellectual Property Basic Act;[61] establishment of the Intellectual Property Strategy Headquarters (*chitekizaisan senryaku honbu*);[62] and the establishment of the Intellectual Property High Court (*chiteki zaisan koto saiban syo*).[63] It is hoped that this proactive initiative will bring advantages throughout the IP sphere.[64]

In relation to trademark law, the following, *inter alia*, have been done:[65] (i) introduction of trademark registration for collective marks;[66] (ii) proposal and ratification of the Anti-Counterfeiting Trade Agreement (the ACTA).[67]

This new system allows registration of the collective trademarks – that is, the name of locally produced goods and/services such as Kobe Beef,[68] Omi Beef[69] or Atami Onsen[70] may be registered as a trademark only by the person(s) entitled to the registration. The concept of protection of regional collective marks is equivalent to that of geographical indications (GIs). However, the main difference between the former and latter is that the former is protected as a *sui generis* right, whilst the latter is not a *sui generis* right, but is protected as one registrable trademark, thereby granting an exclusive property right to the geographical indication in relation to the locally produced goods and/or services.

Since the major policy decision during the Koizumi Cabinet, both the Trademark Act and the Unfair Competition Prevention Act have been amended more or less on an annual basis, so as to reflect changes in the economy and society.[71]

---

61 Act No. 122 of 2002 last amended by Act No. 119 of 2003.
62 Article 24 of Intellectual Property Basic Act.
63 See Section 5.2.1.1.
64 For example, five main points of the Strategic Plan 2014 concerned: (i) consolidation of the employee's patent inventions; (ii) enforcement of the protection of trade secrets; (iii) support for small/medium enterprises and universities; (iv) promotion of the innovative content industry; (v) promotion and utilisation of archives. The full text of the Strategic Plan 2014 is available online at www.kantei.go.jp/jp/singi/titeki2/kettei/chizaikeikaku20140704e.pdf (accessed 6 November 2014).
65 A combination of geographical indication and generic term has been recognised as protectable registered trademark. There is a vast amount of literature concerning this improvement. See, for example, Y. Tamura, 'Chizai rikkokuka niokeru syohyo ho nokaisei to sono ritontekina goi – chiki dantai syohyo to kouri syohyo ho donyu no rinri tekibunseki', *Jurist*, 1326, 2007, 94. For a contrary argument, see T. Imamura, 'Chiikidantai syohyo seido to chiriteki hyoji no hogo – sonoyokisenu hogono kosaku', *Annual Industrial Property Law*, 30, 2006, 274–300, p. 274; Kukida, M, 'Chiiki Brand nituite fuseikyoso boshi ho no syuchi hyoji toshtie hogoga mitomerareta jisei – MIWA SOMEN jiken', *Intellectual Property Law and Policy Journal*, 7, 2005, 201–17. With the introduction of protection of geographical indications, Article 2(1)(13) of the Unfair Competition Prevention Act was added in 2006.
66 Article 7(2) of the Trademark Act.
67 See Section 5.3.1 for further discussion.
68 A word (a combination of *kanji* and *katakana* scripts) mark 神戸ビーフ (KOBE BIF: Kobe beef)' was granted as a registered trademark in 2007, registration number 5068214.
69 A word *kanji* mark '近江牛 (OUMI GYU: Oumi beef)' was granted as a registered trademark in 2003, registration number 5044958.
70 A word (a combination of *kanji* and *hiragana* scripts) mark '熱海温泉 (ATAMI ONSEN: Atami Spa)' was granted as a registered trademark in 2010, registration number 5377749.
71 See K. Doi, 'fuseikyoso boshi ho no kadai', *Jurist*, 1326, 2007, 106; and A. Gomi, 'Chizaigakusetu no ugoki', *IP Annual Report*, 1, 2008, 132–47.

Most recently, the JPO and METI have worked towards an amendment of the Trademark Act in order to include non-traditional signs (such as sound, movement, hologram, colour and position marks) as registrable trademarks.[72] Under the current trademark regime, given that non-traditional signs are not registrable, unlike the EU,[73] it is obvious that Japanese law[74] provides a narrower scope of protectable subject matter in comparison with the EU trade mark regime. Thus it is clear that the JPO intends to depart from the dominant traditional way of looking at the trademarks and transition will be made in the foreseeable future. However, whether such a transition is the way forward needs to be considered with caution.

5.3 Conceptualisation of 'well-known trade mark': the national level

The second part of this chapter undertakes the task of conceptualisation of the definitions of 'well-known trade mark' in the national law of Japan, given that the actual term 'well-known trade mark' is not employed as the language of the Japanese Act[75] (of course, English is not the official national language of Japan); the term 'syuchi-syohyo' is employed as analogous to 'well-known trade mark' and 'trade mark of repute'. Before such an exploration begins, some etymological analysis of the term 'syuchi-syohyo', which is employed in the Trademark Act, is of vital importance.[76]

周知商標 is the kanji for 'syuchi-syohyo'. Of this, the kanji symbols for 'well-known' are: '周知', which consists of two kanji symbols, 周 (Syu) and 知 (Chi). The first symbol 'Syu' has the implicit meaning of 'around, surrounding, or neighbourhood'[77] and the second symbol 'Chi' implies 'known or knowledge'.[78] Therefore, the kanji script '周知 (syuchi or well-known)' implies a scope of 'knownness' emphasising geographic factors rather than depth of knowledge; this is therefore a geographic-based notion. In addition, as was mentioned earlier, Japanese law makes the distinction between 'well-known ('周知', or 'syuchi')[79] and

---

72 Act No. 36 of 2014. The 2014 amendment recognises non-traditional marks as registrable trademarks. Act No. 36 of 2014 was promulgated in May 2014 and will come into force by the end of 2015.

73 See Chapter 4, Section 4.3.1.

74 Trademark Act, Act No. 127 of 1959 last amended by Act No. 84 of 2014.

75 It should be noted here, though, that Article 8(2)(c) imported 'well-known trade mark' cited in the Paris Convention. According to this Article, therefore, it can be speculated that the EU TMD provides protection to 'well-known trade mark' within the meaning of the Paris Convention. However, as was argued in Chapter 2, Section 2.3.1.1, and Chapter 3, Section 3.2.1, the utility of this seems doubtful, as the Paris Convention provides no comprehensive definition of 'well-known trade mark'.

76 The importance of Japanese etymology was indicated in Chapter 1, Section 1.10, and Chapter 2, Section 2.3.3.

77 Shinnmura, Koji-en, p. 1298.

78 Ibid.

79 Please note that the Japanese Trademark Act makes no reference to famous marks: only the term syuchi-syohyo is used.

'famous ('著名' or '*tyomei*').[80] The *kanji* script '周知 (*syuchi* or well-known)' implies that the scope of 'knownness' relies on geographic factors rather than depth of knowledge. It is in '著名' ('*tyomei*' or 'famous') that depth of 'well-knownness' is implied. Thus, a consideration of Japanese etymology indicates that a *syuchi-syohyo* would not have to be known nationwide,[81] whereas a *tyomei-syohyo*, or famous mark, would require a nationwide degree of 'fame' or 'well-knownness'. We will, of course, consider and examine the credibility of the assumption made from the etymological point with reference to the interpretation of the Act itself and its jurisprudence.

5.3.1 'Well-known trade mark' v syuchi-syohyo: are they the same?

The term '*syuchi-syohyo*' appears directly in Articles 4(1)(10) and (19) in the Japanese Trademark Act, although no explicit definition of '*syuchi-syohyo*' is provided (please note that there is also reference to '商標審査基準: *syohyo shinsa kijyun*',[82] which acts as a supplement to the Trademark Act and will be explored in Section 5.3.2 below).

Article 4(1)(10), which was introduced to be compatible with Article 6*bis* of the Paris Convention,[83] attempts to provide protection for unregistered well-known trademarks; this covers well-known trade mark protection principle 1.[84] Article 4(1)(19) was introduced in 1996 and came into force on 1 April 1997,[85] in order to provide stronger *syuchi-syohyo* protection[86] and to be consistent with Article 4(4)(a) of the EU TMD and Article 8(5) of the CTMR in the EU trade mark regime;[87] this therefore covers well-known trade mark protection principle 2. Moreover, the Japanese equivalent to Article 4(4)(a) of the EU TMD (Article 8(5) of the CTMR) is Article 4(1)(19) of the Japanese Trademark Act. Article 4(1) (10) is understood as equivalent to Article 6*bis* of the Paris Convention, and therefore it could be argued that it is equivalent to Article 4(2)(d) of the EU TMD and Article 8(2)(c) of the CTMR.

80　The implicit meanings here are very different. The *kanji* for 'famous' – '著名' – consists of two *kanji* symbols, 著 (*Cho*) and 名 (*Mei*). '*Cho*' implies 'remarkable, significant, or enormous', and '*Mei*' represents notions of name, repute or fame. Therefore, were '*Tyomei*' to be used in relation to a mark, this would imply that the mark in question was remarkably famous, a narrower concept than *syuchi-syohyo*. Japanese speakers automatically understand the differences between well-known and famous marks in Japanese.

81　Shinnmura, *Koji-en*, p. 1050.

82　This is known as the JPO Trademark Examination Guidelines (hereinafter the JPO Guidelines).

83　See Chapter 2, Section 2.3.1.1.

84　H. Goto, *Paris jyoyaku*, Tokyo: Hatsumei-kyokai, 2002.

85　For general information on this, see: JPO, *Kogyosyoyuken ho chikuzi kaisetsu*, Tokyo: Hatsumei-kyokai, 2006; M. Amino, *Syohyo-ho*, Tokyo: Yuhi-kaku, 2004; Y. Tamura, *Syohyo-ho*, Tokyo: Kobun-do, 2004, p. 433.

86　Also, it needs to be noted here that no developments at the academic or statutory level relating directly to well-known trademark protection have been reported since Article 4(1)(19) of the Trademark Act was added in 1996; thus a dearth of legal research can be expected.

87　Ono, *Syohyo ho*, p. 448.

Therefore, this gives the impression that, although the same term, '*syuchi-syohyo*', is employed in Article 4(1)(10) and (19), the interpretation of, '*syuchi-syohyo*' seems to be distinguished from Article 4(1)(10) to (19). In other words, '*syuchi-syohyo*' under Article 4(1)(10) to (19) is most likely to indicate the difference of '*syuchi*' (well-knownness). As was noted above, Article 4(1)(19) is designed to be equivalent to Article 4(4)(a) of the EU TMD, and to Article 8(5) of the CTMR; thus can it be inferred that the scope of protection afforded to 'trade mark of repute' and '*syuchi-syohyo*' should be the same. Or should these terms be interpreted as being synonymous? As evidenced below, the guidance provided as to the interpretation of '*syuchi-syohyo*' does, in fact, suggest that it differs from 'trade mark of repute'.

The Definition Model for the conceptualisation of 'trade mark' is illustrated in Figure 5.3 below.

In the above model, distinctiveness is submitted to be trade mark *concept*. In an ordinary trade mark sense, distinctiveness can be considered as the capacity to distinguish the goods or services of one undertaking from those of another undertaking.

In Chapter 3, one element of the Definition Model for conceptualisation of 'well-known trade mark' was slightly amended: well-known trade mark *concept* is changed from mere distinctiveness to acquired distinctiveness (Figure 5.4).

Thanks to the etymological approach, the conceptualisation of '*syuchi-syohyo*' has already shown progress:

Although the task of conceptualisation has not yet been completed in full, at this stage the *concept* of 'trade mark of repute' and of '*syuchi-syohyo*' can be distinguished: the former is 'reputation', putting equal emphasis on knowledge and geographical area, whilst the latter is '*syuchi*', where the emphasis is predominantly on geographical area.

Briefly, Japanese law divides 'well-known mark' in the purest Article 6*bis* sense into two: well-known (*syuchi-*) and famous (*tyomei-*) trademark (*syohyo*). Given that the conceptualisation of '*syuchi-syohyo*' has yet to be finalised, it is of interest to examine how the Japanese trademark law treats these two differently and whether 'trade mark of repute' and '*syuchi-syohyo*' indicate the same.

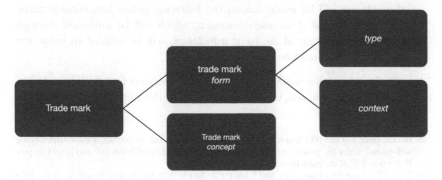

Figure 5.3 The Definition Model

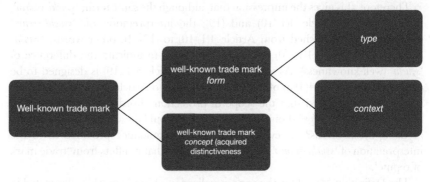

Figure 5.4 The Definition Model – well-known trade mark

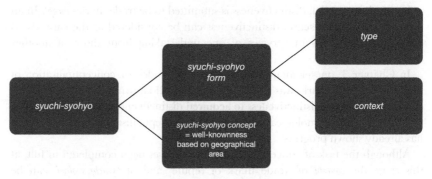

Figure 5.5 Application of the Definition Model – Japan (Stage 1)

Unlike the CTM Guidelines, despite the lack of a clear conceptual definition of '*syuchi-syohyo*', the JPO Guidelines[88] do, in fact, provide criteria to assess whether or not a mark obtaining 'its distinctiveness'[89] leads to well-knownness.

The JPO Guidelines for Article 3(2) provides as follows:

> 3. (1) Judgment as to whether a trademark has come to gain its *distinctiveness* through use will be made, taking the following points into consideration. *Specifically, the level of consumers' awareness,* which will be estimated through a quantitative grasp of *the use of a trademark,* will be utilized to judge the distinctiveness of a trademark.
>
> (i) A trademark actually in use and goods or services for which it is used;
> (ii) The start of its use, the length of its use, or the area where it is used;

---

88 In fact, Item 3 of the JPO Guideline for Article 4(1)(10) sets out 'to provide a trademark's being well-known under the provision of this paragraph, the provisions of Items 2(1) and (2) of Chapter II (Section 3(2)) of the guidelines apply mutatis mutandis'.
89 Item 3(1) of the JPO Guidelines and Chapter 2: Article 3(2) Articles 2(3)(1) and (2) of the JPO Guidelines. Item 3 of Chapter III: Article 4(1)(3) Part 8: Article 4(1)(10) of the JPO Guidelines.

(iii) The volume of production, certification or delivery and a scale of business (number of stores, an area of business, an amount of sales, etc.);

(iv) The method, frequency and contents of advertising;

(v) The number of appearances in general newspapers, trade journals, magazines and the internet, and contents thereof;

(vi) The outcome of the questionnaire regarding consumers' awareness of the trademark. [Emphasis added]

So the *concept* of '*syuchi-syohyo*' being distinctiveness needs to be evidenced. However, distinctiveness might well be more related to geographical extent; whilst, according to Item 3 noted above, the *level of consumers' awareness* – that is, the recognition or knowledge of the mark – seems to be important. This, it is submitted, is where a key inconsistency in the Japanese approach is to be found.

A brief observation relating to Item 3 of the JPO Guidelines for Article 3(2) will now be set out. This Item is followed up by Items 3(2)(i)–(viii) of the JPO Guidelines for Article 3(2).[90] Note that there is a similarity between the criteria set out in Items 3(1)(1)–(6) and Article 2(1) and those of the WIPO Recommendation.

The first factor is related to one of the *preconditions* of a (well-known) trade mark – *commercial use*. Again, a strong emphasis on commercial use can be confirmed.[91] The second factor is very similar to Article 2(1)(b)(2) of the WIPO Recommendation; thus it is submitted that temporal and geographic criteria are proxies for distinctiveness. The third factor is also similar to Article 2(1)(b)(3) of the WIPO Recommendation, and it is submitted that these might well indicate distinctiveness acquired through use. The fourth and the fifth factors can be said to be similar to Article 2(1)(b)(3) of the WIPO Recommendation, and it is submitted that these are proxies for distinctiveness. The last factor might be considered to be similar to Article 2(1)(b)(1) of the WIPO Recommendation; recognition and awareness of the mark are synonyms of distinctiveness (*concept*).

First, these criteria show an emphasis on trademark use (*precondition*). Second, it is held that the earlier the mark starts being used, and the longer the mark is used, the more well known the mark becomes to consumers. Third, the wider geographically a mark is used, the more well known a mark tends to be, although the nature of a trademark shall be taken into consideration. Fourth, the more the products or services are sold, the better the understanding of the products to

90 See Appendix 5. Items 3(2)(i)–(viii) of Chapter II: Article 3(2) of the JPO Guidelines. These can be outlined as follows: that the above *facts* need to be proved *by a method using evidence* such as (i) written publications; (ii) invoices, delivery slips, order slips, bills, receipts, account books, pamphlets, etc.; (iii) evidence of marks being in actual use; (iv) evidence of marks being advertised by an advertisement agency; broadcasting agency, publisher or printer; (v) a certificate by a trade association, business partners or consumers; (vi) a certificate by a public organisation; (vii) tangible publications that show the mark being well-known and advertised; and (viii) questionnaires to show the knowledge of consumers. This is an unofficial translation by the author and is introduced to avoid terminological confusion to readers.

91 See Chapter 2, Section 2.3.3.

which a trademark is attached. Finally, the more a mark is promoted and advertised, the more consumers are aware of the mark.[92]

The following critiques are submitted. First, the criteria to assess whether or not a mark is well known are provided without '*syuchi-syohyo*' being conceptually and comprehensively defined. What seems more bewildering is that distinctiveness of a mark (*shikibetsu-ryoku*[93])[94] will be assessed in order to prove whether the mark is well known or not. This begs the question why the JPO Guidelines do not simply use 'highly distinctive mark' instead of '*syuchi-syohyo*'. Thus, again, the criteria for assessing the '*syuchi*' seem rather inarticulate and there remains a question of how applicable these are in assessing '*syuchi-syohyo*'.

Second, the assessment is determined case by case, based on a bundle of factual evidence, which causes uncertainty and inconsistency in law. For example, the assessment of a mark being distinctive is examined on the grounds of factual evidence: (i) a mark is widely well known in the area; (ii) a mark is well known amongst relevant consumers. Furthermore, in a case of assessing '*syuchi-syohyo*', it is also explicitly stated that the factors listed in the Guidelines are not always overriding factors; thus, other considerations may be taken into account in assessing '*syuchi-syohyo*'.[95] Therefore, yet again, Japan takes the view that '*syuchi-syohyo*' is not something to be defined, but something to be assessed/determined.

To challenge this current approach, it has been argued that it is necessary to conceptualise the definition of 'well-known trade mark' at the international level, on the ground that this would enable a mutual understanding of 'well-known trade mark' throughout different jurisdictions. In consequence, protection of 'well-known trade mark' is likely to become flexible and thus controllable, and will therefore become intuitively consistent.

Also, taking into account all the fact-based criteria above, it is plain that '*syuchi-syohyo*' protection in Japan is *a matter of fact*, not a matter of law.[96] Thus, *factual evidence* is required in order to prove the degree of well-knownness or fame, although the degree of well-knownness is expected to vary case by case due to individual factual evidence and considerations.[97]

5.3.2 The Japanese Trademark Act

Two main Articles that are relevant to well-known trade mark protection are Articles 4(1)(10)[98] and 4(1)(19). Both Articles concern the grounds for refusal of

---

92 See JPO, *Kogyosyoyuken ho chikuzi kaisetsu*.
93 The Japanese term for 'distinctiveness' is '識別性 (*shikibetsu-ryoku*)'. The first two parts of the *kanji* symbols imply 'distinctive'; the last part is equivalent to '-ness'.
94 See Item 3(1) of Chapter II: Article 3(2) of the JPO Guidelines.
95 *Morite*, Tokyo High Court, Heisei13, (Ne) 5748go, sokuho 325–10758.
96 Daihan, syo3nen 3gatus 10ka, (O) 1131, Daihan, syo4nen 11gatsu 30nichi, syo 4nen, (O) 850. Amino, *Syohyo-ho*, p. 351. The same opinion was shared by Mostert, 'When is a Mark "Well-Known"?', p. 377.
97 Japanese scholars seem to be in favour of the case-by-case approach. See, for example, Amino, *Syohyo-ho*; Y. Harima, *Syohyo ho – Riron to Zissai*, Tokyo: Roppo syuppan-sha, 1982; S. Manada, 'Tyomei hyoshiki no mondai no syoso', *Journal of Kanazawa University*, 13, 1967, 2–54, p. 3.

registration (note that there is no distinction between the absolute and the relative grounds for refusal in the EU context) and work as the grounds for refusal of registration of *syohyo*, opposition of the trademark registration[99] and reasoning for invalidation. There are no articles mirroring Article 5(2) of the EU TMD or Article 9(1)(c) of the CTMR, whilst Article 25 of the Act could be considered to have a similar effect to Article 5(2) of the EU TMD or Article 9(1)(c) of the CTMR. (Comparative analysis of these articles will be developed in Chapter 6.)

Article 4(1)(10) is important, since it establishes protection for *syuchi-syohyo* irrespective of registration (well-known trade mark protection principle 1), and Article 4(1)(19) is important, since this sets out occasions where a *syuchi-syohyo* is protected against a third party's registration, which was done with unlawful purposes[100] (well-known trade mark protection principle 2).

98 Article 4(1)(10) of the Japanese Trademark Act states that a mark cannot be registered regardless of Article 3. See Article 3 of the Japanese Trademark Act in full: 'Art. 3. (Requirements for trademark registration) (1) Any trademark to be used in connection with goods or services pertaining to the business of an applicant may be registered, unless the trademark: (i) consists solely of a mark indicating, in a common manner, the common name of the goods or services; (ii) is customarily used in connection with the goods or services; (iii) consists solely of a mark indicating, in a common manner, in the case of goods, the place of origin, place of sale, quality, raw materials, efficacy, intended purpose, quantity, shape (including shape of packages), price, the method or time of production or use, or, in the case of services, the location of provision, quality, articles to be used in such provision, efficacy, intended purpose, quantity, modes, price or method or time of provision; (iv) consists solely of a mark indicating, in a common manner, a common surname or name of a juridical person; (v) consists solely of a very simple and common mark; or (vi) in addition to those listed in each of the preceding items, a trademark by which consumers are not able to recognize the goods or services as those pertaining to a business of a particular person. (2) Notwithstanding the preceding paragraph, a trademark that falls under any of items (iii) to (v) of the preceding paragraph may be registered if, as a result of the use of the trademark, consumers are able to recognize the goods or services as those pertaining to a business of a particular person.'

99 Ibid., Article 43(2). This Article is known as Opposition to registration and states: 'Any person may file with the Commissioner of the Patent Office an opposition to registration within two months from the date of publication of the bulletin containing the trademark, on the grounds that the trademark registration falls under any of the following items. In this case, an opposition to registration may be filed for each of designated goods or designated services if the relevant trademark has been registered in connection with two or more designated goods or designated services: (i) where the trademark registration has been made in violation of Articles 3, 4 (1), 7–2(1), 8(1), 8(2), 8(5), 51(2) (including its mutatis mutandis application under Articles 52–2(2)), 53(2) of this Act or Article 25 of the Patent Act as applied mutatis mutandis under Articles 77(3) of this Act; and (ii) where the trademark registration has been made in violation of a treaty.' Ibid., Article 46(1)(1) in full: 'Art.46(1) Where a trademark registration falls under any of the following items, a request for a trial for invalidation of the trademark registration may be filed. In this case, where the trademark has been registered in connection with two or more designated goods or designated services, a request may be filed for each of the designated goods or designated services: (1) where the trademark registration has been made in violation of Articles 3, 4 (1), 7–2(1), 8(1), 8(2), 8(5), 51(2) (including cases where it is applied mutatis mutandis pursuant to Article 52–2(2)), 53(2) of this Act or Article 25 of the Patent Act as applied mutatis mutandis pursuant to Article 77(3) of this Act.'

100 For instance, Article 4(1)(19) of the Japanese Trademark Act.

Articles 4(1)(10)[101] and 4(1)(19) are set out in full:

Article 4 (Unregistrable trademarks)

(1) Notwithstanding the preceding Article, no trademark shall be registered if the trademark:

   (10) is identical with, or similar to, another person's *trademark which is well known among consumers as that indicating goods or services in connection with the person's business,* if such a trademark is used in connection with such goods or services or goods or services similar thereto;

   (19) is identical with, or similar to, *a trademark which is well known among consumers in Japan or abroad as that indicating goods or services pertaining to a business of another person,* if such trademark *is used for unfair purposes* (referring to the purpose of *gaining unfair profits, the purpose of causing damage to the other person,* or any other unfair purposes, the same shall apply hereinafter) (except those provided for in each of the preceding items). [Emphasis added]

First and foremost, there is no conceptual definition of '*syuchi-syohyo*' in the Japanese Trademark Act, and therefore we will now attempt to conceptualise the definition of '*syuchi-syohyo*', utilising the reformulated Definition Model (Figure 5.4). First, the '*syuchi-syohyo*' *form* (*type* and *context*) will be examined. Very little guidance for '*syuchi-syohyo*' *form* seems to have been provided. Perhaps one element of *type* in *syuchi-syohyo form* that could be added here is that it is an unregistered mark. Article 4(1)(10) and (19) can be read so that trade mark *type* in *form* of '*syuchi-syohyo*' can include *syohyo*, which is narrowly defined (see Article 2).[102] Further,

---

101 Article 4(1)(10) of the Japanese Trademark Act states that a mark cannot be registered regardless of Article 3. See Article 3 of the Japanese Trademark Act in full: 'Art. 3.(Requirements for trademark registration) (1) Any trademark to be used in connection with goods or services pertaining to the business of an applicant may be registered, unless the trademark: (i) consists solely of a mark indicating, in a common manner, the common name of the goods or services; (ii) is customarily used in connection with the goods or services; (iii) consists solely of a mark indicating, in a common manner, in the case of goods, the place of origin, place of sale, quality, raw materials, efficacy, intended purpose, quantity, shape (including shape of packages), price, the method or time of production or use, or, in the case of services, the location of provision, quality, articles to be used in such provision, efficacy, intended purpose, quantity, modes, price or method or time of provision; (iv) consists solely of a mark indicating, in a common manner, a common surname or name of a juridical person; (v) consists solely of a very simple and common mark; or (vi) in addition to those listed in each of the preceding items, a trademark by which consumers are not able to recognize the goods or services as those pertaining to a business of a particular person. (2) Notwithstanding the preceding paragraph, a trademark that falls under any of items (iii) to (v) of the preceding paragraph may be registered if, as a result of the use of the trademark, consumers are able to recognize the goods or services as those pertaining to a business of a particular person.'

102 Having said that, expansion of the protectable trademark subject matter, such as non-traditional trademarks, is very much under discussion. The reader might be interested to know that there is a (limited) Japanese literature relating to the protection of the non-traditional trademarks, namely: R. Kojima, 'Coca-Cola jiken ni mirareru rittai syohyo no hogo – tyomei na mojisyohyoga shiyousareta housoyoki jitai no dedokoro shikibetsu nouryoku kakutoku no annketo tyosa', *CIPIC Journal*, 6, 2008, 209; F. Mityuno, 'Syohyo no rittaiteki keijo nomi karanaru syohyo no torokuyoken handan no kijyun noyukue – mini magligt hanketsukou', *Chizai kanri*, 58, 2008, 191.

syuchi-syohyo context in *form* is essentially (therefore) the same as that found in relation to *syohyo* in Article 2(1) of the Japanese Trademark Act.

Moving on to the *concept* of '*syuchi-syohyo*', this is not explicitly provided either, although some guidance can be inferred from '*syohyo*' *concept* set out in Article 2 of the Japanese Trademark Act (i.e. – distinctiveness[103]), and what might be termed 'back-up legal requirements' within the Trademark Acts – that is, Articles 3(1), (2), (3), (4), (5), 3(2), which all are related to 'distinctiveness'.

Furthermore, how *syohyo concept* might be used to infer that of *syuchi-syohyo* could be made clearer by reference to Article 4(1)(10) and Article 4(1)(19). The former describes 'a person's trademark which is *well known among consumers* as that indicating goods or services in connection with the person's business'. The latter also describes '*a trademark which is well known among consumers in Japan or abroad as that indicating goods or services pertaining to a business of another person*'. Thus, *syuchi-syohyo concept* might indicate a higher level of geographically oriented (as opposed to knowledge-based) distinctiveness amongst consumers. In addition, 'distinctiveness' is implicit in the *kanji* scripts for '*syohyo*', and this term forms part of the phrase '*syuchi-syohyo*'. The *concept* of '*syuchi-syohyo*' is *syuchi*, argued to be acquired distinctiveness, emphasising the degree of geographical area in which the mark is known. Therefore, a conclusion can be drawn that *concept* of '*syuchi-syohyo*' can be: '*syuchi*, which constitutes a high level of *geographically defined* distinctiveness amongst consumers of *syohyo* used in relation to goods or services in connection with the business of the trademark right holder in Japan or abroad'.

Considering the '*syuchi-syohyo*' *concept* further, it may be observed that the emphasis in Article 4(1)(19) (and 64) on the geographical scope of knowledge might be a reflection of a theme-of-origin-style considerations in the Japanese provisions relating to *syuchi-syohyo*.[104] Consequently, in relation to the Definition Model, it could then also be argued that the distinctive nature of '*syuchi-syohyo*' (which clearly falls within *concept*) might be 'highly distinctive in the sense that it functions as an indication of origin'. However, this is not convincing and it is submitted that mere 'indication of origin' reasoning must be insufficient here; otherwise, the *concept* of '*syuchi-syohyo*' would, in this respect, be no different from that of '*syohyo*'.

Finally, in relation to the *preconditions* of the Definition Model, there is no reference to *graphic representation* or *commercial use* in Articles 4(1)(10) or (19). Although not noted in relation to '*syuchi-syohyo*', in relation to a '*syohyo*' it is stated in Article 2 that there must be business use and, it has already been submitted (see Chapter 2, Section 2.3.3), there is indeed a very strong emphasis on business

103 See Chapter 2, Section 2.3.3.
104 Such emphasis is, it is submitted, not limited to the definition of *syuchi-syohyo* and/or to the registration of the same (see Article 4(1) of the Japanese Trademark Act, and see Chapter 2, Section 2.3.3). 'Indication of origin' notions infuse the whole of the Japanese trademark law, it is submitted, with the emphasis on business use made in the Act. In the context of *syuchi-syohyo* in particular, it is provided that where such marks are no longer used in the course of trade, then this has implications for infringement proceedings (ibid., Article 25).

use in the Act. It is considered that 'business use' and 'commercial use' can be regarded as being synonymous. Hence, the *precondition* 'commercial use' is, it is submitted, explicitly present in the Japanese law and is implicitly present for *syuchi-syohyo*. Graphic representation is not a term explicitly seen in the Act, but, from an etymological viewpoint, this is considered to be implicit in the term '*syohyo*', as previously argued in Chapter 2, Section 2.3.3. Hence, both *preconditions* are present.

Nevertheless, in the absence of a detailed statutory definition of '*syuchi-syohyo*', the legal definition[105] and the conceptualisation of the same, using the Definition Model, have made progress, in particular the *concept* of '*syuchi-syohyo*'. This constitutes a high level of *geographically defined* distinctiveness amongst consumers of *syohyo* used in relation to goods or services in connection with the business of the trademark right holder in Japan or abroad.

We shall now examine the JPO Guidelines for further guidance as to how '*syuchi-syohyo*' can be defined and conceptualised with reference to the Definition Model.

5.3.3 The JPO Guidelines

As noted in Section 5.3.1, the JPO Guidelines supplement the Trademark Act (and, indeed, they do so in both a legal and practical context). An exploration of the JPO Guidelines[106] is therefore a reasonable next step in critically considering the definition of '*syuchi-syohyo*'.

Article 4(1)(10) of the Japanese Trademark Act is explained in Items 1, 2 and 3 of Chapter III: Article 4(1)(3) Part 8: Article 4(1)(10) (hereinafter the JPO Guidelines for Article 4(1)(10))[107] and sets out:

1. Trademark which is well known among consumers as prescribed in this paragraph includes not only a trademark which is widely recognized among end consumers but also a trademark which is widely recognized among traders in the industry and also includes not only a trademark which is known throughout the country but also a trademark which is widely recognized in a certain area.[108]

2. A trademark to be cited for the application of the provision of this paragraph needs to be widely recognized among domestic consumers in Japan at a time when an application for the registration of a trademark is filed (refer to Article 4(3)).[109]

---

105 See Amino, *Syohyo-ho*, p. 379.
106 The 'JPO Examination Guidelines for Trademarks' are produced and published to ensure standardisation and uniformity in the examination of trademark applications at the JPO. The Guidelines were updated in 2007. The JPO Guidelines are intended to ensure a consistent standard of assessment made by the JPO, and to provide a fair and transparent account of the trademark system by revealing the Examination Guidelines to the public.
107 See Appendix 3.
108 Item 1 of the JPO Guideline for Article 4(1)(10).
109 Item 2 of the JPO Guidelines for Article 4(1)(10).

Regarding '*syuchi-syohyo*' *type* in *form*, it is disappointing that the Guidelines do not add much. On the contrary, *context* in *form* of '*syuchi-syohyo*' is said to include foreign marks, so here the Guidelines explicitly expand the scope of '*syuchi-syohyo*'. In relation to the *concept* of '*syuchi-syohyo*', this receives more detailed (if implicit) treatment in the Guidelines: (i) a mark that is widely known amongst Japanese end-consumers or relevant traders;[110] (ii) a mark that is known throughout Japan or in a particular area;[111] (iii) a mark that is well known in several foreign countries (full consideration shall be taken into account in assessing foreign '*syuchi-syohyo*').[112]

The provisions above clarify that the *concept* of '*syuchi-syohyo*' is related to the geographical extent of distinctiveness,[113] with emphasis on marks needing to be *geographically* well known.[114] Moreover, the guidance as to consumers seems to be more instructive than that in the Act; end consumers and relevant traders are included in the scope of 'consumers'.

Now, we shall move our attention to Item 3:

> 3.   To prove a trademark's being well known under the provision of this paragraph, the provisions of Items 3(1) and (2) of Chapter II (Article 3(2)) of the Guidelines apply *mutatis mutandis*.

Item 3 asks us to return to Article 3(2) of the Guidelines in order to assess the *syuchi-syohyo*. We will now therefore need to make our way to Items 3(1) and (2) of Chapter II.

Before that, we shall also look at provisions relating to Article 4(1)(19), where well-known trade mark protection principle 2 is established. At this stage, the main focus is on conceptualisation of '*syuchi-syohyo*', and therefore, the conceptual definition of '*syuchi-syohyo*' will be at issue.

Article 4(1)(19) of the Japanese Trademark Act is explained in Chapter III: Part 16: Article 4(1)(19) (hereinafter the JPO Guidelines for Article 4(1)(19)).[115] The relevant provisions for conceptualisation of *syuchi-syohyo* are:

> 2.   Trademarks 'well known among consumers' as stipulated in this paragraph not only mean trademarks widely known to final users but include trademarks widely recognized among traders.

---

110 Items 1 and 2 of the JPO Guidelines for Article 4(1)(10). See Appendix 3.
111 Ibid., Item 2.
112 Ibid., Items 5 and 6.
113 The final version of *concept* of '*syuchi-syohyo*' can thus be stated as follows: '*Syuchi-syohyo*' comprises *syuchi*, which constitutes a high level of geographically defined distinctiveness. National '*syuchi-syohyo*' must be found amongst consumers of *syohyo* throughout or in a particular part of Japan (and traders in Japanese industry), being used and known in relation to goods or services in connection with the business of the trademark right holder in Japan.
114 This geographically oriented *concept* of '*syuchi-syohyo*' can be seen also from Japanese cases in Section 5.3.4.
115 See Appendix 3.

3. Trademarks 'well known among consumers . . . abroad' as stipulated in this paragraph need to be well known in the countries they originate from but not necessarily need to be well known in multiple countries outside those countries. Nor do they in Japan.

6. Judgment of whether the trademark is well known or not apply *mutatis mutandis* Article 3(8) (Article 4(1)(x)) of the guidelines.

According to Items 2 and 3 of the JPO Guideline for Article 4(1)(19), although few additional points to define what constitutes '*syuchi-syohyo*' are provided,[116] a brief point can be made: (i) a '*syuchi-syohyo*' contains a mark which is well known not only in Japan, but in a number of foreign countries;[117] and (ii) a '*syuchi-syohyo*' includes a mark that is widely recognised by relevant traders.[118] Nonetheless, no further guidance concerning *concept* of '*syuchi-syohyo*' is given: here '*syuchi-syohyo*' *concept* (distinctiveness) again appears to focus very much on geographical extent.[119] Therefore, the conclusion made earlier that '*syuchi-syohyo*' *concept* seems to be geographically defined seems reasonably accurate.

Item 6 guides us back to Article 3(8) (Article 4(1)(10)) of the guidelines for the assessment of *syuchi-syohyo*. Article 3(8) (Article 4(1)(10)) then asks us to go to Item 3(1) and (2) of Chapter II (Article 3(2)), where the assessment criteria of *syuchi-syohyo* are clearly listed. We will now pay close attention to Items 3(1) and (2), searching for a number of hints in order to aid conceptualisation of *syuchi-syohyo*.

As described earlier, both Items 3(1) and (2) provide criteria to assess whether the mark has obtained distinctiveness through use. The following factors shall be taken into consideration to determine whether a mark has obtained distinctiveness through use amongst consumers, which can be proved by quantitative evidence:[120]

(i)   actual use of the mark;
(ii) extent, degree, duration, geographical area of the use of the mark;
(iii) market share;
(iv) degree, duration and extent of promoting the mark;
(v)   evidence of advertising and promoting the mark in the press and media;
(vi) market surveys assessing the degree of consumer awareness.

---

116 It should be remembered here that Article 4(1)(19) functions as relative grounds for refusal for third parties to the registration of a mark that is taking an unfair advantage of or is detrimental to with unfair purposes. See Article 4(1)(19) of the Japanese Trademark Act and the supplementary items of the JPO Guidelines.
117 Item 2 of Chapter III: Article 4(1)(3) Part 17: Article 4(1)(19) of the JPO Guidelines. See Appendix 4.
118 Ibid., Item 3.
119 Item 6 of Chapter III: Article 4(1)(3) Part 17: Article 4(1)(19) of the JPO Guidelines.
120 However, due consideration should be given to the objectivity of the questionnaire with respect to the conductor, method and respondents.

Furthermore, the above shall be submitted with evidence such as: (i) printed matter (newspaper clippings, magazines, catalogues, leaflets, etc.) carrying advertisements, public notices; (ii) financial statements, such as invoices, delivery slips, order slips, bills, receipts, account books, pamphlets; (iii) photographs showing the use of a trademark; (iv) a certificate issued by an advertisement agency, broadcasting agency, publisher or printer; (v) a certificate issued by a trade association, fellow traders or consumers; (vi) a certificate issued by a public organisation (e.g. the State, a local public entity, a foreign embassy in Japan, a Chamber of Commerce and Industry); (vii) articles in general newspapers, trade journals, magazines and on the internet; (viii) outcome reports of questionnaires intended for consumers regarding awareness of the trademark.

To summarise, irrespective of efficacy, an exhaustive list of factors to be considered is plainly provided herein. Note that the aim of the list is to assess whether the mark has acquired distinctiveness through use, and the list is not to conceptualise the *syuchi-syohyo*; therefore, no assistance is provided in conceptualising '*syuchi-syohyo*'.

Despite the lack of a complete conceptualisation, what is of utmost interest is that the Japanese trademark regime equates the assessment of *syuchi-syohyo* with that of the mark acquiring distinctiveness through use. This clearly proves the assumption that *concept* of 'well-known trade mark' is '*syuchi*' and this is acquired distinctiveness through use. This can be regarded as the first step to conceptualisation of *syuchi-syohyo*, providing that 'well-known trade mark' is '*syuchi-syohyo*', the concept of '*syuchi-syohyo*' is acquired distinctiveness through use, and the focus is on 'use'. Acquired distinctiveness can only be established through use. As a result, the Definition Model has now been transformed as shown in Figure 5.6.

In the subsequent section, a number of cases will be examined in order to seek further guidance on the conceptualisation of '*syuchi-syohyo*'. Although the cases address more than one issue, the main focus will remain the conceptualisation of the definition of *syuchi-syohyo*.

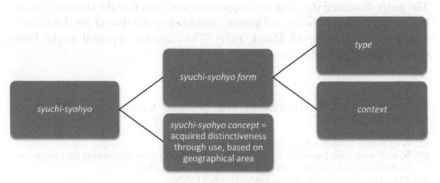

Figure 5.6 Application of the Definition Model – Japan (Stage 2)

5.3.4 Jurisprudence

So far, the conceptualisation of '*syuchi-syohyo*' is the (un)registered trade mark that is well known amongst Japanese end consumers or relevant traders[121] throughout Japan or in a particular area[122] or in several foreign countries.[123] The *concept* of '*syuchi-syohyo*' – *syuchi* (well-knownness) – is argued to be the geographically defined *concept*, as opposed to the knowledge-based.[124] We shall now continue the endeavour of conceptualising the definition of *syuchi-syohyo* by referring to the judicial interpretation[125] of the Act and the JPO Guidelines.

DDC[126] is the first case to be introduced here. This case is known as the very first case that dealt actively with providing guidance as to the geographic extent of 'well-knownness (*syuchi*)' under Article 4(1)(10).[127] The action for revocation of the UCC's later registration of the mark 'DCC' was made by Daiwa Coffee, which holds an unregistered and allegedly not well-known mark, 'DCC'. Daiwa Coffee alleged that by the time of UCC's registrations of 'DCC', which is similar to the earlier mark, the earlier unregistered mark 'DCC' used by the Daiwa Coffee was well known, and therefore UCC's registration should be refused in Article 4(1)(10).

In order to prove the earlier mark was well known, the following were submitted:

(i) The geographical extent of the mark being in trade: in the 1970s, the claimant's trading area was around the Setonaikai area, including 470 cafés in Hiroshima, 40 in Okayama, 15 in Yamaguchi.

(ii) The market share: the claimant had business and trading relations with 30 per cent of the existing coffee shops around the trading area, and became the second or third most dominant company in the relevant trade sector.

(iii) The degree and extent of promoting and advertising the mark: the claimant's mark 'DDC' had been used in, and attached to, for instance, the package of the coffee, the uniforms of employees, business cards and company's vehicles, and also advertisements on billboards, in newspapers and magazines since about 1936. The monthly cost of such advertising was more than ¥300,000 (equivalent to £1,500), which showed a strong commitment to expanding their business.

The judge dismissed the claimant's opposition and held that the claimant's mark had not amounted to being well known (*syuchi*) before the date of the defendant's trademark application (18 March 1971). The claimant appealed to the High Court, which upheld the district court's decision.

---

121 Items 1 and 2 of the JPO Guidelines for Article 4(1)(10). See Appendix 3.
122 Ibid., Item 2.
123 Ibid., Items 5 and 6.
124 See Chapter 4, Section 4.3.4.
125 Note that although Japan is a civil law jurisdiction, the principle of precedent in the case law can be applied in order for the courts to be consistent with each other.
126 *DDC.* Tokyo High Court, Showa 57nen (Gyo Ke) 110go.
127 See the case note of this case. T. Matsumoto, 'DDC jiken', *Jurist*, 11, 2007, 26–7.

The court mentioned that a relationship between a well-known mark and the goods or services to which such a mark is attached needs to be taken into consideration:

> [C]offee beans, and coffee as a beverage are commonly and widely consumed by the general public, and it is difficult to develop locality in such a common product. Therefore, the mark that is attached to common and widely consumed goods or services in Japan needs to be recognised in the significant area, by the relevant major traders throughout Japan or to be well known more than 50 per cent of the relevant traders in at least one prefecture or a few neighbouring prefectures.

The court went on to say:

> Although the claimant's mark 'DCC' has obtained recognition from a significant part of relevant trading circles as the claimant's indication of their trade origin, through use of the mark 'DDC', the claimant's mark is known *only* 30% of the main trading circles . . . the percentage of the claimant's mark being known in neighbouring area, such as Yamaguchi and Okayama, is anticipated to be less than 30%; therefore the claimant's mark shall not be qualified as a well-known mark under Article 4(1)(10).[128]

The court held that, in relation to products (commodities) that are consumed daily, in order for the mark to qualify for protection under Article 4(1)(10) it is required to be significantly well known at least among relevant traders throughout Japan, or the mark is required to be well known at least more than 50 per cent of the relevant prefecture or neighbouring prefectures.

The main point of this case was to examine to what extent geographical well-knownness (*syuchi*) is required in order to grant protection under Article 4(1)(10). For a commodity (coffee beans and coffee) available and used throughout Japan, if the associated *syohyo* was recognised by *almost 50 per cent of the relevant traders* and if the *syohyo* was well known in at least *a few prefectures* in which that business exists (in this particular case, it was known in three prefectures),[129] it is a *syuchi-syohyo*. In this case, '*syuchi-syohyo*' is required to be well known by nearly 50 per cent of the relevant public in three different prefectures (a 'prefecture' is approximately equivalent to an English 'county'). In other words, a significantly higher level of well-knownness (*syuchi*) in both recognition of the mark by the relevant public and wider geographic area of the mark is required. The court seems to put more weight on the geographical extent and degree of recognition of the marks than on the relevant sector of the public. Therefore, this case gives the impression that, in

---

128 Unofficial English translation of this judgment is introduced here due to the lack of an official English translation.
129 *DCCII*. Tokyo High Court, Shyowa 58nen, 6gatsu 16nichi, Mitaisyu 15kan 2go, p. 51.

order to qualify for Article 4(1)(10), a mark needs to be well known in a significant geographic area by a substantial part of the relevant public (or relevant traders). At this stage, the Japanese jurisdiction sets a higher standard for unregistered, allegedly well-known trademark owners to enjoy their well-known status.

In *Iwate haru imidori* [Iwate Spring Green],[130] the locality of the products which bore the mark was taken into consideration in assessing the extent of geographic area that the mark required to qualify as *syuchi-syohyo* under Article 4(1)(10).

The claimant, who was a proprietor of the allegedly well-known collective mark, 'いわて春みどり [Iwate haru midori]' for cabbages originating from Iwate prefecture, opposed the later trade mark registration '岩手春みどり [Iwate haru midori]' for the same category of goods. The court held for the claimant and the claimant's mark was recognised as a *syuchi-syohyo*. The court held that the 'end consumers' under Article 4(1)(10) shall include not only the consumers but also the relevant traders (wholesalers, intermediate agencies and retailers), taking into consideration the circumstances of the trading. Therefore, this case indicates that, in order for the mark to be *syuchi* to both end consumers and the relevant traders, a higher degree of well-knownness is required.

However, in *Shinagawa Inter City*,[131] the court took a different direction for Article 4(1)(10). The estate agency registered a service mark 'Shinagawa Inter City 'for issuing top-up (pre-paid) cards. The request for the revocation of such a trademark registration was made on the grounds that the earlier marks, *inter alia*, 'Inter City' was already well known as an indication of the claimant's estate agent business.

The court held that the 'mark needs to be substantially well-known throughout Japan, or well-known in the substantial number of prefectures in substantially relevant traders or consumers'.[132]

In a similar vein, in *Kitakata ra-men*,[133] the collective mark '喜多方ラーメン' for providing *ra-men* (a type of Japanese noodle) in Kigtakata city, Fukushima prefecture, was rejected by the Intellectual Property High Court, on the grounds that the collective mark in question is not *syuchi* in the Fukushima prefecture or in the neighbouring prefectures among relevant consumers. Furthermore, a *syohyo* that is *syuchi* in only one area within a city (here Nagoya city) cannot be granted as a *syuchi-syohyo*. A service mark (in this case, a service mark for providing food and drinks) was not granted *syuchi-syohyo* status[134] because the mark was only known in a limited area of one prefecture.

Furthermore, *Computer World*[135] provides instruction for a well-known trade mark that is *syuchi* but is not yet registered in Japan. The defendant, a Japanese

---

130 *Iwate haru imidori*. Intellectual Property High Court, Heisei 17 (Gyo Ke) 10041go. Sokuho 398–15111.
131 *Shinagawa Inter City*. Tokyo High Court, Heisei 13nen (Gyo Ke) 430go. Chizai sokuso 307–10825.
132 Ibid.
133 *Kitakata ra-men*. Intellectual Property High Court, Heisei 21 (Gyo Ke) 104335go.
134 Tokyo High Court, Heisei 10nen (Gyo Ke) 7go, sokuhyo 285–8465.
135 *Tenichi*, Tokyo High Court, Heisei 13nen (Gyo Ke) 253go, Chizai sokuso 326–10796.

publishing house, applied for and was granted a trademark registration for the word mark 'Computer World' in relation to newspapers and magazines. The claimant, the US publishing house that publishes the magazine called *Computer World*, and a US trade mark proprietor of such a trade mark, opposed this registration on the grounds of Article 4(1)(10) that the earlier well-known mark, which is similar to the later mark, is well known and therefore qualified for Article 4(1)(10) protection. The claimant submitted the following evidence in accordance with Item 6 of the JPO Guidelines to prove the earlier mark was well known. The claimant had had a US-registered trade mark 'Computer World' (No. 8570665) for a newspaper in relation to computer software since 1968; the volume of sales reached 62,400 copies in 1974 and a further 2,652 were sold outside the US and Canada, including in Japan.

The court held that:

> Well-known mark shall include not only the mark which obtained well-knownness among consumers as that indicating goods or services of one undertaking as a result of such a mark being used as a trademark [in Japan], but also the mark, although is registered and used outside Japan, which obtained well-knownness among consumers as that indicating goods or services of one undertaking through advertisement and reportage.

The court explained the rationale as follows:

> [O]ne of the legitimate purposes of Article 4(1)(10) is to prevent consumers from causing (a likelihood of) confusion. By applying this justification, the distinction between the mark being used in Japan and becoming well known, and the mark, not being used in Japan, but becoming well known through, for example, advertisement amongst Japanese consumers shall not be made. Also, the degree of recognition of the mark is not required to be known to the entire Japanese nationals; this shall be assessed by considering the nature of the goods. A mark can be well known even if it was well known only in the limited and selective range of consumers or traders, so long as there is no confusion.

This case positively recognised that the well-known mark that does not have a Japanese registration and is not in actual use can be afforded protection under Article 4(1)(10). This case seems to have departed from the traditional approach that trademark use was paramount in the Japanese registration system. It illustrates an unnecessary stronger and generous protection afforded to the well-known mark that has not yet had a Japanese trademark registration. This might be justified in the view that the geographic extent to which the mark is well known goes beyond national geographic limitation, since such a mark is well known both outside and in Japan, and such a mark deserves protection. In other words, Article 4(1)(10) becomes automatically applicable as long as the mark is well known in Japan, despite the mark not being used therein. A more generous treatment for such marks can be seen by *Mosrite guitar*.[136]

The trademark registration for the device mark 'Mosrite' for guitars made in California, USA, was held invalid on the grounds that the earlier trade mark 'Mosrite' was well known at the time of the registration in question. Therefore, the registration was barred on the basis of Article 4(1)(10).

It was also noted here that a *syuchi-syohyo* had to be well known throughout Japan by the majority of the relevant parties. Although each criterion in the Guidelines ought to hold equal weight, the overriding factor seems to be the degree of recognition of the mark amongst the relevant public and the geographic extent to which the mark is known. Therefore, other factors, such as duration of the use of the mark,[137] seem less important. In terms of evidence, an incomplete document cannot be treated as legitimate evidence (which is addressed within the Guidelines).[138]

Although the court does not provide conceptualisation of '*syuchi-syohyo*' or a conceptual definition of the same, a moderate amount of guidance can be found with reference to the Definition Model in order to partly delineate a brief overall picture of '*syuchi-syohyo*'. The observation and examination of the JPO Guidelines can be useful.

Regarding '*syuchi-syohyo*' *form*, it is very clear that *form* includes the trade mark that is well known outside Japan but does not yet have a Japanese trademark registration. In other words, the Japanese trademark regime explicitly and proactively recognises and protects a mark without registration; this is compliance with the original purpose of the Paris Convention, Article 6*bis* requirement. In relation to '*syuchi-syohyo*' *concept*, the findings of the JPO Guidelines can be reiterated. *Concept* seems to be equated with the geographic extent of the mark being known. This heavily geographically focused *concept* seems to require a higher degree of well-knownness in Japan. Finally, in relation to the *preconditions* of the Definition Model, there is no explicit reference to *graphic representation* or *commercial use* in the noted cases, although both *preconditions* are inherent in the nature of the case.

Overall, the Japanese courts seem to require a relatively higher degree of recognition of the mark in the relatively broader and wider geographic area. When a mark is known only in the small area of one prefecture, the mark fails to be qualified as '*syuchi-syohyo*',[139] taking into consideration the nature of the goods and/or services to which the mark is attached.[140]

---

136 *Computer World*. Tokyo High Court, Heisei 3nen (Gyo Ke) 29Go, Chitekisaisyu 24ken 1go 182, zai sokuso.
137 *Mosrite Guitar*. Intellectual Property High Court, Heisei 20nen (Gyo Ke) 10415go.
138 A *syohyo* was held not to be a *syuchi-syohyo*, as the length of use was less than five years. Tokyo High Court, Showa 49nen (Gyo Ke) dai 32go, Shinketsu torikeshi syu 529.
139 Showa 56nen shinpan, dai 8843go (3203 go).
140 Ibid.

5.3.5 Summary

So far Section 5.3 has attempted to explore the conceptual definition of *'syuchi-syohyo'* in both the Act (Section 5.3.2) and the JPO Guidelines[141] (Sections 5.3.3), with reference to the Definition Model.

An overview of Section 5.3 is as follows. According to the Definition Model, the conceptual definition of *'syuchi-syohyo'* is not explicitly set out either in the Act[142] or in the JPO Guidelines. Much inference must be employed in applying the Definition Model, with particular concern as to the scope and clarity of *concept* of *'syuchi-syohyo'*. The apparently case-by-case and fact-dependent approach of the courts to this issue appears indicative of the view that *'syuchi-syohyo'* status is a matter of fact. The lack of a comprehensive and precise definition here cannot be helpful for certainty and consistency in the law.

Concerning the JPO Guidelines, *concept* of *'syuchi-syohyo'* is implicitly present, and some similarity to the WIPO Recommendation can be found here. Moreover, a strong emphasis on *commercial use* (one of the *preconditions*) seems to be one of the distinctive characteristics of the Japanese approach. In short, a *syuchi-syohyo* appears to be examined on a case-by-case basis. In terms of a legal definition or more explicit guidance as to *syuchi-syohyo* status, it is concluded that a *syohyo* must be highly distinctive in a (poorly defined) substantial geographic area and also in terms of the scale of sales (with reference to an uncertain definition of consumers). What is clear is that *syuchi-syohyo* status in Japan is unlikely to be achieved by *locally* well-known *syohyo*,[144] but rather by *syohyo* well known on a national scale, if only to a small number of consumers.[145] Further, the JPO Guidelines do state that the extent of the recognition of the mark can be either national or local,[146] depending on the nature of the goods or services. *Concept* of *'syuchi-syohyo'* – geographic-extent-oriented distinctiveness – does appear to play an overriding role in assessing *syuchi-syohyo* status in the JPO Guidelines.[147] But this is not entirely and conceptually clear, since there is significant inconsistency both in the Acts and jurisprudence.

Items 3 and 6 of the JPO Guidelines for Article 4(1)(10) do suggest[148] that there is a test to assess *concept* of *'syuchi'* therein.[149] The term *'syuchi-syohyo'* is then

---

141 Tokyo High Court, Heisei 15nen (Gyo Ke) 32go, Chizai sokuho 342–11811.
142 See Amino, *Syohyo-ho*; Tamura, *Fusei kyoso boshi ho gaisetsu*, Tokyo: Yuhi-kaku, p. 56.
143 See Articles 4(1)(10) and (19) of the Japanese Trademark Act.
144 It is clear that not only can a *syohyo* be well known throughout the country, but it can also be recognised in certain areas (see Item 1 of the JPO Guidelines for Article 4(1)(10)).
145 The JPO Guidelines state that *'syuchi-syohyo'* includes a trademark that is widely recognised not only by end consumers but also by traders in the industry. Traders in industry (in Japan), as well as Japanese consumers, are included in the assessment of distinctiveness.
146 Ibid.
147 See Items 3(1)(i)–(vi) and Items 3(2)(i)–(viii) of Chapter II: Article 3(2) of the JPO Guidelines.
148 See Appendix 3.
149 As Item 3 suggests, in order to assess if the trade mark is *syuchi* or not, we shall refer to Items 3(1) and (2) of Chapter 2 (Article 3(2)) of the JPO Guidelines. Item 3 states that '*To prove a trademark's being well known* under the provision of this paragraph, the provisions of *Items 3(1) and (2) of Chapter 2 (Article 3(2)) of the Guidelines* apply *mutatis mutandis*' [emphasis added].

explicitly addressed in both the items of the JPO Guidelines for Article 4(1)(10)[150] and items of the JPO Guidelines for Article 4(1)(19).[151] Here, in order to assess whether the mark is well known or not under Article 4(1)(19) of the Japanese Trademark Act, the JPO Guideline indirectly refers the reader to the JPO Guidelines for Article 3(2). What is of significance here is that the JPO Guidelines for Article 3(2) speak of successful assessments of *syohyo* requiring distinctiveness. This would therefore appear to confirm the *concept* of '*syuchi-syohyo*' identified in Section 5.3.1 above.[152] More generally, the explicit linking of *syuchi* to distinctiveness supports one of the assumptions made.[153] Here it seems that (in the Japanese context at least) we have: (i) some evidence that this assumption is reasonable; (ii) express recognition that both 'trade mark' and 'well-known trade mark' have to be distinctive; and (iii) the assumption that it is the extent of that distinctiveness that differs between 'trade mark' and 'well-known trade mark' (i.e. in terms of *concept* they are qualitatively similar and quantitatively dissimilar). Finally, it should be noted that neither the Act nor the JPO Guidelines seems to contain any specific or explicit reference to the *preconditions* in relation to '*syuchi-syohyo*' (although, as argued above, these *preconditions* can be implied).

Given the absence of a clear and consistent notion of *concept* of *syuchi-syohyo* in the Act and the Guidelines, it is concluded that *syuchi-syohyo* is not clearly and conceptually defined. This lack of a clear conceptual definition of *syuchi-syohyo* can only impact on the certainty of the scope of the protection of *syuchi-syohyo* against *fuseino mokuteki* (detriment and unfair advantage) in a negative manner. This consideration of *dilution* is the aim of Section 5.4.

5.4 *Syuchi-syohyo* protection against *fuseino mokuteki*

We will now move on to the third part of this chapter: a critical examination of the protection for a *syuchi-syohyo* (equivalent to well-known trade mark) against dilution (*fuseino mokuteki*). The focus will be on the examination of dilution.

The same method employed in Chapter 4 will be employed again here, and the rationale for this was explained therein.[154] A similar structure to that employed in Chapter 4 will be followed: first, the statutory definition of 'dilution' in the Japanese Trademark Act will be explored, before moving on to the JPO Guidelines and relevant jurisprudence.

Having considered the conceptual definition and the conceptualisation of '*syuchi-syohyo*', it can be seen that the task of conceptualising the definition

---

150 See Appendix 3.
151 See Appendix 4.
152 Taking into account the comments in the paragraph above, a slightly expanded version of this can thus be stated as follows: '*Syuchi-syohyo*' comprises *syuchi*, which constitutes a high level of geographically defined distinctiveness amongst consumers and the relevant traders in relation to goods or services in connection with the business of the trademark right holder in Japan, or abroad.
153 See Chapter 1, Section 1.9.
154 See Chapter 4, Section 4.4.

of '*syuchi-syohyo*' has been more fruitful than in the case of the EU 'trade mark of repute'. In particular, the shape of the concept of '*syuchi-syohyo*' has become more clear – acquired distinctiveness through use.

The following questions comprise the central discussion for the third part of this chapter:

(i)   How sufficient are the attempts of law to provide protection against dilution, where there is only an incomplete conceptualisation of a *syuchi-syohyo*?
(ii) How far is the law able to determine the scope of protection where there is so-called dilution without conceptually establishing what it is the law protects?

The main focus of this section is to explore ways in which the *syuchi-syohyo* is protected, and the efficacy of the scope of protection given to the *syuchi-syohyo*. The author argues that the credibility of the scope of protection given to *syuchi-syohyo*, without any conceptual definition, is doubtful.

Having considered the definition of '*syuchi-syohyo*', the main focus of this chapter will now shift to the exploration of *fuseino mokuteki* (dilution concept) and critical analysis of protection against it in the absolute grounds for refusal.

First of all, one of the fundamental differences between the EU and Japanese trademark systems needs to be highlighted. The Japanese regime does not recognise *syuchi-syohyo* protection against dilution in the context of trademark infringement. In other words, Articles equivalent to Article 5(2) of the EU TMD[155] (and Article 9(1)(c) of the CTMR[156]) do not exist herein. The Japanese law only recognises such a protection at the absolute grounds for refusal. Therefore, there is a burden of proof on the well-known trademark proprietor to prove a likelihood of confusion. Instead, there is a defensive trademark registration system, which provides an additional layer of protection only for well-known and/or famous marks, these rights being conferred by the registration. In this regard, it is apparent that the Japanese regime does not appear to provide as broad a protection to well-known trademarks as the EU regime does post-*Bellure*.

5.4.1 Japanese Trademark Act

As was previously noted in Chapter 1, Article 4(1)(19) of the Japanese Trademark Act, which regulates *syuchi-syohyo* protection against dilution, was introduced during the 1996 amendment.[157] This Article also forms the examiner's reasons for refusal (Articles 15(1),[158]) grounds for opposition of the trademark registration

---

155 Directive 2008/95/EC of the European Parliament and of the Council of 22 October 2008 to approximate the laws of the Member States relating to trade marks (Codified version).
156 Council Regulation (EC) No. 207/2009 of 26 February 2009 on the Community trade mark (Codified version).
157 Act No. 68 of 1996.
158 Article 15 of the Japanese Trademark Act. It states: 'Where an application for trademark registration falls under any of the following items, the examiner shall render a decision to the effect that the application is to be refused: (i) the trademark pertaining to an application for

(Article 43(2)[159]) and grounds for invalidation of the trademark registration (Article 46(1)(1)[160]).

Prior to this new development, the trademark examiners and courts utilised either Article 4(1)(7)[161] or Article 4(1)(15)[162] to refuse the registration where the registration contains a mark that is similar or identical to an earlier well-known trademark, and where the purpose of the registration is unfair, and was noted and said to be unsatisfactory and not reflective of current market demand.[163]

Article 4(1)(19) is understood to be equivalent to Article 4(4)(a) of the EU TMD.[164] The main purpose of Article 4(1)(19) is to:

> prevent dilution and so-called free-ride to well-known (trade) marks,[165] and thus to protect distinctiveness of (trade) marks, and thus to enhance the maintenance of *goodwill*[166] established by trademark owners in the course of trade and ultimately protect the interest of consumers.[167] [Emphasis added]

The wider implication of this Article[168] is understood to be the protection of public interests,[169] which stemmed from the fact that Article 4(1)(19)-type protection was dealt with previously by Article 4(1)(7) or Article 4(1)(15). Therefore, such a provision becomes crucial for the well-known trademark owner to prevent such a registration made in bad faith.[170]

---

trademark registration is not registrable pursuant to the provisions of Articles 3, 4(1), 7–2(1), 8(2), 8(5), 51(2) (including the case of its mutatis mutandis application under Articles 52–2(2)), 53(2) of this Act or Article 25 of the Patent Act as applied mutatis mutandis under 77(3) of this Act.'

159 Ibid., Article 43(2).
160 Ibid., Article 46(1)(1).
161 Article 4(1)(7) provides grounds for refusal of registration of any marks that are likely to cause damage to public policy.
162 Article 4(1)(15) provides grounds for refusal of registration of any later mark, where the later mark causes a likelihood of confusion with an earlier mark, because of its similarity to or identity with the earlier marks.
163 See Ono, *Syohyo-ho*, pp. 448–9.
164 Directive 2008/95/EC of the European Parliament and the Council of 22 October 2008 to approximate the laws of the Member States relating to trade marks.
165 However, this current importation and implication of Article 4(1)(15) seems insufficient for well-known trademark protection, in particular when so-called *free-riding* occurs. Now, the current statutory framework of confusion theory will be examined. The term 'free-ride' will be explained shortly and will be used throughout this book. JPO, *Kogyosyoyuken seido hyakunen shi*, Tokyo: Hatsumei Kyokai, 1985, p. 488.
166 The term 'goodwill' is not employed within the Japanese Trademark Act. See Article 1 of the Japanese Trademark Act; the term 'business confidence' is used instead.
167 See Ono, *Syohyo ho*, p. 391; and H. Aoki, *Chiteki zaisan ken toshiteno brand to design*, Tokyo: Yuhi-kaku, 2007, pp. 36–7.
168 Ibid.
169 K. Kudo, *Syohyoho nokaisetsu to saibanrei*, Tokyo: Masterlink, 2011, p. 186.
170 Article 37 of the Japanese Trademark Act provides an exhaustive list of the acts deemed to constitute trademark infringements. It also contains a similar function to Article 9(1)(b) of the CTMR. Article 37 read as follows: 'The following acts shall be deemed to constitute infringement of a trademark right or an exclusive right to use: (i) the use of a trademark similar to the registered trademark in connection with the designated goods or designated services, or the use of the registered trademark or a trademark similar thereto in connection with goods or services similar

Despite the intention behind the introduction of Article 4(1)(19), it was only the concept that was embedded in the law, *not* the actual term 'dilution'. It is speculated that the law assumes that the situation where the trade mark registration was made with unfair purposes equates with the situation where trade mark dilution occurs. The actual term employed herein is 'unfair purposes'. The term *'fuseino mokuteki'* (in English 'unfair purposes') will be used hereinafter.

Returning to the exploration of the definition of *'fuseino mokuteki'*, the English translation of Article 4(1)(19) is as follows:

Article 4:
(19) is identical with, or similar to, a trademark which is *well known* among consumers in *Japan or abroad* as *that indicating goods or services pertaining to a business of another person*, if such trademark is *used for unfair purposes* (referring to the purpose *of gaining unfair profits*, the purpose of *causing damage to the other person*, or any other unfair purposes, the same shall apply hereinafter) (except those provided for in each of the preceding items. [Emphasis added]

In order to apply the Article, the following two elements need to be present: (i) 'well-knownness' and (ii) 'unfair purposes'. As the former was already handled in the previous section, attention will now be turned to analysis of *'fuseino mokuteki'*/unfair purposes.

There are two types of the harm *'fuseino mokuteki'* recognised herein: one is to obtain illicit financial gain from the use of the later mark that is identical/similar to the earlier well-known mark; another is that the later registration damages the

to the designated goods or designated services; (ii) the possession for the purpose of assignment, delivery or export of the designated goods, or goods similar to the designated goods or designated services, affixed with the registered trademark or a trademark similar thereto on the goods or their packages; (iii) possession or importation of articles affixed with the registered trademark or a trademark similar thereto, that are used in the course of the provision of designated services or services similar to the designated services or the designated goods by a person who receives the said services, for the purpose of the provision of the said services through use of the said articles; (iv) the assignment, delivery, or possession or importation for the purpose of assignment or delivery of articles affixed with a registered trademark or a trademark similar thereto, that are used in the course of the provision of designated services or services similar to the designated services or the designated goods by a person who receives the said services, for the purpose of causing the provision of the said services through use of the said products; (v) the possession of products indicating the registered trademark or a trademark similar thereto, for the purpose of using the registered trademark or a trademark similar thereto in connection with the designated goods or designated services, or goods or services similar thereto; (vi) the assignment, delivery, or possession for the purpose of assignment or delivery, of articles indicating the registered trademark or a trademark similar thereto, for the purpose of causing the registered trademark or a trademark similar thereto to be used in connection with the designated goods or designated services, or goods or services similar thereto; (vii) the manufacture or importation of products indicating the registered trademark or a trademark similar thereto, for the purpose of using or causing to be used the registered trademark or a trademark similar thereto in connection with the designated goods or designated services or goods or services similar thereto; and (viii) the manufacture, assignment, delivery or importation, as a business, of products to be used exclusively for the manufacturing of products indicating the registered trademark or a trademark similar thereto.'

earlier well-known trademark owner. The former is indicated by the pecuniary element; the latter is non-pecuniary. With regard to the latter, the law does not indicate the type of damage: measurable (such as financial) or non-measurable (such as non-financial), tangible (such as properties) or intangible (such as reputation) damage. This confers a certain level of flexibility on the court to interpret 'unfair purposes' in the context of each case. It is inevitable therefore that the Japanese courts have exercised their own discretion to interpret unfair purposes depending on the context.

Also, great emphasis is placed on a well-known trademark being used as an indication of origin. As may have been noticed, in the Japanese jurisdiction, emphasis is placed on terms such as '*in the course of trade*' or '*trade mark in business use*'.[171] These are regarded as being tantamount to '*commercial use*',[172] and further emphasise the importance of *commercial use*, in general, in the Japanese Trademark Act.

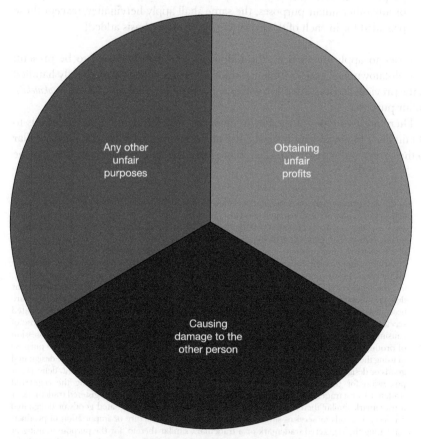

Figure 5.7 Grouping of acts causing harms (*fuseino mokuteki*/unfair purposes)

171 See, for example, Article 2(3) of the Japanese Trademark Act.
172 See Chapter 2, Section 2.2, for the explanation of the Definition Model.

上 'Syuchi-syohyo' in Japan 171

Compared with the EU regime, dilution is classified in a less clear manner.

According to the EU trade mark regime, three types of harm (encroachment) are clearly noted in law: (i) detrimental to the distinctiveness of the mark (dilution by blurring); (ii) detrimental to the reputation of the mark (dilution by tarnishment); (iii) taking unfair advantage of the distinctiveness of and the reputation of the mark (free-riding).

Above all, the definition of '*fuseino mokuteki*/unfair purposes' in the Act and the link between '*syuchi-syohyo*' and '*fuseino mokuteki*/unfair purposes' do appear muddled and less clearly defined than the equivalent interpretation of the EU law.

Furthermore, putting Article 4(1)(19) into a practical context, there seems to be some limitation in the applicability of Article 4(1)(19). The Article becomes applicable and thus utilised when Article 4(1)(1)–(18) is exhausted, thereby making it clear that this provision does *not* overlap with other provisions and the final resort of the absolute grounds for refusal. In practice, a majority of the trademark registration seems to fall within or is able to be dealt by Article 4(1)(15), provided that a likelihood of confusion is present. This criterion is not difficult to satisfy as the law requires the similarity between the earlier and later marks as a prerequisite to protect a trademark being an indication of origin, and the likelihood of confusion is mostly likely to be established. Therefore, Article 4(1)(19), in fact, has little application and appears to become an empty provision. In spite of the initial hope that such an establishment would provide a more stable, consistent and coherent approach to well-known trademark protection against dilution, the practice and jurisprudence suggest that this is not the case.

5.4.2 The JPO Guidelines

This section seeks further guidance in the JPO Guidelines[173] in order to examine the efficacy and credibility of *syuchi-syohyo* protection against *fuseino mokuteki*/unfair purposes. Under the Trademark Act, there are three types of actionable harm: (i) obtaining unfair profits; (ii) causing damage to the other person; and (iii) any other unfair purposes (see Figure 5.7 above).

The relevant Article here is Part 16: Article 4(1)(19).[174] This provision is more instructive in assessing '*fuseino mokuteki*/unfair purposes' than that of the Act.[175] The relevant aspects of the Guidelines are described below.

---

173 The first recorded Examination Guideline was issued around 1932; until recently, such a Guideline was not disclosed to the public. The current Examination Guideline was last amended in 2012. See K. Kudo, *Syohyo shinsa kijyun no kaisetsu*, Tokyo: Hatsumei-kyokai, 2004, p. 3. Item 4 of Chapter 3: Article 4(1)(3) Part 13, Article 4(1)(15) of the JPO Guidelines.

174 Chapter III: Article 4(1)(3) Part 13: Article 4(1)(15) of the JPO Guidelines is provided in full in Appendix 6. See Item 3 of the JPO Guidelines for Article 4(1)(19). There is a difference in the English translation between the Trademark Act and the JPO Examination Guidelines. The former uses the term 'unfair purposes', whilst the latter uses the term 'unfair intention'. This is clearly a cause of further confusion and inconsistency.

175 See Section 5.4.1.

As seen above, there are four main features to be noted and discussed: (i) two types of protectable *syuchi-syohyo* are identified and the interpretations of each *syuchi-syohyo* are submitted; (ii) two types of actionable harm are recognised; (iii) the factors to be taken into consideration in determining that *fuseino mokuteki/* unfair purposes are indicated; (iv) two occasions where the existence of unfair purposes are automatically recognised. We will now examine each point in turn.

The first and second points are discussed together. It is of interest that the type of actionable harm[176] varies depending on the type of protectable *syuchi-syohyo*, and two kinds of protectable *syuchi-syohyo* are noted here. One is the well-known trade mark that is not registered in Japan; the other is the well-known trade mark that is registered in Japan.

Stemming from this distinction, the term 'unfair purposes' can give rise to two different situations.

In the context of the former, three different types of 'unfair purposes' are recognised where the third party registers a register a mark that is well-known but does not yet have a Japanese trademark registration for the purpose of: (i) well-known trademark 'squatting' – in other words, selling such a registration to the person or company who holds the original trademark registration at an inflated price; (ii) preventing the original trademark holder from entering the Japanese market; or (iii) being in an advantageous position to make a licence agreement.

In the context of the latter, unfair purposes occur where the third party makes an application of the mark that is similar or identical to the earlier mark which is well known throughout Japan, even if there is no likelihood of confusion between the earlier and later marks in order to: (i) dilute the function of the trademark being an indication of origin; (ii) tarnish the reputation of the earlier mark. Therefore, it could be argued that the Japanese trademark regime, like the EU TMD, recognises both dilution and free-riding. However, it is not clear, if the protectable mark is a well-known mark that is not registered in Japan, whether the actionable harm is automatically presumed to be 'free-riding' rather than 'dilution'. Does it mean that there is no dilution where a well-known but unregistered trade mark is at issue?

In addition, further guidance on the two different types of protectable *syuchi syohyo* is provided: well-known marks that are registered in Japan can include marks that are well known among more general consumers such as the end users, and marks that are well known among the relevant consumers in the relevant sectors.

The well-known marks that are not yet registered in Japan can include the mark that is well known in the original jurisdictions, but not well known in Japan. Moreover, the mark does not need to be well known in a number of different jurisdictions.

The third point is that six indicative examples of evidence that the claimant can submit to prove whether the registration of the mark is done with 'unfair purposes' are explicitly set out in Item 4 of the Guidelines for Article 4(1)(19).

---

176 There are three types of harms recognised under Article 4(4)(a) of the EU TMD.

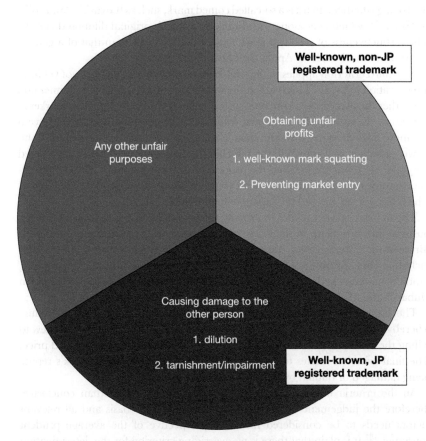

Figure 5.8 Grouping of acts causing harms (*fuseino mokuteki*/unfair purposes) to the *syuchi-syohyo*

The first criterion (evidence to prove that the mark is well known) relates to proving that the mark in question is of *syuchi*.[177] This is reasonable and expected evidence given that the purpose of Article 4(1)(19) is to protect *syuchi-syohyo*. Historically, a higher degree of well-knownness of marks was required under Article 4(1)(19) than Article 4(1)(10) of the Japanese Trademark Act – that is to say, the mark needed to be nationally well known. However, recent cases seem to indicate that a lesser degree of well-knownness (i.e. protection even where the mark is not well known throughout Japan[178]) is required. The next criterion relates

177 It is submitted that well-known trademarks are too famous to be confused and the likelihood of confusion becomes less. Therefore, the conclusion is that well-known trademarks are not dealt with in confusion doctrine. However, Article 4(1)(15) is applied based on the assumption that because well-known trademarks contain stronger distinctiveness and attractiveness to consumers than ordinary marks, the likelihood of confusion might also be greater. It can therefore be inferred that Article 4(1)(15) is implemented as the protector of well-known trademarks in Japan.
178 Tokyo High Court, Heisei 9nen (Gyo Ke) dai 323go, sokuho 283–8377; Tokyo High Court, Heisei 9nen (Gyo Ke) dai 266go, sokuho 286–8524.

to proving whether a mark is a so-called coined mark, such as 'Lexus',[179] 'Sanrio'[180] or 'Sony',[181] which goes along with Frank Schechter's original dilution theory.[182] The distinctiveness of a coined mark tends to be stronger than that of a generic or arbitrary mark such as 'Apple' or 'Oasis'.[183]

The third criterion applies to the well-known trade mark that does not yet have a registration in Japan. This is to test the well-known trade mark owner's intention – whether the owner has a concrete business plan to enter the Japanese market in the future. Examples of well-known trade mark owners that do not yet have a Japanese trademark registration include the proprietor of the trade mark 'John Lewis', which is well known in the UK, but the business itself has not yet entered the Japanese retail market, and the proprietor of the trade mark 'FAGE', a well-known trade mark in relation to Greek yogurt originated and produced in Greece, which has not yet entered the Japanese food market.

The fourth criterion relates to proving the possibility of expanding the existing business into new fields in the foreseeable future. For example, the proprietor of 'Bridgestone'[184] tyres may well expand their business to manufacturing automobiles including cars. Examples of this have occurred in recent times – for example, Prada[185] has launched a new line for mobile phones; Armani has opened hotels in Dubai[186] and Milan.

The fifth criterion relates to evidence of well-known trade mark squatting, whereby a third party attempts to register a well-known trade mark with a view to selling the exclusive trade mark rights to the original owner at an inflated price. The final criterion relates to proving the likelihood of an earlier mark's repute being damaged or diluted by the later use.

All the criteria noted above are merely indicative, rather than conclusive; therefore the judgement will be made on a case-by-case basis and all relevant factors needs to be considered from the perspective of the average prudent consumer.[187] It is plain that there is no overriding criterion for the determination of 'unfair purposes', which means that the scope of 'unfair purposes' is assessed, not defined, rather loosely and incoherently.

Finally, Item 5 of the Guideline for Article 4(1)(19) of the JPO Guidelines clearly sets out two occasions on which Article 4(1)(19) becomes automatically

179 The word mark 'Lexus' is a registered *syohyo* in Japan, Trademark Registration Number 2141029.
180 The word mark 'Sanrio' is a registered *syohyo* in Japan, Trademark Registration Number 1273271.
181 The word mark 'Sony' is a registered *syohyo* in Japan, Japanese Trademark Registration Number 491710.
182 See Schechter, 'The Rational Basis of Trademark Protection'.
183 See Ono, *Syohyo ho*, p. 393; and K. Kudo, *Syohyo shinsa kijyun no kaisetsu*, Tokyo: Hatsumei-kyokai, 2004, p. 315.
184 The word mark 'Bridgestone' is a registered *syohyo* in Japan, Japanese Trademark Registration Number 3002230.
185 The word mark 'Prada' is granted as a registered *syohyo* in Japan, Trademark Registration Number 5737696.
186 More detailed information is available online at www.armanihotels.com/en/index.html (accessed 7 November 2014).
187 Ibid.

applicable. These are as follows: (i) the later mark is identical or similar to the earlier mark that is well known in more than one jurisdiction outside Japan, or is well known throughout Japan;[188] (ii) the earlier mark is a coined mark that contains a very distinctive innate character.[189] Under this Item, a clear distinction is made between three marks: a mark that is (i) well known in Japan; (ii) well known outside Japan and does not have a Japanese trademark registration; and (ii) well known and coined.

It is very interesting that the Japanese law pays positive attention to the coined mark, which puts more emphasis on the inherent distinctiveness of the mark rather than acquired distinctiveness. This approach is echoed in the original dilution theory suggested by Frank Schechter in 1927.[190]

The emphasis on an inherent distinctiveness of the mark and the court's willingness to distinguish inherently distinctive well-known marks from others are the unique characteristics of the Japanese trademark regime. Japanese law openly acknowledges that the potential ramifications of the third party's registration of the mark that is similar or identical to the well-known trade mark 'Lexus', being made with unfair purposes, is greater than that of the mark 'Orange'.

It is a unique feature of the Japanese trademark system that the coined well-known mark is given stronger protection than ordinary and less distinctive marks. This is one of the most significant differences between the Japanese and EU trade mark systems.

Overall, what has been found in the Guidelines seems rather useful, but it has limitation in conceptualisation as to the situations in which unfair purposes can arise. In terms of well-known non-Japanese-registered trademarks, the presence of unfair purposes is likely to be evidenced where there is an illicit financial gain or intention of financial gain by the third party. However, the law becomes less clear and useful when the well-known Japanese mark is considered. The law under Article 4(1)(19) does not give the impression of being maturely developed.

A notable aspect of the Japanese trademark regime is the different legal treatment of *syuchi-syohyo* (as opposed to *syohyo*) where a third party's registration includes a mark that is similar or identical to *syuchi-syohyo*; here, the existence of *fuseino nokuteki*/ unfair purposes is *automatically assumed*.[191] Thus, the Japanese law takes a strongly pro-*syuchi-syohyo* stance in this regard. Moreover, Japanese law appears to give very strong protection to coined, well-known marks, as originally suggested by Frank Schechter in 1927.[192] There is potentially different treatment when the earlier mark in question contains a coined mark or part of a distinctive character.[193] Note that determination of well-known marks needs to refer back to guidance on Article 4(1)(10).

188 Item 5(1) of the JPO Guidelines for Article 4(1)(19).
189 Ibid., Item 5(2).
190 See Schechter, 'The Rational Basis of Trademark Protection'.
191 See Item 3 of the JPO Guidelines for Article 4(1)(15).
192 See Schechter, 'The Rational Basis of Trademark Protection'.
193 JPO Guidelines, Item 4.

More centrally to this book, nevertheless, it still must be conceded that the *precise* scope of the protection of *syuchi-syohyo* against unfair purposes is not clear; the Japanese trademark jurisdiction appears to provide more generous but less flexible protection to *syuchi-syohyo* against dilution than is provided to trade marks of repute against dilution in the EU trade mark regime.

5.4.3 Jurisprudence

So far, some useful guidance in exploring 'unfair purposes' in the context of *syuchi-syohyo* has been evidenced in the Act and the Guidelines. We will now seek further guidance in delineating the overall picture of dilution in the Japanese context. Note that since Article 4(1)(19) was introduced in 1992, the Article has been little used by the judiciary and/or the examiners. Despite a lack of application, the Japanese jurisprudence will be critically examined to see how the courts interpret Article 4(1)(19) and provide protection against unfair purposes.

By way of background, a number of points need to be made. The burden of proof is on the claimants: *syuchi-syohyo* owners are required to be proactive in gathering evidence for any violation/infringement.[194] Furthermore, in assessing whether *syuchi-syohyo* is at risk of being *diluted* or not, the court and/or trademark examiners consider not only the marks in question but also the factual and circumstantial evidence of the current business world.[195] An overall picture of the protection under Article 4(1)(19) was noted earlier in Figures 5.7 and 5.8.

We shall also attempt to complete the task of conceptualisation of *syuchi-syohyo* protection against dilution and see how the Japanese model will be transformed.

The first case to be introduced here is *Microsoft*.[196] This case involved a well-known non-Japanese-registered mark. According to the Japanese model of protecting the *syuchi-syohyo* against dilution, the actionable harm can be presumed to be causing unfair profits, and we will see whether this assumption is correct. The US-based company Microsoft made an announcement in the US in June 1998 that the updated version of their products was to be called 'Office 2000', for which the company held a US-registered trade mark 'Office 2000' (the earlier mark). The Japanese branch made the same announcement in Japan in November 1998. The defendant's business developed and sold the computer software, and registered a trade mark 'Office 2000' (hereinafter the contestant's mark/later mark) in December 1998. The proprietor of the earlier mark relied on Article 4(1) (19), alleging that the contestant's Japanese registration was made with unfair purposes and thus should be rejected and revoked. The court accepted the claimant's argument and, taking into consideration the fact that both the owner of the earlier mark and the contestant were competitors in the same sector, held that it was reasonable to believe that the contestant had knowledge that the owner

---

194 K. Doi, 'syohyo ho 4jyo 1kou 15jyo ni kiteisusu kondo no igi', *Chizai Kanri*, 4, 1995, 589–93.
195 T. Katsube, 'Syohyo ho niokeru kondo gainen no bunse', *Patent*, 3, 1996, 25–31, p. 26.
196 *Microsoft*. Tokyo High Court, Heisei 13nen (Gyo Ke), dai 205. Sokuho 320–10452.

of the earlier mark was launching a new product called 'Office 2000' and that, at the time of the contestant's trademark registration, the earlier mark was already well known in Japan. It was held that the defendant intended to free-ride on the reputation of the earlier mark 'Office 2000'. It was also concluded that it was likely that allowing the defendant's registration would dilute the well-knownness of the claimant's mark.

The court relied on the latter sense of unfair purposes – that is, the purpose of *causing damage to the other person* – which is explained further in the Guidelines:

> [An] application is filed *with an intention to dilute the distinctiveness of the well-known trademark to indicate the source of goods or impair the reputation, etc. of the trademark owner;* however, the trademark of that application per se is *not liable to cause confusion over the source of goods.*[197]

Based on the facts presented, the defendant's registration of 'Office 2000' in relation to similar goods was made with unfair purposes intending to free-ride on the reputation of the earlier mark.

This case did not at all follow the Japanese model of protecting the *syuchi-syohyo* (see Figure 5.7); the well-known trademark that is not yet registered in Japan can apply for the second harm – causing the damage to the person.

Briefly speaking, the court seems to take rather a simple and direct approach to decide the existence of dilution and impairment, irrespective of the type of *syuchi-syohyo*.

Whether the contestant had prior knowledge that the earlier well-known mark did not have a Japanese trademark registration plays a chief role in determining whether the later registration was made in order to dilute and impair the reputation of the earlier mark.

Manhattan Portage[198] was brought under Article 4(1)(19). The issue involved the proprietor of an earlier well-known trade mark 'Manhattan Portage' which, at the time of the contestant's registration for 'Manhattan Passage', did not have a Japanese trademark registration. Thus, according to the original Japanese model of protecting the *syuchi-syohyo* against dilution, only the harm of obtaining unfair profits should be recognised. The contestant's mark was registered in 1991 as a composite mark – the shape of the tall buildings of Manhattan with the English words 'Manhattan Passage' – in relation to Class 21 goods (Nice Classification). The earlier well-known mark was also a composite mark – the shape of the tall buildings with the English words 'Manhattan Portage' (hereinafter the earlier mark). The proprietor of the earlier well-known trade mark opposed the later registration, alleging that the later mark was registered in bad faith, and unfair purposes were evidenced as the later mark was visually, phonetically and semantically similar to the earlier well-known trade mark. There were two key

---

197 Item 1(b) of the JPO Guidelines for Article 4(1)(19).
198 *Manhattan Portage*. Tokyo High Court, Heisei 14nen (Gyo Ke) 514go and 515go (unreported).

issues to be determined: (i) whether the earlier mark was famous under Article 4(1)
(19); and (ii) whether the contestant's registration was made with 'unfair purposes'.
With relation to the second point, whether the contestant had prior knowledge
of the earlier well-known mark plays an important role in establishing 'unfair
purposes', and relevant evidence is required to be submitted (see Item 4 of the
JPO Guidelines for Article 4(1)(19)). The following evidence was submitted by the
owner of the earlier mark in order to prove that the contestant had knowledge
of the earlier well-known mark and how the contestant obtained such knowledge:
(i) the earlier mark's owner had changed its name, in 1983, from Wolverine
Mountain Products Inc. to Manhattan Portage Ltd; (ii) the design of an earlier
composite mark was published and distributed in the product catalogue before
October 1998 (prior to the contestant's registration); (iii) both parties were in the
same industry.

From the above, the court concluded that earlier mark was well known amongst
the relevant consumers in the US and the products which bore the defendant's
mark were popular amongst the consumers; therefore, it was clear that the
claimant had knowledge of the defendant's mark in 1988.

This case seems compatible with the Japanese model of protecting the *syuchi-
syohyo* in that the actionable harm for the well-known non-Japanese-registered
trade mark is to obtain unfair financial profits. In order to prove that the
contestant's registration was made with 'unfair purposes' to obtain illicit financial
gain, the owner of the earlier mark submitted the following evidence: (i) in 1998,
both parties had a number of meetings to discuss the possibility of an exclusive
licensing agreement, but the negotiations broke down and the parties failed to
reach agreement; (ii) the contestant without an agreement with the claimant made
an order to produce, in Korea, bags which bore logos and shapes that were very
similar to the earlier mark and attempted to import those goods back to Japan;
(iii) the contestant had not informed the owner of the earlier mark that they
registered a similar mark 'Manhattan Passage' in Japan. Taking all the elements
into consideration, the court accepted the claimant's argument and held that such
trademark registration was made with unfair purposes. The Japanese model of
protecting the *syuchi-syohyo* (see above) is compatible with the interpretation of
Manhattan Portage.[199] It may be inferred that it is less troublesome for the proprietors
of well-known non-Japanese-registered trade marks to prove the presence of
unfair profits being taken than prove dilution/impairment of the reputation of a
well-known trade mark.

The interpretation of 'obtaining unfair profits' suggested by the JPO
Guidelines was confirmed by the court. The judicial approach to the hypothetical
situations where obtaining unfair profits can be evidenced is mirrored in the JPO
Guidelines. This includes, at the time of the contestant's registration, that the
contestant had knowledge of the earlier mark being famous in the US and the
mark not having a Japanese registration, with a view to preventing the proprietor

199 *Manhattan Portage*. Tokyo High Court, Heisei 14nen (Gyo Ke) 514go and 515go (unreported).

of the earlier well-known trademark from entering the Japanese market, or to be in a better and stronger position in a business deal for the purpose of a licensing agreement.

The next case is *Marie France*.[200] The trademark owner of the well-known magazine *Marie France* opposed a registration (made in 1993) of a word mark 'Marie France' in relation to women's clothes, alleging that the registration in question was done with unfair purposes. This case was again in relation to a well-known mark that is not yet registered as a Japanese trademark; based on the Japanese model of protecting the *syuchi-syohyo*, the actionable harm was presumed to be 'obtaining unfair profit'. Note that there have been several cases in which 'Marie France' has been involved.

The magazine *Marie France* was first launched and published in France in 1944. Since then, it has become a well-known magazine. During 1980s, the volume of sales reached between 500,000 and 520,000, and the magazine was sold in a number of countries, including Italy, Belgium, Switzerland and Canada. However, the proprietor of the earlier mark had not yet launched, at the time of the contestant's registration, the Japanese version of *Marie France*. The proprietor of the earlier mark submitted that the mark was famous in France when the registration of the mark in question was submitted to the JPO in 1993.

The trademark in question was a word mark 'MARIEFRANCE', which was visually, phonetically and semantically identical to the earlier well-known mark 'Marie France', although the mark was applied to women's clothes.

The court pointed out first that the earlier mark and the later mark share similarities for the relevant consumers (both dealt with women's fashion) by reflecting on the fact of Japanese women being interested in current fashion trends in France. Therefore, because of the likelihood of confusion between the earlier and the later mark amongst the consumers, the earlier mark owner may be discouraged from entering the Japanese market. The court held that the registration in question was made with unfair purposes and in bad faith, and was therefore invalid.

This case was interesting in that it appears that because of the identity of the earlier and the contestant's marks, the court automatically assumed the existence of 'unfair purposes'; this approach is in accordance with the Guidelines. Also the court relied on the evidence that the earlier mark was well known not only in its home country but also neighbouring countries such as Belgium, Switzerland, Holland and Italy. This relative fame seems to have led to establishing unfair purposes. This case is a triumph for the well-known trade mark owner who has not yet obtained the Japanese trademark registration. This broader approach to well-known trademark protection in the absolute grounds for refusal completely departs from the geographical limitation arising in domestic law. The Japanese trademark law provides the strongest protection for well-known trademark owners

---

200 *MARIE FRANCE.* Examination Reference 20007–25958. See Kudo, *Syohyo shinsa kijyun no kaisetsu*, pp. 384–5.

who do not have a Japanese registration – in particular, when their well-known mark becomes well known outside Japan – and departed from the necessity of the trademark being used or at least there being an intention of use.

The last case to be introduced here is *Zanotta Sacco*.[201] This case deals with a well-known trade mark that does not hold a Japanese trademark registration, and therefore the presumed harm is 'taking unfair profit'.

The issue here was the word marks 'Zanotta' and 'Sacco' for furniture and related products such as leather cushions and chairs. The contestant registered two marks, 'Zanotta/ザノッタ' (in *katakana* form) and 'Sacco/サッコ' (in *katakana* form) in relation to furniture and related products such as outdoor benches. The Italian proprietor of the earlier well-known mark opposed such a registration, applying Article 4(1)(19), and asked for revocation of the contestant's marks. In order to assess whether the registration in question was rejected on the grounds of Article 4(1)(19), the court needed to establish: (i) the well-knownness of the earlier mark; and (ii) the existence of unfair purposes. In relation to the first point, the court took the nature of the products (furniture) and consumers into consideration and held for the Italian owner:

> Products such as furniture offer customers a great range of choices such as different patterns, designs, colours and prices. This is particularly true when it comes to imported furniture. It is a plain fact that, based on the information that they have gathered via magazines, exhibitions, catalogues, customers make a careful purchase depending on their preference for designs and according to their budgets by comparing different pieces of furniture. The consumers do the overall assessment, including designs and luxuriousness, of the piece of furniture, and consumers might pay extra attention to the unique feature of imported furniture, which the Italian furniture offers. Italian imported furniture, which is famous for its unique design, is of course included in the choices of the consumers and even if the consumer did not, in fact, purchase the product, they were likely to remember the origin of the products and who the manufacturer was. Therefore, although it may be true that the proprietor of the earlier well-known mark is not the best seller of the furniture in the Italian furniture industry, we cannot conclude that the earlier mark is not well-known in Article 4(1)(19) sense.

In relation to the second point, the court found the existence of unfair purposes: at the time of the contestant's trademark registration, the proprietor of the earlier mark came to the end of a contractual relationship on a licensing agreement, and this contract was not renewed. The registration was made seven months after the termination of the licensing agreement (the owner had already found a new agent in Japan to deal with their products). This would clearly and intentionally

---

201 *Zanotta*. Tokyo High Court, Heisei 13 (Gyo Ke) 175/176.

put a burden on the owner of the earlier mark and the new agent. Therefore, the Japanese model was compatible with the decision of the case.

The last case to be considered here is the trademark registration of 'MAC'.[202] The case involves a well-known mark that does not have a Japanese trademark registration. The earlier well-known trade mark was a word mark 'MAC', which was proved to be internationally well known for make-up and cosmetic products in countries including the USA, Canada, the UK and Hong Kong. Before the registration of such a mark, the products, which bore the mark 'MAC', were often introduced and advertised in a number of fashion magazines in Japan. Therefore, the mark was alleged to be well known amongst the relevant traders and consumers in Japan. The contestant's mark was a word mark, which consisted, in part, of the earlier mark. The later mark was registered in relation to similar goods. The court held that the contestant had knowledge of the existence of the earlier mark, its reputation and the fact that the earlier mark had not obtained Japanese registration. Based on that, the registration of the contestant's trademark was made with unfair purposes: the contestant intended to prevent the proprietor of the earlier mark from entering the Japanese market and/or force them to make a licensing agreement or dilute and free-ride the attractive force of the earlier mark for customers.

It is noted that, under Article 4(1)(19), the courts seem to recognise trademark registration with unfair purposes when the contestant has a prior knowledge of the earlier mark not having a Japanese trademark registration and where the earlier mark has (international) recognition. Therefore, the Japanese model of protecting the syuchi-syohyo can be amended as shown in Figure 5.9 below.

It is interesting to note that there is a distinctive differentiation in treatment between a well-known mark whose fame remains at the domestic level and an internationally well-known mark that has not obtained Japanese registration.

This gives a rather generous scope of protection to the well-known trade mark owners who have not yet obtained Japanese trademark registration.

It is true that the Japanese courts give a very strong protection to the well-known trademark owners to prevent well-known mark 'squatting'; however, there are a number of cases in which the applicability of Article 4(1)(19) was rejected. It is also interesting to observe that the grounds for rejecting the application of Article 4(1)(19) are more linked to the principle of Article 4(1)(19), which is the protection for syuchi-syohyo, and therefore syuchi-syohyo must be well known.

For instance, in the Diesel Vox trademark registration,[203] involving the contestant mark 'Diesel Vox' for clothing and the earlier well-known mark 'Diesel' for clothing, the existence of unfair purposes was denied, since the earlier mark, at the time of the contestant's registration, could not be deemed to be well known. Another case illustrating the principle is the Macross trademark registration. The contestant mark 'Macross' was for Classes 16, 25 and 41 and the earlier

202 MAC trademark registration. Examination Reference: 92239.
203 Diesel Vox Trademark Registration. Examination reference 1999-35105.

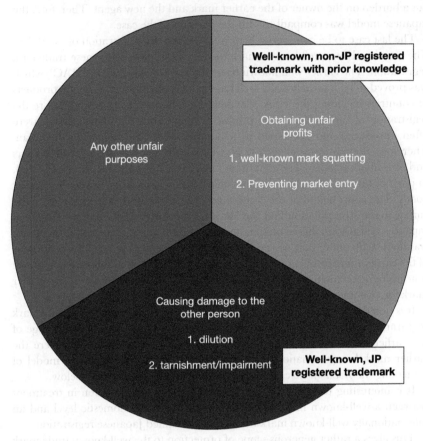

Figure 5.9 Grouping of acts causing harms (*fuseino mokuteki*/unfair purposes) to the
'*syuchi-syohyo*' – final

well-known mark 'Macross' and/or 'マクロス (in a *katakana* form)' was for similar
goods.[204] The application of Article 4(1)(19) failed on the grounds that the earlier
mark was not deemed to be well known in Japan.

The cases above emphasise the importance of the principle of Article 4(1)(19),
and that the application was rejected on the grounds that the earlier mark did not
qualify as well known under Article 4(1)(19).

The application of 'unfair purposes' was also rejected in the *Sky Boss* trademark
registration[205] by referring to one of the key features of Article 4(1)(19): the later
mark must be identical or similar to the earlier *syuchi-syohyo*. The contestant
mark was 'Sky Boss', and the earlier well-known mark was 'Boss'. The court found
that those two marks were not phonetically and visually similar; therefore, the

204 *Macross* Trademark Registration. Examination Reference 2001-90383.
205 *Sky Boss* Trademark Registration. Examination reference 2003-90096.

contestant mark was not similar to the earlier well-known mark, and no 'unfair purposes' could be observed.[206] Another example is the *Speed Arena* trademark registration. The contestant mark was 'Speed Arena' underneath スピードアリーナ (in *katakana* form) for Class 25, and the earlier well-known marks were 'Speed' and 'Arena'.[207] The similarity of those marks was not established, since there was a significant difference in the phonetic and semantic sense. The two cases noted above place emphasis on the similarity of the contestant's and the earlier mark; due to the dissimilarity of the marks, the existence of the unfair purposes was rejected.

5.4.4 Summary

A summary of the Japanese jurisprudence can be outlined as follows. First, the well-knownness of the earlier marks and existence of 'unfair purposes' must be present in order to give rise to an application of Article 4(1)(19). Second, it appears that Article 4(1)(19) is utilised only by the non-Japanese proprietors of well-known trade marks that do not yet have a Japanese trademark registration, and therefore its application for Japanese well-known trademark owners has become dormant. Third, in order to assess the well-knownness of the contestant's and earlier marks, the similarity and identity of both marks are taken into consideration. Fourth, the fact of the contestant having a prior knowledge of the earlier well-known mark that does not have a Japanese trademark registration plays a chief role in determining whether the later registration was made in order to dilute and impair the reputation of the earlier mark. Finally, Japanese law seems to appreciate the inherent distinctiveness of the mark more than the acquired distinctiveness of the mark, as jurisprudence confirms that unfair purposes are established where the earlier mark is the mark with inherent distinctiveness.

5.5 Alternative mechanisms for *syuchi-syohyo* protection: a different paradigm?

We have now reached the fourth part of this chapter. This part explores a number of the alternative and supplementary ways in which the proprietor of *syuchi-syohyo* can enjoy the broader scope of protection afforded to *syuchi-syohyo*.[208] Note that the counterfeited goods can be regulated and/or seized by import suspension or border control (*mizugiwa kisei*).[209] In recent years[210] the Japanese legislature and policy-makers have been proactive in combatting the problem of counterfeited good at border control.[211] For example, the Japanese Government has led the way

---

206 Ibid.
207 *Speed Arena* Trademark Registration. Examination Reference 902278.
208 See, for example, M. Miyazaki, 'Tyomei-syohyo no hogo', *Japan Industrial Property Right Annual Report*, 31, 2008, 99–222.
209 In the Japanese script – 水際規制: *mizugiwa kisei*. This is usually translated as 'border control'.
210 This has been on the Strategic Plan since 2002.
211 For example, 74 per cent of counterfeit goods or reproductions seized in Japan were related to trade mark infringements. The estimated economic loss for one company is reported to be about

in proposing the international treaty known as the Anti-Counterfeiting Trade Agreement (the ACTA).[212] Consultation on ratifying the ACTA has started and is still in progress.[213] Although this is outside the scope of this section, a brief summary will be given.[214]

There are two complementary ways in which fuller *syuchi-syohyo* protection may be obtained. These are by utilising (i) the defensive trademark registration system (albeit in the domain of trademark law) and (ii) the Unfair Competition Prevention Act (*fusei kyoso boshi ho*).[215] These are explained in the following sections.

5.5.1 Defensive registered trademark system

The first alternative is to utilise the defensive trademark system or the *bogo-syohyo toroku* system available under the trademark law. Article 64 of the Japanese Trademark Act[216] introduces the extra registration system for marks that have already obtained the status of well-known and/or fame, called *bogo-syohyo* (defensive trademark),[217] in order for the proprietor of the earlier well-known

¥190 million (= £1.5 million), and the estimated total loss caused by the counterfeiting produces are ¥98.3 billion. (= £75 million, at the exchange rate of October 2014). See JPO, 'FY2013 Survey Report on Counterfeit Losses Caused by Counterfeiting'. This report is only available in Japanese. Available online at www.jpo.go.jp/torikumi/mohouhin/mohouhin2/jittai/pdf/2013_houkoku/2013gaiyou.pdf (accessed 31 October 2014). Because well-known trade marks are highly likely to be valuable, these marks are certain to be a target of counterfeit goods or dead-copy. For instance, 'Seiko' for watches, 'Sony' for MP3 players, 'Louis Vuitton' for bags, and 'Burberry' for clothes. These trade marks are not only well known but also valuable. For example, 93 per cent of counterfeit goods seized at the EU border in 2013 are related to trade mark infringement, and 66 per cent of the total amount of any counterfeited articles originated from China. A full text of the 2014 EU Report, 'Report on EU Customs Enforcement of Intellectual Property Rights' is available online at http://ec.europa.eu/taxation_customs/resources/documents/customs/customs_controls/counterfeit_piracy/statistics/2014_ipr_statistics_en.pdf (accessed 31 October 2014).

212 The main purpose of the ACTA is to prevent and regulate globally the dissemination of counterfeit goods and piracy. Other purposes include: (i) reinforced multilateral cooperation; (ii) promotion of forceful enforcement; (iii) criminal, civil and administrative sanctions and sanctions at border control.

213 The 'Strategic Plan 2009' (see Strategic Plan 2009 at 44–5) mentions that the Government is to make an effort to reach agreement on the ACTA as early as possible. The expected signatory nations are: Japan, the EU, US, Switzerland, Canada, New Zealand, Mexico and Korea. In practice, well-known trade marks are highly likely to be victimised by those illegal actions, and it can therefore be submitted that the enforcement of regulating those issues will implicitly provide legal protection to well-known trade marks. It is commented that the contribution of the ACTA needs to be observed and that slight reform of the Trademark Act can be expected.

214 The efficacy of border control coupled with regulation by the unfair competition law is reported in the JPO Report in 2005, 'Chitikizaisan shingaibutsunitaisuru mizugiwaseidono arikata nikansuru cyosakenkyu (Report on the efficacy of the border control to seize goods infringing IP rights)'. Available online at www.jpo.go.jp/shiryou/toushin/chousa/pdf/zaisanken/17mizugiwabunnsatu1.pdf (accessed 7 November 2014).

215 In Japanese *kanji* script – 不正競争防止法: *Fusei kyoso boshi ho*. This is officially translated as the Unfair Competition Prevention Act. Act No. 47 of 1993, last amended by Act No. 12 of 2012.

216 Ibid.

217 Although the abolition of the *bogo-syohyo* registration system has been on the agenda, it is yet to happen.

trade mark to prevent the third party from registering/using the mark that is similar or identical to the earlier mark, in relation to dissimilar goods or services.

In order to satisfy the criteria for enjoying the extra protection as a defensive mark under Article 64, first, the earlier mark must be well known amongst the relevant public. Second, the later mark must be similar or identical to the earlier mark. Third, the later mark's use in respect of dissimilar goods or services must cause the likelihood of confusion with the earlier mark amongst the consumers.

The key point of the defensive trademark registration is that the use of the later mark that is similar or identical to the earlier well-known mark in relation to dissimilar goods or services must cause a likelihood of confusion amongst consumers. Therefore, the law protects the trademark being an indication of trade origin. Hypothetically, a third party's registration of the word mark 'Toyota' in relation to a restaurant would be prevented as long as the proprietor of the 'Toyota' mark in relation to the automobile could establish the likelihood of confusion between the marks amongst consumers. The drawback of this system is that, as in this hypothetical scenario, although the relevant consumers might make an association between the two marks, those consumers are very unlikely to be confused between the two Toyotas. As a result, the registration of such is most likely to fail.

We shall now look at a number of examples of successful and unsuccessful registration of the defensive trademark system. The earlier famous mark 'Seiko', in relation to soaps, attempted to register the mark 'Seiko' in relation to scientific, photographic, cinematographic, optical, weighing, measuring apparatus and instruments. Fame of the sign 'Seiko' was recognised and the defensive trademark registration was granted.[218] Similarly, the earlier famous mark 'Haisee [ハイシー]', in relation to chemical products, attempted to register the mark 'Haisee [ハイシー]' in relation to confectionery and sweets as a defensive mark. Fame of the sign Haisee [ハイシー]' was recognised and the defensive trademark registration was granted.[219] The earlier mark 'Toyota', in relation to automobiles, attempted to have a defensive trademark registration in relation to metals, and this application succeeded.[220] The earlier mark 'Kurabit [クラビット]', in relation to pharmaceutical and veterinary preparations, attempted to seek a defensive trademark registration for 'Kurabit [クラビット]' in relation to cleaning preparations and toilet preparations. This application was rejected on the grounds that the earlier mark had not obtained the sufficient level of fame required under Article 64.[221]

The defensive registered trademark system appears to be ineffective in practice and this registration has become a mere label,[222] although it might still be useful for foreign syuchi-syohyo owners to secure additional protection in Japan.

218 *Seiko defensive trademark application.* No. 3460 of 1963.
219 *Haisee defensive trademark application.* No. 24034 of 1981.
220 *Toyota defensive trademark application.* No. 21655 of 1981.
221 *Kurabit defensive trademark application.* No. 11427 of 1999.
222 See, for example, H. Kudo, *Syohyou no kaisetu to saiban rei*, Tokyo: MasterLink, 2011, p. 215.

5.5.2 Well-known trade mark protection: the Unfair Competition Prevention Act

The second route is through the Unfair Competition Prevention Act (*fusei kyoso boshi ho*).[223] This can be the main vehicle for *syuchi-syohyo* protection, accompanied by the trademark law. The first part of this section introduces an overview of unfair competition law and the second part explores how the well-known and/famous marks are protected in the unfair competition law with reference to case law.

The current form of the Japanese Unfair Competition Prevention Act[224] was born in 1993,[225] completely replacing the old 1934 Act,[226] and since then a number of major amendments have been made.[227]

One of the main characteristics of the 1993 Act is that prohibited acts are listed – that is, the Act employs the closed-list system in which an exhaustive list of acts that amount to unfair competition is provided. As a result, when a new type of unfair competition arises, the law could incrementally add such an act into the list; for example, the unauthorised use of and illicit possession of domain names were added in 2003.[228] One of the concerns of adopting the closed-list system is the fear that new law cannot come into force in a timely manner: by the time the law came into force, it might already be too late.[229]

The purpose of the unfair competition law is not to create a stand-alone natural right, but to regulate the 'act' – that is, to confer the right to take an action against the situation where there is an infringement of the right. In other words, the person cannot take an action if there is no right infringed.

5.5.2.1 The Japanese Unfair Competition Prevention Act

The Act differentiates well-known marks (*syuchi-syohyo*) and famous marks (*tyomei-syohyo*) in Articles 2(1)(1) and (2) respectively.

Article 2(1)(1) regulates the use of a sign that is similar or identical to an earlier *unregistered* well-known sign, which, because of its similarity to and identity with that sign, causes a likelihood of confusion to relevant consumers.[230] The scope of

---

223 Act No. 47 of 1993, last amended by Act No. 12 of 2012. The full text of the Act is available online at www.japaneselawtranslation.go.jp/law/detail/?ft=2&re=01&dn=1&yo=&ia=03&kn[]=%E3%81%B5&_x=19&_y=24&ky=&page=4 (accessed 7 November 2014).
224 Act No. 47 of 1993, last amended by Act No. 12 of 2012.
225 Ibid.
226 Act No. 14 of 1934.
227 Such as 1993, 1998 and 2001.
228 Act No. 46 of 2005.
229 See one example of the protectable subject matter in the Unfair Competition Act in J. Thessensohn and S. Yamamoto, 'Japan: Unfair Competition – Pharmaceuticals – Trade Dress', *European Intellectual Property Review*, 29, 2007, N43–4.
230 Article 2(1)(1) sets out as follows: 'Article 2(1) The term "unfair competition" as used in this Act means any of the following: (1) the *act of creating confusion* with another person's goods or business by using an indication of goods or business (meaning a name, trade name, trademark, mark, container or packaging for goods which is connected with a person's operations, or any other

the category of the sign is set out rather broadly and includes a name, trade name, trademark, mark, container or packaging for goods that is connected with a person's operations, or any other indication of a person's goods or business. Further to this, Article 2(1)(1) attempts to protect the local goodwill (of the traders) that is attached to the well-known unregistered sign of the goods or services, by preventing third parties from free-riding on the goodwill. Article 2(1)(1) thus plays a vital role for local traders who have no intention of registering the sign as a trademark and expanding their business on a larger scale. The requirement of Article 2(1)(1) is that: (i) the earlier sign must be well known, as an indication of origin, amongst the public; (ii) there must be a similarity between the earlier and later signs; (iii) the use of the later sign that is similar or identical to the earlier sign must cause the likelihood of confusion, because of that similarity or identity.

Article 2(1)(2),[231] which was newly added in the 1993 Amendment, prohibits third parties from using a mark that is identical or similar to the earlier famous mark, and prevents them from assigning, delivering or displaying the goods to which the earlier famous mark is attached. The purpose of this is understood to protect the trader's goodwill and their incentive in establishing business goodwill, and to prevent the famous mark from being diluted and/or tarnished (note that the Unfair Competition Prevention Act does not refer to the exact term 'dilution' *per se*). Article 2(1)(2) demands a higher degree of well-knownness than Article 2(1)(1); it requires the sign to be famous, but there is no need to prove the likelihood of confusion.

The requirement of Article 2(1)(2) is that (i) the earlier sign must be famous as an indication of origin; and (ii) there must be similarity between the earlier famous sign and the later sign.

5.5.2.2 Unfair competition jurisprudence

This section will look at the judicial application of Article 2(1)(1) and (2), considering how the unfair competition law protects well-known and famous marks, and will evidence the supplementary nature of the law of trademark and unfair competition. As a reminder, the former provision regulates the act whereby a third party uses the affiliation that is similar or identical to the claimant's well-known affiliation, where its being identical or similar to that affiliation causes confusion (on the part of the consumer). The latter provision regulates the unauthorised act whereby the third party, without consent, uses the claimant's famous affiliation as if it is theirs.

indication of a person's goods or business; the same shall apply hereinafter) that is identical or similar to an indication of goods or business *that is well-known* among consumers as that of another person, or by assigning, delivering, displaying for the purpose of assignment or delivery, exporting, importing or providing through a telecommunications line goods that uses such an indication' [emphasis added].

231 The full text of Article 2(1)(2) is as follows: 'use as one's own of an indication of goods, etc. identical or similar to another person's famous indication of goods, etc., or assignment, delivery display for the purpose of assignment or delivery, export, import or provision through a telecommunications line of goods bearing such an indication of the goods, etc.'

5.5.2.2.1 WELL-KNOWN (UNREGISTERED) MARKS: ARTICLE 2(1)(1)

Under the old unfair competition law regime, Article 1(1)(1) was applied to protect the name of a product, such as 'Walkman' for Sony.[232] We will now look at a number of cases – *Katsuretsu an*,[233] *Jeans stitch*,[234] *Micro diet*[235] and *GEKI manjyu*[236] – in order to examine well-known signs under Article 2(1)(1).

The first case to be introduced here is *Katsuretsu an*.[237] The case illustrates how being well known in the context of geographic area plays a role in determining the well-known nature under Article 2(1)(1). In 1927, the claimant started a Japanese restaurant called 'Katsuretsu an' – represented in the *kanji* script, 勝烈庵 – in Yokohama City. His restaurant business gradually expanded and resulted in having 20 branches in neighbouring cities, including Kawasaki, Fujisawa and Machida (in Tokyo), and 2,000 employees. The annual net income reached over ¥1,200,000,000 (equivalent to £8,125,276 in 1980), and the number of customers visiting the restaurant each day reached more than 4,000. In the meantime, the claimant undertook intensive advertising campaigns to promote the business in newspapers, on the train and underground, on TV and in magazines. The first defendant opened a restaurant called 'Katsuretsu an' (represented in a combination of the *hira-gana* and *kanji* scripts, かつれつ庵) and/or 'Katsuretsu an tosa (かつれつ庵佐渡) in the city of Kamakura. The sign of the first defendant was vocally identical but visually dissimilar to the claimant's earlier sign. The second defendant opened the restaurant 'Katsuretsu an', represented entirely in the *hira-gana* script (かつれつあん) in the city of Fuji, Shizuoka. The sign of the second defendant was vocally identical but not visually identical to the claimant's earlier sign. The claimant sued both defendants, seeking damages and an injunction, in order to prevent them from using the name 'Katsuretsu an' in both Kamakura and Fuji, a measure to prevent any use the sign 'sano katsuretsu an' in the future. The court granted an injunction to the claimant. The court held that to apply for Article 2(1)(1) the sign is required to be known in a certain geographical area, but is not required to be known in the wider area, and the rights conferred shall be limited to the area in which the sign is known. The court accepted that 'Katsuretsu an' is well known in Kamakura, but not in Fuji. *Katsuretsu an* illustrates that the well-knownness in the geographical area does not require national well-knownness; local well-knownness is sufficient for the application of Article 2(1)(1).

232 Chiba District Court, Heisei 3nen (Wa) 1746.
233 *Katsuretsu an.* Yokohama District Court, Showa 56(wa) 2100. The decision of the Yokohama District Court, 9 December, 1983.
234 *Jeans stitch.* Tokyo High Court, Heisei 12nen (Ne) 3882. Appeal from Tokyo District Court, Heisei 8nen (Wa) 12929.
235 *Micro diet,* Tokyo High Court, Heisei 15nen (Ne) 1430go.
236 *GEKI manj.* Tokyo District Court, Heisei 16nen (Wa) 3137go.
237 *Katsuretsu an.* Yokohama District Court, Showa 56(wa) 2100. The decision of the Yokohama District Court, 9 December, 1983. *Katsuretsu an.* Showa 56(wa) 2100.

In *GEKI manjyu*,[238] on the other hand, the mark could not pass the hurdle of the extent of the geographical area in which the mark needs to be known under Article 2(1)(1). The claimant is a manufacturer of the Japanese traditional sweets, *manjyu*, named '擊 GEKI'. The defendant sold sweets named '擊 GEKI' at military bases. The claimant proceeded litigation against the defendant, alleging that the defendant's use of the name '擊 GEKI' had amounted to unfair competition under Article 2(1)(1) and that the claimant's mark was well known. The following evidence was submitted to prove the *syuchi* status of '擊 GEKI'. First, the duration of the mark being used: the *manjyu* in question had been on the market since February 2004; by December 2004, 19,000 boxes of '擊 GEKI' *manjyu* were sold, which was not a great number. Second, the degree of advertisement: the product was mentioned in a TV programme on September 2003. The defendant argued that the advertisement made a significant contribution to an increase in sales between October and December 2003. However, the court looked at the volumes and it was found that 75 per cent of sales in that period were concentrated on one particular shop, which gave rise to doubt about the geographical area in which the mark was well known. Of more than 400 shops, the '擊 GEKI' *manjyu* were sold in only 20. As a result, it cannot be said that the volume of sales was increased in *all* of the shops, and the mark was not considered to be well known under Article 2(1)(1).

To briefly summarise, the threshold of the geographical area of well-knownness of the mark under Article 2(1)(1) does not seem high; the mark does not need to be known throughout Japan, but needs to be known in a certain area of Japan.

Next, we will examine the issues surrounding the degree of knowledge and recognition of the mark in the relevant public: to what extent the mark needs to be known to consumers in order for the mark to be qualified as a well-known mark under Article 2(1)(1). *Jeans stitch*[239] provides some guidance as to the degree of knowledge and recognition of the mark in the relevant public. The claimant, the US company Levi's, and the defendant, the Japanese company Edwin, are both well-known manufacturers of clothes, whose strength lies in producing jeans. The claimant sued the defendant in Article 2(1)(1) (and 2(1)(2)), alleging that the defendant's use of the arch-shaped stitching to the pocket was very similar to that of the claimant, and this had amounted to the prohibited act under Article 2(1)(1). In order for the claimant to prove that the arch-shaped stitching to the pocket is well known, a series of questionnaire results were submitted as evidence. The first questionnaire was conducted with consumers who had purchased their products in the past six months. The second questionnaire was conducted with both male and female consumers between the ages of 15 and 34 who had purchased either the claimant's or the defendant's products in the past year. The third questionnaire was conducted with consumers who had no relation to this retail industry. In the

238 *GEKI manjyu*. Tokyo District Court, Heisei 16nen (Wa) 3137go.
239 *Jeans stitch*. Tokyo High Court, Heisei 12nen (Ne) 3882. Appeal from Tokyo District Court, Heisei 8nen (Wa) 12929.

first questionnaire, 46 per cent of consumers between the ages of 15 and 29 were able to recognise the trade origin when the stitching was shown, and 31 per cent of consumers between the ages of 15 and 69 were able to do so. In the second questionnaire, 86 per cent of consumers were certain that they had recognised the stitching in question and 37 per cent of those identified correctly that the stitching in question belonged to the claimant. In the third questionnaire, 18 per cent of the general public identified the stitching in question as belonging to the claimant. Taking this evidence into account, the court held for the claimant and accepted that the claimant's stitching is well known under Article 2(1)(1). Irrespective of the credibility of the questionnaires, this gives us the impression that the knowledge threshold is high. Therefore, it can be said that the degree of the recognition of the mark in the relevant consumers sets a higher hurdle for the proprietor of the well-known trade mark.

The degree of any promotion of the mark is linked with the assessment of well-knownness under Article 2(1)(1), as became evident in the case of *Micro diet*.[240] The court assessed the *syuchi* status of the mark solely based on the factual evidence submitted by the claimant. The claimants produced and sold low-calorie food products called 'Micro Diet' and/or 'マイクロダイエット'. The sign, 'Micro Diet' and/or 'マイクロダイエット' is attached to the product and applied to the packaging. The defendant produced and sold similar products named 'Micro Silhouette' and/or 'マイクロシルエット'. The claimant brought an action against the defendant under Article 2(1)(1) and (2), alleging that the claimant's sign is deemed to be a protectable subject matter under Article 2(1)(1). The court held for the claimant and accepted that the mark in question is well known under Article 2(1)(1).

The following factual evidence was taken into consideration for assessing *syuchi* status: newspaper advertisements, the volume of sales, the number of purchasers, the number of magazines containing the advertisement and degree of advertising. There had been a gradual increase in the frequency of advertising since 1994. For example, in 1992 the number of magazine titles in which the advertisement was included increased from one to 19 titles, and the frequency increased from one to 23 times. In 1995, the frequency of advertisements had increased to 48 times and, by 1996, the average number of the advertisement circulated in the magazines was 92 times in 35 different titles. With regard to the volume of sales, between 1988 and 1994 the overall volume of sales reached 119 million packages, which the court held to be a considerable number.

Above all, the court held that, considering the well-knownness and sales volume of the magazines, this evidence was sufficient to conclude that the mark obtained *syuchi* status under Article 2(1)(1). An increase in the frequency of advertisements and number of magazine titles that contain the advertisement is compatible with an increase in the volume of sales. Thus, the mark was deemed well known in the sense of Article 2(1)(1). The court also made a remark on the relevant consumers:

---

240 *Micro diet*. Tokyo High Court, Heisei 15nen (Ne) 1430go.

the relevant consumer shall include not only those who actually purchase the product to which the mark is attached, but also those who do not purchase. Therefore, the mark needs to be well known in the wider range of consumers, who are not direct consumers of the product. In other words, under Article 2(1) (1), the mark does not need to be nationally well known, but does need to be well known in the general public.

Therefore, the mark cannot be said to be well known only to relevant consumers – in the *GEKI manjyu* case,[241] introduced above, this was those who worked for the Self-Defence Force – but it must also be relevant to consumers more generally. In this case, the court denied the application of Article 2(1)(1), holding that the mark in question did not amount to being well known.

Above all, *syuchi* under Article 2(1)(1) requires a mark to be well known throughout Japan not only to relevant consumers, but also to the general public. The court seems to take a restrictive approach in assessing *syuchi*, since a higher degree of *syuchi* is required to apply Article 2(1)(1). Furthermore, in order to prove *syuchi*, the court heavily relies on the factual evidence, as, for instance, in the case of *Jeans stitch*.[242] The higher degree of *syuchi* in the geographical area as well as among relevant consumers is required; in other words, *syuchi*, is assessed on the grounds of the geographic extent to which the mark is known and to whom the mark is known.

5.5.2.2.2 FAMOUS MARKS: ARTICLE 2(1)(2)

Article 2(1)(2) regulates the act of unfair competition where the third party uses the mark that is identical or similar to the earlier famous mark. For example, 'Maxell' for cassettes[243] and 'J-Phone' for telecommunication services[244] are recognised as famous marks under Article 2(1)(2). The purpose of Article 2(1)(2) is to protect the trader's goodwill, allow the trader to establish business goodwill, and to prevent dilution and/or tarnishment. A series of cases will be considered to highlight the interpretation of *syuchi-syohyo* under Article 2(1)(2) and to compare the differences between the requirement of well-knownness in Article 2(1)(1) and (2). As a reminder, well-knownness under Article 2(1)(1) is assessed by the geographical extent of the use and recognition of the mark, the degree of the recognition of the mark in the relevant sectors of the population and the degree of promotion of the mark.

The first case to be introduced is *Moschino*.[245] Here the earlier mark is 'Moschino'. The later mark is 'Moschino Camerio Italy'. The proprietor of the earlier mark brought the action against the later use of the mark, applying for Article 2(1)(2).

---

241 *GEKI manjyu.* Tokyo District Court, Heisei 16nen (Wa) 3137go.
242 Ibid.
243 *Maxell.* Osaka District Court, Heisei 15nen (wa) 6624go.
244 *J-Phone.* Tokyo District Court, Heisei 13nen, 4gatsu, Hanketsu, Heisei 12nen (wa) 3545go, Hanji 1755go 43.
245 *Moschino.* Tokyo District Court, Heisei 8nen (Wa) 21631go.

The claimant was the famous Moschino producers of luxury goods. The defendant started producing the products to which the mark 'Moschino Camerio Italy' was attached. The claimant sued the defendant for Article 2(1)(2), alleging that the defendant's use of the mark, which was similar to that of the claimant, had amounted to acts prohibited under Article 2(1)(2). In order to show that the earlier mark was famous in the Article 2(1)(2) sense, the following evidence was submitted:

(i)   the degree of the recognition of and any promotion of the mark: Moschino was listed as one of the most luxurious products in the world in 1991 and 1996;

(ii) the degree of the recognition of the mark: the publication of a newspaper article (the main article) extracted from an interview with the general manager of the Moschino in relation to their business plan after the death of the founder of Moschino (Franco Moschino) in 1996;

(iii) the degree of any promotion of the mark: from 1898 to 1996, Moschino goods, such as bags, clothes, leather goods, jewellery, eyewear, sunglasses, shoes and bags, were advertised in a great number of different magazine titles (the total sales of these magazines were 90,000 to 780,000) across different age groups and genders.

The court took the factual evidence into consideration in the assessment of Article 2(1)(2), and held that at the time (1995), the claimant's mark was famous not only to relevant traders and consumers, but also to the general public. It is of interest that all the evidence submitted appears to demonstrate the degree of promotion of the mark, and the evidence to prove whether the mark has been promoted seems to be the sole and overriding criterion in deciding the famousness of the mark under Article 2(1)(2).

Trussardi[246] followed a similar vein of reasoning to *Moschino*. The issue was between the earlier mark 'Trussardi' and the later mark 'Trussardi' and/or 'Trussardi Johns' and/or 'トラサルディ' in combination with 'Made in Italy'. The claimant was the manufacturer, owner, authorised distributor and licensee of Trussardi in Japan. The licensed products are sold under the name of 'Trussardi' and/or 'トラサルディ'. The defendant started deploying the mark, 'Trussardi' and/or 'Trussardi Johns' and/or 'トラサルディ' in combination with 'Made in Italy', which was identical or similar to the claimant's mark. The claimant sued the defendant, alleging that the defendant's use of the marks that were identical or similar to those of the claimant amounted to the act under Article 2(1) (2). In order to prove that the claimant was famous, the following was submitted to the court:

(i)   the record of the exclusive rights: an authorised licensing agreement between Trussardi and the Japanese exclusive authorised licensee, Ito, and the legitimate transfer of the trademark rights of the marks to Ito;

246 *TRUSSARDI*. Tokyo District Court, Heisei 9nen (Wa) 3588go.

(ii)   the degree of any promotion of the mark: the claimants had actively undertaken advertising promotion (e.g. advertising in newspapers, magazines, billboards and posters at train stations), the annual cost of which was ¥400,000,000 (equivalent to £2,683,596). For instance, between November 1992 and February 1995, advertisements for clothing, watches, shoes, glasses, bags, golf products and accessories were published in a number of monthly magazines, broadsheet newspapers and on billboards, including the airport. Since 1995, the claimant's products, to which the mark is attached, had been advertised in magazines including *Figaro*, *President* and *Esquire*. Four of the major regional newspapers, covering the area of Tokyo, Osaka and Nagoya, publicised the claimant's products. By applying a similar approach to that taken by *Moschino*, the court held that the claimant's mark was of fame throughout the nation at the time (1995).

Yet again, the degree of any promotion of the mark seems to be the sole consideration under Article 2(1)(2).

Next to be examined is *Alinabig A25*.[247] The issue was between the earlier mark 'Alinamin A25' and the later mark 'Alinabig 25'. The proprietor of the earlier mark was Takeda Pharmaceutical Company, which manufactures and sells, *inter alia*, the nutritious drink 'Alinamin A25'. The later mark was used by the defendant, Toyo Pharma, which started selling a similar product called Alinabig 25. The claimant sued the defendant, arguing that the defendant's use of Alinabig had amount to an act of unfair competition under Article 2(1)(2). In order to prove that the claimant's mark is famous, the following evidence was submitted:

(i)   the duration of the use of the mark: the product, in which the earlier mark was attached, in question has been on the market since 1954 and the range of the products, such as Alinamin A, Alinamin A50, Alinamin EX, had been expanded;
(ii)   the record of the market share: more than 99 per cent of pharmacies in Japan sell the range of the claimant's products and the claimant's products is fourth best-selling product in the field of energy drinks;
(iii) the record of the annual revenue: the products in question generated the annual sum of ¥11,100,000,000 (equivalent to £74,473,301) and between 1967 and 1997 the overall sales reached ¥349,000,000,000 (equivalent to £2,341,547,962 at the time of the case);
(iv)   the degree of any promotion of the mark: the claimant had advertised their products, including a photographic image of the product as well as the name, through the national, regional and local papers and magazines. The cost of advertising the products between 1980 and 1996 was: TV – ¥18,300,000,000 (equivalent to £122,778,647); radio – ¥400,000,000 (equivalent to £2,683,686); newspapers – ¥5,041,000,000 (equivalent to £33,820,042); magazines – ¥2,300,100,000 (equivalent to £15,432,245).

---

247 *Alinabig A25*. Osaka District Court, Heisei 10nen (Wa) 5743go.

Taking this evidence into consideration, the court held for the claimant and held that it was plainly obvious that the mark in question was a famous mark. In addition to the degree of any promotion of the mark, the court attempted to consider the market share and volume of sales of the product throughout the nation.

The next case is *Toraya*.[248] The claimant, who uses '虎屋 [toraya]' and '虎屋黒川 [toraya kurokawa]' as their business affiliation, started proceedings against the defendant, alleging that the defendant's identical or similar names amounted to an act of unfair competition under Article 2(1)(2) of the Unfair Competition Prevention Act.

The point of law was whether the claimant's mark amounted to a 'famous mark' and therefore qualified for protection under Article 2(1)(2). In order to prove that the claimant's affiliation was 'famous', the following categories of evidence were submitted:

(i)   duration of the continuous use of the mark: the mark has been in use since 1869;
(ii) the geographical extent of the use of the mark is used: all products bore the 'Toraya' mark, and multiple branches were in operation throughout Japan and outside Japan. At the time of the litigation, there were 68 shops, including one in every major city in Japan, as well as outside Japan in cities such as Paris and New York. The claimant also operated nine cafés throughout Japan under the name of Toraya;
(iii) evidence of proactive promotion of the mark *via* intensive advertising: intensive advertising to promote the mark was done not only through nationwide magazines and newspapers but also on the company's webpage, which had recorded a large number of hits by consumers. Exhibitions and seminars in relation to the Japanese sweets were regularly held, and the company's products are used as a souvenir given by the Japanese emperor and empress to their visitors;
(iv) the degree of the recognition of the mark: questionnaires conducted around the greater Tokyo area showed that 96 per cent of people knew Toraya.

Taking the evidence into account, the court held that the claimant's mark did amount to a famous mark, and therefore qualified for protection under Article 2(1)(2). This case demonstrates yet again the current Japanese approach to the assessment of fame and well-knownness in the context of unfair competition law.

Maxell[249] also applied the evidence to prove whether the mark is famous. The issue is between 'Maxell' and the later domain name 'maxellgrp.com'.

Here the claimant held the famous mark 'Maxell' for cassettes. The defendant obtained a domain name 'maxellgrp.com', which the claimant alleged is very similar to the claimant's mark, and created a website for advertising the

248 *Toraya*. Tokyo District Court, Heisei 17(wa) 14972go, the appeal from Heisei 11(wa) 29234go.
249 *Maxell*. Osaka District Court, Heisei 15nen (wa) 6624go.

defendant's business (adult entertainment). Taking into account the evidence that the claimant's mark is registered under AIPPI (International Association for the Protection of the Intellectual Property) Japan and is listed as one of the most well-known and famous marks in Japan, the court held for the claimant and recognised the claimant's mark as being famous. In this case, the record of the successful registration by the competent authority (AIPPI Japan) was the decisive evidence in assuming the mark of fame.

Aoyma Gakukin[250] is a leading case of the application of Article 2(1)(2). Here the issue was between the earlier marks ('Aoyama Gakuin'/'青山学院' and 'Aoyama Gakuin Chutogu'/'青山学院中等部') and the later use of a mark containing the word 'Aoyama' as part of that later mark, including '呉青山学院中学校' 'Kure Aoyama Gakuin' and 'Kure Aoyama Gakuin Junior High School'.

The claimant's mark was alleged to be a famous sign for both the university and the junior high school. The claimant argued that the later use of the signs '呉青山学院中学校', 'Kure Aoyama Gakuin' and 'Kure Aoyama Gakuin Junior High School', which are similar to the earlier mark, was likely to dilute the value and distinctiveness of the name of the school. The claimant submitted the following evidence to prove that the claimant's name is of fame:

(i)   the duration of and the degree and geographical extent of the recognition of the business in trade: the claimant had been in business for more than 125 years and, since its establishment, the number of schools had been increased and expanded; applications to the school were sent from all over Japan, from Hokkaido to Okinawa, and open days were held for those prospective students. Throughout the long-established history of the school, each prefecture has had graduates, and networking and alumni events take place throughout Japan. The questionnaire, conducted with prospective students for the claimant's university, showed that 2,089 out of 3,799 students gave positive answers that the claimant's school is famous;

(ii) the degree of any promotion of the mark: the claimant's institutions are proactively publicised and advertised through national TV, magazines and newspapers in order to improve their reputation and value;

(iii) the record of the successful registration of the trademark.

The court held for the claimant and accepted that the mark is a mark of fame under Article 2(1)(2). Therefore, the use of a similar mark 'Kure Aoyama Gakuin' constitutes infringement under Article 2(1)(2).

The final case to be considered here is *Sweet Lover*.[251] *Sweet Lover* is the Japanese equivalent to *Bellure*, which was discussed at length in the Chapter 4. Owing to the similarity of the facts of these cases, it is interesting to examine how *Sweet Lover* was handled by the Japanese judiciary under the unfair competition law.

---

250 *Aoyma Gakukin*. Tokyo District Court, Heisei 13nen (wa) 967go, Hanji 1815go, 148.
251 *Sweet Lover*, Tokyo High Court, Syowa 55nen, 1gatsu 28 Mutaisyu 12kan 1go 1.

The issue was first brought to the court in 1980 under the old Unfair Competition Prevention Act. The defendant, a producer of a perfume called *Sweet Lover*, created an advertisement comparing the smell of *Sweet Lover* to *Miss Dior*, *Chanel No. 5* and *Mitsouko*, whose marks are owned by the claimant. The main issue was whether this use of famous names as part of a comparative advertisement could amount to unfair competition under the old Article 1(1)(1) (equivalent to Article 2(1)(1) of the current law). The perfume *Sweet Lover* was sold as if the smell was very similar to one of the claimant's perfumes (*Miss Dior* and *Chanel No. 5*), when it was, in fact, not similar at all.

The trial judge dismissed the claim and the claimant appealed to the High Court. The High Court upheld the first instance decision and denied the application of Article 1(1)(1). It was held that the defendant advertised their products as *smelling like Miss Dior* or *Chanel No 5*; they had not advertised their products *as Miss Dior* or *Chanel No. 5*. The court explained that average consumers were aware that they were not buying *Miss Dior* or *Chanel No. 5*. In other words, the relevant consumers received clear information that the products of the defendant contained a similar smell to that of the claimant's. This decision gives the impression that the state of the consumer's mind is the key factor in relation to third-party use of a well-known mark in comparative advertising.

Clearly, in the domain of unfair competition law, the court took a rather stringent and restrictive approach to the well-known mark. Interestingly, the reasoning presented by the Japanese court is completely different from that of *Bellure*. The Japanese jurisprudence considers that any third party's use of the earlier famous mark A, being part of the comparative advertising to sell the third party's product B, appears not to amount to trademark infringement or an act of unfair competition, so long as the consumers are not misled to buy B, believing that they are buying the product A. It is clear that the protected interest under the unfair competition law is the well-known mark being an indication of origin. Provided that such a function is not being violated, there is nothing that the law can protect.

Although *Sweet Lover* is still an authority, it is useful to introduce more recent developments in respect of the judicial treatment of the third party's use of a well-known trade mark in comparative advertising. The recent trend is that when the issue concerns comparative advertising, Article 2(1)(14) is more likely to be made applicable than Article 2(1)(1) or (2).

In *Pos-cum*[252] the claimant and defendant were confectionery manufacturers, whose business included manufacturing and selling chewing gum. The defendant launched a new range of chewing gum called 'Pos-cum (very clear and dry taste)' and created an advertisement accordingly. In the advert, the following statement was made: 'a "Pos-cum" is five times more effective in teeth whitening than the normal xylitol contained in chewing gum.' Note that the claimant's chewing gum contained the substance called xylitol plus two.

---

252 *Pos-cum.* Intellectual Property High Court, Heisei 18nen (ne) 10059go (unreported).

The claimant alleged that the defendant's advertisement contained a false and inaccurate statement and that such a comparative advertisement amounted to unfair competition pursuant to Article 2(1)(14), and sought an injunction. The trial judge dismissed the claim and the claimant appealed to the Intellectual Property High Court. The court overruled the first instance's decision and held that the comparative advertisement containing the false statement ought not to be permitted. The focus was not on the use of the well-known or famous mark but on the advertisement being false or inaccurate.

Above all, it can be concluded (as agreed by Japanese legal academics[253]) that use of a famous mark (*tyomei-syohyo*) (which does not cause any false indication of origin) in the context of comparative advertising does not amount to an act of unfair competition. In other words, an accurate reference to the well-known/ famous mark in a comparative advertisement is legitimately permitted in Japan for the purpose of preventing unfair competition and promoting sound and healthy competition amongst traders. Although the extent to which the decision of *Bellure* has an implication for the Japanese trademark regime is worth observing, under the current regime it appears that Japan is unlikely change its approach to comparative advertising under the domain of the Unfair Competition Prevention Act.

5.5.3 Summary

Under the current legal system in Japan, *syohyo* and *syuchi-syohyo* can be protected by both the Trademark Act[254] and the Unfair Competition Prevention Act, which work closely together and are complementary to each other. The Trademark Act operates under the registration system, which provides an exclusive right to use the registered mark in relation to the goods/services. The Unfair Competition Prevention Act, on the other hand, directly regulates acts that are considered to amount to unfair competition. One of its purposes is to ensure fair competition amongst business operators and to provide measures for the prevention of unfair competition.[255]

The scope of protectable subject matter under the Unfair Competition Prevention Act is broader than that of the Trademark Act. For example, indications including personal names, trade names, trademarks (*syohyo*), trade symbols, appellations,[256] well-known unregistered trademarks,[257] reproduction of get-ups[258] and single colour *per se* are more likely to be protected in unfair competition law than trademark law.[259] In fact, not only is the scope of the

253 For example, Tamura, *Fusei kyoso boshi ho*, p. 56.
254 Act No. 127 of 1959 amended by Act No. 84 of 2014.
255 See Article 1 of the Unfair Competition Prevention Act for the purpose of the Act.
256 Ibid., Article 2(1).
257 Ibid., Article 2(2).
258 Ibid., Article 2(3).
259 Gomi, 'Chizaigakusetu no ugoki', pp. 145–7.

protectable subject matter in the Unfair Competition Prevention Act broader than that of the Trademark Act, but the Unfair Competition Prevention Act appears to provide the more flexible protection too, and this (it is submitted) also holds true for *syuchi-syohyo*.[260] Due to this flexible nature of the Act, it seems that *syuchi-syohyo* protection is more developed under the Unfair Competition Prevention Act.[261]

Overall, in order to apply for Article 2(1)(1), the following criteria must be satisfied: (i) the earlier sign must be well known, as an indication of origin, amongst the public; (ii) there is a similarity between the earlier and later signs; (iii) the use of the later sign, which is similar or identical to the earlier sign, must cause a likelihood of confusion because of the similarity or identity. In order to apply for Article 2(1)(2), a famous mark of A must be in use as a mark of B. Therefore, no infringement is established when the third party's use of the earlier famous mark does not cause consumers confusion as to the origin of the famous mark. Therefore, in principle, the proprietor of a famous mark is unable to bring a claim when the use of the mark correctly indicates the proprietor of the famous mark. Therefore, it makes sense the Unfair Competition Prevention Act has been seen as providing an effective mechanism for the protection of *syuchi-syohyo*.[262]

In relation to the assessment of the provisions above, the geographic extent and the degree of the recognition of the mark are the two dominant criteria for Article 2(1)(1), whilst the degree of promotion and advertising of the mark becomes dominant in assessing Article 2(1)(2). In other words, the court focuses

---

260 Articles 2(1) and (2) of the Unfair Competition Prevention Act.
261 The Japanese government does appear to recognise the importance of providing appropriate protection for *syuchi-syohyo*. For example, in 1992, the Japanese Government commissioned a study of the need to have special protection for well-known marks. It concluded as follows: 'In the current information society, product or business appellations are being more broadly used via a variety of different media. These brand images are becoming well known. These independent brand images have specific customer appeal. As such, they have attained an independent value of their own. Through use of these famous appellations, for example even when there is no confusion, such a user can gain the customer appeal of this famous appellation even though he did nothing to achieve it. This is known as "free-riding". As a result, consumers might become confused that this new comer is the same as the company that endeavoured to obtain high trust and repute. In this case, the good image of the first comer would be damaged. This is known as "dilution". (In such a case in the past,) courts have simply presumed confusion even though the facts of the case made confusion impossibility. Judges have deemed such a conclusion to be appropriate; however, they have come to question the notion of presuming confusion. Therefore, frankly speaking, it is appropriate to create a new cause of action where confusion is not necessary in order to protect famous appellations.' See JPO, '*Sangyo Kozo Shingikai Chiteki Zaisan Seisaku Bukai Hokokusho* (Report of the Intellectual Property Policy Committee of the Industrial Structure Council)', Tokyo: JPO, 1992.
262 Article 2(1)(1) prohibits acts of unfair competition defined in the Unfair Competition Prevention Act. The well-known trademark and the famous trademark are protected in accordance with the relevant provisions stipulated in the Unfair Competition Prevention Act. Non-exhaustive lists of acts considered to be unlawful acts against fair and just competition are explicitly addressed in the Unfair Competition Prevention Act. Note that a so-called dilution-related article can be found herein: in order to establish 'dilution' under Article 2(1)(2), the plaintiff must establish the following: (i) use of the plaintiff's goods or other appellation by the defendant; (ii) the plaintiff's appellation is famous; and (iii) the defendant's appellation is the same as or similar to the plaintiff's.

more on the degree of financial expenditure, frequency and means of advertising the mark in the assessment of Article 2(1)(2). This plainly indicates the transformation of a *syuchi-syohyo*: once the *syuchi-syohyo* obtains *über* status, it becomes a *tyomei-syohyo*, which can be considered to be the finished or advanced product of a *syuchi-syohyo*.

5.6 Conclusion

The main aim of this chapter has been to explore the Japanese framework for protecting '*syuchi-syohyo*' against *dilution* and to assess the efficacy of this. It was mentioned that a Japanese translation of 'well-known trade mark' is '*syuchi-syohyo*', and the transliterated term '*syuchi-syohyo*' has been applied in this chapter.

Similar to the approach taken by the EU trade mark regime, the Japanese trademark regime does not define what constitutes '*syuchi-syohyo*'. Therefore, conceptualisation of '*syuchi-syohyo*' was undertaken by making reference to the definition of 'trade mark' (see Chapter 2). In summary, no conceptualisation of '*syuchi-syohyo*' was evidenced; the protection of '*syuchi-syohyo*' against *fuseino mokuteki* is based on contextualisation.

The examination of the Japanese approach to the protection of '*syuchi-syohyo*' against *fuseino mokuteki* and the assessment of the certainty of the same lead to the conclusion that '*syuchi-syohyo*' protection against *fuseino mokuteki* in Japan is not certain and lacks clarity.

Not having a clear and comprehensive definition of '*syuchi-syohyo*' and *fuseino mokuteki* is submitted to be the cause of potential uncertainty.

The following have been presented:

(i) the absence of well-known trademark protection against *fuseino mokuteki* at the trademark infringement level: the likelihood of confusion must be present for an action in trademark infringement;
(ii) the absence of any particular legal treatment of the protection afforded to '*syuchi-syohyo*' against *fuseino mokuteki* in the Trademark Act (see Sections 5.2 and 5.3);
(iii) the fact that alternative routes to protect '*syuchi-syohyo*' seem to be in favour in Japan (see Section 5.5);
(iv) the strong emphasis on the inherent distinctiveness of the earlier mark to determine whether and when a *syohyo* becomes a '*syuchi-syohyo*' (see Sections 5.3.2–5.3.3), and;
(v) the strong emphasis on non-exclusive factual-based criteria to determine whether and when a *syohyo* is registered with unfair purposes (see Sections 5.3.3–5.3.4).

Whether this lack of certainty and clarity is an acute problem is not clear from the findings of this chapter.

In Chapter 6, the following will be undertaken: (i) a critical comparison of the definitions of 'trade mark of repute' and '*syuchi-syohyo*'; and (ii) an assessment of the scope and clarity/certainty of protection afforded to both 'trade mark of repute' and '*syuchi-syohyo*' against detriment/unfair advantage and *fuseino mokuteki*.

It will be then considered what can be learned from these two systems in terms of the future development of well-known trade mark protection.

Above all, it might be concluded that '*syuchi-syohyo*', in particular coined marks, enjoy stronger protection under Article 4(1)(19) of the Japanese Trademark Act,[263] although assessments of '*syuchi-syohyo*' and *fuseino mokuteki* are based on non-exclusive fact-based criteria, and thus assessments of '*syuchi-syohyo*' and *fuseino mokuteki* are likely to vary case by case.[264]

---

263 Ono, *Syohyo ho*, p. 393. Having said this Article is intended to protect well-known trademarks, the majority of legal academics (e.g. Manda, Tamura, Miyazaki, Ono) still consider that well-known trademark protection should be dealt with under Article 2(1)(1) of the Japanese Unfair Competition Prevention Act.
264 H. Nishi, 'Tyomei syohyo wo hukumi syohyo to dedokoto kondo no osore', *Chizai Kanri*, 52, 2002, 361–71, p. 369.

6 Comparative analysis

6.1 Introduction

This chapter introduces a critical comparison between the positions set out in the EU and the Japanese systems.[1] The chapter is structured as follows. First, a comparison of the scope, clarity and function of well-known trade mark protection in the EU and Japan will be undertaken. Second, critical consideration will be offered as to how these two jurisdictions differ in their approach to trade marks of repute and *syuchi-syohyo*, and detriment/taking unfair advantage and *fuseino mokuteki*. Third, comparison will be made of the similarities between these two jurisdictions in their approach to trade marks of repute against detriment/ taking unfair advantage, and to *syuchi-syohyo* against *fuseino mokuteki*. Finally, some consideration will be given to the question: is it necessary (or helpful) to have a comprehensive conceptualisation of 'well-known trade mark' protection against 'detriment/unfair advantage'?

6.2 Conceptualisation of 'well-known trade mark'

Before starting the critical comparison of the well-known trade mark defined in the EU and Japan, the following points need to be repeated.

The first is the transformation, suggested by the author, from the most general to the most distinctive: trade mark → well-known trade mark → famous mark

---

1 A comparative legal analysis is employed. See K. Zweigert and H. Kötz, *An Introduction to Comparative Law*, Oxford: Clarendon Press, 1998, p. 19 and 31. See, further, M. Hoechke, *Epistemology and Methodology of Comparative Law*, Oxford: Hart Publishing, 2004, p. 39. See also A. Saidov, *Comparative Law*, London: Wildy, Simmons & Hill, 2003. Some of the generally accepted benefits of comparative law are as follows: (i) as an aid to legislators; (ii) as a tool of construction; (iii) as a component of the curriculum of universities and law schools; and (iv) as a contribution to the systemic unification of law. Furthermore, it can be said that the method of comparative law 'can provide a much richer range of model solutions than a legal science devoted to a single nation, simply because the different systems of the world can offer a greater variety of solutions' (Hoechke, *Epistemology and Methodology of Comparative Law*, p. 39): it is here that the central benefit of comparative methodology is to be found – in other words, enhancing the legal scholar's ability to critique and offer possible directions for legal reform of well-known trade marks by comparing the EU and Japanese systems.

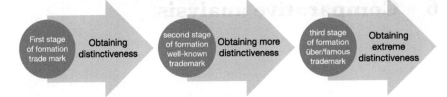

Figure 6.1 Formation of well-known trade mark

(see Figure 6.1). Therefore, the passport to becoming a well-known trade mark is obtaining *a certain degree of distinctiveness*.

Second, the principle of well-known trade mark protection, coupled with the ordinary trade mark principle, needs to be remembered. Protection of the well-known mark goes beyond the normal trade mark protection principle in two ways:

(i) Trade mark protection principle 1: statutory trade marks are protected through registration ('registration principle').

   Well-known trade mark protection principle 1: protection can be given irrespective of whether or not the mark is registered. Therefore, this goes beyond the 'registration principle'.

(ii) Trade mark protection principle 2: trade mark protection operates on the principle that the later registration, which would be likely to cause confusion as to trade origin amongst consumers/public ('beneficiaries') of the earlier mark, shall be refused in order to protect the beneficiaries from such confusion ('confusion principle').

   Well-known trade mark protection principle 2: the well-known trade mark protection expands the scope of protection to situations in which there is no likelihood of confusion between the earlier well-known trade mark and the later mark to the relevant public, even though these two marks are used for dissimilar goods or services.

Since well-known trade mark protection gives proprietors an extra layer of protection, it is not surprising that well-known trade mark proprietors are keen to enjoy such protection. The next step is for the proprietor to ask: 'What is a well-known mark?' In Chapter 1 this was called the key question. The answer to the key question was quite simple: we do not know. The main reason for such a proposition is that well-known trade mark protection is not a matter of law, but a matter of facts. In other words, well-known trade mark protection has been developed contextually, rather than conceptually. The author named this the contextualisation of the well-known trade mark protection, and suggested that the conceptualisation of well-known trade mark protection should be more encouraged.

In Chapter 3, the attempt was made to conceptualise the definition of 'well-known trade mark' at the international level. It was found that well-known trade mark protection has developed in the context (contextualisation of well-known trade mark protection), not in the concept (conceptualisation of well-known trade mark protection), and therefore the notion of 'well-known trade mark' is not conceptually defined at the international level. So we do not know exactly what a 'well-known trade mark' *is*. We then learnt that well-known trade mark protection is something to be contextualised (contextualisation of well-known trade mark protection, instead of conceptualisation). In short, the international regime does not provide a sufficient yardstick by which to understand the conceptual definitions of 'trade mark of repute' and '*syuchi-syohyo*' (to be found in the EU and Japanese systems, respectively). As a result of the inadequate tools provided by the international instruments, the Definition Model, as developed in Chapter 2, becomes the *de facto* yardstick by which to compare these concepts analogous to 'well-known trade mark' (although, obviously, consideration of the international guidance on defining 'well-known trade mark' remains important).

Before undertaking the comparison of the definitions of 'trade mark of repute' and '*syuchi-syohyo*', a gentle reminder of the Definition Model[2] is helpful:

> well-known trade mark *form* consists of trade mark *type* and trade mark *context*;
> well-known trade mark *concept* is a high level of acquired distinctiveness, and;
> the two *preconditions* are *graphical representation* and *commercial use*.

6.2.1 'Well-known trade mark': the international level

We now know that there is no conceptual definition of 'well-known trade mark' at the international level. In consequence, a composite definition of 'well-known trade mark', achieved by mosaicing elements of the Paris Convention,[3] GATT TRIPS[4] and the WIPO Recommendation,[5] is offered[6] as follows: well-known trade mark *form* explicitly includes registrable trade marks, service marks, business identifiers and domain names. Well-known trade mark *concept* lies in the

---

2 See Chapter 2, Section 2.2.
3 A summary of the Paris Convention is as follows. No comprehensive and conceptual definition of 'well-known trade mark' is provided. It is submitted that guidance in the Paris Convention as to the *form* of 'trade mark' can be used to infer the *form* of 'well-known trade mark'. It is also submitted that *concept* of 'trade mark' is present; however, there are no provisions on *concept* that are particular to well-known trade marks, so, exercising the assumption that we can infer the latter through the former, we can say that (well-known) trade mark *concept* is distinctive character, and that such distinctive character needs (at least) to be national in nature. See Chapter 3, Section 3.2.1.
4 A summary of GATT TRIPS is as follows. In Article 16 of GATT TRIPS, both *form* (*context*) and *concept* of 'well-known trade mark' can be recognised. First, the *form* of 'well-known trade mark' is limited to *context* (there is no explicit reference to *type*) – that is, the reference to service marks in Article 16(2). Second, at first reading, *concept* of 'well-known trade mark' in the Definition Model does not appear to be found in GATT TRIPS as the term 'distinctiveness' is not used. However, unlike the Paris Convention, some explicit guidance as to when a mark is well-known is provided – that is, recognition of marks. See Chapter 3, Section 3.2.2.
5 It is argued that this division is necessary as the WIPO Recommendation is not legally binding. See Chapter 3, Section 3.2 5, for the nature of the WIPO Recommendation.
6 See Chapter 3, Section 3.2.5.

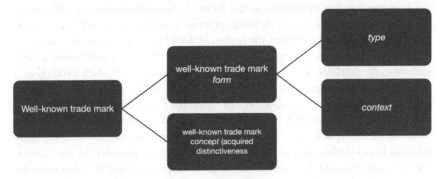

Figure 6.2 Definition Model – well-known trade mark

consideration of to what extent a mark is well known (well-knownness) in signatory nations of the Paris Convention and GATT TRIPS and in the knowledge of the relevant public, in which the promotion of trade marks needs to be taken into consideration in assessing if a mark is well known or not.

The factors that may be used in assessing whether or not a mark is well known include: the degree of knowledge or recognition of the mark in the relevant sector of the public; the duration, extent and geographical area of any use of the mark; promotion of the mark; trade mark registration or applications; a record of successful enforcement of rights in the mark, and the value of the mark.[7]

In Chapter 3, a newly formulated Definition Model was suggested. With reference to the newly formulated Definition Model (see Figure 6.2 above), well-known trade marks under the Paris Convention are simply trade marks that are well known in the country of registration or use. Thus, there is no explicit specific guidance as to *form* or *concept* of 'well-known trade mark' here. Well-known trade marks under GATT TRIPS are trade marks (including service marks) for which there is sufficient knowledge in the relevant sector of the public (including knowledge obtained as a result of promotion of the trade mark). Service marks are explicitly included. There is some attention to *context* in *form*, and the *concept* lies in knowledge. However, (well-known) trade mark *preconditions* are not addressed in GATT TRIPS. The composite definition also contains some elements of the WIPO Recommendations – in particular, the criteria used to assess whether or not the mark is well known.[8] It has become clear that 'well-known trade mark' is something to contextualise, but not to conceptualise.

6.3 Conceptualisation of 'trade mark of repute' and '*syuchi-syohyo*'

The conceptual definition of 'well-known trade mark' at the regional and national levels was explored in Chapters 4 and 5 respectively. Interestingly, in both

---

7 See Chapter 3, Section 3.3.
8 Article 2 of the WIPO Recommendation.

jurisdictions, the term 'well-known trade mark' used in Article 6*bis* of the Paris Convention is not employed; alternatively – and, arguably, equivalently – 'trade mark of repute' and '*syuchi-syohyo*' are employed. The compatibility of those two terms with the well-known trade mark defined in Article 6*bis*, and thus the credibility of the protection conferred, can be questioned, given that that there is a possibility of the terminological differences being substantive.

The extent to which the definitions of 'trade mark of repute' under the EU TMD[9] and '*syuchi-syohyo*' under the Japanese Trademark Act[10] are compatible with the various elements of the Definition Model will now be considered. Figures 6.3 and 6.4 encapsulate the overall picture of conceptualisation of 'trade mark of repute' and '*syuchi-syohyo*'.

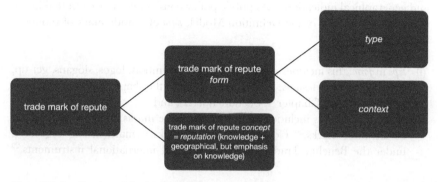

Figure 6.3 Application of the Definition Model – EU

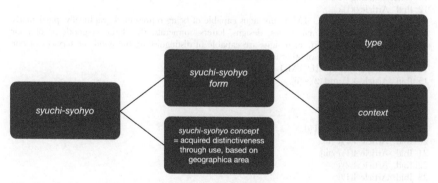

Figure 6.4 Application of the Definition Model – Japan (Stage 2)

9 Articles 4(4)(a) and 5(2) of the EU TMD (correspondingly Articles 8(5) and 9(1)(c) of the CTMR).
10 Articles 4(1)(10) and 4(1)(19) of the Japanese Trademark Act.

6.3.1 The form of 'trade mark of repute' and 'syuchi-syohyo'

A comparison of Article 4(4)(a)[11] (and corresponding Article 5(2)[12] in the EU TMD) and Article 4(1)(10) of the Japanese Trademark Act relating to *form* will now be undertaken.

With respect to the EU system, 'trade mark of repute' includes trade marks defined in Article 2 of the EU TMD[13] and Community trade marks,[14] marks being registered under the Benelux Trade Mark Office[15] and international instruments,[16] and well-known marks stated in the Paris Convention.[17] EU trade marks include signs under Article 2 of the EU TMD, but excluded under Article 3 is subject matter such as mere description of the indications of trade origin or goods,[18] a mark which has become common,[19] shapes of goods which achieve the technical result[20] or add substantive value,[21] emblems or national escutcheons[22] and geographical indication.[23] As public policy considerations are omitted in the definitional emphasis of the Definition Model, *form* of a trade mark of repute in the EU TMD is thus:

(i) *type* in *form*: this includes any signs, including symbols, logos, slogans, get-up, personal names, designs, letters, numerals and the shape of goods or of their packaging[24] (see Chapter 4, Section 4.3.1.1); and

(ii) *context* in *form*: this includes trade marks, service marks, geographic marks,[25] certification marks,[26] Community trade marks,[27] marks being registered under the Benelux Trade Mark Office[28] and international instruments,[29]

---

11 Correspondingly Article 8(5) of the CTMR.
12 Ibid., Article 9(1)(c).
13 See Article 2 of the EU TMD (any signs capable of being represented graphically, particularly words, including personal names, designs, letters, numerals, the shape of goods or of their packaging, provided that such signs are capable of distinguishing the goods or services of one undertaking from those of other undertakings).
14 Article 4(2)(a)(i) of the EU TMD.
15 Ibid., Article 4(1) and (2)(a)(ii).
16 Ibid., Article 4(2)(a)(iii).
17 Ibid., Article 4(2)(d).
18 Ibid., Article 4(1)(c).
19 Ibid., Article 4(1)(a) and (d).
20 Ibid., Article 4(1)(e)(ii).
21 Ibid., Article 4(1)(e)(iii).
22 Ibid., Article 4(2)(c).
23 Ibid., Article 4(1)(g).
24 Some similarities between the EU TMD and GATT TRIPS are as follows: Article 3 of the EU TMD and Article 15(1) of GATT TRIPS appear to be rather similar; 'trade mark' is defined both in the EU TMD and GATT TRIPS as a sign that is capable of being distinguished and of being graphically represented, including personal names, designs, letters and colours.
25 Article 3(1)(g) of the EU TMD. See B. O'Connor, 'The EC Need Not Be Isolated on GIS', *European Intellectual Property Review*, 8, 2007, 303–6, p. 303.
26 Article 1 of the EU TMD.
27 Article 4(2)(a)(i) of the EU TMD.
28 Ibid., Article 4(1) and (2)(a)(ii).
29 Ibid., Article 4(2)(a)(iii).

and well-known marks stated in the Paris Convention[30] (see Chapter 4, Section 4.3.1.1).

One of the trade mark *preconditions (graphic representation)* is present in the EU system.

With reference to the Definition Model, *form (type* and *context)* of '*syuchi-syohyo*' can be found within Articles 4(1)(10) and 4(1)(19). It includes unregistered trademarks and any registered trademarks in the context of Article 2(1) of the Japanese Trademark Act. An overview of '*syuchi-syohyo*' *form* is thus:

 (i) *type* in *form*: this is as for *syohyo*, and, as such, is relatively narrow (see Article 2),[31] and includes characters, figures, signs or three-dimensional shapes, or any combination thereof, or any combination thereof with colours; and

 (ii) *context* in *form*: this is essentially the same as that in relation to *syohyo* in Article 2(1) of the Japanese Trademark Act, and this therefore includes character marks, design marks, symbol marks, colour marks, three-dimensional marks, combined marks; and *context* in *form* of 'trade mark' includes merchandising marks, service marks, business marks, collective marks, geographical indications, grade marks, manufacturer marks, retailer marks, certification marks, family marks, coined marks, stock marks, and promotional marks (see Chapter 2, Section 2.3.3).[32]

(iii) The trade mark *precondition* of *commercial use* is present in the Japanese trademark system.

Comparison of the EU and Japanese trademark regimes leads to the following inference: although some similarity is found, '*syuchi-syohyo*' *form* in the Japanese Trademark Act is narrower than that of 'trade mark of repute' in the EU TMD. This is because non-traditional trademarks are most likely to be excluded from the protectable subject matter under the Japanese system (see Chapter 2, Section 2.3.3,

---

30 Ibid., Article 4(2)(d).
31 In June 2009, the JPO announced that it was considering broadening the trademark subject matter to non-traditional trademarks – that is, movement marks and sound marks – and that it was setting up a working group under the industrial structure committee. See the JPO press release *Sangyo kozo shingikai ni working group wo secchishi, ugoki oto tou wo riyoushita atarashii type no syohyo nitsuite kennto wo kaishi shimashita* (no longer available on website).
32 Trademark subject matters are narrowly indicated in the Japanese law whilst the future expansion of trade mark subject matter in the EU regime is implicit in Article 2 of the EU TMD. Non-traditional trade marks are highly unlikely to be protected. See also Item 4 of Part 2: Principal Paragraph of Article 3(1) of the Guidelines. In Japan, the functional aspects of trademarks can have an impact on the classification of trademarks. The legal aspects of 'trademarks' are seen in the statutory definition of 'trademark', such as signs, symbols, characters, etc.; see Article 2 of the Japanese Trademark Act. The functional aspect can be classified as character marks, design marks, symbol marks, colour marks, three-dimensional marks, combined marks related to merchandising marks, service marks, business marks, collective marks, geographical indications, grade marks, manufacturer marks, retailer marks, certification marks, family marks, coined marks, stock marks, promotional marks. In the EU regime, on the other hand, the lesser categorisation of 'trade mark' can be seen.

and Chapter 5, Section 5.4.1.1), whereas the EU system does recognise these marks as being part of a well-known trade mark *type* (see Chapter 2, Section 2.3.2, and Chapter 4, Section 4.3.1.1).[33]

6.3.2 The concept of 'trade mark of repute' and 'syuchi-syohyo'

Although the EU trade mark legislation does not explicitly state the *concept* of 'trade mark of repute', the *concept*, with reference to the Definition Model, was construed as the reputation and distinctive character. As noted above, such trade marks have to have *a reputation* in the Community or Member States, and the *distinctive character* or *the repute* of such marks is protected (see Chapter 4, Section 4.3.1.2).

In relation to the EU trade mark regime, the term 'reputation' implies a higher level of knowledge-based *distinctiveness* – that is to say, a trade mark of repute is known by a significant part of the public concerned with the products or services covered by the mark, in a substantial part of the Member States concerned.[34] Regarding the *concept* of 'trade mark of repute', this can be implied to be a very high level of acquired distinctiveness, which can possibly contain 'image'. The examples of 'image' that can be included in acquired distinctiveness are 'prestigious image of the goods in question' and 'their aura of luxury',[35] which is also reflected in the goods or services to which the mark is attached. It is also held that a particular type of message can be conveyed in the mark, but in order to argue that image is the reputation of the mark, the trade mark owner must submit the evidence to prove that relevance.[36] Hence, the trade mark may also serve as 'a medium for a message associated with it, which must be protected along with it'.[37] Evidence of the existence of image, which includes the allure/prestigious/ luxurious image of the mark is required to be submitted by the proprietor of the alleged trade mark of repute.

Therefore, the *concept* of trade mark of repute under the Definition Model can be amended as follows: a degree of reputation (= acquired distinctiveness), which might be affected by the allure/prestigious/luxurious image of the mark. The mark of repute can therefore be said to be the mark having reputation, which includes the positive image of allure, prestige and luxury. This approach implies the possibility that certain types of trade marks – those that are known, yet do not possess any such 'positive image' – can be excluded from being a 'trade mark of repute'.

---

33 An important update is made here. The Japanese government passed the Bill to amend the scope of protectable subject matter. The Bill recognises so-called non-traditional trademarks as being protectable subject matter, and therefore they will become subject to trademark registration.
34 *Intel* [2009] ETMR 13, para 23; Advocate General Sharpston summarised *General Motors* in his opinion.
35 *Dior* [1998] ETMR 26, para 45.
36 Ibid., para 68.
37 Ibid., para 66.

Likewise, the Japanese Act does not directly speak of *concept* of '*syuchi-syohyo*' therein; nonetheless, this can be inferred from '*syohyo*' *concept* as set out in Article 2 of the Japanese Trademark Act (i.e. distinctiveness).[38] In addition, 'distinctiveness' is implicit in the *kanji* scripts for *syohyo*, and this term forms part of the phrase '*syuchi-syohyo*'. '*Syuchi-syohyo*' *concept* can also be implicitly defined as being a high level of distinctiveness in relation to the geographical extent of knowledge of the *syuchi-syohyo* by the consumers, rather than as a degree of knowledge *per se*. Thus, '*syuchi-syohyo*' *concept* appears to constitute a high degree of geographically defined distinctiveness amongst consumers.

Concerning the JPO Guidelines, *concept* of '*syuchi-syohyo*' is implicitly present, and some similarity to the WIPO Recommendation can be found here. It is concluded that a *syohyo* must be highly distinctive in a (poorly defined) substantial geographic area and in terms of the scale of sales (with reference to an uncertain definition of consumers). What is clear is that *syuchi-syohyo* status in Japan is unlikely to be achieved by *locally* well-known *syohyo*,[39] but is likely to be achieved by *syohyo* that are well known on a national scale, even if only to a small number of consumers.[40] Further, the JPO Guidelines do state that the extent of the recognition of the mark can be either national or local,[41] depending on the nature of the goods or services. *Concept* of '*syuchi-syohyo*' – geographical-extent-oriented distinctiveness – does appear to play an overriding role in assessing *syuchi-syohyo* status in the JPO Guidelines.[42] But this is not entirely and conceptually clear, since there is significant inconsistency both in the Acts and in jurisprudence.

Moving on to the *preconditions* – graphic representation and commercial use – Article 2 of the EU TMD makes explicit reference to *graphic representation*, but not to *commercial use*. The Japanese regime takes the opposite approach: *commercial use* is explicitly present,[43] but *graphic representation* is not explicit (being, instead, linguistically implicit). It is suggested that the different position on *commercial use* probably has very little import in practice. In relation to *commercial use*, in the EU TMD, marks cannot be registered in bad faith[44] and non-use can be grounds for trade mark revocation.[45] In relation to *graphic representation*, the real issue is that this explicit criterion appears to be interpreted rather generously and broadly in the EU regime, whereas the equivalent implied criterion in Japan is, in fact, stricter.

---

38 See Chapter 2, Section 2.3.3.
39 It is clear that not only can a *syohyo* be well known throughout the country, but it can also be recognised in certain areas (see Item 1 of the JPO Guidelines for Article 4(1)(10)).
40 The JPO Guidelines states that '*syuchi-syohyo*' includes 'a trademark which is widely recognised among end-consumers but also traders in the industry'. Traders in the industry (in Japan), as well as Japanese consumers, are included in the assessment of distinctiveness.
41 Ibid.
42 See Items 3(1)(i)–(vi) and Items 3(2)(i)–(viii) of Chapter II: Article 3(2) of the JPO Guidelines.
43 Article 2 of the Japanese Trademark Act.
44 Article 3(2)(d) of the EU TMD.
45 See Article 12 of the EU TMD. Thus, although *commercial use* is not an explicit element of the definition of a 'trade mark of repute', it is relevant to the trade mark registration process and is relevant to the continued protection of marks in the EU.

To conclude, the substance of *concepts* of 'trade mark of repute' and '*syuchi-syohyo*' are similar, since both relate to a higher level of distinctiveness. However, there is a significant difference: the former emphasises knowledge-based distinctiveness,[46] whilst the latter emphasises geographic-based distinctiveness.[47] Therefore, the Japanese system, *per se*, can be observed to set a higher hurdle for well-known trade mark proprietors than the EU regime. This can be mitigated in practice by the alternative routes to *syuchi-syohyo* protection.[48] Given that the well-developed support mechanism outside the trademark law is one of the unique features of well-known trademark protection in Japan, fuller protection for '*syuchi-syohyo*' proprietors can be achieved by utilising, for example, defensive trademark registration[49] and protection under the unfair competition law regime.[50] (Note that the author argued that '*syuchi-syohyo*' should be appropriately protected under the trademark laws, and the fact that alternative protection is available elsewhere should not be used as an excuse to give limited scope to the definition of '*syuchi-syohyo*' under the Trademark Act.) Finally, it might be interesting to observe whether, in future, the Japanese trademark regime takes a more EU (knowledge-based) approach and how that would affect '*syuchi-syohyo*' protection in Japan.

6.3.3 Assessment of 'trade mark of repute' and 'syuchi-syohyo'

So far, it has become apparent that the protection of the well-known trade mark is not something to be conceptualised, but to be contextualised. As a result of undertaking the contextual approach (as opposed to the conceptual approach), 'trade mark of repute'[51] and '*syuchi-syohyo*' are not conceptually or coherently *defined* in laws, but are *assessed and determined* by non-exclusive fact-based criteria.

We shall now discuss the similarities and dissimilarities in the assessments of the EU and Japanese regimes. There are a couple of differences in the administrative context of the assessments. In the EU TMD, a list of the non-exclusive fact-based criteria seems to have been developed by the cases (see Chapter 4, Section 4.3.3), whilst in Japan the list of the criteria is suggested in the JPO Guidelines (see Chapter 5, Section 5.4.2).

Broadly speaking, both 'trade mark of repute' criteria (see Chapter 4, Section 4.3.3) and '*syuchi-syohyo*' criteria (see Chapter 5, Sections 5.4.2–5.4.3) contain similar elements with different emphasis. Under the EU regime, the *concept* of 'trade mark of repute' is assessed by the knowledge-based requirements – that is to say, to what extent trade marks are known to the relevant consumers. In order to assess whether a trade mark is a mark of repute, a certain degree of knowledge

---

46 See Chapter 4, Section 4.3.3.
47 See Chapter 5, Section 5.4.3.
48 See Chapter 5, Section 5.3.
49 See Chapter 5, Section 5.3.3.
50 See Chapter 5, Section 5.3.4.
51 *El Corte Ingles* [2007] ETMR 81.

on behalf of the relevant public must be achieved, with the factual criteria outlined in *General Motors*[52] being indicative (but not conclusive) of this. Similarities between these criteria and those of the WIPO Recommendation can be noted (thus, many of the same criticisms can apply to the EU approach; see Chapter 3, Section 3.2.4).

The factors to be considered are set out as follows: '(i) the inherent characteristics of the mark, including the fact that it does or does not contain an element descriptive of the goods or services for which it has been registered; (ii) the market share held by the mark; (iii) how intensive, geographically widespread and long-standing use of the mark has been; (iv) the amount invested by the undertaking in promoting the mark; (v) the proportion of the relevant section of the public which, because of the mark, identifies the goods or services as originating from a particular undertaking; and (vi) statements from chambers of commerce and industry or other trade and professional associations'.[53]

Under the Japanese trademark regime, the *concept* of *syuchi-syohyo* appears to be geographically defined – an assessment as to the geographical extent the *syohyo* is known to the consumers. The following factors are taken into consideration: '(i) A trademark actually in use and goods or services for which it is used; (ii) The start of its use, the length of its use, or the area where it is used; (iii) The volume of production, certification or delivery and a scale of business (number of stores, an area of business, amount of sales, etc.); (iv) The method, frequency and contents of advertising; The number of times of appearance in general newspapers, trade journals, magazines and the internet, and contents thereof; (v) The outcome of the questionnaire regarding consumers' awareness of the trademark'.[54]

Comparing those two lists of criteria, although the wording is different, the substance seems rather similar, except that the EU looks into the inherent distinctiveness of the mark, whilst Japan looks into the mark being used in the course of trade. To a certain extent, the Japanese criterion of the mark being used seems very odd, as it is highly unlikely that the mark could establish well-knownness without being used. However, it does make sense if this is directed towards a mark that is well known outside Japan but is not yet actually used in Japan. It is rather interesting that the Japanese approach makes reference to the well-known mark that does not yet have a Japanese trademark registration.

The requirement of the actual commercial use of the mark in assessing whether the mark is *syuchi-syohyo* echoes with the strong emphasis made by the Japanese Trademark Act generally – that is, the commercial part of the trade use (mark *precondition*). The actual commercial use requirement under the EU regime seems to have less emphasis; the EU looks at the nature of the mark itself – that is to say, the distinctiveness of the mark (*concept* of 'well-known trade mark'). So the EU regime is about *concept* of the trade mark – distinctiveness – and the Japanese regime is about the *preconditions* – commercial use.

52 *General Motors* [1998] ETMR 950.
53 *Lloyd Schuhfabrik Meyer & Co. GmbH v Klijsen Handel BV* (C-342/97) [2000] FSR 77, para 24.
54 The JPO Guidelines for Article 3(2).

The author is in favour of the EU approach, which puts more weight on the substance of the trade mark, whilst the Japanese approach emphasises the administrative side.

6.4 A comparison of 'detriment/taking unfair advantage' and *'fuseino mokuteki'*

This section begins with a comparison of well-known trade mark protection against 'detriment/unfair advantage' in the EU and *'fuseino mokuteki'* in Japan. First, some terminological comments. As explained in Chapter 1, the original term 'dilution' developed by Frank Schechter[55] is not employed in the law of either the EU or Japan. The term 'dilution' was transformed into an expression of 'detriment' and 'unfair advantage' in EU law, and the EU has developed its own approach to well-known trade mark protection against dilution (correspondingly, the protection of the trade mark of repute against encroachment[56]).

Likewise, the Japanese law does not speak directly of 'dilution'; instead, the Japanese law introduced 'unfair purposes' with the underlying aim of preventing the highly distinctive nature of the well-known trade mark from being diluted.[57] Given that Japanese law does not employ the original term 'dilution' and also that the equivalent EU term of detriment and unfair advantage is not explicitly employed, the first task was to identity whether such a concept is present in Japan. The answer was yes: such a protection *de facto* exists and is reflected in law (Article 4(1)(19)) where it is termed as protection against unfair purposes.

The characteristics of dilution in the EU and Japan will be reiterated briefly in Figures 6.5 and 6.6, and the comparison of the EU and Japan will then begin.

The EU legislation distinguishes and thus divides 'trade mark' *concept* (referring to the Definition Model) of the mark of repute into two: distinctiveness and reputation. This confirms the argument submitted earlier that 'trade mark' *concept* is distinctiveness, and 'trade mark' *concept* of 'trade mark of repute' is reputation.

Second, four types of actionable harm are clearly recognised in the EU: (i) detriment to the distinctiveness of the mark (dilution by blurring); (ii) detriment to the repute of the mark (dilution by tarnishment); (iii) unfair advantage of the distinctiveness; and (iv) unfair advantage of the repute of the mark (free-riding).[58]

In other words, the EU law recognises the difference between 'detriment' and 'taking unfair advantage', and differentiates between the 'distinctiveness' of the mark and the 'reputation' of the mark. At this point, the author argues that an attempt at conceptualisation of the dilution was evidenced.

By contrast, the Japanese Act does not make a distinction between distinctiveness and reputation. The subject matter here is very simple: the *syuchi-syohyo*

55 See Schechter, 'The Rational Basis of Trademark Protection'.
56 See the New CTM Guidelines Part C, Article 8(5) CTMR at 49.
57 See Ono, *Syohyo ho*, pp. 447–9.
58 See Chapter 4, Section 4.4.1.

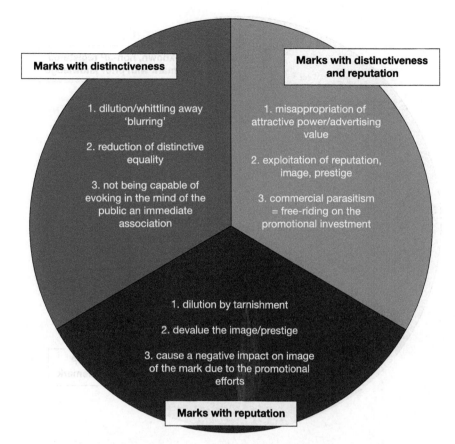

Marks with distinctiveness

1. dilution/whittling away 'blurring'

2. reduction of distinctive equality

3. not being capable of evoking in the mind of the public an immediate association

Marks with distinctiveness and reputation

1. misappropriation of attractive power/advertising value

2. exploitation of reputation, image, prestige

3. commercial parasitism = free-riding on the promotional investment

1. dilution by tarnishment

2. devalue the image/prestige

3. cause a negative impact on image of the mark due to the promotional efforts

Marks with reputation

Figure 6.5 Full map of 'trademark of repute against detriment/unfair advantage'

– well-known mark.[59] Japanese law recognises only a single type of harm – 'unfair purposes', which is understood to equate with 'unfair advantage' in the EU TMD phrase. A further difference compared with the EU regime can be seen in the Japanese trademark legislation. The Japanese legislation provides two categories of unfair purposes: (i) gaining unfair profits; (ii) causing damage to the other person. The second example can be interpreted in a broad way and therefore may work as double-edged sword.

It is observed that both the EU and Japanese systems introduced trade mark protection against dilution without referring to the actual term, although they seem to show a constructive way of approaching trade mark dilution and are clearer in terms of identifying the types of actionable harm. Overall, it seems obvious that the EU legislation provides a clearer and more constructive conceptual framework for protection against dilution than the Japanese Trademark Act.

59 Note that the difference between well-known (*syuchi-syohyo*) and famous (*tyomei-syohyo*) is made in the Unfair Competition Prevention Act (Article 2(1)(1) and (2)).

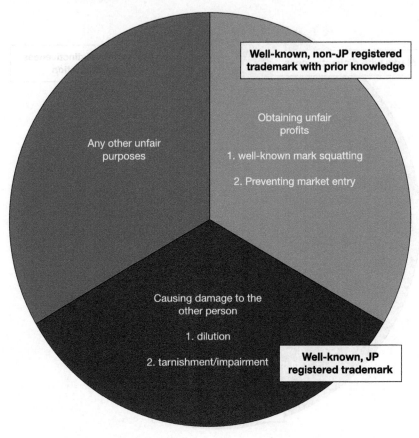

Figure 6.6 Grouping of acts causing harms (*fuseino mokuteki*/unfair purposes) to the
'*syuchi-syohyo*' – final

6.4.1 Contextualisation of 'detriment/taking unfair advantage' and 'fuseino mokuteki'

This section will make a comparison between the two jurisdictions in order to seek some guidance in assessing whether the conduct by a third party amounts to causing detriment to or taking unfair advantage of the marks of repute and acting with unfair purposes under Article 4(4)(a) of the EU TMD and Article 4(1)(19) of the Japanese Trademark Act.

Although it can be conceded that, in both cases, the contextualisation for these legal notions may require a factually based and therefore unfixed approach, it is submitted that clear and comprehensive definitions of the same could only increase clarity, consistency and coherency for the application of such contextualisation.

In relation to the assessment of detriment/taking unfair advantage and *fuseino mokuteki*, unlike the EU regime, the Japanese law does provide reasonably clear guidance as to the test for *fuseino mokuteki vis-à-vis* the JPO Guidelines (see Chapter 5, Section 5.4.2). In contrast, the primary source of the test is EU jurisprudence (see Chapter 4, Sections 4.4.2–4.4.4). A cursory view of this might lead one to conclude that the difference in the source of dilution and *kisyakuka* tests is simply a reflection of the types of jurisdiction at issue, but (i) although Japan is a civil law country, the EU is not a common law jurisdiction, so this conclusion is questionable; and (ii) the source of the tests may have influenced the clarity of the test contents: it is argued that the piecemeal development of EU jurisprudence has not led to a clear and consistent test of dilution/detriment or taking unfair advantage in the EU system, whereas the Japanese approach appears a little clearer.

Thus, at this stage, it is believed that a composite of the various guidelines provided in both *Intel* and *Bellure* to establish detriment and unfair advantage can be collated and the following submitted.

First, detriment to the distinctiveness of the mark can be regarded as 'dilution', 'whittling away' or 'blurring'. Such detriment is caused when that mark's ability to identify the goods or services for which it is registered is weakened, since use of an identical or similar sign by a third party leads to weakening of the identity and hold upon the public mind of the earlier mark.

Second, in order to prove whether the third party's use amounted to detriment of the distinctiveness or the reputation of the mark, a link between the earlier and the later marks needs to be evidenced, although a mere link is not sufficient in establishing detriment or unfair advantage. Establishing a link should be assessed globally, taking into account all the relevant factors.

Third, such factors are as follows: (i) the similarity of the mark; (ii) the nature of the parties' goods or services and whether their relevant consumers overlap; and (iii) the distinctiveness of the earlier mark and whether the mark is unique or essentially unique.

In addition, the court also referred to the strength of the earlier mark, which might encourage a link to be made between two marks. The fact that the average consumer calls the earlier mark to mind is tantamount to there being such a link. A link that includes a change in the economic behaviour of the average consumer of the earlier goods or services as a consequence of the use of the later mark, or some likelihood that such a change will occur in the future, must be present.

Fourth, taking unfair advantage can be paraphrased as 'parasitism' or 'free-riding'. This concept relates not to the detriment caused to the mark but to the advantage taken by the third party as a result of the use of the identical or similar sign. It covers, in particular, cases where, by reason of a transfer of the image of the mark or of the characteristics that it projects to the goods identified by the identical or similar sign, there is clear exploitation on the coat-tails of the mark with a reputation.[60]

The advantage arises where a third party uses a sign similar to a mark of repute or distinctive character in order to: (i) benefit from the power of attraction, the reputation and the prestige of that mark; and (ii) exploit, without paying any

---

60 *Bellure* [2009] ETMR 55, para 41.

financial compensation, the marketing effort expended by the proprietor of the mark in order to create and maintain the mark's image.

To recapitulate, under Article 4(4)(a) (and therefore Article 5(2)), three types of actionable harm are recognised: detriment to the distinctive character of the mark, detriment to the repute of the mark and unfair advantage of the distinctive character and repute of the mark. The traditional 'dilution', which was explored by Frank Schechter,[61] is now recognised as one type of detriment. By way of comparison, the following needs to be summarised: although there is no conceptual definition of either detriment or unfair advantage, it can be submitted that there have been attempts to show contextualisation of the concepts. Putting aside any discussion of whether or not those terms are comprehensively conceptualised and whether such a contextualisation is legitimate, such an effort ought to be acknowledged.

The approach taken by the Japanese trademark regime appears to share, to a certain extent, some similar characteristics with the EU trade mark regime.

Trade mark protection against dilution under the Japanese trademark regime was very slow to develop, since such protection was conferred under the umbrella of the Japanese unfair competition law, which was deemed to be sufficient and satisfactory to the trademark proprietors. However, the introduction of Articles 4(4)(a) and 5(2) of the EU TMD seems to have had the effect of introducing a similar Article into Japanese domestic law, and Article 4(1)(19) was incrementally added into the absolute grounds for refusal.

One of the most important and overriding differences between the EU TMD and the Japanese Trademark Act is that trademark protection against dilution is not recognised in the trademark infringement. In other words, the equivalent to Article 5(2) of the EU TMD and Article 9(1)(c) of the CTMR does *not* exist under the Japanese trademark system. Trademark infringement operates under the confusion doctrine;[62] therefore, the proprietor of the (well-known) trademark must prove there is a likelihood of confusion, and the onus is on the trademark proprietors in Japan.[63] The tradition that the unfair competition law provides protection for well-known marks against dilution has discouraged the trademark law from developing in such a way as to offer well-known trademark protection against dilution.

Japanese trademark law does not employ the actual term 'dilution' or the EU equivalent, 'detriment' and 'unfair advantage'; instead, it employs the term 'unfair purposes'.

Notwithstanding the absence of clarification of those terms,[64] the main purpose of Article 4(1)(19) was clearly communicated: to 'prevent dilution and so-called

61 See Schechter, 'The Rational Basis of Trademark Protection'.
62 See Article 37 of the Trademark Act for trademark infringements, and Article 25 for rights conferred by the trademark proprietor.
63 See Chapter 5, Section 5.4.1.
64 Note that Japan is a civil law country, and not much importance is given to the juridical interpretation.

free-ride to well-known (trade) marks, and thus to protect distinctiveness of (trade) marks, and thus to enhance the maintenance of *goodwill*[65] established by trademark owners in the course of trade and ultimately protect the interest of consumers'[66] [emphasis added].

With reference to the Definition Model, under the EU system, two categories of trade mark *concept* are identified: one is the distinctiveness of the mark, and the other is the reputation of the mark. Under the Japanese system, two sets of two categories of trademark *type* are identified. In the first set, one is a well-known mark that is registered in Japan; the other is a well-known mark that is not yet registered in Japan. In the second set, one is a non-coined mark; the other is a coined mark. No trademark *concept* is of consideration here: *concept* is well known.

Unfair purposes are expected to occur where: '(i) the later mark is *identical or very similar to an earlier well-known trademark in other countries* or a trademark *well known throughout Japan*; and (ii) the earlier well-known mark *is composed of a coined word or particular in composition*'[67] [emphasis added].

Furthermore, the following evidence is taken into consideration when determining whether a third party's application amounted to unfair purposes under Article 4(1)(19):

(i)   evidence that the earlier mark is well known to the relevant public;
(ii) evidence that the earlier mark consists of a coined mark;
(iii) evidence that the proprietor of the earlier mark has: (a) a concrete future plan for entering the Japanese market; (b) a plan to expand their business in the future;
(iv) evidence that the proprietor of the earlier mark was being aggressively approached to enter the licensing agreement without due cause;
(v)   evidence that the third party's use of the earlier well-known trademark causes damage to the goodwill (reputation, creditability, attractive force for consumers) attached to the earlier mark.

The criteria to assess whether the later mark amounted to unfair purposes are indicatively set out in the JPO Guidelines, although it should be noted that, obviously, the assessment of *unfair purposes* does vary from case to case.

The criteria summarised above and critically discussed in Chapter 5, Section 5.4.2, show that in Japan the Guidelines provide that *unfair purposes* is assessed comprehensively with reference to the five fact-based criteria noted above. As noted in Chapter 5, Section 5.3.3, this approach can be criticised for a lack of clarity and certainty, although the JPO Guidelines clearly set out the criteria. Assessments of '*syuchi-syohyo*' and *unfair purposes* are based on non-exclusive

---

65 No term 'goodwill' is employed within the Japanese Trademark Act. In Article 1 of the Japanese Trademark Act, the term 'business confidence' is used instead.
66 See Ono, *Syohyo-ho*, p. 391; and Aoki, *Chiteki zaisan ken toshiteno brand to design*, pp. 36–7.
67 The relevant text of the JPO Guidelines for Article 4(1)(19) is to be found in Appendix 6.

fact-based criteria, and thus assessments of '*syuchi-syohyo*' and *unfair purposes* are likely to vary case by case. It is interesting that the JPO Guidelines suggest two situations in which the existence of *unfair purposes* is *prima facie* positively recognised.

In contrast, in the EU trade mark regime, two types of actionable harm are recognised for two types of marks (the mark of distinctiveness and the mark of repute): the assessment of finding detriment and unfair advantage varies depends on the jurisdiction and includes dilution by blurring, tarnishment, free-riding or parasitism, and takes a consistent and harmonised approach with one 'catch all' provision relating to distinctiveness and another relating to similarity (between the earlier and later marks, *not* between the goods and services). As was noted in Chapter 4, Section 4.4.3, this approach is more rationalised in comparison with the Japanese approach, and can be preferred to the Japanese approach as it provides, to a certain extent, legitimate contextualisation of 'detriment' and 'unfair advantage'.

How, then, do the approaches of Article 4(4)(a) and Article 4(1)(19) compare? In terms of similarities, there seem to be two common themes: one is the rationale of establishing the trade mark protection against dilution; and the other lies in the assessment of such protection. Both the EU regime and the Japanese Trademark Act require similarity between the earlier and later marks. Other similarities in assessment include the fact that both jurisdictions rely on non-exhaustive fact-based criteria, and both determine on a case-by-case basis.

However, differences in the detriment/unfair advantage approaches are significant. For example:

(i) Japan does not provide trademark protection against dilution at the trademark infringement level whereas the EU TMD does (Article 5(2)).

(ii) The concept of detriment and unfair advantage seems clearer under the EU TMD (Articles 4(4)(a)) than the Japanese Trademark Act (Article 4(1) (19)) (various types of *dilution* are recognised and addressed within the EU TMD).

(iii) The Japanese system seems to provide a less instructive and comprehensive approach to *unfair purposes*, in comparison with the EU system.

(iv) The EU regime seems to provide a more detailed and contextualised approach to detriment and unfair advantage. The EU jurisprudence provides more instructive rationale on the test for detriment and unfair advantage (i.e. how to apply for the context) but there seems to be a lack of *criteria*. The Japanese system, on the other hand, gives very little indication as to how to assess *unfair purposes*, whilst the Guidelines provide a list of criteria needed to be considered when *unfair purposes* is assessed.[68] Overall, the Japanese Guidelines seem be more simplified and less rationalised, contextualised and thus seem to be lacking rationalisation and contextualisation.

68 See Chapter 4, Section 4.4.4.

(v) Japan provides different but unclearly defined treatment for uncoined and coined *syuchi-syohyo* against *unfair purposes*, whereas in the EU TMD this differentiation seems not to be explicit.

(vi) Article 37 of the Japanese Trademark Act provides more precise causes of actions regarding trademark infringements in comparison with Article 5 of the EU TMD.

So far, the similarities and dissimilarities of 'trade mark of repute' and '*syuchi-syohyo*' against dilution and *kisyakuka* in the EU TMD and the Japanese trademark system have been critically compared and examined. With relation to Article 4(4) (a) and Article 4(1)(19), it is a challenging task even to attempt to draw a conclusion as to which is more effective.

It is submitted that both the EU and Japanese trademark laws take rather similar approaches to contextualisation of the term 'dilution'. To conclude, the EU approach is preferable as its detriment and unfair advantage doctrine seems clearer than that of *fuseino mokuteki* in the Japanese system.

6.5 Conclusion

This chapter has attempted to critically compare the definitions afforded to 'trade mark of repute' and '*syuchi-syohyo*' and dilution in the EU and Japan.

It has been concluded that, in terms of the definitions offered, the scope of '*syuchi-syohyo*' is narrower than that of 'trade mark of repute' by virtue of a more restrictive approach to *type* in *form*, and *concept*.

We will now turn to the tests or general approach used for determining well-known status in these two jurisdictions. Although they are rather similar, assessment of 'trade mark of repute' seems to be based on the knowledge threshold requirement, whereas assessment of '*syuchi-syohyo*' seems to be based on the geographic threshold requirement. Moreover, the Japanese system seems to take a more concise and indicative approach to assessment of '*syuchi-syohyo*' than the EU TMD. However, the scope of protection afforded to 'trade mark of repute' seems to be broader than in the Japanese trademark regime. On this point, the EU system takes a broader approach to the scope of 'trade mark of repute' protection than does the Japanese.

In terms of defining detriment/unfair advantage and unfair purpose, the Japanese law seems to take a less rationalised and contextualised approach than the EU system. In terms of the tests for detriment/unfair advantage and unfair purpose, the EU approach is more indicative and instructive than that of the Japanese approach, as the EU cases provide guidelines in greater narrative detail.

Overall, it is suggested that the following comparisons can be drawn in relation to the certainty of the scope of protection for trade marks of repute and *syuchi-syohyo* against detriment/taking unfair advantage and *fuseino mokuteki*, respectively.

First, the *legal origins* of this protection. In the EU, much is defined in the case law (see Chapter 4, Sections 4.3.4 and 4.4.4), whereas in Japan it is the JPO Guidelines that are more important. It is argued that this means that protection for marks of repute against dilution has developed and is developing in an inherently piecemeal fashion in the EU, whereas the Japanese system, although there are some uncertainties in protection (in the Guidelines), has been developed in an inherently more systematic way. Further, the JPO Guidelines can be reviewed and changed as required (see Chapter 5, Section 5.4.2), whereas in the EU the greater emphasis on the courts means that this process is less predictable and more reactive.

Second, the *specificity* of this protection. Although the legal framework to provide protection for trade marks and *syohyo* against detriment/unfair advantage and *fuseino mokuteki* is in operation – even if it is not always clear (a lack of clarity that, given the assumption made in this book as to the relationship between trade marks and well-known trade marks, has import for marks of repute and *syuchi-syohyo*) – the extent to which dilution *explicitly* applies to trade marks of repute/ *syuchi-syohyo* is less clear. Here, it is submitted that the Japanese law takes a clearer approach to 'legal treatment for '*syuchi-syohyo*' than does the EU in respect of 'trade mark of repute', whilst the EU regime provides a clearer and more coherent approach to detriment and unfair advantage than the Japanese law.

Third, in the *key areas of uncertainty* as to scope of protection, three areas are identified.

The first area is certainty as to the conceptual *definition* of 'trade mark of repute' in the EU and '*syuchi-syohyo*' in Japan. As earlier evidenced (see Chapter 4, Section 4.3, and Chapter 5, Section 5.3), no conceptual definition was provided, and thus the scope seems particularly uncertain.

The second area is certainty as to the *appropriateness* of the approach to identifying 'trade mark of repute' and '*syuchi-syohyo*'. As earlier evidenced (see Chapter 5, Sections 5.4.2–5.4.3), it is very clear that *syuchi-syohyo* status is judged with reference to a geographically drawn expression of *concept*, whilst the EU criteria are more knowledge-based, and the indicators of 'trade mark of repute' status include proxies for distinctiveness, together with a reference to value and image (see Chapter 4, Section 4.3). Clearly, '*syuchi-syohyo*' is the narrower concept and it is harder to satisfy the threshold of '*syuchi-syohyo*' than the EU threshold.

The third area is the *suitability* of detriment/unfair advantage and unfair purposes as forms of protection for trade marks of repute and *syuchi-syohyo* respectively. This is a significant and interesting point, because the Japanese Trademark Act does not recognise such a right conferred to the proprietor of *syuchi-syohyo* in a trademark infringement. Plainly, the Japanese jurisdiction does not consider such a protection to be necessary. As noted in relation to *unfair purposes* (see Chapter 5, Section 5.4), there is ambiguity and incoherent argument surrounding the scope of protection afforded to the trade mark of repute and *syuchi-syohyo* against detriment/unfair advantage and unfair purposes. Provided that the definitions of the protectable subject matter (the trade mark of repute and *syuchi-syohyo*) are not clearly delineated, to what extent the protection can be conferred also becomes ambiguous and incoherent in consequence. The suitability of detriment/unfair advantage and unfair purposes as forms of protection for trade marks of repute and *syuchi-syohyo* is explicit in the law, but perhaps this legitimacy can be questioned.

7   Well-known trade mark: a way forward

7.1 Introduction

We have now reached the final stage of the exploration of well-known trade mark protection against dilution in the EU and Japan. This final chapter is divided into two parts. The first part revisits the journey made so far in exploring the conceptual definition of well-known trade mark and in examining the efficacy and credibility of well-known trade mark protection against dilution in EU and Japan.

In the second part, and in conclusion, a number of recommendations will be proposed for well-known trade mark protection in the future.

The main features of the book are: (i) a detailed comparative analysis of well-known trade mark protection against dilution in the EU and Japan; (ii) the employment of an etymological approach to the analysis of the relevant Japanese laws – it is hoped that this approach, implicit to native Japanese speakers and fluent Japanese readers, will aid non-Japanese speakers to further understand Japanese law; and (iii) development of the Definition Model. This Model, it is submitted, is of import and interest as it both conceptualises the definitions of 'trade mark' and 'well-known trade mark' *and* offers a concise yet simple structure for analysing and understanding these two key trade mark notions.

In addition, the book has attempted to explore and analyse well-known trade mark protection against dilution in, respectively, the EU[1] and Japan.[2] A detailed comparative analysis of these two jurisdictions has been undertaken in order to assess the efficacy of well-known trade mark protection. Furthermore, a critical examination of well-known trade mark protection at the international level has been carried out, as this is an area that has been subject to some international harmonisation,[3]

---

1 See Chapter 4.
2 See Chapter 5.
3 See Chapter 3, in particular the examination of the Paris Convention (Section 3.2.1), GATT TRIPS (Section 3.2.2) and the WIPO Recommendation (Section 3.2.5).

222 Well-known trade marks

7.2 Summary and findings

In Chapter 1, the following quotation was illustrated:

> What is a 'well-known trade mark'? . . . A well-known mark is . . . well, we
> can all recognise one when we see it, can't we? But can we verbalise that
> recognition? As St Augustine said: 'If no one asks me, I know what it is. But
> if I wish to explain it to him that asks me, I do not know.'[4]

The heart of the book was based on the analysis of the established norm of well-known trade mark protection (contextualisation of well-known trade mark protection) – 'we know what it is when we see it, but we cannot explain what it is' and 'well-known trade mark protection is a matter of facts, not law' – and an attempt to challenge this and to establish the conceptualisation of 'well-known trade mark' at the international, the regional and the national level. It is believed that the conceptualisation of 'well-known trade mark', in particular at the international level, would help individual nations to provide a sufficient scope of protection to the well-known trade mark.

A summary of the main findings can be outlined as follows.

In Chapters 2 and 3, the lack of conceptualisation was identified and the establishment of a conceptualised definition of a well-known trade mark was attempted. This lack of conceptualisation has determined the choice of the terms used in law: 'well-known trade mark' in the Paris Convention sense is translated to a 'trade mark of repute' and '*syuchi-syohyo*'. 'Well-known trade mark protection against dilution' is translated to 'protection for a trade mark of repute against detriment/taking unfair advantage' and '*syuchi-syohyo* (well-known mark) protection against *fuseino mokuteki* (unfair purposes)'. An inherent uncertainty and incoherency in the choice of the relevant terms has encouraged well-known trade mark protection to grow out of the international context.

In determining the scope of well-known trade mark protection under the EU regime, it is important to note that it operates essentially on a case-by-case basis as a result of the contextualisation of the protection for trade mark of repute. 'Trade mark of repute', 'detriment' and 'taking unfair advantage' are essentially *factual* questions in the current law; this should be supplemented first by the conceptualisation of 'trade mark of repute' and then by determining 'detriment' and 'taking unfair advantage'. The current EU approach to the trade mark of repute against 'detriment' and 'taking unfair advantage' might work for providing a certain level of flexibility and autonomy. However, this advantage may well outweigh the disadvantage, which is the degree of uncertainty caused. This uncertainty, it is submitted, has only been increased by the divergent policy messages as to the protection of trade marks of repute sent out by *Intel* and *Bellure*

4 Tatham, 'WIPO Resolution on Well-Known Marks: A Small Step or a Giant Leap?', p. 129.

(see Chapter 4, Section 4.4.4), *Bellure* in particular.[5] Both *Intel* and *Bellure* are heavily criticised since they can be seen as creating uncertainty as to the scope of protection afforded to marks of repute in general. Why? Given that there is no clear definition of 'mark of repute', the narrow *Intel* and broader *Bellure* approaches create uncertainty, if not conflict, as to the scope of protection for the trade mark of repute: an uncertainty that can only raise further questions as to the extent to which such marks are protected against detriment/taking unfair advantage.

Turning to the protection of *syuchi-syohyo* against *fuseino mokuteki* in Japan, the most fundamental difference between Japan and the EU was noted: the Japanese Trademark Act does not offer the EU TMD equivalent of Article 5(2) – well-known trade mark protection against dilution, when the trademark infringement is at issue, is not recognised in law. Putting this fact into the comparative context, it is plain that the EU TMD provides a broader scope of protection to the trade mark of repute than the Japanese Trademark Act, even though alternative routes were developed in order to bridge the gap in practice.

Regarding the issue of conceptualisation of the definition of well-known trade mark, it should be emphasised that there is no comprehensive definition of *syuchi-syohyo* either in the Japanese Act or the JPO Guidelines. At the registration level, protection afforded to *syuchi-syohyo* is also uncertain for much the same reason as the protection for the trade mark of repute – the test for *syuchi-syohyo* status is a factual one:[6] this is hardly surprising, as these tests are necessarily applied on a case-by-case basis, rather than on a rationalised and principled basis. In relation to the assessment of the well-known trade mark, both jurisdictions have established rather similar criteria to assess whether the mark is well known, despite the difference in format: in Japan, the criteria for assessment are provided in the JPO Guidelines, whilst in the EU TMD the criteria have developed through cases. Should the EU take the same approach as Japan? The codification of the criteria for assessment within the law might enhance consistency and coherency in approach. Returning to protection of *syuchi-syohyo* against *fuseino mokuteki*, the Japanese trademark regime appears to generate a similar result to the EU regime; yet again, the Japanese trademark system endorses contextualisation in the fact-based approach to protection of *syuchi-syohyo* against *fuseino mokuteki*.

It must be conceded that the EU and Japanese systems for protecting trade marks of repute and *syuchi-syohyo* against detriment, taking unfair advantage and

5 It is submitted that, in the context of dilution, the importance of the advertising function of marks of repute was inadequately recognised and interpreted in the *Bellure* decision. As a result, it is argued that protection of marks of repute against dilution has become more uncertain. If the *Bellure* approach is to be favoured in the EU in the future, clearly a broader scope of protection would be offered to 'trade mark of repute'. This would be unfortunate, because *Bellure* unhelpfully confuses the legal relationship between trade marks and comparative advertising, and trade mark law and unfair competition law. This can only result in further uncertainty. It was pondered whether the scope of the protection for 'trade mark of repute' would be better determined by reference to a conceptual definition of marks of repute, rather than an ever-widening notion of the function(s) of marks of repute.

6 See Chapter 5, Sections 5.4.3.

fuseino mokuteki are, in a number of ways, very similar. Clearly, the relevant laws may reflect influences from the international regime[7] and, interestingly, some influence of the EU regime on the Japanese system can also be seen (thus it could be said that there is horizontal, as well as vertical, influence on Japanese law). However, despite the number of apparent similarities, it has been shown that there *are* significant differences between the EU and the Japanese trademark regimes in practice, if not in the Directives and Act themselves. For instance, Japanese trademark law emphasises trademarks being in commercial use in the course of trade (see Chapter 2, Section 2.3.3). This surely limits the scope of protection afforded to both ordinary and well-known trademarks in Japan. It is interesting to observe that this emphasis on use in the course of trade in Japan means that it would be highly unlikely that a *Bellure*-type claim would ever appear before a Japanese court. Therefore, it appears that the Japanese law delineates the clear division between the domains of trade mark law and unfair competition law, and therefore the limits in determining the scope of trade mark protection are appropriately drawn.

7.3 Conceptualisation of well-known trade mark: a way forward

Notwithstanding a strong belief that conceptualisation of well-known mark would only contribute to increase in coherency and certainty of the well-known trade mark protection, a fundamental question can be posed here. Is it necessary to have a conceptual definition of 'well-known trade mark' in order to determine the scope of protection for such a mark in practice? It is strongly argued that such a definition could only increase certainty and coherence, but the examination of whether such a definition is a prerequisite for such certainty (and, indeed, whether true certainty could ever be achieved) is an issue for future research.

In conclusion, a recommendation for the future is made in accordance with the following points.

The conceptualisation of a well-known mark and the embracement of a definition of 'well-known trade mark'. As has been seen in Chapters 4 and 5, the respective definitions of 'mark of repute' and '*syuchi-syohyo*' can both be criticised and it is proposed that clearer definitions of these terms should be introduced. It is also suggested that a geographically defined concept of well-knownness would be useful to set a higher degree of well-knownness than that of 'reputation' or 'well-knownness', so that a sufficient scope of protection could be granted to the class of 'well-known' trade marks. Conceptualisation would also change the tradition of 'we know what it is when we see it, but we cannot explain what it is' to 'we know what it is when we see it, and we can also explain what it is!'

A more systematic approach to the protection of well-known trade marks against dilution in particular. When the conceptualisation of a well-known trade mark, alongside the

---

7 See Chapter 4, Section 4.3.1, for EU; and Chapter 5, Section 5.4.1, for Japan.

conceptualisation of dilution, is adequately achieved, the determination of the scope of well-known trade mark protection can be done in a more systematic and therefore more coherent manner. Conceptualisation would provide the exhaustive and overarching framework for a well-known trade mark, which generates a certain degree of flexibility and autonomy within the framework.

Limitation: the limited sphere of the trade mark law regime. As the scope of the protectable subject matter broadens, the scope of protection available to the (well-known) trade mark proprietor is expanded equally. In consequence, the spheres of trade mark law and the unfair competition law (including the issue of comparative advertising) are muddied. A clear division between these two laws may well allow trade mark law to expand sufficiently, and would therefore achieve adequate determination of the scope of protection afforded to the (well-known) trade mark.

Appendix 1
Defining 'trade mark'

Law	Form of 'trade mark' (trade mark type and context)	Concept of 'trade mark' (what is trade mark?)	Trade mark preconditions (graphic representation and commercial use)
International law			
Paris Convention	*Trade mark type* – signs and indications[1] *Trade mark context* – indications of source or appellations of origin;[2] well-known trade marks;[3] service marks;[4] collective marks;[5] and trade names[6]	Distinctiveness[7]	No reference
Trademark Law Treaty	*Trade mark type* – *visible* marks; also includes three-dimensional marks[8] and excludes hologram marks, non-visible signs, sound marks, and olfactory marks[9] *Trade mark context* – marks relating to goods,[10] service marks[11]	No reference	*Graphic* (visual) *representation*
Singapore Treaty	*Trade mark type* – no reference *Trade mark context* – e.g. service marks are protected[12]	No reference	No reference

Law	Form *of 'trade mark' (trade mark* type *and* context*)*	Concept *of 'trade mark' (what is trade mark?)*	*Trade mark* preconditions *(*graphic representation *and* commercial use*)*
GATT TRIPS	*Trade mark type –* signs, words, personal names, letters, numbers and figurative marks, combination of colours, and combination of signs[13] *Trade mark context –* trade marks,[14] service marks, geographical indication might also be included herein[15]	'Signs which are capable of *distinguishing*'. It is to be noted that Article 15(1) distinguishes between what might be conceptualised as inherent distinctiveness ('capable of distinguishing') and acquired distinctiveness ('where signs are not inherently capable of distinguishing the relevant goods or service, members may make registrability depend on distinctiveness acquired through use')	*Graphic representation*[16]
Regional law			
CTMR	*Trade mark type –* any signs, including symbols, logos, slogans, get-up, personal names, designs, letters, numerals and the shape of goods or of their packaging[17] *Trade mark context –* context in *form* includes trade marks, service marks, geographic marks and certification marks[18]	Distinctiveness[19]	*Graphic representation*[20]
National law			
National – the Japanese Trademark Act	*Trade mark type –* characters, figures, signs, three-dimensional shapes or any combination thereof[21] *Trade mark context –* trade marks or goods marks with a trade mark is attached to the goods, and service marks[22]	Distinctiveness[23]	*Commercial use*[24]

1 Article 6*ter*(1)(b) of the Paris Convention.
2 Ibid., Article 1(2).
3 Ibid., Article 6*bis*.
4 Ibid., Article 6*sexies*. Service marks are recognised, but there is no obligation to protect them.

5 Ibid., Article 7*bis*.
6 Ibid., Article 8.
7 *Concept* of 'trade mark' is both indirectly stated and is implicit within the Article 6*quinquies* B(ii) of the Paris Convention as follows: marks, which are 'devoid of any distinctive character'; and marks which 'consist exclusively of signs or indications which may serve, in trade, to designate the kind, quality, quantity, intended purpose, value, place of origin, of the goods, or the time of production, or have become customary in the current language'.
8 Article 1(1)(a) of the TLT.
9 Ibid.
10 Ibid., Article 2(2)(a).
11 Ibid.
12 Article 2(2)(a) of the Singapore Treaty.
13 Article 15(1) of GATT TRIPS.
14 Ibid.
15 Article 22 of GATT TRIPS.
16 Ibid., Article 15(1).
17 Article 4 of the CTMR.
18 Ibid.
19 *Concept* of 'trade mark' can be found in the criterion that signs have to be capable of *distinguishing* the goods or services of one undertaking from those of others: i.e. trade mark *concept* is distinctiveness.
20 Article 4 of the CTMR.
21 Article 2 of the Japanese Trademark Act.
22 Ibid.
23 Distinctiveness is implicitly present in the *kanji* symbols.
24 Article 2 of the Japanese Trademark Act.

Appendix 2

Illustrations of the Definition Model

Well-known and valuable trade mark		
Form	*Coca-Cola*	*Toyota*
Context	A trade mark (for a product).	A trade mark (for a product)
Types	A combination of a word mark and colour. The word is represented in a stylised manner applying the colour red on a white background with combination of the colour red.	A logo, which in this case comprises a figurative element consisting of a two-dimensional graphic representation of circles and a silver colour elements.
Concept	A highly distinctive nature, which enables consumers to select 'Coca-Cola' drinks from other cola drinks.	A highly distinctive nature, which enables consumers to distinguish 'Toyota' cars from those of other competitors.

Appendix 3

An annotated[1] version of the JPO Trademark Examination Guidelines Relating to *Syuchi-Syohyo*: Chapter III: Article 4(1)(3) Part 8: Article 4(1)(10)

1. 'Trademark which is well known among consumers' as prescribed in this paragraph includes *not only a trademark which is widely recognised among end consumers* but also a trademark which is *widely recognised among traders in the industry* and also includes not only a trademark which is known *throughout the country* but also a trademark which is *widely recognised in a certain area.*
2. A trademark to be cited for the application of the provision of this paragraph needs to be widely recognised among domestic consumers in Japan at a time when an application for the registration of a trademark is filed (refer to Article 4(3)).
3. *To prove a trademark's being well known under the provision of this paragraph, the provisions of Items 3(1) and (2) of Chapter II (Article 3(2)) of the Guidelines apply mutatis mutandis.*

---

1 Emphasis added in the text by the author.

Appendix 4

An annotated[1] version of the JPO Trademark Examination Guidelines Relating to Well-known Trademarks and *Fuseino mokuteki*: Chapter III: Article 4(1)(3) Part 16: Article 4(1)(19)

1. For example, trademarks presented below fall under the provision of this paragraph.

   (a) A trademark of which the registration is sought to, taking advantage of a well-known foreign trademark or a trademark similar thereto being not registered in Japan, force its purchase, prevent a market entry by the owner of that foreign trademark or force the owner of that foreign trademark to conclude an agent contract

   (b) A trademark identical with or similar to a trademark well known throughout Japan, for which an application is filed with an intention to dilute the distinctiveness of the well-known trademark to indicate the source of goods or impair the reputation, etc. of the trademark owner' however the trademark of that application per se is not liable to cause confusion over the source of goods.

2. Trademarks 'well known among consumers' as stipulated in this paragraph not only mean trademarks widely known to final users but include trademarks widely recognised among traders.

3. Trademarks 'well known among consumers ... abroad' as stipulated in this paragraph need to be *well known in the countries they originate from* but *not* necessarily need to be well known *in multiple countries outside those countries*. Nor do they in Japan.

4. A judgment on 'unfair purposes' needs to be made with full consideration given to the following materials, if available.

   (a) Materials proving a fact that *another person's trademark is well known among consumers* (the period, scope, frequency of its use);

   (b) Materials showing that a well-known trademark is composed of a *coined word* or particular in composition;

   (c) Materials proving a fact that the owner of a well-known trademark has a *concrete plan* to make a market entry in Japan (such as, for example, exportation to Japan, sales in Japan, etc.);

---

1 Emphasis added in the text by the author.

(d)   Materials proving a fact that the owner of a well-known trademark *has a plan to expand its business* in the near future (such as, for example, the start of a new business, development of its business in new areas, etc.);

(e)   Materials proving a fact that the owner of a well-known trademark is forced to accept a demand from a trademark applicant for the purchase of a trademark in question, the conclusion of an agent contract, etc., and;

(f)   Materials showing that a trademark, if used by its applicant, is liable to impair credit, reputation, consumer attractiveness built up in a well-known trademark.

5.   A trademark in correspondence to (1) and (2) is *prima facie* assumed to have been used with unfair intention.

(1)   A trademark which is identical or very similar to a well-known trademark in other countries or a trademark well-known throughout Japan.

(2)   The above-mentioned well-known trademark is composed of a coined word or particular in composition.

6.   *Judgment of whether the trademark is well known or not shall apply mutatis mutandis Article 3(8) (Article 4(1)(x)) of the Guidelines.*

Appendix 5

An annotated[1] version of the JPO
Trademark Examination Guidelines
Relating to *Distinctiveness*: Chapter II:
Article 3(2)

3. (1) Judgment as to *whether a trademark has come to gain its distinctiveness through use will be made*, taking the following points into consideration. Specifically, *the level of consumers' awareness*, which will be estimated through *a quantitative grasp of the use of a trademark*, will be utilized to judge the distinctiveness of a trademark.

(i) A trademark *actually in use* and goods or services for which it is used;
(ii) The start of *its use,* the length of *its use,* or the area where it is used;
(iii) The volume of production, certification or delivery and a scale of business (number of stores, an area of business, an amount of sales, etc.);
(iv) The method, frequency and contents of advertising;
(v) The number of times of appearance in general newspapers, trade journals, magazines and the internet, and contents thereof;
(vi) The outcome of the questionnaire regarding consumers' awareness of the trademark.

(2) The above *facts need to be proved by a method using evidence,* including:

(i) Printed matter (newspaper clippings, magazines, catalogues, leaflets, etc.) carrying advertisements, public notices, etc.;
(ii) Invoices, delivery slips, order slips, bills, receipts, account books, pamphlets, etc.;
(iii) Photographs, etc. showing the use of a trademark;
(iv) A certificate by an advertisement agency, broadcasting agency, publisher or printer;
(v) A certificate by a trade association, fellow traders or consumers;
(vi) A certificate by a public organization, etc. (the state, a local public entity, a foreign embassy in Japan, a Chamber of Commerce and Industry, etc.);
(vii) Articles in general newspapers, trade journals, magazines and the internet;
(viii) Outcome reports of the questionnaire intended for consumers regarding awareness of the trademark.

---

1 Emphasis added in the text provided by the author.

However, due consideration will be given to the objectivity of the questionnaire with respect to the conductor, method, and respondents.

(3) *Judgment as to whether a trademark has come to gain its distinctiveness through use* will be made with consideration given to the frequency of use by people other than the applicant ('other than the applicant and the members' in the case of a collective trademark), and the status of use.

Selected bibliography

Primary materials

International (in chronological order)

- Paris Convention for the Protection of Industrial Property (of 20 March 1883, as revised at Brussels on 14 December 1900, at Washington on 2 June 1911, at The Hague on 6 November 1925, at London on 2 June 1934, at Lisbon on 31 October 1958, and at Stockholm on 14 July 1967, and as amended on 28 September 1979) (the Paris Convention).
- Berne Convention for the Protection of Literary and Artistic Works (of 9 September 1886, completed at Paris on 4 May 1896, revised at Berlin on 13 November 1908, completed at Berne on 20 March 1914, revised at Rome on 2 June 1928, at Brussels on 26 June 1948, at Stockholm on 14 July 1967, and at Paris on 24 July 1971, and amended on 28 September 1979) (the Berne Convention).
- Nice Agreement Concerning the International Classification of Goods and Services for the Purposes of the Registration of Marks (of 15 June 1957, as revised at Stockholm on 14 July 1967, and at Geneva on 13 May 1977, and amended on 28 September 1979) (the Nice Agreement).
- Nairobi Treaty on the Protection of the Olympic Symbol (adopted at Nairobi on 26 September 26) (Nairobi Treaty).
- Protocol Relating to the Madrid Agreement Concerning the International Registration of Marks (adopted at Madrid on 27 June 1989, as amended on 3 October 2006 and on 12 November 2007) (the Madrid Protocol).
- The General Agreement on Tariffs and Trade and the Agreement on Trade Related Aspects on Intellectual Property Rights (GATT TRIPS).
- Trademark Law Treaty (adopted at Geneva on 27 October 1994).
- WIPO, Joint Recommendation Concerning Provisions on the Protection of Well-Known Marks adopted by the Assembly of the Paris Union for the Protection of Industrial Property and the General Assembly of the World Intellectual Property Organization (WIPO) at the Thirty-Fourth Series of Meetings of the Assemblies of the Member States of WIPO 20–29 September 1999) (Publication 833(E)) (the WIPO Recommendation).
- Singapore Treaty on the Law of Trademarks (2006).

Regional

- First Directive 89/104/EEC of the Council, of 21 December 1988, to Approximate the Laws of the Member States Relating to Trade Marks (OJ EC No. L 40 of 11.2.1989, p. 1).
- Directive 2008/95/EC of the European Parliament and of the Council of 22 October 2008 to approximate the laws of the Member States relating to trade marks (Codified version).
- Council Regulation (EC) No. 40/9 of 20 December 1993 on the Community trade mark.
- Council Regulation (EC) No. 207/2009 of 26 February 2009 on the Community trade mark (Codified version).
- Council Regulation (EEC) No. 2081/92 of 14 July 1992 on the Protection of Geographical Indications and Designations of Origin for Agricultural Products and Foodstuffs.
- Council Directive 84/450/EEC of 10 September 1984 relating to the approximation of the laws, regulations and administrative provisions of the Member States concerning misleading advertising.
- Community Trade Mark Examination Guidelines.

National

- United States Code Title 15 Chapter 22, subchapter III § 1125.
- *Syohyo jyorei* [商標条例明治17年6月7日].
- *Syohyo ho* [商標法　昭和三十四年四月十三日法律第百二十七号: The Trademark Act (Act No. 127 of 13 April 13 1959)].
- *Syubyo ho* [種苗法　平成十年五月二十九日法律第八十三号: Plant Variety Protection and Seed Act (Act No. 83 of 29 May 29 1998)].
- *Chiteki zaisan koto saibansyo setti ho* [知的財産高等裁判所設置法　平成十六年六月十八日法律第百十九号: Act for Establishment of the Intellectual Property High Court (Act No. 119 of 18 June 18 2004)]
- *Fusei kyoso boshi ho* [不正競争防止法　平成五年五月十九日法律第四十七号: Unfair Competition Prevention Act (Act No. 47 of 19 May 1993)].
- *Min po* [民法　明治二十九年四月二十七日法律第八十九号: Civil Code
- (Act No. 89 of 27 April 1896).
- *Syohyo shinsa kijyun* [商標審査基準: Examination Guidelines for Trademarks].

European Union jurisprudence

- *Adam Opel GmbH v Autec* (I ZR 88/08) [2010] ETMR 50 (GER).
- *Adidas AG v Marca Mode CV* (Case C-102/07) [2008] ETMR 44.
- *Adidas-Salomon AG v Nike Europe Holding BV Arrondissementsrechtbank (Den Haag)* [2007] ETMR 12.
- *Alcon Inc v Office for Harmonisation in the Internal Market (Trade Marks and Designs) (OHIM)* (Case C-412/05 P) [2007] ETMR 68.

- *Alecansan SL v Office for Harmonisation in the Internal Market (Trade Marks and Designs) (OHIM)* (Case T-202/03) [2006] ETMR 93.
- *Antarctica Srl v Office for Harmonisation in the Internal Mark*et (Trade Marks and Designs) (Case T-47/06) [2007] ETMR 77.
- *Assembled Investments (Proprietary) Ltd v Office for Harmonisation in the Internal Market (Trade Marks and Designs) (OHIM)* (Case T-105/05) (Unreported, 12 June 2007) (CFI).
- *Beko Plc v Socks World International Ltd* [2011] RPC 11.
- *Betty's Kitchen Coronation Street TM* [2000] RPC 825.
- *Bovemij Verzekeringen NV v Benelux-Merkenbureau* (Case C-108/05) [2007] ETMR 29.
- *Canon Kabushiki Kaisha v Metro Goldwyn Mayer Inc* (Case C-39/97) [1999] ETMR 1; [1998] ETMR 366 (Opinion of Advocate General Francis Jacobs).
- *Cartoon Network v Cartoon Triangle Apparel* [2003] EWHC 3375.
- *Castellani SpA v Office for Harmonisation in the Internal Market (Trade Marks and Designs) (OHIM)* (T-149/06) [2008] ETMR 22.
- *Citigroup Inc v Office for Harmonisation in the Internal Market (Trade Marks and Designs) (OHIM)* (Case T-181/05) [2008] ETMR 47.
- *Claude Ruiz-Picasso v Office for Harmonisation in the Internal Market (Trade Marks and Designs)* (Case C-361/04 P) [2006] ETMR 29.
- *Coty Germany GmbH v eBay International AG* [2012] ETMR 29 (Berlin).
- *Davidoff & Cie SA, Zino Davidoff SA v Gofkid Ltd* (Case C-292/00) [2003] ETMR 42.
- *Digipos Store Solutions Group Ltd v Digi International Inc* [2007] EWHC 3371 (Ch).
- *Dyson Ltd v Registrar of Trade Marks* (Case C-321/03) [2007] RPC 27.
- *El Corte Ingles SA v Office for Harmonisation in the Internal Market* (Case T-443/05) [2007] ETMR 81.
- *Elleni Holding BV v Sigla SA* (Case R 1127/2000–3, 2003) [2005] ETMR 7.
- *Ellerman Investments Ltd v C-Vanci* [2006] EWHC 1442 (Ch).
- *Environmental Manufacturing LLP v Office for Harmonisation in the Internal Market (Trade Marks and Designs) (OHIM) (T-570/10)* [2012] ETMR 54.
  Esure Insurance Ltd v Direct Line Insurance Plc [2007] EWHC 1557 (Ch).
- *European Ltd v Economist Newspaper Ltd* [1998] ETMR 307.
- *Floris (J) Ltd v Istrad Ltd* (R 470/2001–2) [2005] ETMR 8.
- *General Motors Corporation v Yplon SA* (Case C-375/97) [1999] ETMR 950, [1999] ETMR 122 (Opinion of Advocate General Francis Jacobs).
- *Giersch v Google Inc (B 795 569) Office for Harmonisation in the Internal Market* (Opposition Division) [2007] ETMR 41.
- *Google France Sarl v Louis Vuitton Malletier SA* (Case C-236/08) [2010] ETMR 30.
- *Helena Rubinstein SNC and L'Oréal SA v Office for Harmonisation in the Internal Market (Trade Marks and Designs) (OHIM)* (Case C-100/11 P) [2012] ETMR 40.
- *Hollywood S.A.S. v Souza Cruz S.A.* (Case R-283/1999–3) [2002] ETMR 64.
- *House of Donuts International v Office for Harmonisation in the Internal Market (Trade Marks and Designs) (OHIM)* (Case T-333/04) [2007] ETMR 53.

- *Hoya Kabushiki Kaisha v Office for Harmonisation in the Internal Market (Trade Marks and Designs) (OHIM)* (Case T-9/05) [2008] ETMR 29.
- *IG Communications Ltd v Office for Harmonisation in the Internal Market (Trade Marks and Designs) (OHIM) (T-301/09)* [2013] ETMR 17.
- *Il Ponte Finanziaria SpA v Office for Harmonisation in the Internal Market (Trade Marks and Designs) (OHIM)* (Case C-234/06) [2008] ETMR 13.
- *Intel Corporation Inc. v CPM United Kingdom Limited* (Case C-252/07) [2009] ETMR 13.
- *Interflora Inc and Interflora British Unit v Marks & Spencer Plc and Flowers Direct Online Limited* (Case C-323/09) [2012] ETMR 1.
- *Interflora Inc v Marks and Spencer Plc* [2012] EWHC 1722 (Ch).
- *Interflora Inc v Marks and Spencer Plc* [2012] EWCA Civ 1501.
- *Kingspan Group Plc v Rockwool Ltd* [2011] EWHC 250 (Ch).
- *Koipe Corporacion SL v Office for Harmonisation in the Internal Market (Trade Marks and Designs) (OHIM)* (T-363/04) [2008] ETMR 8.
- *Koninklijke Philips Electronics NV v Remington Consumer Products Ltd* (Case C-299/99) [2002] ETMR 81.
- *Kraft Foods Schweiz Holding GmbH v Office for Harmonisation in the Internal Market (Trade Marks and Designs) (OHIM) (T-357/10)* [2012] ETMR 51.
- *La Mer Technology Inc v Office for Harmonisation in the Internal Market (Trade Marks and Designs) (OHIM)* (Case T-418/03) [2008] ETMR 9.
- *Leidseplein Beheer B.V. and Others, other parties v Red Bull GmbH and Others* (Case C-65/12).
- *Libertel Groep BV v Benelux-Merkenbureau* (Case C-104/01) [2003] ETMR 63.
- *Lloyd Schuhfabrik Meyer & Co. GmbH v Klijsen Handel BV* (Case C-342/97) [2000] FSR 77.
- *Lodestar Anstalt v Austin Nichols & Co Inc Irish Patents Office* [2008] ETMR 54.
- *L'Oréal SA v Bellure NV* (Case C-487/07) [2009] ETMR 55.
- *L'Oréal SA v Office for Harmonisation in the Internal Market (Trade Marks and Designs)* (C-235/05 P).
- *Madaus AG v Office for Harmonisation in the Internal Market (Trade Marks and Designs) (OHIM)* (Case T-202/04) [2006] ETMR 76.
- *Mango Sport System S.R.L. Socio Unico Mangone Antonio Vincenzo v Diknah S.L.* (Case R-308/2003–1) [2005] ETMR 5.
- *Marca Mode CV v Adidas AG and Adidas Benelux BV* (Case C-425/98) [2000] ETMR 723.
- *Market Tools Inc v Optimus Telecomunicacoes SA* (Case R-253/2006–2) [2007] ETMR 74.
- *Maurer + Wirtz GmbH & Co KG v Office for Harmonisation in the Internal Market (Trade Marks and Designs) (OHIM) (T-63/07)* [2010] ETMR 40.
- *Medion AG v Thomson Multimedia Sales Germany & Austria GmbH* (Case C-120/04) [2006] ETMR 13.
- *Mostaza Claro v Centro Movil Milenium SL* (Case C-168/05) [2007] 1 CMLR 22.
- *Muhlens GmbH & Co KG v Office for Harmonisation in the Internal Market (Trade Marks and Designs) (OHIM)* (Case C-206/04 P) [2006] ETMR 57.

- *Nieto Nuno v Monlleo Franquet* (Case C-328/06) [2008] ETMR 12.
- *Oasis Stores Ltd's Trade Mark Application* [1999] ETMR 531.
- *O2 Holdings Ltd v Hutchison 3G UK Ltd* (Case C-533/06) [2008] ETMR 55.
- *Office for Harmonisation in the Internal Market (Trade Marks and Designs) (OHIM) v Kaul GmbH* (Case C-29/05) [2007] ETMR 37.
- *Parfums Christian Dior SA v Evora BV* (Case C-337/95) [1998] ETMR 26.
- *Portakabin Ltd v Primakabin BV* (C-558/08) [2010] ETMR 52.
- *Procter & Gamble Co v Reckitt Benckiser (UK) Ltd* [2008] FSR 8.
- *Principe SpA v Principles Retail Ltd Irish Patents Office* [2007] ETMR 56.
- *Quelle AG v Office for Harmonisation in the Internal Market (Trade Marks and Designs) (OHIM)* [2007] ETMR 62.
- *Ralf Sieckmann v Deutsches Patent- und Markenamt* (Case C-273/00) [2003] ETMR37.
- *Red Bull GmbH v Sun Mark Ltd* [2012] EWHC 1929 (Ch).
- *Rousselon Freres ET CIE v Horwood Homewares Limited* [2008] EWHC 881 (Ch).
- *Ruiz-Picasso v Office for Harmonisation in the Internal Market (Trade Marks and Designs) (OHIM)* (Case C-361/04 P) [2006] ETMR 29.
- *Sabel BV v Puma AG, Rudolf Dassler Sport* (Case C-251/95) [1998] ETMR 1.
- *S.A. Cnl-Sucal NV v Hag GF AG* (Case C-10/89) [1990] 3 CMLR 571.
- *SA Spa Monopole, Compagnie Fermié de Spa, En Abrégé SA Spa Monopole NV v Spa-Finders Travel Arrangements Ltd* (Case R 131/2003–1) [2005] ETMR 9.
- *Sergio Rossi v Office for Harmonisation in the Internal Market (Trade Marks and Designs)* (T-169/03) [2005] ECR II-68.
- *SIGLA SA v Office for Harmonisation in the Internal Market (Trade Marks and Designs) (OHIM)* (T-215/03) [2007] ETMR 79.
- *Spa Monopole, compagnie fermière de Spa SA/NV v Office for Harmonisation in the Internal Market, Spa-Finders Travel Arrangements Ltd Intervening* (Case T-67/04) [2005] ETMR 109.
- *Sunrider Corp (t/a Sunrider International) v Vitasoy International Holdings Ltd* [2007] EWHC 37 (Ch).
- *Uluslararasi Saat Ticareti ve dis Ticaret AS v Office for Harmonisation in the Internal Market (Trade Marks and Designs) (OHIM)* (Case C-171/06) [2007] ETMR 38.
- *Van Zuylen v Hag AG* (Case 192/73) [1974] 2 CMLR 127.
- *Windsurfing Chiemsee Produktions-und Vertriebs GmbH v Boots- und Segelzubehör Walter Huber and Franz Attenberger* (Joined Cases C-108/97 and C-109/97) [1999] ETMR585.
- 2333–2000 Telefonica on line/t-online (EN).
- 1243/2000 CAMPBELL'S et al./CAMPBELL CATERING (EN).

Japanese jurisprudence

- 大判昭 3.3.10　昭 2（オ）1311　大判昭 4.11.30　昭4（オ）850. Daihan, syo3nen 3gatus 10ka, (O) 1131, Daihan, syo4nen 11gatsu 30nichi, syo 4nen, (O) 850.

- サントリーシャツ事件 [SANTRY shirts jiken: this can be translated as SANTRY shirts case].
  昭和 32 年　審判大　564 号.
  Syowa 32 shinpan dai 564go.
- New Yorker 事件 [New Yorker jiken: this can be translated as the New Yorker case].
  東京高等裁　昭和36年　(行ナ)第35号　審決取消集 昭和42年　460.
  Tokyo High Court, Syowa 36nen, (Gyo Na) dai 35go, shinketsu torikeshi-yu 460.
- SONY FOOD事件 [SONY FOOD jiken: this can be translated as SONY FOOD case].
  昭和40年10月20日　昭和36年審判　第654号.
  Showa 40nen 10gatsu 20ka, Showa 36nen, shinpan dai 654go.
- 東京高等裁　昭和49年　(行ケ)第32号　審決取消集　25　昭和56年 審判　第8843号(3203号) [the case name is not available].
  Tokyo High Court, Showa 49nen, (Gyo Ke) dai 32go, shinketsu torikeshi syu 529.
- 東京高等裁　昭和53年　(行ケ)第22号　審決取消集　709　[the case name is not available].
  Tokyo High Court, Sowa 53 nen, (Gyo Ke) dai 22go, shinketu sorikeshi-syu 709.
- ハーレーダビットソン事件 [Harley-Davidson jiken: this can be translated as Harley-Davidson case].
  東京地方裁　昭和55年1月28日　無体集1巻5562号42ページ.
  Tokyo District Court, Syowa 55nen 1gatsu 28 nichi, mutaishi-shu 5562go at 42.
- スイートラバー事件 [*SWEET LOVER* jiken]
  東京地裁　昭和55年1月28日　無体集12巻1号1ページ.
  Tokyo District Court, Syowa 55nen, 1gatsu 28 Mutaisyu 12kan 1go 1.
- 昭和56年審判第8843号(3203号) [the case name is not available].
  Showa 56nen shinpan dai 8843 go (3203 go).
- 昭和56年8月11日　昭和50年審判　第6097号　2119号　[the case name is not available].
  Showa 56nen 8gatsu 11nichi, Showa 50nen shinpan dai 6097go 2119go.
- 最高裁判　昭和56年　(オ)第1166号　判例時報1119号34ページ　[the case name is not available].
  The Supreme Court, Showa 56nen, 9(O) dai 1166 go, hanrei jiho 1119go at 34.
- ＤＣＣ事件 [DDC jiken: this can be translated as DDC Case].
  東京高裁昭和57年(行ケ)110号)　東京高等裁　昭和58年　無体集 15巻2号501頁.
  Tokyo High Court, Shyowa 58nen, 6gatsu 16nichi, mitaisyu 15kan 2go at 501.
- ピアジェ社事件 [PIAGE sya jiken: this can be translated as PIAGE case].
  東京高等裁　昭和63年　(行ケ) 第100号　審決取消集　6号399頁.

Tokyo High Court, Showa 63nen, (Gyo Ke) dai 100go, shinketsu rotikeshi-syu (6)P399.

- コンピューターワールド事件 [Computer World jiken: this can be translated as the Computer World case].
東京高等裁　平成3年(行ケ)　29号　知財　集　24巻1号182頁.
Tokyo High Court, Heisei 3nen, (Gyo Ke) 29 go, Chizai-syu 24 kan 1go at 182.
- 東京高等裁　平成7年 27 巻4号855頁 [the case name is not available].
Tokyo High Court, Heisei 7nen, 11gatsu 22nichi, 27kan 4go at 855.
- スナックシャネル事件Snack CHANEL jiken.
最高裁　平成 7 年　(オ)　637 号
Supreme Court, Heisei 7nen, (o) 637go.Hanji 1665go 160.
- 東京高裁　平成8年250-7123号 [the case name is not available].
Tokyo High Court, Heisei 8nen, 3gatsu 27nichi, 250-7123go.
- 東京高等裁　平成8年250-7027号 [the case name is not available].
Tokyo High Court, Heisei 8nen, 2gatsu 7ka, 250-7027go.
- 東京高等裁　平成8年 250-7077号 [the case name is not available].
Tokyo High Court, Heisei 8nen, 2gatsu 15nichi, 250-7077go.
- 東京高等裁　平成9年(行ケ)　323号　速報　283-8377 [the case name is not available].
Tokyo High Court, Heisei 9nen, (Gyo Ke) dai 323go, Sokuho 283-8377.
- 東京高等裁　平成9年(行ケ)　266号　速報　286-8524 [the case name is not available].
Tokyo High Court, Heisei 9nen, (Gyo Ke) dai 266go, Sokuho 286-8524.
- 東京高等裁　平成9年 (行ケ)　278号　判例時報1669号129頁 [the case name is not available].
Tokyo High Court, Heisei 9nen, (Gyo Ke) dai 278go, hanjirei jiho 1669go at 129.
- 東京高等裁　平成 9 年 (行ケ)　139号　特許ニュース判例10年6月25日 [the case name is not available].
Tokyo High Court, Heisei 9nen, (Gyo Ke) dai 139go, Tokkyo News Heisei 10nen 6gatu 25, 29nich and 7gatsu 1ka.
- 東京高等裁　平成10年　(行ケ)　第74号　速報　285-8465 [the case name is not available].
Tokyo High Court, Heisei 10nen, (Gyo Ke) dai 74 go, sokuhyo 285-8465.
- 最高裁　平成 10 年　(行ヒ)　85号　判例時報1721号141頁 [the case name is not available].
Supreme Court, Heisei 10nen, (Gyo Hi) dai 85go, Hanrei jiho 1721go at 141.
- レールデュタン [*L'AIR DU TEMPS* jiken: this can be translated as *L'AIR DU TEMPS* case].
Supreme Court, Heisei 10nen (gyo ke) 85go, minsyu 54kan 6go 1848, hanji 1721go 141.
最高裁判第3　平成10年 (行ヒ)　85号.
Supreme Court, the Third Petty Bench, Heisei 10nen, (Gyo Hi) dai 85go, Hanrei jiho 1721go at 141.

- ユーロポート株式会社 v 特許庁長官   C (known as the Royal Prince Polo Club jiken) [yuro port kabushiki geisha v tokkyo cyo c: this can be translated as Yuro Port Kabushiki gaisha v JPO (known as Royal Prince Polo Club case)].
  東京高等裁　平成11年 (行ケ)　290号　知財速報　297-9181.
  Tokyo High Court, Heisei 11nen, (Gyo Ke) 290go, Sokuho 297-9181.
- 株式会社セント•ローラ　v 特許庁長官 [kabushikigaisya saint ro-ran tokkyocyo cyokan: this can be translated as Kabushiki gaisya St. Lauran v the JPO (known as Lancel case)].
  東京高等裁　平成11年(行ケ)　217号　知財速報　298-9218.
  Tokyo High Court, Heisei 11nen, (Gyo Ke) dai 217go, Sokuho 298-9218.
- J-PHONE事件 [J-PHONE jiken].
  東京地裁平成12年　(ワ)　3545号　判時　1755号　43.
  Tokyo District Court, Heisei 13nen, 4gatsu, Hanketsu, Heisei 12nen (wa) 3545go, Hanji 1755go, 43.
- 呉青山学院中学校事件　 [Kure aoyama gakuin cyugakko jiken: this can be translated as Kure Aoyama Gakuin Junior High School case].
  東京地裁平成12年　(ワ)　967号　判時　1815号　148.
  Tokyo District Court, Heisei 13nen (wa) 967go, Hanji 1815go, 148.
- 株式会社天一 v株式会社天一 [kabushiki gaisya tenichi v kabushiki gaisha tenichi: this can be translated as kabushiki gaisya tenichi v kabushiki gaisha tenichi (known as Tenichi case)].
  東京高等裁　平成13年 (行ケ)　253号　知財速報　326-10796.
  Tokyo High Court, Heisei 13nen, (Gyo Ke) 253go, chizai sokuso 326-10796.
- 富士工業株式会社　特許庁　v ジェット天秤 [Fuji koGyo kabushiki gaisya v tokkyo cyo; this can be translated as Fuji koGyo kabushiki gaisya v JPO (known as Jet Tenbin case)].
  東京高等裁　平成13年(行ケ)　48号　知的所有権判決速報 322-10555.
  Tokyo High Court, Heisei 13nen, (Gyo Ke) 48 go, chiteki syoyuken hanketsu Sokuho 322-10555.
- 有限会社黒雲製作所　A v MOSRITE [Yugen gaisya kokuunn seisakusyo v Mosrite: this can be translated as Yugen gaisya kokuunn seisakusyo v Mosrite].
  東京高等裁　平成13年　(ネ)　5748号　速報　325-10758.
  Tokyo High Court, Heisei 13nen, (Ne) 5748 go, Sokuho 325-10758.
- インターシティー株式会社 v 興和不動産株式会社 [Intercity kabushiki gaisya v Kowa fudosan kabushiki gaisya: this can be translated as Intercity kabushiki gaisya v Kowa fudosan kabushiki gaisya].
  東京高等裁　平成13年 (行ケ)　430号　知財速報　307-1825.
  Tokyo High Court, Heisei 13nen, (Gyo Ke) 430go, Chizai sokuso 307-1825.
- 金盃酒造株式会社v 特許庁 [kanesakazuki syuzo kabishiki gaisya v tokkyo cho: this can be translated as kanesakazuki syuzo kabishiki gaisya v the JPO].
  東京高等裁　平成13年(行ケ)　494号　知財速報　32-10797.
  Tokyo High Court, Heisei 13nen, (Gyo Ke) dai 494go, Sokuho 32-10797.

- マイクロソフトオフィス事件[Microsoft: this can be translated as Microsoft case]
  東京高等裁　平成13年(行ケ)　205号　速報32-10452.
  Tokyo High Court, Heisei 13nen, (Gyo Ke), dai 205. Sokuho 320-10452.
- ザノッタ，サッコ事件[Zanotta and Sacco: this can be translated as Zanotta and Sacco case]
  東京高等裁　平成13年 (行ケ)　175，176号
  Tokyo High Court, Heisei 13(Gyo Ke) 175/176.
- 品川インターシティー事件　[*Shinagawa Inter City*: this can be translated as Shinagawa Inter City case]
  東京高等裁　平成13年 (行ケ)　430号.　知財速報　307-10825.
  Tokyo High Court, Heisei 13nen, (Gyo Ke) 430go. Chizai sokuso 307-10825.
- Manhattan Portage 事件　[Manhattan Portage jiken: this can be translated as Manhattan Portage case].
  東京高裁　平成14年　(行ケ)　514号　(判例集未登載).
  Tokyo High Court, Heisei 14nen (gyo Ke) 514go (unreported).
- アイーフロー •コーポレーションv 有限会社丼親堂本舗「Ｏｎ•Ｑ」
  [Ai Flow Corporation v Yugen gaisya seishindo honpo: this can be translated as I Flow Corporation v Yugen gaisya seishindo honpo (known as On Q case)].
  東京高等裁　平成15年 (行ケ)　32号　知財速報　342-11811.
  Tokyo High Court, Heisei 15nen, (Gyo Ke) 32go, Chizai Sokuho 342-11811.
- (有)二鶴堂（株）v ひよ子 [Yu nikaku do v kabushiki gaisya Hiyoko: this can be translated as Yu nikaku do v kabushiki gaisya Hiyoko (known as Hiyoko case)].
  知的財産高等裁　平成17年　(行ケ)10673.
  Intellectual Property High Court, Heisei 17nen, (Gyo Ke) 10673.
- キシリトールガム比較広告事件 [*xylitol gum hikaku kokoku* jiken *xylitol gum hikaku kokoku* jiken: this can be translated Xylitol Chewing Gum comparative advertisement case].
  知的財産高等裁　平成17年　(ネ)　10059号　判例集未登録.
  Intellectual Property High Court, Heisei 18nen (ne) 10059go unreported.
- 岩手春みどり事件[Iwate haru imidori: this can be translated as Iwate Spring Green case].
  知的財産高等裁　平成17年 (行ケ)　10041号，速報398-15111.
  Intellectual Property High Court, Heisei 17 (Gyo Ke) 10041go. Sokuho 398-15111.
- ジェ　ア　モドゥフィヌ　エス　アー　特許庁 [Je a modou finne esu a v tokkyo cyo: this can be translated as Je A Modo fin SR v JPO (known as AJ case)].
  知的財産高等裁　平成19年 (行ケ)10243.
  Intellectual Property High Court, Heisei 19nen, (Gyo Ke) 10243.
- 喜多方ラーメン事件[*Kitakata ra-men* Kitakata Japanese noodle (ra-men) case]

知的財産高等裁　平成21年 (行ケ)104335号
Intellectual Property High Court, Heisei 21 (Gyo Ke) 104335go.
*   マクロス商標　[*Macross* Trademark Registration]
    異議2001-90383.
    Examination Reference 2001-90383.
*   スピードアリーナ商標[*Speed Arena* Trademark Registration]
    異議902278.
    Examination reference 902278.
*   スカイボス商標[*Sky Boss* Trademark Registration].
    異議2003-90096
    Examination reference 2003-90096.
*   ディーゼル商標　[*Diesel* Trademark Registration.]
    異議1999-35105
    Examination reference 1999-35105.
*   マック商標 [MAC trademark registration]
    異議92239
    Examination Reference: 92239.
*   マリーフランス商標[*Marie France* Trademark Registration]
    異議2007-25958
    Examination Reference 2007-25958.

American jurisprudence

*   *Nabisco v P F Brands Inc* 191 D 3d 208. 227-8 (2nd Cir 1999).
*   *Mosely et al., dba Victor's Little Secret v V Secret Catalogue Inc* 537 US 418, 123 Sup Ct 1115 (2003).
*   *Times Mirror Magazine Inc v Las Vegas Sports News LLC* 212 F 3d 157, 167 (3rd Cir 2000).

Secondary materials

Books (English language)

D. Aaker, *Building Strong Brand*, Detroit: Free Press, 1996.
D. Aaker, *Managing Brand Equity/Capitalising on the Value of a Brand Name*, Canada: Maxwell Macmillan, 1991.
D. Aaker and A. Biel, *Brand Equity and Advertising: Advertising's Role in Building Strong Brands*, Hillsdale, NJ: Lawrence Erlbaum Associates, 1993.
D. Aaker and E. Joachimsthaler, *Brand Leadership*, Detroit, MI: Free Press, 2000.
R. Allen, *The Concise Oxford Dictionary of Current English*, Oxford: Clarendon Press, 1990.
R. Annand and H. Norman, *Blackstone's Guide to the Community Trade Mark*, London: Blackstone Press, 1998.
N. Caravalho, *The TRIPS Regime of Trademarks and Designs*, London: Kluwer Law International, 2006.
W. Cornish, *Intellectual Property: Omnipresent, Distracting, Irrelevant?*, Oxford: Oxford University Press, 2004.

W. Cornish and D. Llewelyn, *Intellectual Property: Patents, Copyright, Trade Marks and Allied Rights*, 5th edition, London: Sweet & Maxwell, 2007.

S. Davis, *Brand Asset Management: Driving Profitable Growth Through Your Brands*, London: John Wiley and Sons, 2002.

M. Franzos, *European Community Trade Mark: Commentary to the European Community Regulation*, London: Kluwer Law International, 1977.

J. Gaines, *Contested Cultures: The Image, the Voice and the Law*, London: BFL Publishing, 1992.

D. Gervais, *The TRIPS Agreement: Drafting History and Analysis*, London: Sweet & Maxwell, 2003.

C. Health, *Intellectual Property Law in Asia*, London: Kluwer Law International, 2003.

C. Health and L. Kung-Chung, *The Protection of Well-Known Marks in Asia*, London: Kluwer Law International, 2000.

U. Hildebrandt, *Harmonised Trade Mark Law in Europe: Case-Law of the European Court of Justice*, Cologne: Carl Heymanns Verlag, 2005.

M. Hoechke, *Epistemology and Methodology of Comparative Law*, Oxford: Hart Publishing, 2004.

B. Issac, *Brand Protection Matters*, London: Sweet & Maxwell, 2000.

INTA EU, Canada, Middle East Dilution Subcommittee, *The Protection of Well-Known Marks in the European Union, Canada and the Middle East: A Country and Regional Analysis*, INTA, October 2004.

S. Kane, *Trademark Law: A Practitioner's Guide*, New York: City Practising Law Institute, 1987.

J. Kaufmann, *Passing off and Misappropriation: An Economic and Legal Analysis of the Law of Unfair Competition in the United States and Continental Europe*, Weinheim, Germany: Wiley-VCH, 1986.

D. Kitchin, *Kerly's Law of Trademarks and Trade Names*, 13th edition, London: Sweet & Maxwell, 2001.

N. Klein, *No Logo*, London: Flamingo, 2001.

W. Landes and R. Posner, *The Economic Structure of Intellectual Property Law*, Cambridge, MA: Harvard University Press, 2003.

T. McCarthy, *McCarthy on Trademarks and Unfair Competition*. New York: Clark Boardman Callaghan, 1995.

S. Maniatis, *The Communicative Aspects of Trade Marks: A Legal, Functional and Economic Analysis*, PhD thesis, University of London, 1998.

S. Maniatis, *Trade Marks in Europe: A Practical Jurisprudence*, London: Sweet & Maxwell, 2006.

T. Martino, *Trademark Dilution*, Oxford: Clarendon Press, 1996.

A. Michaels, *A Practical Guide to Trade Mark Law*, London: Sweet & Maxwell, 2003.

F. Mostert, *Famous and Well-Known Marks: An International Analysis*, London: Butterworths, 1997.

F. Mostert and L. Apolzon, *From Edison to iPod: Protect Your Ideas and Make Money*, New York: DK Publishing, 2007.

M. Perelman, *Steal This Idea: Intellectual Property and the Corporate Confiscation of Creativity*, New York: Palgrave, 2002.

J. Phillips, *Trade Mark Law: A Practical Anatomy*, Oxford: Oxford University Press, 2003.

J. Phillips, *Trade Marks at the Limit*, London: Edward Elgar Publishing, 2006.

C. Pickering, *Trade Mark in Theory and Practice*, Oxford: Oxford University Press, 1998.

D. Pope, *The Making of Modern Advertising*, New York: Basic Book, 1983.

L. Rahanasto, *Intellectual Property Rights, External Effects and Anti-Trust Law: Leveraging IPRs in the Communications Industry*, Oxford: Oxford University Press, 2003.

A. Saidov, *Comparative Law*, London: Wildy, Simmons & Hill, 2003.

I. Simon, *Trade Mark Dilution in Europe and the United States*, Oxford: Oxford University Press, 2011.

G. Smith, *Trademark Valuation*, Oxford: John Wiley & Sons, 1997.

D. Tatham, *Well-Known Trade Marks: A Clip Seminar Report* (1997). The Intellectual Property Institute ECTA (European Communities Trade Mark Association) '15 The Opposition. A Cornerstone of the European Trade Mark System' Conference organised by ECTA Brussels, 10–13 June 1998 (Publisher ECTA 1998).

G. Tritton, *Intellectual Property in Europe*, London: Sweet & Maxwell, 2007.

L. Wittgenstein, *Philosophical Investigations*, Oxford: Blackwell, 1958.

World Intellectual Property Organization (WIPO) *Introduction to Intellectual Property: Theory and Practice*, London: Kluwer Law International, 1997.

J. Zaichowsky, *The Psychology Behind Trademark Infringement and Counterfeiting*, Lawrence Erlbaum, 2006.

K. Zweigert and H. Kötz, *An Introduction to Comparative Law*, Oxford: Clarendon Press, 1998.

Books (Japanese language)

H. Aizawa, T. Obuchi, N. Koizumi and Y. Tamura, *Chitekizaisanho no riron to genzaiteki kadai: Nakayama Nobuhiro sensei kanrekikinen ronbun syu* [知的財産法の理論と現在的課題：中山信弘先生還暦記念論文集: this can be translated as *A Theory of Intellectual Property Law and its Problems: Professor Nakayama Nobuyuki 60th Birthday Anniversary Edition*], Tokyo: Kobun-do, 2005.

H. Aoki, *Chiteki zaisan ken toshiteno brand to design* [知的財産権としてのブランドとデザイン: this can be translated as *Brands and Designs as Intellectual Property Rights*, Tokyo: Yuhi-kaku, 2007.

K. Aoyama, *Chizai 20 ko: Chiteki zaisan no sozo, hogo, katsuyo tou no genjyo to kadai* [知財２０講：知的財産の創造、保護、活用等の現状と課題: this can be translated as *Lessons 20 on Intellectual Property: Problems of Creation, Protection and Facilitation of Intellectual Property*, Tokyo: Keizai Sangyo Chosa-kai, 2004.

K. Aoyama, *Fusei kyoso boshi ho* [不正競争防止法: this can be translated *Unfair Competition Prevention Act*], Tokyo: Hogaku-syoin, 2005.

M. Amino, *Syohyo arekore* [商標あれこれ: this can be translated as *Various Aspects of Trademarks*], Tokyo: Tokyo Nunoi-syupppan, 1989.

M. Amino, *Syohyo-ho* (商標法: this can be translated as *Trademark Law*), Tokyo: Yuhi-kaku, 2004.

M. Amino, *Syohyo ho no syomondai* [商標法の諸問題: this can be translated as *Problems of Trademark Law*], Tokyo: Tokyo Nunoi-syuppan, 1978.

M. Amino, *Zoku Syohyo ho no syomondai* [続商標法の諸問題: this can be translated as *Problems of Trademark Law II*], Tokyo: Tokyo Nunoi-syuppan, 1983.

T. Doi, *Chiteki syoyuken kihon hanrei (syohyo Fuseikyoso)* [知的所有権基本判例 (商標、不正競争): this can be translated as *Cases on Intellectual Property Rights (Trademarks, Unfair Competition)*], Tokyo: Dobun-kan, 1996.

T. Doi, *Tokkyo Syohyo Chosakuken no kokusai mondai* [特許、商標、著作権保護の国際問題: this can be translated as *International Problems of Protection for Patents, Trademarks, Copyrights*], Tokyo: Sakai-syoten, 1970.

K. Doi, *Chiteki Zaisan Ho Nyumon* [知的財産法入門: this can be translated as *Intellectual Property Law*], Tokyo: Tyuokeizai-sha, 2005.

J. Eguchi, *America syohyo ho niokeru tsuyoi mark, yowai mark no hori nitsuite* [アメリカ商標における強いマーク、弱いマークの法理について: this can be translated as *Legitimacy in Protecting Strong and Weak Marks in US Trademark Law*], Osaka: Osaka Daigaku, 1982.

T. Fukai, *Ruijisyogo wo meguru hunso: saishinhanrei nimiru fuseikyoso syohyokenshingai* [類似商号をめぐる紛争 最新判例にみる不正競争・商標権侵害: this can be translated as *Trade Mark Litigations Concerning Similar Marks: The Current Case Studies on Trademark and Unfair Competition Infringement*], Tokyo: Nihon horei, 2006.

H. Goto, *Paris jyoyaku* [パリ条約: this can be translated as *The Paris Convention*], Tokyo: Hatsumei-kyokai 2002.

Y. Harima, *Q&A Fuseikyoso boshi ho nyumon* [Q&A 不正競争防止法入門: this can be translated as *Introduction to the Unfair Competition Law*], Tokyo: Sekaishisosya kyougakusya, 1988.

Y. Harima, *Sohyo ho – Riron to Zissai* [商標法 – 理論と実際: this can be translated as Trademark: Theory and Practice], Tokyo: Roppo-syuppan, 1982.

M, Hirao, *Syohyo ho* [商標法: this can be translated as *Trademark Law*], Tokyo: Gakuyo-syobo, 2002.

Y. Iida, *Osyukyodotai syohyoseido shinkou* [欧州共同体商標制度新講: this can be translated as *Guidelines Concerning the European Community Trade Mark*, Tokyo: Hatsumei kyokai, 1997.

S, Kanei, T. Yano, Y. Akiyama, A. Takahashi and H. Hosoda, *Chitekizaisanho jyuyo hanrei* [知的財産法重要判例: this can be translated as *Case Studies on Intellectual Property Law*], Tokyo: Gakuyo syobo, 2005.

S. Kanei, M. Yamaguchi and H. Ogura, *Fusei kyoso boshi ho komentar* [不正競争防止法コメンタール: this can be translated as *Comments on Unfair Competition Prevention Act*], Tokyo: LexisNexis Japan, 2004.

Keizai Sangyosyo chitekizaisan seisakushitsu, *Fuseikyoso boshi ho* 不正競争防止法: this can be translated as *Unfair Competition Prevention Act*], Tokyo: Yuhi-kaku, 2005.

S. Kidana, *Kokusai chitekizaisanken shingaisosyo no kisoriron* [国際知的財産侵害訴訟の基礎理論: this can be translated as *Fundamental Theory of International Intellectual Property Infringements*], Tokyo: Keizai sangyo tyosa kai, 2003.

Kokusai chitekizaisansyoyuken kenkyu group (this can be translated as International Intellectual Property Rights Research Working Group), *Kokusai jidaino chitekizaisan syoyuken: sekaino cyoryu ha ima* [国際化時代の知的所有権：世界の潮流はいま: this can be translated as *Intellectual Property Rights in the Global Century*], Tokyo: Nikkan kyogyo shinbun-sya: 1998.

Kubo Katsusori Tokkyo jimusyo (this can be translated as Kubota Katsunori Patent Office), *Net jidaino syohyo to syogo* [ネット時代の商標と商号: this can be translated as *Trademarks and Trade Names in the Web Era*], Tokyo: Nexus Media-sya, 2006.

H. Kudo, syohyo shinsakijyun no kaisetu, *syohyo no kaisetu to saiban rei* [商標の解説と裁判例: this can be translated as *Trademark: Commentary and Court Cases*], Tokyo: Masterlink, 2011

K. Kudo, *c* [商標審査基準の解説: this can be translated as *Introduction of the JPO Examination Guideline for Trademarks*], Tokyo, Hatsumei-kyokai, 2004.

T. Makio, and T. Iimura, *Shin saibanjitsumutaikei 4: Chitekizaisan kankei sosyo ho* [新裁判実務大系４：知的財産関係訴訟法: this can be translated as *Lawsuits in Intellectual Property Rights*], Tokyo: Seirin-syoin, 2001.

M. Miyake, *Syohyoho zakkan: sono kyukyokuni arumono wo tazunete* [商標法雑感：その究極にあるものを尋ねて: this can be translated as *Trademark Law*], Tokyo: Tomiyama-bo, 1973.

M. Monya, *Syohyoho 50 kou* [商標法50講this can be translated as *Trademark Law: 50 Lessons*], Tokyo, Yuhi-kaku, 1978.

N. Nakayama, *Chitekizaisanken kenkyu II* [知的財産権研究 II: this can be translated as *Studies in Intellectual Property Rights II*], Tokyo: Nunoi syuppan, 1991.

N. Nakayama, *Chitekizaisanken kenkyu III* [知的財産権研究 III: this can be translated as *Studies in Intellectual Property Rights III*], Tokyo: Nunoi syuppan, 1995.

H. Nasuno, *Fuseikyoso boshiho niyoru chizai boei senryaku* [不正競争防止法による知財防衛戦略: this can be translated as *Intellectual Property Asset Protection by the Unfair Competition Prevention Act*], Tokyo: Nippon Keizai Hinbunsha, 2005.

S. Ono, *Syohyo ho* [注解商標法 新版: this can be translated as *Trademark Law*], Tokyo: Seirin-syoin, 2005.

S. Ono, *Overview of the Japanese Trademark Law* (Tokyo, IIP, 1999). This is available in English at www.iip.or.jp/translation/ono/ch2.pdf (accessed 30 January 2015).

Sangyo Kozo Shingikai Chiteki Zaisan Seisaku Bukai, *Sangyo Kozo Shingikai Chiteki Zaisan Seisaku Bukai Hokokusho* [産業構造審議会知的財産政策部会 報告書: this can be translated as *Report of the Intellectual Property Policy Committee of the Industrial Structure Council*], Tokyo: Sangyo Kozo Shingikai Chiteki Zaisan Seisaku Bukai, 1992.

T. Shibuya, *Syohyo ho no rion* [商標法の理論: this can be translated as *Trademark Law in Theory*], Tokyo: Tokyo University Press, 1973.

I. Shimamura, *Koji en* [広辞苑: this cannot be translated but known as *Japanese–Japanese Dictionary*], Tokyo: Iwanami-syoten, 1998.

W. Sueyoshi, *Syohyo ho* [商標法: this can be translated as *Trademark Law*], Tokyo: Cyuo Keizaisya, 2008.

Y. Tamura, *Fusei kyoso boshi ho gaisetsu* [不正競争防止法概説: this can be translated as *Unfair Competition Prevention Act*], Tokyo: Yuhi-kaku, 2003.

Y. Tamura, *Fusei kyoso boshi ho* [不正競争防止法: this can be translated as *The Unfair Competition Prevention Act*], Tokyo: Iwanami-syoten.

Y. Tamura, *Syohyo ho* [商標法: this can be translated as *Trademark Law*], Tokyo: Kobun-do, 2004.

Y. Tamura, *Kinouteki Chitekizaisanho no riron* [機能的知的財産法の理論: this can be translated as *Theory of Functional Intellectual Property Law*], Tokyo: Intellectual Property Research Institute Shinzansya, 1996.

Y. Tamura, *Shijyo, Jiyu, Chitekizaisan* [市場•自由•知的財産: this can be translated as *Market, Freedom, Intellectual Property*], Tokyo: Yui-kaku, 2003.

Y. Tamura, *Syohyoho Gaisetsu* [商標法概説: this can be translated as *Trademark Law*], Tokyo: Kobun-do, 2000.

Y. Takahashi, *Gendai Keiei to Chitekizaisanken: Gijyutsu to Keizai to ho no sojyokoka* [現代経営と知的財産権2版 – 技術と経済と法の相乗作用: this can be translated as *Modern Management and Intellectual Property Rights – Synergic Effect on Technology, Economy and Law*], Tokyo: Sosei-sya, 2003.

S. Takakura, *Chitekizaisanhosei to kokusaiseisaku* [知的財産法制と国際政策: this can be translated as *Intellectual Property Law Regime and International Policy*]. Tokyo: Yuhi-kaku, 2001.

K. Takamura, *Dotei* [道程: this cannot be translated], Tokyo: Iwanami syoten, 1942.

Tokkyo cho (JPO), *Kogyosyoyuken seido hyakunen shi* [工業所有権制度百年史: this can be translated as JPO, *100-Year History of the Industrial Property Right*], Tokyo: Hatsumei kyokai, 1985.

Tokkyo cho (JPO), *Kogyosyoyuken ho chikuzi kaisetsu* [工業所有権法逐次解説: this can be translated as *Guidelines for Industrial Rights*], Tokyo: Hatsumei kyokai, 2001.

M. Toyosaki, *Kogyo syoyuken* [工業所有権: this can be translated as *Industrial Property Law*], Tokyo: Yuhi-kaku, 1980.

S. Ui, *Syohyo to shiteno shiyou: Saiban jitsumu taikei 9* [商標としての使用 裁判実務大系 9: this can be translated as *Trade Mark Use in the Course of Trade: Case Studies*], Tokyo: Seirin-syoin, 1985.

Y. Yamamoto, *Yosetsu Fusei kyoso boshi ho* [要説 不正競争防止法: this can be translated as *Explanation of the Unfair Competition Prevention Law*], Tokyo: Hatsumei kyokai, 2006.

Reports and official documents (English)

AIPPI, 'Question 100, Protection of Unregistered but Well-Known Trademarks (Art. 6*bis* Paris Convention and Protection of Highly Renowned Trademarks', AIPPI Yearbook 1991/I. Available online at www.aippi.org/download/commitees/100/RS100English.pdf (accessed 17 June 2013)

European Commission, 'Amended Proposal for a Council Regulation on the Community Trade Mark, Doc. COM(84) 470 final; 27 OJ [1984] C230', 31 August 1984.

European Commission, 'Amended Proposal for a Regulation on the Community Trade Mark, Doc. COM(88) 5865 draft (IP/36)', 11 May 1988.

European Commission, 'Memorandum on the Creation of an EEC Trade Mark' (SEC (76) 2462 final, 6 July 1976), Bulletin of the European Communities (Supp. August 1976)'. Available online at http://aei.pitt.edu/5363 (accessed 17 June 2013)/

European Commission, 'Report on EU Customs Enforcement of Intellectual Property Rights'. Available online at http://ec.europa.eu/taxation_customs/resources/documents/customs/customs_controls/counterfeit_piracy/statistics/2012_ipr_statistics_en.pdf (accessed 17 June 2013)

WIPO, 'Compare Protection of Well-Known Marks, World Intellectual Property Organisation (WIPO)', (Document SCT/1/3/ (14 May 1998)). Available online at www.wipo.int/edocs/mdocs/sct/fr/sct_1/sct_1_3.pdf (accessed 18 February 2015). (This document is no longer available in English.)

WIPO, 'Dr. Idris Opens Diplomatic Conference to Revise Key Trademark Treaty', Press Release 439 (Geneva/Singapore, 14 March 2006). Available online at www.wipo.int/pressroom/en/prdocs/2006/wipo_pr_2006_439.html (accessed 17 June 2013).

WIPO, *Intellectual Property Handbook*. Available online at www.wipo.int/about-ip/en/iprm (accessed 17 June 2013).

WIPO, 'Main Program 09 WIPO Program and Budget for the biennium 1998–99' Main Program 09' (Document A/32/2-WO/BC/18/2).

WIPO, 'Report on the 18th Session of WIPO'S Standing Committee on the Law of Trademarks, Industrial Designs and Geographical Indications' (Document SCT/18/2). Available online at www.wipo.int/edocs/mdocs/sct/en/sct_18/sct_18_2.doc (accessed 17 June 2013).

WIPO, 'Representation and Description of Non-Traditional Marks: Possible Areas of Convergence' (Document SCT/19/2). Available online at www.wipo.int/edocs/mdocs/sct/en/sct_19/sct_19_2.pdf (accessed 17 June 2013).

WIPO, 'Singapore Treaty on the Law of Trademarks (2006): Summary'. Online. Available online at www.wipo.int/treaties/en/ip/singapore (accessed 17 June 2013).

WIPO, 'Standing Committee on the Law of Trademarks, Industrial Designs and Geographical Indications, Twenty-First Session, Geneva, June 22 to 26, 2009'. Available online at www.wipo.int/edocs/mdocs/sct/en/sct_21/sct_21_7.pdf (accessed 17 June 2013).

WIPO, 'Summary of the Paris Convention for the Protection of Industrial Property (1883)'. Available online at www.wipo.int/treaties/en/ip/paris/summary_paris.html (accessed 17 June 2013).

Interbrand Survey, 'Best Global Brands 2012'. Available online at www.interbrand.com/en/best-global-brands/2012/Best-Global-Brands-2012.aspx (accessed 17 June 2013).

Articles (English language)

A

M. Abell and B. Cookson, 'Beware the Pitfalls of Co-branding', *Managing Intellectual Property*, 15, 1997–1998, 15–18.

G. Adams and D. McLennan, 'Intellectual Property Licensing and Part IV of the TPA: Are the TPA's Pro-Competitive Provisions Anti-Intellectual Property Commercialisation?', *Intellectual Property Forum*, 51, 2003, 13.

L. Akazaki, 'Source Theory and Guarantee Theory in Anglo-American Trade Mark Polity: A Critical Legal Study', *Journal of the Patent and Trademark Office Society*, 72, 1990, 255–78.

R. Annand and I. Davies, 'European Court of Justice: Sabel v Puma', *Trademark World*, 103, 1998, 18–21.

H. Aoki, 'Protection for Three-Dimensional Trademarks: An Examination of Maglight case', *CIPIC Journal*, 180, 2007, 20.

Arnold and Siedsma, 'The Benelux Influence on European Decisions', *Managing Intellectual Property*, 74, 1997, 46.

M. Attridge, 'Lucky Lucky, Arsenal: Infringing Use of Trade Marks', *Intellectual Property Quarterly*, 4, 2001, 389–97.

B

D. Bainbridge, 'Changes to the Community Trade Mark', *Intellectual Property and Information Technology Law*, 9, 2004, 18–20.

Z. Ballantine, 'Legal Loophole: UK Companies May Not Be Able to Rely on Their Well-Known Trade Marks under the Paris Convention – Imperial Tobacco Ltd. v. Berry Bros & Rudd Ltd', *European Intellectual Property Review*, 24, 2004, 415.

E. Barraclough, 'Introducing the Singapore Treaty', *Managing Intellectual Property*, 159, 2006, 16–18.

H. Becher, 'The Protection of Well-Known Trade-Marks', *Trade Mark Reporter*, 42, 1952, 606–14.

G. Benjamin and B. Paster, 'Trademarks – Their Early History', *Trade Mark Reporter*, 59, 1969, 551–72.

D. Bereskin, 'Afterthoughts', *Trademark World*, 215, 2009, 66.

J. Bernett, 'Shopping for GUCCI Canal Street: Reflection Status Consumption, Intellectual Property and the Incentive Thesis', *Virginia Law Review*, 91, 2005, 1381–424.

S. Bernnet and J. Marshall, 'How Far Does Reputation Alone Get You?', *Trademark World*, 214, 2009, 17–19.

A. Bertrand, 'French Trade Mark Law: From the Well-Known Brand to the Famous Brand', *European Intellectual Property Review*, 15, 1993, 142–5.

Bird and Bird, 'Trade Mark Dilution', *Practical Law Companies*, 20, 2009, 94.

R. Black and R. Guthrie, 'Intel v Intelmark: An INTEL-Ligent Way Forward?', *Trademark World*, 210, 2008, 16–17.

M. Blakeney, 'Trade Marks and the Promotion of Trade', *International Trade Law and Regulation*, 5, 1999, 140–6.

S. Blakeney, 'Adverse to AdWords? An Overview of the Recent Cases Relating to Google AdWords', *Computer and Telecommunications Law Review*, 13, 2007, 83–7.

A. Blythe, 'Attempting to Define Unfair Advantage: an Evaluation of the Current Law in light of the Recent European Decisions', *European Intellectual Property Review*, 34, 2012, 754–61.

P. Bicknell, '"Without Due Cause" – Use of the Defendant's Sign Before the Claimant's Mark is Filed: Leidseplein Beheer and de Vries v Red Bull GmbH and Red Bull Nederland BV, (C-65/12)', *European Intellectual Property Law Review*, 36, 2014, 402–4.

S. Blakeney, 'Google AdWords: Searching for More Answers', *Computer and Telecommunications Law Review*, 16, 2010, 152–5.

B. Boad, 'Co-Branding Comes of Age', *Managing Intellectual Property*, 20, 1999–2000, 20–6.

V. von Bomhard, 'Dormant Trade Marks in the European Union – Swords of Damocles?', *Trademark Reporter*, 96, 2006, 1122–36.

R. Bond, 'Business Trends in Virtual Worlds and Social Networks – An Overview of the Legal and Regulatory Issues Relating to Intellectual Property and Money Transactions', *Entertainment Law Review*, 20, 2009, 121–8.

D. Bowen, 'Trademarks and Psychology', *Journal of Patent Office Society*, 41, 1956, 633–67.

D. Bowen, 'Applied Psychology and Trademarks', *Trade Mark Reporter*, 51, 1961, 1–26.

A. Bowler and E. Hughes-Jones, 'No Confusion: Less Joy for Trademark Owners', *Trademark World*, 214, 2009, 13–15.

A. Breitschaft, 'Intel, Adidas & Co – Is the Jurisprudence of the European Court of Justice on Dilution Law in Compliance with the Underlying Rationales and Fit for the Future?', *European Intellectual Property Review*, 31, 2009, 497–504.

S. Brevetti, 'European Community: Trade Marks – Just How Well Known Must a Well-Known Trade Mark Be? The "Chevy" Case Question Answered', *European Intellectual Property Review*, 22, 2000, N46–7.

N. Briggs, 'Infringement under Section 10(2) and 10(3) of the 1994 Trade Marks Act in Perspective', *European Intellectual Property Review*, 22, 2000, 429–34.

P. Brock, 'Merchandising Value of Trade-Marks', *Trade Mark Reporter*, 42, 1952, 701–7.

A. Brown, 'Post Harmonisation Europe – United, Divided or Unimportant?', *Intellectual Property Quarterly*, 3, 2001, 275–86.

E. Bruzga, 'Sophisticated Purchaser Defence Avoid Where Pre-Sale Confusion is Harmful – A Brief Note', *Journal of Patent and Trademark Office Society*, 71, 1989, 32.

J. Bugge and E. Greegersen, 'Requirement of Use of Trademarks', *European Intellectual Property Review*, 25, 2003, 309–21.

S. Burstein, 'Dilution by Tarnishment: The New Cause of Action', *Trade Mark Reporter*, 98, 2008, 1189–252.

C

A. Carboni, 'Confusion Clarified: Sabel BV v Puma AG', *European Intellectual Property Review*, 20, 1998, 107–9.

A. Carboni, 'Two Stripes and You're Out! Added Protection for Trade Marks with a Reputation', *European Intellectual Property Review*, 26, 2004, 229–33.

A. Carney, 'Setting Sights on Trademark Piracy: The Need for Greater Protection Against Imitation of Foreign Trademarks', *Trade Mark Reporter*, 81, 1991, 30–57.

H. Carty, 'Registered Trademarks and Permissible Comparative Advertising', *European Intellectual Property Review*, 24, 2002, 294–300.

H. Carty, 'Do Marks With a Reputation Merit Special Protection?', *European Intellectual Property Review*, 19, 1997, 684–8.

H. Carty, 'Passing off at the Crossroads (Case Comment)', *European Intellectual Property Review*, 18, 1996, 629–32.

H. Carty, 'Character Merchandising and the Limits of Passing Off', *Legal Studies*, 12, 1993, 289–307.

H. Carty, 'Advertising, Publicity Rights and English Law', *Intellectual Property Quarterly*, 3, 2004, 209–58.

S. Casparie-Kerdel, 'Dilution Disguised: Has the Concept of Trade Mark Dilution Made its Way into the Laws of Europe?' *European Intellectual Property Review*, 23. 2001, *EIPR* 185–95.

S. Chapman, A. Chillingworth, J. Halens, B. Kist, J. Nurton and M. Reynolds, 'Pushing at the Boundaries of Protection', *Managing Intellectual Property*, 18, 2002–2003, 18–27.

E. Coffin, 'Fraud as an Element of Unfair Competition', *Harvard Law Review*, 16, 1902–1903, 272–90.

L. Cohen, 'Brands and Valuations', *Managing Intellectual Property*, 25, 1994–1995, 23–5.

W. Cornish, J. Drexl, R. Hillty and A. Kur, 'Procedures and Remedies for Enforcing IPRs: The EU Commission's Propose Directive', *European Intellectual Property Review*, 25, 2003, 447–9.

D

L. Daniels, 'The History of the Trade Marks', *Trade Mark Bulletin*, 7, 1991, 239–70.

C. Davies, 'To Buy or Not to Buy – The Use of a Trade Mark as a Communication Tool Rather than as a Link Between a Product and Its Source: A Further Consideration of the Concept of Dilution', *European Intellectual Property Law Review*, 35, 2013, 373–82.

J. Davis, 'The Value of a Reputation', *Cambridge Law Journal*, 57, 1998, 38–42.

J. Davis, 'European Trade Mark Law and the Enclosure of the Commons', *Intellectual Property Quarterly*, 4, 2002, 342–67.

J. Davis, 'To Protect or Serve? European Trade Mark Law and the Decline of the Public Interest', *European Intellectual Property Review*, 25, 2003, 180–7.

J. Davis, 'Locating the Average Consumer: His Judicial Origins, Intellectual Influences and Current Role in European Trade Mark Law', *Intellectual Property Quarterly*, 2, 2005, 183–203.

J. Davis, 'The European Court of Justice Considers Trade Mark Dilution', *Cambridge Law Journal*, 68, 2009, 290–2.

S. Dillbary, 'The Role of Trademarks in Intra-Brand Settings: An Economic Analysis', *University of Alabama Public Law Research Paper*, 2008, No. 1126857.

G. Dinwoodie, '(National) Trademark Laws and the (Non-National) Domain Name System', *University of Pennsylvania Journal of International Economic Law*, 21, 2000, 495.

G. Dinwoodie, 'The Integration of International and Domestic Intellectual Property Lawmaking', *Columbia-VLA Journal of Law and Art*, 23, 2000, 307–15.

G. Dinwoodie, 'The Architecture of the International Intellectual Property System', *Chicago-Kent Law Review*, 77, 2002, 993–1014.

G. Dinwoodie, 'The Seventh Annual Honourable Helen Wilson Nies Memorial Lecture in Intellectual Property Law: The Trademark Jurisprudence of the Rehnquist Court', *Marques Intellectual Property Law Review*, 8, 2004, 187–210.

G. Dinwoodie, 'Trademarks and Territory: Detaching Trademark Law from the Nation-State', *Houston Law Review*, 41, 2004, 885–974.

G. Dinwoodie and M. Janis, 'Confusion over Use: Contextualism in Trademark Law', *Trade Mark Reporter*, 98, 2008, 1086–159.

T. Drescher, 'The Transformation and Evolution of Trade Marks: From Signals to Symbols to Myth', *Trade Mark Reporter*, 82, 192, 301–40.

J. Drexl, A. Hilty and A. Kur, 'Proposal for a Directive on Measures and Procedures to Ensure the Enforcement of Intellectual Property Rights', *International Review of Intellectual Property and Competition Law*, 34, 2003, 530–5.

P. Dryberge and M. Skylv, 'Does Trade Mark Infringement Require that Infringing Use be Trade Mark Use and If So, What is "Trade Mark Use"?', *European Intellectual Property Review*, 25, 2003, 229–32.

D. Dryden and T. Gold, 'ECJ: Trade Mark with a Reputation', *Trademark World*, 114, 1999, 12–14.

T. Dunlop, 'The Average Consumer's Opinion', *European Intellectual Property Review*, 22, 2000, 177–81.

S, Dunstan, 'Smells and Shapes in the United Kingdom: Continuing Pitfalls of Non-Traditional Trademarks', *Trademark World*, 197, 2007, 41–6

E

N. Economides, 'The Economics of Trade Marks', *Trade Mark Reporter*, 78, 1988, 523–39.

F

G. Fearon, 'The Importance of Goodwill', *Managing Intellectual Property*, 24, 2003–2004, 24–7.

A. Folliard-Monguiral and D. Rogers, 'The Community Trade Mark and Designs System and the Enlargement of the European Union', *European Intellectual Property Review*, 26, 2004, 48–58.

G

J. Gardner, 'NOTE: Trademark Infringement, Likelihood of Confusion, and Trademark Parody: *Anheuser-Busch, Inc. v. L & L Wings, Inc.*', *Wake Forest Law Review*, 28, 1993, 705–46.

P. Gerland and V. Wilson, 'Trade Marks: What Constitutes Infringing Use?', *European Intellectual Property Review*, 25, 2003, 373–6.

W. Geert, 'Protecting "Famous Brands" in Germany', *European Intellectual Property Review*, 11, 1989, 158–61.

D. Gervais, 'The TRIPS Agreement: Interpretation and Implementation', *European Intellectual Property Review*, 21, 1999, 156–62.

F. Gevers, 'ECJ: Sabel v Puma: Three More Lion-Tamers Visit the Wildlife Park', *Trademark World*, 106, 1998, 18–20.

G. Goble, 'Where and What a Trade-Mark Protects', *Illinois Law Review*, 22, 1927, 379–96.

G. Ghidini, 'European Trends in Trade Mark Law', *European Competition Law Review*, 12, 1991, 122–5.

C. Gielen, 'A Benelux Perspective: Sabel v Puma', *European Intellectual Property Review*, 20, 1998, 109–11.

C. Gielen, 'European Community: Use of BMW Trade Mark in Advertisements of a Garage Business', *European Intellectual Property Review*, 21, 1999, N100.

C. Gielen, 'Harmonisation of Trade Mark Law in Europe: The First Trade Mark Harmonisation Directive of the European Council', *European Intellectual Property Review*, 14, 1992, 262–9.

C. Gielen, 'Netherlands: Trade Marks – Likelihood of Dilution and the Possibilities for a Licensee to Request an Injunction', *European Intellectual Property Review*, 21, 1999, N83.

C. Gielen and N. Dutilh, 'L'Oréal v Bellure (C-487/07) and Dior v Copad (C-59/08): EU – Trade Marks – Protection of Well-Known Brands', *European Intellectual Property Review*, 31, 2009, N70–1.

C. Gielen and B. Strowel, 'The Benelux Trademark Act: A Guide to Trademark Law In Europe', *Trademark Reporter*, 86, 1996, 543–75.

E. Gilmour, 'European Union: Advocate General Issues Opinion on Confusion, Association Tests', *World Licensing Law Report*, 2, 2000, 7–8.

E. Goldman, 'International Trademark Licensing Agreements: A Key to Future Technological Development', *California Western International Law Journal*, 16, 1986, 178–204.

J. Green and P. Hariss, 'Case Comment; European Community: Trade Marks', *European Intellectual Property Review*, 21, 1999, N13–15.

M. Grabrucker, 'Marks for Retail Services – An Example for Harmonising Trade Mark Law', *International Review of Intellectual Property and Competition Law*, 34, 2003, 503–20.

D. Greenberg, 'To Dilute Your Trade Mark – Just Add Parody', *European Intellectual Property Review*, 27, 2005, 436–8.

J. Battersby and C. Grimes, 'Merchandising Revised', *Trade Mark Reporter*, 76, 1986, 271–307.

A. Griffiths, 'The Impact of the Global Appreciation Approach on the Boundaries of Trade Mark Protection', *Intellectual Property Quarterly*, 4, 2001, 326–60.

A. Griffiths, 'Modernising Trade Mark Law and Promoting Economic Efficiency: An Evaluation of the Baby-Dry Judgment and its Aftermath', *Intellectual Property Quarterly*, 1, 2003, 1–37.

A. Griffiths, 'The Trade Mark Monopoly: An Analysis of the Core Zone of Absolute Protection under Art. 5(1)(a)', *Intellectual Property Quarterly*, 3, 2007, 312–49.

A. Griffiths, 'Trade Marks Plus? The Role of Trade Marks in the Global Economy and the Danger of Over-Protection', *Liverpool Law Review*, 28, 2007, 107–41.

M. Grinberg, 'The WIPO Joint Recommendation Protecting Well-known Marks and the Forgotten Goodwill', *Chicago-Kent Journal of Intellectual Property*, 5, 2005, 1–11.

P. Groves, 'Trademarks: The Directive Grows Up – The Puma Case: More Confusion about Association?', *Student Law Review*, 24, 1998, 46–7.

N. Gross, 'Trade Mark Exhaustion: The UK Perspective', *European Intellectual Property Review*, 23, 2001, 224–37.

H

J. Hager, 'Infringement of Shape Trademarks', *International Review of Intellectual Property and Competition Law*, 34, 2003, 403–17.

K. Halmen, 'The Effects on the Corporate Diversification Trend on Trademarks', *Marques Intellectual Property Law Review*, 10, 2006, 459–76.

M. Handler and C. Pickett, 'Trade-Marks and Trade Names – An Analysis and Synthesis: I', *Columbia Law Review*, 30, 1930, 168–201.

D. Hall, 'Trade Mark Infringement', *Practical Law Companies*, 10, 1999, 74–5.

D. Hall, 'Reputation: Dissimilar Goods or Services', *Practical Law Companies*, 10, 1999, 77–8.

M. Handler, 'Trade Marks Dilution in Australia?', *European Intellectual Property Review*, 29, 2007, 307–18.

M. Hanson and W. Walls, 'Protecting Trademark Good Will: The Case for a Federal Standard of Misappropriation', *Trade Mark Reporter*, 81, 1991, 480–533.

J. Hatton, 'European Union: Relevance of Reputation of Trade Mark in Determining Whether Similarity Between Goods or Services is Sufficient to Give Rise to Likelihood of Confusion', *International Trade Law Quarterly*, 1, 1999, 39–43.

M. Harris and M. Shillito, 'ECJ Clarifies Trade Mark Directive', *Communications Law*, 74, 1998, 74.

I. Hering, 'Pushing at the Boundaries of Protection', *Managing Intellectual Property*, 114, 2001, 23–32

F. Hide and B. Clark, 'ECJ Clarifies Dilution Test for Well-Known Brands'. *Managing Intellectual Property*, 186, 2009, 28–30.

K. Holt and S. Duvall, 'Chasing Moseley's Ghost: Dilution Surveys under the Trademark Dilution Revision Act', *Trade Mark Reporter*, 98, 2008, 1311–44.

A. Horton, 'The Community Trade Mark Regulation', *European Intellectual Property Review*, 16, 1994, 1.

A. Horton, 'The Implications of L'Oréal v Bellure   A Retrospective and a Looking Forward: The Essential Functions of a Trade Mark and When is an Advantage Unfair?', *European Intellectual Property Review*, 33, 2011, 550–8.

C. Howell, 'Intel: A Mark of Distinction?' *European Intellectual Property Review*, 29, 2007, 441–5.

L. Howard, 'Dilution Versus Deception – Are State Anti-Dilution Laws an Appropriate Alternative to the Law of Infringement?', *Trade Mark Reporter*, 77, 1987, 273–98.

L. Huisman, and G. Bergj, 'Judgment in Baby-Dry Leaves Door Wide Open for Registration of Descriptive Trade Marks', *Trademark World*, 142, 2001, 11.

I

A. Inglis, 'Registrability and Enforcement of Inherently Non-distinctive Trade Marks in the United Kingdom', *European Intellectual Property Review*, 19, 1997, 138–41.

B. Isaac, 'European Court of Justice: Trade Marks – Trade Mark Infringement in Relation to the Advertising of Parallel Products', *European Intellectual Property Review*, 20, 1998, 13–14.

N. Isaacs, 'Infringement Criteria Under the European Trade Mark Directive', *European Business Law Review*, 10, 1999, 508–16.

D. Ivor, 'WIPO News – Harmonisation of Trade Mark Law', *European Intellectual Property Review*, 12, 1990, D60.

B. Issac and J. Ravji, 'What does Identical Mean?', *European Intellectual Property Review*, 27, 2005, 184–7.

J

L. Jaeschke, 'The Quest for a Superior Registration System for Registered Trade Marks in the United Kingdom and the European Union: An Analysis of the Current

Registration System in the United Kingdom, the Community Trade Mark (CTM) Registration System and Coming Changes', *European Intellectual Property Review*, 30, 2008, 25–33.

J. Jacoby, 'The Psychological Foundations of Trademark Law: Secondary Meaning, Genericism, Fame, Confusion and Dilution', *Trade Mark Reporter*, 91, 2001, 1013–71.

P. Jaffey, 'Likelihood of Association', *European Intellectual Property Review*, 24, 2002, 3–8.

M. Janssens, 'The "Toblerone" Chocolate Bar Case in Belgium (Case Comment)', *European Intellectual Property Review*, 29, 2004, 554–9.

B. Joachim, 'Harmonising Trade Mark Law in Europe: The Stephen Stewart Memorial Lecture (March 4, 1999)', *Intellectual Property Quarterly*, 3, 1999, 283–303.

V. Jones, 'Smell-Alikes: A Bed of Roses or a Crown of Thorns?', *New Law Journal*, 156, 2006, 1862–4.

K

P. Kaeding, 'Cleary Erroneous review of Mixed Questions of Law and Fact: The Likelihood of Confusion Determination in Trademark Law', *University of Chicago Law Review*, 59, 1992, 1291–314.

S. Kamperman, 'The Wagamama Decision: Back to the Dark Ages of Trade Mark Law', *European Intellectual Property Review*, 18, 1996, 3–5.

I. Karet, 'Passing off and Trade Marks: Confusing Times Ahead', *European Intellectual Property Review*, 17, 1995, 3–5.

J. Kakinuki, 'Protection of Trade Marks and Anti-Counterfeiting Law in Japan', *European Intellectual Property Review*, 12, 1990, 6–11.

J. Kakinuki and H. Sekine, 'How Japan Protects Famous Trade Marks', *Managing Intellectual Property*, 54, 1995, 21–3.

J. Kakinuki and Y. Ishimura, 'Japan: Practical Tips for Combating Counterfeits', *Managing Intellectual Property*, 92, 1999, 36–8.

S. Khwaja, 'A Ticket to Ride?', *Trademark World*, 216, 2009, 12–15.

F. Kindred, 'When is a Trade Mark Not a Trade Mark? A Commentary on the COCA-COLA Case', *European Intellectual Property Review*, 12, 1986, 377–9.

M. Kleespies and M. Hoffmann, 'Global Protection of Intellectual Property', *International Company and Commercial Law Review*, 12, 2001, 267–75.

L. Kuczma and A. Mullenholz, 'Global Harmonisation of Trademark Law: Not Quite There Yet', *World Intellectual Property Report*, 21, 2007, 29–30.

G. F. Kunze, 'WIPO Standing Committee on the Law of Trade Marks, Industrial Designs and Geographical Indications', *World Licensing Law Report*, 2, 2000, 3–4.

A. Kur, 'Well-Known Marks, Highly Renowned Marks, and Marks Having a (High) Reputation – What's It All About?' *International Review of Intellectual Property and Competition Law*, 23, 1992, 218–31.

A. Kur, 'The WIPO Recommendations for the Protection of Well-Known Marks', *International Review of Intellectual Property and Competition Law*, 31, 2000, 824–45.

A. Kur, 'Use of Trade Marks on the Internet – the WIPO Recommendations', *International Review of Intellectual Property and Competition Law*, 33, 2002, 41–7.

A. Kur, 'The TRIPS Agreement Ten Years Later – a Conference Commemorating the 10th Anniversary of the TRIPS Agreement', *International Review of Intellectual Property and Competition Law*, 36, 2005, 558–62.

M. Kurt, 'Confusion is the Key: A Trademark Law Analysis of Keyword Banner Advertising', *Fordham Law Review*, 71, 2003, 543–78.

L

C. Lackert, 'International Efforts Against Trademark Counterfeiting', *Columbia Business Law Review*, 1988, 1988, 161–76.

P. Lambert, '"Likelihood of Confusion" and "Likelihood of Association" Under EC Trade Mark Law: A Case Note on Sabel BV v Puma KG', *Irish Law Times*, 16, 1998, 218–9.

S. Lane, 'Goodwill Hunting: Assignments and Licences in Gross after Scandecor', *Intellectual Property Quarterly*, 2, 1999, 264–79.

M. Leaffer, 'Protecting United States Intellectual Property Abroad: Toward a New Multilateralism', *Iowa Law Review*, 76, 1990–1991, 273–308.

M. Leaffer, 'The New World of International Trademark Law', *Marques Intellectual Property Law Review*, 2, 1998, 1–32.

C. Lee, 'Parody and Domain Names', *European Intellectual Property Review*, 26, 2004, 263–5.

J. Lee, 'Comparative Advertising, Commercial Disparagement and False Advertising', *Trade Mark Reporter*, 71, 1981, 620–40.

H. Leeds, 'Confusion and Consumer Psychology', *Trade Mark Reporter*, 46, 1956, 1–7.

M. Lemley, 'The Modern Lanham Act and the Death of Common Sense', *Yale Law Journal*, 108, 1998–1999, 1687–716.

N. Jenkins, 'ECJ Confirms Flexible Approach to Assessment of Likelihood of Confusion', *Trademark World*, 113, 1998, 16–19.

P. Levy, 'The Trademark Dilution Revision Act – A Consumer Perspective', *Fordham Intellectual Property Media & Entertainment Law Journal*, 16, 2005–2006, 1189–222.

J. Litman, 'Breakfast with Batman: The Public Interest in the Advertising Age', *Yale Law Journal*, 108, 1998–1999, 1717–36.

R. Litowitz and D. Rettew, 'What is "Dilution" under the New US Federal Trademark Dilution Act?', *European Intellectual Property Review*, 18, 1996, 618–20.

J. Lunsford, 'Proper Typographical Treatment for Trademarks', *Trade Mark Reporter*, 39, 1949, 3–6.

J. Lunsford, 'Consumers and Trademarks: The Function of Trademarks in the Market Place', *Trade Mark Reporter*, 64, 1974, 75–96.

N. Loon, 'The Polo Match in Singapore: England v Europe? The Polo/Lauren Co LP v Shop in Department Store Pte Ltd', *European Intellectual Property Review*, 28, 2006, 250–5.

P. Loughlan, 'Trade Marks: Arguments in a Continuing Contest', *Intellectual Property Quarterly*, 3, 2005, 294–308.

D. Lyons, 'Community Trade Mark Office: Trade Marks – Seniority; Part 1', *European Intellectual Property Review*, 18, 1996, D311–3.

D. Lyons, 'Fierce Creatures', *Paisner Intellectual Property Briefing*, 14, 1997, 4.

M

J. McAuliffe, 'Commercial Names in International Trade', *Trade Mark Reporter*, 61, 1971, 61–8.

F. McBridge, 'The Mark of a Dominant Industry Maker', *Legal Week*, 11, 2009, 22.

I. McCabe, 'Dilution-By-Blurring: A Theory Caught in the Shadow of Trademark Infringement', *Fordham Law Review*, 68, 2000, 1827–77.

J. McCarthy, 'Compulsory Licensing of a Trademark: Remedy or Penalty?', *Trade Mark Reporter*, 67, 1977, 197–254.

J. McCarthy, 'Important Trends in Trademark and Unfair Competition Law During the Decade of the 1970s', *Trade Mark Reporter*, 71, 1981, 93–126.

J. McCarthy, 'Lanham Act §43(a): The Sleeping Giant is Now Wide Awake', *Law & Contemporary Problems*, 59, 1996, 45–74.

J. McCarthy, 'Dilution of a Trademark: European and United Sates Law Compared', *Trade Mark Reporter*, 94, 2004, 1163–81.

J. McCarthy, 'Proving a Trademark Has Been Diluted: Theories or Facts?', *Houston Law Review*, 41, 2004, 715–48.

B. McGrady, 'TRIPS and Trademarks: The Case of Tobacco', *World of Trade Review*, 3, 2004, 53–82.

C. McLeod, 'Well-Known Mark, Likelihood of Confusion and Dilution – A Gauling Judgment', *Entertainment Law Review*, 15, 2004, 56–7.

C. McLeod, 'Adidas AG v Marca Mode', *Trademark World*, 208, 2008, 22–3.

B. Malkawi, 'Well-Known Marks in Jordan: Protection and Enforcement', *Communications Law*, 12, 2007, 119–24.

R. Mallinson, 'Trade Marks in the EU: One Right, One Law, One Decision – or Not?' *European Intellectual Property Review*, 29, 2007, 432–7.

D. Mangis, 'When Almost Famous Just Isn't Famous Enough: Understanding Fame in the Federal Trademark Dilution Act as a Term of Art Requiring Minimal Distinctiveness', *Review of Litigation*, 21, 2002, 455–92.

S. Maniatis, 'New Bottles, But No Wine', *Yearbook of Copyright & Media Law*, 5, 2000, 208–18.

S. Maniatis, 'Trade Mark Law and Domain Names: Back to Basics?' *European Intellectual Property Review*, 24, 2002, 397–408.

S. Maniatis, 'Trade Mark Rights: A Justification Based on Property', *Intellectual Property Quarterly*, 2, 2002, 123–71.

S. Maniatis, 'Whither European Trade Mark Law? Arsenal and Davidoff: The Creative Disorder Stage', *Marques Intellectual Property Law Review*, 7, 2003, 99–148.

S. Maniatis and S. Kamperman, 'A Consumer Trade Mark: Protection Based on Origin and Quality', *European Intellectual Property Review*, 15, 1993, 406–15.

S. Maniatis and S. Kamperman, 'A Quixotic Raid Against the Tobacco Mill', *European Intellectual Property Review*, 19, 1997, 237–42.

S. Maniatis and S. Chong, 'Case Comment: The Teenage Mutant Hero Turtles Case: "Zapping" English Law on Character Merchandising Past the "Embryonic" Stage', *European Intellectual Property Review*, 13, 1991, 253–7.

S. Maniatis and E. Gredley, 'Case Comment: "People You Know, Yet Can't Quite Name . . .": Fair or Foul in the "Wet Wet Wet" Case', *Entertainment Law Review*, 7, 1996, 9–102.

S. Maniatis and E. Gredley, 'Parody: A Fatal Attraction? Part 1: The Nature of Parody and its Treatment in Copyright', *European Intellectual Property Review*, 19, 1997, 339–44.

S. Maniatis and E. Gredley, 'Parody: A Fatal Attraction? Part 2: Trade Mark Parodies', *European Intellectual Property Review*, 19, 1997, 412–20.

S. Maniatis and E. Gredley, 'Case Comment: One Door Closes; Another One Opens? The Opinion of the Advocate General in Marca Mode v. Addidas', *Entertainment Law Review*, 11, 2000, 127–30.

S. Maniatis and A. Sander, 'A Consumer Trade Mark: Protection Based on Origin and Quality', *European Intellectual Property Review*, 15, 1993, 406–51.

R. Marks, '"Dressing"' A Trademark to Project a Modern Image Requires Careful "Tailoring"', *Trade Mark Reporter*, 66, 1976, 12–27.

T. Martino, 'Trade Mark Dilution: I Hear You Knocking but You Can't Come in: Mead Data Central v Toyota', *European Intellectual Property Review*, 12, 1990, 141–5.

T. Martino, 'Passing off and the Ninja Turtles', *Solicitors Journal*, 135, 1991, 1266–7.

J. Mercer, 'Trademark Dilution: Only the Truly "Famous" Need Apply', *Boston University Journal of Science & Technology Law*, 5, 1999, 281–5.

S. Middlemiss and J. Phillips, 'Bad Faith in European Trade Mark Law and Practice', *European Intellectual Property Review*, 25, 2003 397–405.

S. Middlemiss and C. Badger, 'Nipping Taste Marks in the Bud', *European Intellectual Property Review*, 26, 2004, 152–4.

S. Middlemiss and S. Warner, 'The Protection of Marks with a Reputation: Intel v CPM', *European Intellectual Property Review*, 31, 2009, 195–201.

G. Middleton, 'Some Reflection on Dilution', *Trade Mark Reporter*, 42, 1952, 175–87.

J. Mitchiner, 'Intellectual Property in Image – A Mere Inconvenience', *Intellectual Property Quarterly*, 1, 2003, 163–208.

C. Morcom, 'L'Oréal v Bellure – Who Has Won?', *European Intellectual Property Review*, 31, 2009, 627–35.

C. Morcom, 'Extending Protection for Marks Having a Reputation: What is the Effect of the Decision of the European Court of Justice in Davidoff v Gofkid?', *European Intellectual Property Review*, 25, 2003, 279–82.

R. Montagnon, '"Strong" Marks Make More Goods "Similar"', *European Intellectual Property Review*, 20, 1998, 401–4.

R. Montagnon and M Shillito, '"Strong" Marks Have Broader Protection', *Communications Law*, 29, 1998, 85.

T. Moore and B. Lehman, 'Striking a Balance in Trade Mark Protection', *Managing Intellectual Property*, 25, 2003–2004, 25–8.

R. Morgan, 'Recent Trademark Decisions of the European Court of Justice', *Trademark World*, 107, 1998, 42–6.

J. Moskin, 'Dilution or delusion: the Rational limits of trademark Protection' *Trade Mark Reporter*, 83, 1993, 122–48.

F. Mostert, 'Is Goodwill Territorial or International? Protection of the Reputation of a Famous Trade Mark Which Has Not Been Used in the Local Jurisdiction', *European Intellectual Property Review*, 11, 1989, 440–6.

F. Mostert, 'The Parasitic Use of the Commercial Magnetism of a Trade Mark on Non-Competing Goods', *European Intellectual Property Review*, 8, 1996, 342–8.

F. Mostert, 'Well-Known and Famous Marks: Is Harmony Possible in the Global Village?', *Trade Mark Reporter*, 86, 1996, 103–43.

F. Mostert, 'When is a Mark "Well-Known"?', *Intellectual Property Quarterly*, 3, 1997, 377–83.

F. Mostert, 'The Burning Question: Which Brands are Famous Where?', *Trademark World*, 166, 2004, 21–2.

A. Muhlendahl, 'ECJ on 22 November 2007: "Notorious" Or "Well-Known" Marks – What Must Their Territorial Scope Be?', *IP News*, 12/01, 2007–2008, 8.

A. Muhlendahl, 'Community Trade Mark Riddles: Territoriality and Unitary Character', *European Intellectual Property Review*, 30, 2008, 66–70.

A. Muhlendahl, 'Blue Sky in Luxembourg for Trademarks: L'Oréal v Bellure (C-487/07)', *IP News*, 7/8, 2009, 8.

N

S. Nelson, 'The Wages of Ubiquity in Trademark Law', *Iowa Law Review*, 88, 2003, 731–808.

A. Nette, 'Multinational Trademark Protection in the European Union', *Trademark World*, 86, 1996, 22–6.

X. Nguyen, 'New Wild West: Measuring and Proving Fame and Dilution under the Federal Trademark Dilution Act', *Alabama Law Review*, 63, 2000, 201–40.

H. Norman, 'Davidoff v Gofkid: Dealing with the Logical Lapse or Creating European Disharmony?', *Intellectual Property Quarterly*, 3, 2003, 342–54.

H. Norman, 'Perfume, Whisky and Leaping Cats of Prey: A UK Perspective on Three Recent Trade Mark Cases before the European Court of Justice', *European Intellectual Property Review*, 20, 1998, 306–12.

H. Norman, 'Protecting the Advertising Function of Trade Marks', *Communications Law*, 6, 2001, 39–45.

H. Norman, 'Time to Blow the Whistle on Trade Mark Use?', *Intellectual Property Quarterly*, 1, 2004, 1–34.

J. Nurton, 'ECJ Clarifies Well-Known Definition', *Managing Intellectual Property*, 175, 2007, 14.

J. Nurton, 'Enforcement Blow for Weak Marks in EU', *Managing Intellectual Property*, 178, 2009, 18.

J. Nurton, 'L'Oréal Opinion Welcomed as Positive for Brand Owners', *Managing Intellectual Property*, 187, 2009, 8.

O

L. O'Callaghan, 'Intel-Ligent Way Forward? The ECJ Rules on Dilution', *Journal of Intellectual Property Law & Practice*, 4, 2009, 237–9.

B. O'Connor, 'The EC Need Not Be Isolated on GIS', *European Intellectual Property Review*, 8, 2007, 303–6.

H. Onishi. 'Revisiting the Japanese Unfair Competition Law: Post-Bellure', *European Intellectual Property Review*, 33, 2011, 368–74.

P

J. Palm, 'Canon, Waterford . . . How the Issue of Similarity of Goods Should be Determined in the Field of Trade Mark Law', *European Intellectual Property Review*, 29, 2007, 475–9.

A. Papandreou, 'The Economic Effect of Trademarks', *California Law Review*, 44, 1956, 503–10.

B. Pattishall, 'Two Hundred Years of American Trademark Law', *Trade Mark Reporter*, 68, 1978, 121–47.

B. Pattishall, 'Dawning Acceptance of the Dilution Rationale for Trademark-Trade Identity Protection', *Trade Mark Reporter*, 74, 1984, 289–310.

B. Pattishall, 'The Dilution Rationale for Trademark – Trade Identity Protection, its Progress and Prospects', *Trade Mark Reporter*, 67, 1997, 607–24.

J. Phillips, 'Analysis: Pariah, Pirahna or Partner? The New View of Intellectual Property in Europe', *Intellectual Property Quarterly*, 1, 1998, 107–12.

J. Phillips, 'Man's Best Friends: Time to Take a Lesson from Trigger and Fido', *Trademark World*, 66, 2004, 167.

J. Phillips, 'Trade Mark Law and the Need to Keep Free', *International Review of Intellectual Property and Competition Law*, 36, 2005, 389–401.

J. Phillips, 'An Agenda for Europe's Trade Mark Regime', *Managing Intellectual Property*, 155, 2005–2006, 43–6.

J. Phillips, 'Strong Trade Marks and the Likelihood of Confusion in European Law', *Journal of Intellectual Property Law & Practice*, 1, 2006, 385–97.

J. Phillips, 'Court of First Instance takes Firm Line on Appeals Against Refusal to Register Community Trade Marks of Marginal Distinctiveness', *Journal of Intellectual Property Law & Practice*, 1, 2006, 96–7.

J. Phillips, 'BOA Constricted by Community Trade Mark Law', *Journal of Intellectual Property Law & Practice*, 1, 2006, 824–5.

J. Phillips, 'Information Overload and IP Practice', *Journal of Intellectual Property Law & Practice*, 4, 2009, 301.

I. Ping, and D. Reitman, 'Why Are Some Products Branded and Others Not?', *Journal of Law & Economics*, 39, 1995, 207–24.

T. Pinto, 'Putting Advertising Claims to the Test', *Managing Intellectual Property*, 38, 2003–2004, 38–61.

K. Port, 'Trademark Dilution in Japan', *William Mitchell Legal Studies Research Paper*, 30, 2005.

H. Porter and L. Albertini, 'ECJ Makes its Mark', *New Law Journal*, 159, 2009, 303.

B. Pretnar, 'Is the Future Enlargement of the European Union an Immediate Issue for the Community Trade Mark System?', *European Intellectual Property Review*, 14, 1997, 185–7.

N. Prentoulis, 'The Omega Ruling: Trade Mark Co-Existence Agreements in the Tension Between "Public" and "Private" Trade Mark Law', *European Intellectual Property Review*, 30, 2008, 202–5.

Q

X. Qing, 'Protection of Well-Known Trademark: The Comparison of Trademark Examination Standard and Trademark Law Systems Between Japan and China', Japanese Patent Office, 2002.

R

H. Rangel-Ortiz, 'Well-known Trademarks Under International Treaties: Part 1: Paris Convention and TRIPS', *Trademark World*, 94, 1997, 14–16.

N. Ramires, 'Will the Anticybersquatting Consumer Protection Act Create More Problems than it Solves?' *Washington University Journal of Law and Policy*, 8, 2002, 395–418.

T. Richards, 'Trade Marks – A Round-up of Some Recent Development', *Communications Law*, 13, 2008, 151–4.

M. Richardson, 'Copyright in Trade Marks? On Understanding Trade Mark Dilution', *Intellectual Property Quarterly*, 1, 2000, 66–83.

M. Rijsdijk, 'Brand Awareness in the Benelux Countries', *Managing Intellectual Property*, 96, 2000, 51.

C. Roche and J. Rosini, 'Trade Marks in Europe 1992 and Beyond', *European Intellectual Property Review*, 13, 1991, 404–12.

D. Rogers, 'The TRIPS Regime of Trademarks and Designs', *European Intellectual Property Review*, 29, 2007, 76–8.

E. Rogers, 'Some Suggestions Concerning the International Trade Mark Situation', *Yale Law Journal*, 36, 1926, 235–44.

E. Rogers, 'Some Historical Matter Concerning Trade Marks', *Trade Mark Reporter* 62, 1972, 239–54.

E. Rogers, 'The Lanham Act and the Social Function of Trade Marks', *Trade Mark Reporter*, 62, 1972, 255–61.

G. Rogers, 'From Eveready to Park 'n Fly: Has a Decade of Development for the Lanham Act Re-Charged Trademark Law or Left the Customer Without a Place to Park?', *New England Law Review*, 22, 1987–1988, 165–208.

P. Roncaglia, 'Should We Use Guns and Missiles to Protect Famous Trade Marks in Europe?', *Trade Mark Reporter*, 88, 1998, 551–63.

D. Rose, 'Season of Goodwill: Passing off and Overseas Traders', *European Intellectual Property Review*, 18, 1996, 356–62.

H. Rosler, 'The Rationale for European Trade Mark Protection', *European Intellectual Property Review*, 29, 2007, 100–7.

G. Ruston, 'On the Origin of Trade Marks', *Trade Mark Reporter*, 45, 1955, 127–44.

C. Rutz, 'Germany: Trade Marks – Well-Known Marks and Similar Goods', *European Intellectual Property Review*, 26, 2004, N208–9.

S

J. M. Samuels and L. B. Samuels, 'The Changing Landscape of International Trademark Law' (1993–1994)', *George Washington Journal of International Law and Economics*, 27, 433–56.

S. Sandri and S. Rizzo, 'Non-Conventional Trade Marks?', *Managing Intellectual Property*, 138, 2004, 8–10.

S. Sanghera, 'Facebook v Facetime: So What Do You Do?' *Times*, 23 August 2007.

F. Schechter, 'The Rational Basis of Trademark Protection', *Harvard Law Review*, 40, 1927, 813–33.

F. Schechter, 'Fog and Fiction in Trade-Mark Protection', *Columbia Law Review*, 36, 1936, 60.

H. Schmidt, 'Likelihood of Confusion in European Trade Marks – Where Are We Now?' *European Intellectual Property Review*, 24, 2002, 463–5.

L. Schmidt, 'Definition of a Trade Mark by the European Trade Marks Regime – A Theoretical Exercise? , *International Review of Intellectual Property and Competition Law*, 30, 1990, 738–52.

K. Schmit, J. Laurence and L. Cohen, 'Is the English Law of Passing off Discriminatory to Continental European Trade Mark Owners?', *European Intellectual Property Review*, 21, 1999, 88–92.

M. Senftleben, 'The Trademark Tower of Babel – Dilution Concepts in International, US and EC Trademark Law', *International Review of Intellectual Property and Competition Law*, 40, 2009, 45–77.

T. Shafran, 'ECJ Intel Decision Clarifies What Will Amount to a "Link" Between an Earlier Mark with a Reputation and a Later Mark', *Computer and Telecommunications Law Review*, 15, 2009, 81–3.

D. Shanahan, 'The Trademark Right: Consumer Protection or Monopoly?', *Trade Mark Reporter*, 72, 1982, 233–50.

R. Shaughnessy, 'Trademark Parody: A Fair Use and First Amendment Analysis', *Virginia Law Review*, 72, 1986, 1079–118.

A. Shaw, 'A Victory for Strong Brands' *Managing Intellectual Property*, 128, 2003, 44–9.

I. Simon, 'The Actual Dilution Requirement in the United States, United Kingdom and European Union: A Comparative Analysis', *Boston University Journal of Science & Technology Law*, 12, 2006, 271–309.

I. Simon, 'Dilutive Trade Mark Applications: Trading on Reputation or Just Playing Games?', *European Intellectual Property Review*, 26, 2004, 67–74.

I. Simon, 'How Does "Essential Function" Doctrine Drive European Trade Mark Law?', *International Review of Intellectual Property and Competition Law*, 36, 2005, 401–20.

I. Simon, 'Embellishment: Trade Mark Use Triumph or Decorative Disaster', *European Intellectual Property Review*, 28, 2006, 321–8.

I. Simon, 'Brand Owners Left in the Dark over Scope of Rights', *Managing Intellectual Property*, 5, 2006, 66–9.

I. Simon, 'Nominative Use and Honest Practices in Industrial and Commercial Matters – A Very European History', *Intellectual Property Quarterly*, 2, 2007, 117–47.

I. Simon, 'Dilution by Blurring – A Conceptual Roadmap', *Intellectual Property Quarterly*, 1, 2010, 44–87.

I. Simon, 'Exploring the Roots of European Dilution', *Intellectual Property Quarterly*, 1, 2012, 25–8.

A. Simonson, 'How and When Do Trademarks Dilute: A Behavioural Framework to Judge "Likelihood" of Dilution', *Trade Mark Reporter*, 83, 1993, 149–74.

A. Smith and B. Heard, 'Every BULLDOG Has its Day: An Analysis of "Due Cause": Leidseplein Beheer BV and de Vries v Red Bull GmBH', *European Intellectual Property Law Review*, 36, 2014, 536–9.

E. Smith, 'Dyson and the Public Interest: An Analysis of the Dyson Trade Mark Case' *European Intellectual Property Review*, 29, 2007, 469–73.

G. Smith, 'Brand Valuation; Too Long Neglected' *European Intellectual Property Review*, 12, 1990, 159–64.

G. Smith, 'Intellectual Property Rights, Developing Countries and TRIPS', *Journal of World Intellectual Property*, 6, 1999, 969–75.

J. Smith and D. Meale, 'EU: Trade Marks – Revocation – Similar Mark for Dissimilar Goods', *European Intellectual Property Review*, 31, 2009, N23–4.

C. Steele, 'Famous Trademark Owners' Bid to Stop Dilution of Their Trademarks Suffers Setback', *Intellectual Property News*, 2, 2009, 1–2.

K. Stephens, and Z. Fuller, 'Trade Marks: Translated Evidence Submitted out of Time', *Chartered Institute of Patent Agents Journal*, 36, 2007, 459.

K. Stephens and Z. Fuller, 'Trade Mark Dilution', *Chartered Institute of Patent Agents Journal*, 37, 2009, 405–6.

K. Stephens and Z. Fuller, 'Trade Marks: Smell-Alike – Advocate General's Opinion', *Chartered Institute of Patent Agents Journal*, 38, 2009, 211–2.

K. Stephens, Z. Fuller and, A. Sculthorpe, 'Trade Marks: Construction of the Term "Reputation in the Community"', *Chartered Institute of Patent Agents Journal*, 38, 2009, 359–60.

G. Stewart, 'The Source Theory and Trade Mark Law Reform: A Functional Analysis', *University of Western Ontario Law Review*, 20, 1982, 337–58.

D. Stone, 'EC: Trademarks – ECJ Overrules German Pragetheorie', *European Intellectual Property Review*, 28, 2006, N4–5.

D. Stone and J. Barker, 'Own-Brand and Look-Alike Products', *Trademark World*, 216, 2009, 24–6.

J. Swann 'The Validly of Dual Functioning Trademarks: Genericism Tested by Consumer Understanding Rather Than by Consumer Use', *Trade Mark Reporter*, 69, 1979, 357–76.

J. Swann, 'An Interdisciplinary Approach to Brand Strength' *Trade Mark Reporter*, 96, 2006, 943–76.

J. Swann, D. Aaker and M. Reback, 'Trademarks and Marketing', *Trade Mark Reporter*, 91, 2001, 787–836.

J. Swann and T. Davis, 'Dilution, an Idea Whose Time has Gone: Brand Equity as Protectable Property, The New/Old Paradigm', *Trade Mark Reporter*, 84, 1994, 267–99.

T

D. Tatham, 'WIPO Resolution on Well-Known Marks: A Small Step or a Giant Leap?', *Intellectual Property Quarterly*, 2, 2000, 127–37.

D. Tatham and F. Gervers, 'The Continuing Story of the Examination of Seniority Claims by the OHIM in Alicante', *European Intellectual Property Review*, 21, 1999, 228–35.

D. Tatham and A. Edward, 'The Community Trade Mark: Comments on the Latest Draft Directive and Implementing Rules for the Regulation', *European Intellectual Property Review*, 8, 1986, 135–8.

J. Thessensohn, 'Holy Hand Tools, Batman! Well-Known BATMAN Mark Faces Peril in Japan', *Trademark World*, 117, 1999, 44–50.

J. Thessensohn and S. Yamamoto, 'Japan: Trademarks – Changes to Law', *European Intellectual Property Review*, 28, 2006, N236–7.

J. Thessensohn and S. Yamamoto, 'Japan: Unfair Competition – Pharmaceuticals – Trade Dress', *European Intellectual Property Review*, 29, 2007, N43–4.

P. Torremans, 'The Likelihood of Association of Trade Marks: An Assessment in the Light of the Recent Case Law of the Court of Justice', *Intellectual Property Quarterly*, 3, 1998, 295–310.

B. Trimmer, 'The Power of Attraction: Do Trade Marks Have an "Image" Problem in the English Courts?', *European Intellectual Property Review*, 31, 2009, 195–201.

B. Trimmer, 'An Increasingly Uneasy Relationship – the English Courts and the European Court of Justice in Trade Mark Disputes', *European Intellectual Property Review*, 30, 2008, 87–92.

B. Trimmer, 'Comparative Advertising Trumps Trade Marks Rights: O2 Holdings Ltd v Hutchinson 3G UK Ltd', *European Intellectual Property Review*, 30, 2008, 302–5.

K. Troller, 'Switzerland: Trade Marks – Distinctiveness', *European Intellectual Property Review*, 33, 2001, N154–5.

A. Tsoutsanis, 'The Biggest Mistake of the European Trade Mark Directive and Why the Benelux is Wrong Again – Between the European Constitution and European Conscience', *European Intellectual Property Review*, 28, 2006, 74–82.

P. Turner-Kerr, 'Confusion or Association under the European Trade Mark Directive', *European Intellectual Property Review*, 23, 2001, 49–51.

P. Turner-Kerr, 'Trade Mark Tangles: Recent Twists and Turns in EC Trade Mark Law', *European Intellectual Property Review*, 29, 2004, 345–65.

P. Turner-Kerr, 'EU Intellectual Property Law: Recent Cases Development', *Intellectual Property Quarterly*, 4, 2004, 448–519.

V

G.-J. Van De Kamp, 'Protection of Trade Marks: The New Regime – Beyond Origin?', *European Intellectual Property Review*, 20, 1998, 364–70.

E. Vassallo and M. Dickey 'Protection in the United States for "Famous Marks": The Federal Trademark Dilution Act Revised' (1998–1999)', *Fordham Intellectual Property, Media and Entertainment Law Journal*, 9, 503–28.

D. Vaver, 'Unconventional and Well-known Trade Marks', *Singapore Journal of Legal Studies* 2005, 1–9. The full text of this Article is available online at http://law.nus.edu.sg/sjls/articles/SJLS-2005j-1.pdf (accessed 30 January 2015).

W

C. Wadlow, '"Including Trade in Counterfeit Goods": The Origin of TRIPS as a GATT Anti-Counterfeiting Code', *Intellectual Property Quarterly*, 3, 2007, 350–402.

A. Wagner, 'Infringing Trade Marks: Function, Association and Confusion of Signs According to the EC Trade Marks Directive', *European Intellectual Property Review*, 21, 1999, 127–32.

M. Walmsley, 'Trade Mark Dilution – Court of Appeal Waters Down Trade Mark Owners' Rights', *European Intellectual Property Review*, 30, 2008, 109–11.

T. Watkins, 'What Price Good Will', *Trade Mark Reporter*, 56, 1966, 67–90.

J. Watts and G. Faeron, 'Defining the Limits of Trade Mark Protection', *Managing Intellectual Property*, 51, 2003–2004, 51–6.

D. Welkowitz, 'Re-Examining Trademark Dilution', *Vandebilt Law Review*, 44, 1991, 531–87.

P. Wheeler, 'ECJ Decision on Reputation of Chevy Mark in Europe', *Communications Law*, 5, 2008, 31–2.

S. Wilf, 'Who Authors Trademarks?', *Cardozo Arts and Entertainment Law Journal*, 17, 1999, 1–46.

S. Willimsky, 'Comparative Advertising: An Overview', *European Intellectual Property Review*, 18, 1996, 649–53.

E. Winner, 'Right of Identity: Right of Publicity and Protection for a Trademark's "Persona"', *Trade Mark Reporter*, 71, 1981, 193–214.

J. Wolff, 'Non-Competing Goods in Trademark Law', *Columbia Law Review*, 27, 1937, 582–608.

K. Wong and L. Nathan, 'Well-Known Brands Enjoy Better Protection', *Managing Intellectual Property*, 148, 2005, 57–8.

A. Wood, 'Case Comment: EU: Trade Marks–OHIM Procedure–Evidence' *European Intellectual Property Review*, 27, 2005, N66–7.

G. Wurtenberger, 'Recent Decisions of the Federal Supreme Court on the Exploitation of Reputation', *European Intellectual Property Review*, 9, 1987, 239–44.

G. Wurtenberger, 'A Risk of Confusion in Community Trade Mark Law: First Contours in Case Law of the European Court of Justice and the Harmonisation Office', *European Intellectual Property Review*, 21, 1999, 508–18.

G. Wurtenberger, 'Risk of Confusion and Criteria to Determine the Same in European Community Trade Mark Law', *European Intellectual Property Review*, 24, 2002, 20–9.

G. Wurtenberger, 'Enforcement of Community Trade Mark Rights', *Intellectual Property Quarterly*, 4, 2002, 402–17.

G. Wurtenberger, 'Case Comment; Community Trade Mark Law Astray or Back to the Roots', *European Intellectual Property Review*, 28, 2006, 549–51.

Y

S. Yu-Sheng, 'Trademark Infringement and Unfair Competition Case Study: Toyota Motors vs. Zhejiang Geely' (2003/4) *China Law & Practice*. Available online at www.

chinalawandpractice.com/Article/1692947/Channel/9930/Trademark-Infringement-
and-Unfair-Competition-Case-Study-Toyota-Motors-vs-Zhejiang-Geely.html(accessed
30 January 2015).

Reports and Official Documents (Japanese)

Chitekizaisan suishin hon bu (知的財産推進本部: this can be translated as Intellectual
Property Strategy Headquarters), 'Chiteki zaisan suishin keikaku 2009 [知的財産推進
計画2009: this can be translated as the Strategic Plan 2009]'.
The full text of the Strategic Plan 2009 is available online at www.kantei.go.jp/jp/singi/
titeki2/090624/2009keikaku.pdf (accessed 30 January 2015).
JPO (特許庁), 'atarashii type no syohyo nikansuru tyosa hokoku syo: tyomei syohyo ni
kakaru jogo no kakudai to ni kansuru syousa kenkyu hokokusho [新しいタイプの商
標に関する調査報告書著名商標にかかる保護の拡大の等に関する調査研究報
告書: this can be translated as Report of New Protectable Trademarks: Expanding the
Scope of the Protection for Famous Marks]' March 2008.
JPO (特許庁), 'syuchi/tyomei syohyo no hogo touni kansuru shinsa kijyun nokaisei
nitsuie [周知•著名商標の保護等に関する　審査基準の改正について: this can be
translated as Amendment of the JPO Examination Guidelines of Well-Known and
Famous Trade Mark Protection]'.
JPO (特許庁), 'Sangyo Kozo Shingikai Chiteki Zaisan Seisaku Bukai Hokokusho
[産業構造審議会知的財産政策部会報告書: this can be translated as Report of the
Intellectual Property Policy Committee of the Industrial Structure Council], 1992.
JPO (特許庁), 'Kogyo syoyuken no rekishi [工業所有権の歴史: this can be translated as
History of Industrial Property Rights]'. The full text of this Article is available online at
www.jpo.go.jp/seido/rekishi/rekisi.htm (accessed 18 February 2015).
The former Prime Minister, Koizumi, '2002 Policy Statement by Prime Minister Koizumi'.
(This statement is no longer officially or electronically available.)
The former Prime Minister, Koizumi, 'Prime Minister's Decision; Concerning the
Strategic Council on Intellectual Property in 2005'. (This is no longer electronically
available.)
JPO (特許庁), '2009 nenndo moho shigai cyosa hokoku syo [２００9年度 模倣被害調査
報告書: this can be translated as JPO 2009 Report on Counterfeited Goods]'. The full
text of the report is available online at www.jpo.go.jp/torikumi/mohouhin/mohouhin2/
jittai/pdf/2009_houkoku/higai_shousai.pdf (accessed 18 February 2015).
JPO (特許庁), 'Rittai syohyo toshiteno Hiyoko Rittai syohyo tourokuyouken [ひよこ型の
立体商標登録要件: this can be translated as IP News: Registrability of a Three-
Dimensional Chick Shape in JPO]' (11 August 2005).
Kondo, T, 'Roles of the Intellectual Property Rights System in Economic Development in
the Light of Japanese Economy', 16 November 1999, Tokyo (Official Speech of the
JPO).

Articles (Japanese language)

A

H. Aizawa, (相澤英孝) 'Kondo (2) – Snack CHANEL jiken [混同（２）－スナックシャネル
事件: this can be translated as Confusion (2) – Bar CHANEL case]', *Jurist*, 11, 2007,
148–9.

H. Aoki, (青木博通) 'Syuchi, Tyomei syojyo no hogo kyoka [周知•著名商標の保護強化: this can be translated as Strong Protection for Well-Known and Famous Trademarks]', *Chizai Kanri* [知財管理], 50, 2000, 629–47.

M. Amino, (網野誠) 'Syohyo ho kaiseini tomonau syohyono teigi sonota ni san no mondaiten nitsuite [商標法改正に伴う商標の定義その他二•三の問題点について: this can be translated as A Few Problems of Amendment of Trademark Law]', *Patent*, 49, 1996, 11–28.

C

S. Chaen, (茶園成樹) 'Hyoji noyusuru kati no fusei boshi ho ni yoru hogo [表示の有する価値の不正競争防止法による保護: this can be translated as Protection of the Value Attached to Marks in the Unfair Competition Prevention Act]', *Jurist*, 1018, 1993, 31–6.

D

K. Doi, (土肥一史) 'Syohyo ho 4jyo 1kou 15jyo ni kiteisuru kondo no igi [商標法４条１項１５条に規定する混同の意義: this can be translated as Definition of Likelihood of Confusion in Article 4(1)(15)]', *Chizai Kanri*, 4, 1995, 589–93.

K. Doi, (土肥一史) 'Fuseikyoso boshi ho no kadai [不正競争防止法の課題: this can be translated as Current Situation and Issues of the Unfair Competition Law]', *Jurist*, 1326, 2007, 106.

E

J. Eguchi, (江口順一) 'America syohyo-ho niokeru tsuyoi mark, yowai mark no hori nituite' [アメリカ商標法における強いマーク•弱いマークの法理について: this can be translated as Legal Theory of Weak Marks and Strong Marks in the US Trademark Law], Osaka University 30th University Essay, Osaka University, 1982.

G

A. Gomi, (五味飛鳥) 'Chizaigakusetu no ugoki [知財学説の動き: this can be translated as A Report of Movement in Legal Theory – Unfair Competition, Trademark and Design]', *IP Annual* Report, 2008, 132–47.

H

T. Higuchi, (樋口豊治) 'Syohyo ho 4jyo 1kou 15go niui kondo no osore [商標法４条１項１５号にいう混同のおそれ: this can be translated as Risk of Confusion in Article 4(1)(15) of the Japanese Trademark Act]', *Chizai Kanri* (知財管理), 53, 2003, 1901–1991.

T. Higuchi, (樋口豊治) 'syohyo ho jyo no syohin yakumu to so no ruihi [商標法上の商品•役務とその類否: this can be translated as Similarity of Goods or Services in the Trademark Law]', *Patent*, 54, 2001, 53–67.

F. Hirose, (広瀬文彦) 'Kaisei syohyo ho no youten [改正商標法の要点: this can be translated as Key Points of the Amendment of the Japanese Trademark Act]', *Patent*, 49, 1996, 5–10.

I

T. Imamura, (今村哲也) 'Chiikidantai syohyo seido to chiriteki hyoji no hogo – sono yokisenu hogono kousaku [地域団体商標制度と地理的表示の保護—その予期せぬ保護の交錯—: this can be translated as Protection of Geographical Collective Trademarks and Geographic Indications – Unexpected Overlapping]' *Nippon Kogyo shoyukenhougakukai nenpo* (日本工業所有権法学会年報), 30, 2006, 274.

Y. Inoue, (井上由利子) 'Syohyo saisei to kongo nokadai [商標法改正と今後の課題: this can be translated as the Amendment of the Trademark Law and its Problems]', *IPR Forum*, 23, 1995, 20.

K

T. Katsube, (勝部哲雄) 'Syohyo ho niokeru kondo gainen no bunseki [商標法における混同概念の分析: this can be translated as Analysis of the Concept of Confusion in the Trademark Act]', *Patent*, 3, 1996, 25–31.

N. Koizumi, (小泉直樹) 'Dilution [ダイリューション: this can be translated as Dilution]', *Jurist*, 1005, 1992, 29–32.

N. Koizumi, (小泉直樹) 'Iwayuru "akuino syutsugan" nitsuite [いわゆる悪意の出願について: this can be translated as Trademark Application Made in Bad Faith?]', *Nippon Kogyo shoyukenhougakukai nenpo*, 31, 2008, 153–68.

N. Koizumui, (小泉直樹) 'Dai sansya no shiyo ni yori tokuteino engyo syutai no hyoji toshite syuchi to natta hyojito kyuu fuseikyoso boshi ho 1jyo1kou2go "[第三者の使用より特定の営業主体の表示として周知となった表示と旧不競法1条1項2号: this can be translated as Well-Known Marks Through Use by Third Parties and Article 1(i)(2) of the Unfair Competition Prevention Law]', *Cizai Kanri*, 45, 1995, 533–6.

R. Kojima, (小島立) 'Rittai syohyo no toroku yoken: Maglight rittai syohyo jiken [立体商標の登録用件 Maglight立体商標事件: this can be translated as Trademark Registration Requirements for Three-Dimensional Marks: Maglight Case]', *Chizai Kanri*, 58, 2008, 259.

R. Kojima, (小島立) 'Coca-Cola jiken ni mirareru rittai syohyo o hogo – tyomei na mojisyohyoga shiyousareta housoyoki jitai no dedokoro shikibetsu nouryoku kakutoku no annketo tyosa [Coca-Cola事件に見られる立体商標の保護—著名な文字商標が使用された包装容器自体の出所識別能力獲得のアンケート調査: this can be translated as Protection for Three-Dimensional Trade Marks – Coca-Cola Case – Acquired Distinctness Through Use of the Shapes of the Packaging to Which a Famous Mark is Attached]', *CIPIC Journal*, 184, 2008, 6.

H. Koseki, (古関宏) 'Kosyo ruiji to kannen no kankei [呼称類似と観念の関係: this can be translated as Relation Between Oral Similarity and Conceptual Similarity]', *Patent*, 54, 2001, 11–16.

H. Koseki, (古関宏) 'Syuchi syoho "ASAHI" to syotai ga kokuji suru "AsaX" no ruihi nisuite [周知商標ASAHI と書体が酷似するAsaXの類否について: this can be translated as Similarity Between Well-Known Trademark ASAHI and AsaX]', *Chizai Kanri* , 45, 1995, 523–32.

M. Kukida, (久木田百香) 'Chiiki Brand nitsuite fuseikyoso boshi ho no syuchi hyoji toshite hogoga mitomerareta jirei: MIWA somen jiken [地域ブランドについて不正競争防止法の周知表示として保護が認めらた事例　三輪素麺事件: this can be translated as Cases on Protection of Local Collective Brand Being a Well-Known Mark under the Unfair Competition Prevention Act]', *Intellectual Property Law and Policy Journal*, 7, 2005, 201–17.

Y. Kyo, (蕎優美) 'Toroku syohyo no shiyou to kenri noranyo [登録商標の使用と権利の濫用: this can be translated as Use of Registered Trademark and Abuse of Rights]' *Horitsu no Hiroba*, 19, 2008, 11.

M

S. Manada, 'Tyomei hyoshiki no mondai no syoso' [著名標識の問題の諸相: this can be translated as Mapping the Problems of Protecting Famous Signs], *Journal of Kanazawa University*, 13, 1967, 2–54.

K. Matsuo, (松尾和子) 'Syohyo ho no kaisei to syohyo no teigini tuise [商標法の改正と商標の定義について: this can be translated as Definition of a Trademark and the Amendment of the Trademark Law]', *Patent*, 48, 1995, 2–13.

N. Matsumura, (松村信夫) 'Fusei kyoso boshi ho to kogyo syoyuken ho [不正競争防止法と工業所有権法: this can be translated as Unfair Competition Prevention Act and Industrial Property Law]', *Patent*, 52, 1998, 23–41.

K. Matsumura, (松村信夫) 'Syohyo no ruiji [商標の類似: this can be translated as Similarity of Trademarks]', *Nippon Kogyo shoyukenhougakukai nenpo*, 31, 2008, 73–98.

T. Matsumoto, (松本司) 'DDC 事件 [DDC jiken: this can be translated as DDC case]', *Jurist*, 11, 2007, 26–7.

S. Monda, (満田重昭) 'Tyomei hyoshiki no mondai no syoso [著名標識の問題の諸相: this can be translated as Problematic Aspects of Well-Known Mark Protection]', *Kanazawa hogaku* (金沢法学),13, 1967, 2–54.

K. Miura, (三浦一紀) 'Chiiki Brand ni syohyo ken nintei dai 1go [地域ブランドに商標権 認定第1号: this can be translated as Local Collective Brand as a Registered Trade Mark]', *Chiho Gyosei*, 9864, 2006.

K. Miura, (三浦一紀) 'Chiiki no brand kanrenshisaku no gejyo to kadai [地域のブランド関連施策の現状と課題: this can be translated as Problematic Aspects of the Local Collective Marks as Brands]', *Economic Review*, 3, 2006, 30.

F. Mitsuno, (光野文子) 'Syoho no rittaiteki keijo nomi karanaru syohyo no torokuyoken handan no kijyun noyukue – mini magligt hanketsukou [商標の立体的形状のみからなる商標の登録要件判断の基準の行方―　ミニマグライト判決考一: this can be translated as A Perspective of Trademark Registration for Mere Shape Marks: Mini Maglight Case]', *Chizai Kanri*, 58, 2008, 191.

F. Mityuno, 'Syohyo no rittaiteki keijyo nomi karanaru syohyo no torokuyoken handan no kijyun noyukue – mini magligt hanketsukou' [商標の立体的形状のみからなる商標の登録用件の基準の要件　ミニマグライト判決考: this can be translated as Problems of the Requirement of a Three-Dimensional Shape as a Trademark, *Chizai kanri*, 58, 2008, 191.

K. Mizuno, (水野勝文) 'Syohyo ho kaisei no dokou nitsuite [商標法改正の動向について: this can be translated as Amendment of Trademark Act: A Future Perspective]', *Patent*, 48, 1995, 36–46.

M. Miyake, (宮脇正晴) 'Tyomei syohyo no hogo [著名商標の保護: this can be translated as Famous Trademark Protection]'. *Nippon Kogyo shoyukenhougakukai nenpo*, 31, 2008, 99–122.

S. Miyake, (三宅俊司) 'Fusei kyoso boshi ho ni okeru tyomeihyoji to syuchi hyouji no kankei [不正競争防止法における著名表示と周知表示の関係: this can be translated as Well-Known Marks and Famous Marks in the Unfair Competition Law]'. *Patent*, 51, 1998, 15–26.

K. Miyata, (宮田金雄) 'Syohin Yakumu no ruijini tuiteno ichi kousatsu [商品・役務の類似についての一考察: this can be translated as One Analysis of Similarity Between Designated Goods and Services' Intellectual Property Management]', *Patent*, 50, 2000, 181–220.

M. Miyawaki, (宮脇正晴) 'Syohyo kinou to syohyo ho no mokuteki [商標の機能と商標法の目的: this can be translated as Function of Trademark and Purposes of Trademark Law]', *Kokusai kokyu seisaku kenkyu*, 9, 2000, 275–85.

M. Miyazaki, 'Tyomei-syohyo no hogo' [著名商標の保護: this can be translated as Protecting Famous Trademarks], *Japan Industrial Property Right Annual Report*, 31, 2008, 99–222.

K. Morioka, (盛岡一夫) 'Dilution [ダイリューション: this can be translated as Dilution]', *Jurist*, 960, 1997, 64–5.

N

N. Nakayama, (中山信弘) 'Fukyoho kaisei no houkou to kongono kadai [不競法改正の方向と今後の課題: this can be translated as Suggestions for Future Developments of the Unfair Competition Prevention Act]', *Jurist*, 1019, 1993, 8–10.

H. Nishi, (西博幸) 'Tyomei syohyo wo hukumi syohyo to dedokoto kondo no osore [著名商標を含む商標と出所混同のおそれ: this can be translated as Well-Known Trademark and Risk of Confusion of Origin]', *Chizai Kanri*, 53, 2002, 361–71.

O

M. Ozaki, (尾崎雅彦) 'Dilution no tyomei yoken nitsuite [ダイリューションの著名要件について: this can be translated as The Requirements of Fame in Trademark Dilution]', *Patent*, 49, 1996, 65–7.

S. Ono, (小野昌延) 'Syohyo ho to Goodwill [商標法とGOODWILL: this can be translated as Trademark Law and Goodwill]', *Nippon Kogyo shoyukenhougakukai nenpo*, 31, 2008, 137–52.

S

M. Saito, (斉藤方秀) 'Sychi hyoji to syohyoken no yusen kankei [周知表示と商標権の優先関係: this can be translated as Earlier Unregistered Well-Known Marks and Trademark Rights]', *Patent*, 48, 1995, 34–58.

T. Sato, (佐藤恒雄) 'Syohyo no kino to syohyo ken no shingai [商標の機能と商標権の侵害: this can be translated as Functions of Trademarks and Trademark Infringements]', *Patent*, 51, 1998, 39–60.

T

N. Taniguchi, (谷口登) 'Syohyo ken no koryoku ga oyobanai hani nitsuite [商標権の効力が及ばない範囲について: this can be translated as Beyond the Scope of Trade Mark Rights]', *Chizai Kanri*, 54, 2004, 1039–48.

K. Tamai, (玉井克哉) 'Doitsu Fusei kyoso boshi ho niokeru ippanjyoko no keiken [ドイツ不正競争防止法における一般条項の経験: this can be translated as General Provisions of German Unfair Competition Law]', *Jurist*, 1018, 1993, 11–14.

K. Tamai, (玉井克哉) 'Free-ride to Dilution [フリーライドとダイリューション: this can be translated as Free-Ride and Dilution]', *Jurist*, 108, 1993, 37–45.

Y. Tamura, (田村善之) 'Syohin no keitai ya moyou no syohin hyoji gaitousei ni tsuite [商品の形態や模様の商品表示該当性について: this can be translated as Protection of Shape of Goods or Its Design in the Unfair Competition Prevention Act]', *Jurist*, 1018, 1993, 18–23.

Y. Tamura, (田村善之) 'Taninno syohinno mohou koui to fusei kyoso boshi ho [他人の商品の模倣行為と不正競争防止法: this can be translated as Free-ride, Dead Copy and the Unfair Competition Prevention Act]', *Jurist*, 1018, 1993, 24–30.

Y. Tamura, (田村善之) 'Chizai rikkokuka ni okeru syohyo ho no kaiseito sono rirontekina goi – chiikidantai syohyo to kourisyohyo no donyu no rinnriteki bunnseiki [知財立国化における商標法の改正とその理論的な合意－地域団体商標と小売商標の導入の倫理的分析: this can be translated as Logical Agreement and Amendment of Trademark Law – Moral Analysis of an Introduction of Local Collective Trademarks and Service Retail Trademarks]', *Jurist*, 1326, 2007, 94–115.

Z. Tatsumura, (龍村全) 'Fusei kyoso boshi ho niokeru kondo gainen nokyakkan ka – wagakokuni okeru Post sale confusion ni tsuiteno kaisyakuronnteki taiou [不正競争防止法における混同概念の客観化－わが国におけるポストセールコンフュージョンについての解釈論的対応: this can be translated as Conceptualisation of Confusion Theory in Unfair Competition Prevention Act – Logical Interpretation of Post-Sale Confusion]', *IP Annual Report*, 2006, 297–310.

N. Tsutsumi, (堤信夫) 'Syohyo kinou no gendaiteki kosatsu [商標機能の現代的考察: this can be translated as Modern Analysis of Trademark Functions]', *Cizai kanri*, 54, 2004, 619–32.

M. Terushima, (照嶋美智子) 'Syohyo to brand – konogoro no jyokyo [商標とブランドーこのごろの状況―: this can be translated as Trademark and Brand: Current Situation]', *Patent*, 57, 2004, 72–5.

M. Toba, (鳥羽みさを) 'Syohyo no kinou to Globalisation [商標の機能とグローバリゼーション: this can be translated as Function of Trademark and Globalisation]', *Patent*, 55, 2002, 34–40.

M. Toyokaki, (豊崎光衛) 'Takahashi korekiyo to syohyo jyorei [高橋是清と商標条令: this can be translated as Takahashi Korekiyo and the Trademark Regulation]', *Gakisyuin University Law Journal*, 8, 1973, 187–239.

U

R. Uki, (牛木理一) 'Syohyo "AJ" and syohyo ho 3jyo 1kou jiken [商標AJ 商標法3条1項事件: this can be translated as a Trademark "AJ" And Article 3(1) of the Trademark Law Case]', *Tokkyo News (Patent news)*, 12249, 2008, 1–6.

Y

T. Yamamoto, (山本隆) 'Fusei kyoso boushi ho to benrishi no yakuwari – iMac jiken no mondai wo cyushinni [不正競争防止法と弁理士の役割―iMac事件の問題点を中心に―: this can be translated as Unfair Competition Prevention Act and the Role of Attorney Considering the iMac case]', *Chizai Kanri*, 45, 1993, 523–32.

W

M. Wakabayashi, (若林元伸) 'Syohyo niokeru ruijiseihanndan to dedokoro kondo no osore [商標における類似性判断と出所混同のおそれ: this can be translated as Assessments in Similarity of Trademarks and Risk of Confusion in the Trademark Law]', *Chizai Kanri*, 52, 2002, 1857–62.

Index

For Product Safety Concerns and Information please contact our
EU representative GPSR@taylorandfrancis.com Taylor & Francis
Verlag GmbH, Kaufingerstraße 24, 80331 München, Germany